Keeping PACE

25 YEARS OF THEOLOGY, EDUCATION, AND MINISTRY FROM PACE

Padraic O'Hare, editor

BROWN-ROA

A Division of Harcourt Brace & Company

Dubuque, Iowa

Book Team
President—Matthew J. Thibeau
Executive Editor—Janie Gustafson
Production Manager—Marilyn Rothenberger
Marketing Manager—Ginny Schumacher
Art Director—Cathy Frantz
Editorial Assistant—Barbara J. Tucker

Printed in the United States of America

ISBN 0-15-950217-9

Table of Contents

Part II: Issues

Part III: Strategies

Dedicated to
Mary Perkins Ryan (1913–1993)
With gratitude and love

Acknowledgements

Special gratitude is expressed to Damien Steger, FSC, founding publisher of *PACE* and to Sheila Moriarty, founding editor.

Over the years, the following have contributed, and many continue to contribute, mightily: Mary Dalton, James Lockwood, Ernest Nedder, Matthew Thibeau, Ginny Schumacher, and Jill McDermott. Thanks to Janie Gustafson for her work on this volume.

Finally, special thanks go to Maria Harris, teacher and friend, with whom I co-edited *PACE* for three years, to Joanmarie Smith, associate editor, to Art Kubick, assistant editor, and to Marilyn Bowers Gorun, copy editor.

Prologue

Mary Perkins Ryan

The more we Catholics move out of our isolation to work in ecumenical programs and to concern ourselves with the future of religion and education in our society, the more we need to be aware of the fact that "religious education" can mean different things to different people in different contexts. Such an awareness also helps us better define our own task. The purpose of this reflection, then, is to indicate some of these meanings.

Any education, formal or informal, should certainly be called *irreligious* if it is not carried out with a reverence for persons and for reality in all its aspects, with a sense of wonder at the mystery of reality and of our human approaches to it. "Secular" education, to be truly humanistic, ought to be "religious" in this sense, offering people the possibility of recognizing what Berger calls "signals of transcendence."[1] There is no need to point out how desperately American education—as given not only in schools, but also in homes, churches, and by the mass media—needs to regain this "religious" quality if our society and our world are to survive.

Education about religion is also "religious education." This can constitutionally be given in public schools as part of a properly human education. "Religion has played such a vital role in civilization that to avoid it or omit it, or fail to deal with it adequately, would represent faulty scholarship and academic folly. No one interested in good education would deny this essentiality. Religion must be studied where it falls logically and naturally into the regular curriculum areas."[2]

As the same article points out, this education about religion should be carried out on three levels:

1. "The first approach, and certainly the most elementary and perhaps the least controversial, is the factual or informational level. For example, in studying the Bible as literature, the materials would have to stand on their own, without interpretation."

This article was first printed in PACE 1 (1970).

xi

2. "Good education, however, involves the search beyond the facts for the meaning. Professor Philip Phenix . . . . rejects the idea that religious materials should be studied only at the factual level . . . . 'As soon as one is concerned with the import of what is read, interpretation is required. The only point in reading the Bible or in studying any other religious entity is to understand what it means, and this is the goal of interpretation.' The test of objectivity in such teaching, according to Phenix, is the acknowledgement of possible alternative patterns of interpretation."

3. "Still further, beyond the process of examining various alternative interpretations and points of view, comes the internalization of meaning for the student. Where does he or she stand? Does he have a response, perhaps even a commitment, freely chosen? Education that is concerned with what is ultimately meaningful necessarily takes on a religious dimension."

People who are concerned with promoting this kind of education about religion are usually also concerned about education in *valuing,* that is, in examining the values one is living by and in consciously choosing the values one intends to live by. This kind of training, to be given in the state schools, is advocated, for example, in *Religious Information and Moral Development,* the Report of the Committee on Religious Education in the Public Schools of the Province of Ontario. Methods for carrying it out are proposed in detail in *Values and Teaching,* by Louis E. Raths, Merrill Harmin, and Sidney B. Simon (Merrill, Columbus, Ohio, 1966).

"Religious education," in this sense of education about religion and the values on the basis of which moral choices are made, raises some pertinent questions for Catholic religious educators. Should we not be cooperating with other religious bodies, in whatever ways are open to us, to work out practical methods of including such education in public schools, training teachers, creating a climate of acceptance in the community, etc.? To what extent should we ourselves be giving to Catholic students this kind of education about other religions and value-systems besides our own? If this kind of "religious education" were being given *well* in non-sectarian schools, what would be our proper task as Catholic religious educators?

Most usually, at least to Catholics, of course, "religious education" means education in the beliefs, values, attitudes, practices, history, etc., of a particular religious body. Protestants prefer to call their programs "Christian education." But in his encyclical, *On Christian Education,* Pius XI used this term to refer to the total formation to be given by the *Catholic* home, Church, and formal schooling. "Catholic education," in turn, has come to mean what is done in Catholic schools and colleges.

Thus it happens that the more general term, "religious education," is, in the minds of most Catholics, narrowed down to the education given in the religion classes in Catholic schools and in similar, more or less formal, programs outside Catholic schools. Of course, this usage has a very practical value: to distinguish between the "secular" subjects taught in Catholic schools which might be paid for by public funds, from the "religion class" which obviously cannot.

But, although "religious education" has this narrow school-and-classroom meaning to the majority of Catholics, many Catholic religious educators are coming to see it much more deeply and widely, as a lifelong and life-extensive process—a process which is the professional religious educator's work to facilitate, but by no means necessarily in a classroom.

Most Catholics would probably agree, if they thought about it, that all education ought to be "religious" in the sense of the attitude of reverence toward reality, mentioned earlier in this article—although so much of the education given in Catholic as well as public schools is "irreligious" in this same sense. How many Catholics would think it desirable to have their children given in their schooling education about religions other than the Catholic and training in valuing, rather than in the imposing of a given value-system, is certainly a question. And how many will be willing to consider religious education as something for adults as well as children, and to undertake their own religious education as an ongoing process, is an even greater question.

All the same, it seems to me that Catholic religious educators should try to get people concerned about "religious education" in all these three senses.

Endnotes

1. Peter L. Berger, *A Rumor of Angels* (Garden City, NY: Doubleday & Co., 1969).
2. J. Blaine Fister, "Teaching Religion in the Public Schools," *The Living Light*, (Fall, 1969).

Mary Perkins Ryan (1912–1993), the founding editor of The Living Light and editor of PACE for fifteen years, was a pioneer in bringing liturgical, educational, and social justice concerns to the forefront of Church life in the United States.

Introduction

Padraic O'Hare

From its inception, the journal *Professional Approaches For Christian Educators, (PACE),* has embodied one overriding conviction: Religious education is not a narrow, sectarian enterprise engaged in by people who live in their own closed world, on the margin of the world inhabited by everyone else. Instead, religious education is practice in the midst of the world, the only world the Holy One created. Religious education is the practice of faithfulness, helping one another make our individual and collective lives into masterpieces of compassion, peace, reverence, gratitude, justice, and joy. What makes practice "Christian" is that the clues to a path of spiritual potentiality are derived primarily, not exclusively, from Jesus, the Christ. What makes Christian religious education "Catholic" is participation in the practice common to one, diverse, community of Christians, their predominant interpretations, patterns of faithful response, and ways of giving thanks and sharing love.

Mary Perkins Ryan knew this. In the very first issue of *PACE,* as you read in the prologue to this collection, she challenged Catholics to view religious education as practice that is broadly ecumenical, multi-dimensional, and deeply particular all at the same time. No feature of *PACE* better reveals this vision of Mary Perkins Ryan than its threefold structure: Foundations (theology), Issues, (religion and society), and Strategies (the practical how-tos).

Issues of *PACE* begin with authentic, rather than erudite, theological reflection. This is because one crucial mode of religious education is thoughtful, reasoned *expression* about the experience of being faithful or trying to be faithful. (This is a reverential reversal of Bernard Lonergan: Here theology is the functional specialty, or communication, of religious education). The theologians who have contributed these articles are noteworthy for their sensitivity to concrete human practice now, to the relationship between tradition and experience, and to the political function (the public function) of religious thinking. So we are grateful for the contributions of Chittister, McBrien, Sloyan, Brueggemann, Cooke, (E.) Johnson, and many others.

A cursory look at the "Issues" sections over the years reveals the breath of concern to bring Christian yearning for faithfulness to every aspect of human life—prayer and parenting, homophobia and militarism, and an endless variety of human concerns. These articles have not, however, failed to engage the thoughtful reader in careful analysis of a vast range of proper ecclesial questions. Many of the most renown religious educators of the last twenty-five years have contributed here, as well as in "Foundations'" and "Strategies." So we give thanks to Boys, Groome, Durka, Fowler, Harris, Moran, Walters, Smith, and a host of others.

From the first day Mary Ryan asked me to help on the editorial team of *PACE,* I have adopted a relatively simple formulaic way of explaining the difference between "Strategies" essays in *PACE* and many of the "how to for catechist" articles that appear elsewhere. Year in, year out, the renown and not so well known practitioners who contribute here adopt a tone of expression which makes it clear that they not only practice, but that they have *reasons* for doing what they do and for what they are sharing with the reader. In an era in which some Church leaders speak of the desirability of "re-amatuerizing" religious education, I give thanks for our "Strategies" contributors and their inspiring practice.

There is another feature of *PACE* which has been, over the years, a source of pride and gratitude to our founders who started us on this path. This feature is a reverence for persons. Children who are disabled, people who suffer the pangs of being victimized, and people in marginal communities feature prominently in the pages of *PACE.* I am especially grateful and honored to continue a tradition of providing the pages of the journal for sustained and caring conversation between Jews and Christians. In this regard, the contributions of Gene Fisher and Leon Klenicki should be noted as but one example.

Please forgive me if I have left out your favorite *PACE* essay, including one of your own authorship. This volume is not "the *best* of *PACE.*" It is a sampling of writings which, for the past twenty-five years, have helped to set the pace in religious education. I hope that paging through this volume gives readers a good deal of hope. It is clear that the state of some "problems" is pretty much as it was twenty-five years ago or fifteen years ago. But, reading the essays in this volume is an opportunity to acquaint yourself or reacquaint yourself with a remarkable company of women and men whose fidelity to humane society, thoughtfulness in practice of religious education, and commitment to the church are inspiring.

Padraic O'Hare is a member of the Religious Studies faculty at Merrimack College, North Andover, Massachusetts, and the editor of PACE.

Foundations

The God of Human Transformation

Donald Gray

G regory Baum has observed that "we have to be taught to take our own experience seriously." He goes on to say that "a contact with our own life story is for us a way to self-knowledge and, beyond that, an entry into wisdom."[1] It is within our own experience that we discover God to be present for us in a profoundly personal way. In reflecting back on our own life stories, we begin to perceive the many ways in which our God is truly Emmanuel, God with us. We also begin to perceive that this God is the source and support of the many significant transformations which have marked our journey and enabled us to grow, even if we may feel that we still have far to travel and much growing yet to accomplish. In this essay I would like to reflect on three transformative experiences which have touched me personally in my own life as a Catholic and which I believe have altered the lives of many other Catholic Christians. I shall refer to these as the ecumenical transformation, the secular transformation, and the spiritual transformation. Each of the transformations has required a conversion, a death in order to attain new life. Each has meant that a limited but perhaps more comfortable and secure standpoint has had to be surrendered in order that a more inclusive, more demanding, and more enriching standpoint might be taken up.

Ecumenical Transformation

In his book *Man Becoming,* Gregory Baum[2] has pointed to two experiences which have been ecumenically transformative of Catholic life. The first involves a new sense of fellowship with others beyond the boundaries of our own tradition and community. We have discovered, often to our surprise, the presence of gospel values in others. We have seen how deeply committed they are to the cause of God which is at the same time the cause of human life.[3] We have come to admire their selfless dedication to the needs of the human community. We believe that we can discern in their goodness and compassion the signs of God's presence to their lives. The mystery of salvation which we experience among ourselves we see also at work among them. We feel solidarity with them, a new sense of wider

This article appeared in PACE 10 (1979).

community. It becomes possible to struggle at their side for the transformation of the earth. This experience of new fellowship with others leads to a second experience, a new openness to truth. Others have something to teach us. We have something to learn from them. Human life is seen to require conversation, mutuality, dialogue. While it remains true that we have much to offer to others, we find, again often to our surprise, that we have much to receive from them as well.

This new openness to fellowship and dialogue can be costly. We are forced to die to a certain narrowness in ourselves, to give up cherished prejudices, to abandon aloofness and an arrogant superiority, to resist the attraction of belonging to an in-group. We may feel that our identity has become uncertain and that consequently our security has been jeopardized. We may long for the clearer boundaries of the past, the limits which unambiguously set us apart from others and put them in their proper place at a distance. It is painful to hear others addressing us in a prophetical way, calling us into question and summoning us to reform and renewal, challenging our most precious presuppositions. It is difficult to listen when you have been accustomed only to talking. Why must life be purchased with death?

To experience ecumenical transformation is to make contact with the divine saving mystery in other people, people whom we may have once learned to shun and disparage. To experience this transformation is also to make contact in a new way with the divine saving mystery in ourselves as a creative source of new relationships and attitudes, of change and growth. When we look back on our lives we are surprised, perhaps amazed, to see what has happened to us along life's way, what God's graciousness has enabled us to become, how the improbable has become possible for us. In the experience of ecumenical transformation, we have experienced God's presence and influence; through death we have found new life. We are not alone, left to our own devices. We have heard God's Word questioning and challenging us, inviting us to break camp and move on. For this great gift we can only be grateful.

Secular Transformation

God is present as saving mystery in our own lives and in the lives of other people, in whatever traditions and communities they find themselves. But God is also present as saving mystery within all the circumstances of human life; God is not limited to the context of Church and Sacrament, although this God is also certainly to be found there as well. "The first and foremost means of grace is life itself."[4] To realize this is to experience secular transformation.

The word *secular* in this sense is probably confusing to Christians who are only familiar with a godless secularism. The word *saeculum,* however, refers simply to this world and to this life. It is possible for a Christian to love and cherish this world and his or her life in it without falling into secularism, without turning away from the Church which exists precisely to minister to this world, and without surrendering hope for another life which complements and completes this life. To experience secular transformation is to turn toward this world and one's life, precisely as a Christian, in order to discover God's gracious presence there as creative source of new life. For the Christian, it is not a matter of choosing between the Church and the world but rather of choosing both of them together as the context within which God is met.[5]

When we turn toward our own life histories in attentive listening we discover the many ways in which our lives have been marked by crises and transition, by separation and change. We are able to delineate the principal points of passage on life's journey, the many alterations of standpoint[6] required of us on the way. We may also be able to discern some pattern of growth toward larger openness and greater responsibility. We find ourselves invited over and over again to become more compassionate from out of our own experience of suffering and struggle and our exposure to what is so frequently the overwhelming suffering and struggle of others. Perhaps we are even surprised by the awareness that we have a surer sense of ourselves as individuals at the same time as we manage now and again to set aside self-interest and self-preoccupation for the sake of others. We have seen so many hopes end in disappointment, so many dreams in illusions; but not all. What is it that has enabled us to continue, called us to go forward, supported our efforts, made possible growth, brought us to this place and time in our lives? There is a mystery that goes beyond us and yet is present in the midst of our lives,[7] a mystery that is the source and support of our becoming human. "To be human is the gift of God."[8]

When we turn toward the world in attentive listening, we discover many tasks awaiting us. There is an earth waiting to be developed and yet protected. There are victims of oppression waiting to be liberated. There are ominous issues of war and injustice waiting to be addressed. There are the sick and distressed waiting to be consoled and healed. There are the hungry waiting to be fed. There are the poor waiting for resources and opportunity. There are the prisoners waiting to be helped. There are the dying waiting for understanding. There are the children, the aged, the homeless, the refugees, the helpless, the hopeless. All waiting. What is it that enables us to respond, to reach out, to forget ourselves, to be concerned? There is a gracious and compassionate mystery present to and active in human society and human history on behalf of life. This mystery invites us to be sensitive and responsive instruments of new life.

When we enter deeply into our own lives and into the lives of other people, we discover not only ourselves or others but also the mystery graciously present to us all within the solidarity of the human community. In the experience of secular transformation we have experienced the God who, in the interests of life, stands against the destructive powers at work in the human community. For this great gift we can only be grateful.

Spiritual Transformation

Many Catholics have recently experienced a spiritual transformation in their lives. Some have turned toward the great spiritual traditions of the East for meditative techniques. Some have interested themselves in the rich mystical traditions of both Eastern and Western cultures. Some have found help in the psycho-therapeutic traditions which have enabled them to become attentive to their inner life and especially their dreams. Some have reached out to movements—Charismatic Renewal, Cursillo, Marriage Encounter, Foculari, and many others—for nurture.

There is a desire for a more prayerful life, for experiential contact with the deep places in ourselves and with the divine Spirit alive within us and around us. There is a desire for closer contact with other people, for sharing and support, for community and a sense of belonging. There is a desire to express feelings and to communicate openly and freely. There is a desire to be of service, to seek out new and meaningful forms of ministry. There is a desire to achieve solitude as a basis for a life of hospitality.[9] We are often surprised to find in the midst of this spiritual renewal how cut off from the riches of our spiritual tradition we actually were because of our own religious upbringing. Once again this gracious God appears unexpectedly in our lives, opening new avenues of access to his presence, new paths of growth. In the experience of spiritual transformation we have experienced God at work in our lives as creative source of new life and vitality. For this great gift we can only be grateful.

The God of our tradition is not simply a God of the past whom we are asked to believe in on the authority of others' experience. Our God is a great mystery available to us in our own experience—in our experiences of ecumenical transformation, secular transformation, and spiritual transformation. The God we know at first hand in our lives is a God who is the source and support of transformation; a God who invites us over and over again to be converted to the way, the truth, and the light so that we can be saved from ourselves for ourselves, from the limitations we have imposed on our lives that prevent us from entering into our own special humanity.

Endnotes

1. *Journeys,* ed. Gregory Baum (New York: Paulist Press, 1975), 2–3. Baum tells his own story in a chapter entitled "Personal Experience and Styles of Thought," 5–33.
2. *Man Becoming* (New York: Herder and Herder, 1970), 32–34. See also Baum's *Faith and Doctrine* (New York; Paulist Press, 1960), 2–5.
3. Hans Kung speaks of the Kingdom of God, which is the central motif of the proclamation of Jesus, as the cause of God which is simultaneously the cause of humanity. See *On Being a Christian* (New York: Doubleday, 1976), Section C, chaps. 2–3.
4. *Man Becoming,* XIV.
5. Perhaps no one has made this point more powerfully in recent Catholic history than Teilhard de Chardin, especially in his classic study of Christian spirituality, *The Divine Milieu* (New York: Harper Torchbooks, 1965).
6. On the notion of standpoint, see Michael Novak, *Ascent of the Mountain, Flight of the Dove* (New York: Harper and Row, 1978; 2nd revised edition), 53–59.
7. The expression is that of Dietrich Bonhoeffer, who inspired a great deal of the so-called secular theology of the sixties.
8. David Jenkins, "What does salvation mean to Christians today?" *Living Faiths and Ultimate Goals,* ed. S. J. Samartha (Maryknoll, NY: Orbis Books, 1974), 34.
9. The relationship between solitude and hospitality has been sensitively explored by Henri Nouwen, *Reaching Out* (New York: Doubleday, 1975).

At the time of this writing, Donald Gray was professor of religious studies at Manhattan College, Bronx, New York. His book, Jesus: The Way to Freedom (Saint Mary's Press, 1979), was an expanded version of his articles in PACE 8 and 9.

7

Educational and Pastoral Approaches to Scripture: Biblical Criticism and the Church Today

Mary C. Boys

In the original essay of this series, I proposed that biblical interpretation sheds significant light on life in a changing church. Accordingly, I suggested in the second article that reexamination of a very old dilemma, the relationship between the Testaments, now compels the Church to consider anew its claims vis-à-vis Judaism.[1] In recognizing, moreover, that every age has had to confront the Scriptures in the light of its own presuppositions, concerns, and methodologies—the topic of the third essay—I intended to place twentieth-century modes of interpretation in their historical context and thus to offer some perspective on the premises and practices of contemporary biblical scholars. By sketching the contours of the fundamentalist debate in the fourth essay, I sought to illumine by way of contrast precisely why historical criticism is so important today. In this final two-part article, I aim to demonstrate how historical criticism, complemented by contemporary theories of interpretation, can be of service to the educational and pastoral dimensions of ecclesial life.

A. Historical Criticism in a Post-Critical Age

During the first two-thirds of the twentieth century, the general thrust of biblical scholarship has been directed toward refinement of the methodologies so daringly proposed in the nineteenth century. Because the basic premise of historical criticism lies in the axiom that the meaning of a passage cannot be understood apart from its historical context and literary form, the guild of scholars has developed highly refined methodologies for ferreting out these foundational determinants. Whereas nineteenth-century scholars amplified textual criticism (the search for the most reliable, authentic wording and texts) with a basic kind of literary and source criticism (respectively, the recognition of literary genre and the sources of

This article appeared in PACE 11 (1981).

the texts, e.g., the documentary theory of the Pentateuch or the two-source hypothesis of the Synoptic Gospels), their twentieth-century colleagues have cultivated even more precise techniques. Among the most prominent contemporary tools are:

- *literary criticism,* dealing with particular units of texts and their internal arrangement (e.g., themes, structure, style) as well as with the historical settings in which the literature was produced.
- *redaction criticism,* studying the history of the oral transmission of the text with the goal of identifying the theological perspectives of a writer by analyzing the editorial and compositional techniques. This is often termed *tradition criticism* when referring to the Hebrew Scriptures.
- *form criticism,* concentrating primarily on smaller units (e.g., parables, proverbs, miracle stories) rather than on whole documents and examining the sociological setting within the life of Israel or the early Church in which particular forms took shape; this is often referred to as the *Sitz im Leben,* the "setting in life."

Involved in these methodologies is the use of philology and archaeology. The former assists scholars to deal with the text in its original language and also to translate it in accord with either the cognate languages (in the case of the Hebrew Scriptures, Akkadian, Ugaritic, and Arabic), or in light of more extensive literature (in the case of the New Testament, Greek literature). Archaeological discoveries have provided other ancient texts that have offered significant linguistic data and comparative literature; most famous among recent finds are the Dead Sea Scrolls, discovered at Qumran in 1947. In addition, archaeology has contributed a further means of evaluating the historical character of biblical texts.[2]

A new demand confronts scholars in the latter third of the century: to integrate the results of their study with the daily life of believers.[3] Without doubt, historical criticism has provided an immense body of knowledge to the Church, but its function thus far has seemed to many non-specialists to be largely negative and predominantly restricted to technicians. In a very real way, it has served to make the Bible more difficult to read as well as dispelling some long-treasured sentiments—as by pointing out the literary character of the infancy narratives. Moreover, it has spawned a proclivity to arrogance, as Leander Keck cleverly suggests in his play on the Pharisee's prayer (Luke 18:11b): "Lord, I thank thee that I am no longer the pious conservative I once was. I know that some psalms were composed for the enthronement festival borrowed from Mesopotamia. I know that 2

9

Corinthians is a compilation of at least four later fragments. I know that most of the Fourth Gospel does not report accurately Jesus' words. Above all, I am thankful that I have been liberated from my past by what I know."[4]

On the other hand, historical criticism has already provided considerable richness to the Church. Let me suggest five specific contributions:

1. Historical criticism has offered a substantial and intellectually honest tool appropriate to modern modes of thought. No longer, for instance, need one feel compelled to defend Genesis against evolutionary theorists or to harmonize the conflicting accounts of the four evangelists.

2. It provides a means for differentiating what the author said from what another age assumes or wishes he had said. Likewise, it corrects ways in which particular passages have been distorted or oversimplified and provides criteria against which we might check our reading of them. Two examples illustrate this clearly. Exegetes have drawn our attention to the eschatological context of 2 Cor. 7:25–39 (Paul's recommendations to the Corinthians cautioning against marriage [unless one's passions are too strong] and extolling celibacy). They have thereby demonstrated that Paul's view of marriage is shaped by his conviction of "impending disaster" (v. 26, the end of the world) and that, in another context, he might well have a very different perspective. By implication, 1 Cor. 7 ought not to function in today's Church as the principal basis of a theology of sexuality. Another illustration from Paul: His distinction between spirit and flesh has long been a foundation for a spirituality which denigrates material things (including the body) and honors only the immaterial. Historical critical exegesis shows the inadequacy of this interpretation of the dualism; "flesh," in Pauline terms, does not mean the physical or material but everything (including ideas) which might lead one away from God. Unfortunately, the faulty distinction, in league with a misunderstanding of the Johanine usage of "world" and later Neo-Platonic concepts, has legitimized a spirituality which holds, in Thomas a Kempis's famous phrase, that "everytime one goes out into the world, he returns less a man." Even more disastrously, the misunderstanding of Paul's usage of spirit and flesh has tragically legitimized an anti-Semitic ideology, in which "we, the Church, seek the spiritual,

invisible realities. . . . whereas *they*, the Jews, seek only fleshly, earthly goals."[5]

3. It enables readers to gain insight into the specific, concrete issues that originally occasioned the text so that they might gain some sense of how the text might function in a comparable manner in their own era. For instance, recent scholarship has made evident that the negative portrayal of the Pharisees in the Gospels reflects the late first-century Church's intense struggle for identity vis-à-vis Judaism. The Church's polemic led it to read its hostility to Judaism back into the ministry of Jesus, thus presenting the Pharisees in an excessively negative fashion.[6] By calling attention to this exaggeration, exegetes suggest not only that we must revise our opinion of Pharisees as hypocrites and legalists, but also that most of us are very much like the Pharisees (middle-class, earnest, dedicated) and hence susceptible to the sort of critique the Gospel gives.

4. It provides comparative literature that sheds light on the Scripture texts and thereby helps to unlock layers of meaning easily overlooked. Here the Dead Sea Scrolls have been of particular value, as James Sanders demonstrates in a sermon on Luke 14:7–24.[7] In the Lukan account, Jesus attends a dinner at the home of a ruler of the Pharisees and tells two parables, one on the seating arrangements at a marriage feast ("for everyone who exalts himself will be humbled, and he who humbles himself will be exalted") and another on a large banquet to which the invited guests did not come, causing the host to instruct his servant to "go out quickly to the streets and lanes of the city, and bring in the poor and maimed and blind and lame." Sanders calls attention to a pertinent parallel from the Qumran Rule of the Congregation dealing with the membership of the Essene congregation and the seating arrangement at their messianic banquet (1 Q Sa II, 5–22). No one "afflicted in his flesh, crippled of feet or hands, lame or blind or deaf or dumb . . . of poor eyesight or senility" is to be admitted to the community; in contrast, Jesus has instructed the Pharisee: "But when you give a feast, invite the poor, the maimed, the lame, the blind, and you will be blessed, because they cannot repay you. You will be repaid at the resurrection of the just" (vv. 13–14).

The provisions for seating the "men of renown" at the Essene banquet when the messiah comes are equally revealing: The high priest is to sit at the head of the banquet table, followed in turn by the elders of the priests, then the heads of the divisions of Israel, then the heads of the elders of the congregation and, finally, the scribes. That is to say, each is seated "according to his status," and the poor and lame are excluded lest they offend the holy angels. Against such a background, Jesus' parables function as a stinging criticism of the religious mores of one group of his contemporaries; the radicality of his parables is made more evident in this case by the stark contrast with the Essene rule.

5. It provides a basis for utilizing the Scripture in coming to a greater maturity of faith. Historical criticism has helped to reveal an "adult Christ at Christmas" and to clear away some of the pietistic accretions that distorted some of the great figures of early Christianity (such as Mary and Peter).[8] By so doing, it allows believers to come to a more realistic understanding of discipleship.

In sum, historical criticism offers the Church an important lens through which the Scriptures can be more clearly put in focus. But a question arises: need one always wait on the expertise of the exegete before understanding a passage? Or, as Joseph Parker more sharply framed the question in the nineteenth century, "Have we to await a communication from Tubingen or a telegram from Oxford before we can read the Bible?"[9] His questions will be considered in the continuation of this article in the next issue.

Endnotes

1. See Paul van Buren, *Discerning the Way: A Theology of the Jewish-Christian Reality* (New York: Seabury, 1980).
2. See John J. Collins, "Methods and Presuppositions of Biblical Scholarship," *Chicago Studies* 17 (Spring 1978), pp. 5–28. Fortress Press publishes brief Guides to Biblical Scholarship; the series includes, for instance Edgar Krentz, *The Historical Critical Method* (Philadelphia: Fortress, 1975).

3. Raymond E. Brown, *Biblical Reflections on Crises Facing the Church* (New York: Paulist, 1975), p. vii.

4. Leander E. Keck, *The Bible in the Pulpit: The Renewal of Biblical Preaching* (Nashville: Abingdon, 1978), p. 25.

5. van Buren, p. 57. See also Erwin Rosenthal, "The Study of the Bible in Medieval Judaism," G. W. H. Lampe, ed., *The Cambridge History of the Bible,* Vol. 2 (Cambridge: University Press, 1969), pp. 252–279.

6. See Daniel Harrington, *God's People in Christ* (Philadelphia: Fortress, 1980) and John Koenig, *Jews and Christians in Dialogue* (Philadelphia: Westminster, 1979) for a thorough expose of early Christian views of the Pharisees.

7. James A. Sanders, *God Has a Story Too: Sermons in Context* (Philadelphia: Fortress, 1979), pp. 80–91.

8. See Raymond E. Brown, *An Adult Christ at Christmas: Essays on the Three Biblical Christmas Stories* (Collegeville: Liturgical Press, 1975–77); R. E. Brown *et al.,* eds., *Peter in the New Testament* (Minneapolis: Augsburg, 1973, and New York: Paulist, 1973); R. E. Brown *et al.,* eds., *Mary in the New Testament* (Philadelphia Fortress, 1978, and New York: Paulist, 1978).

9. Cited in W. Neil, "The Criticism and Theological Use of the Bible," in S. L. Greenslade, ed., *The Cambridge History of the Bible,* Vol. 3 (Cambridge: University Press, 1963), p. 286.

At the time of this writing, Mary C. Boys, SNJM, was assistant professor at the Institute of Religious Education and Pastoral Ministry at Boston College and the author of Biblical Interpretation in Religious Education (Religious Education Press, 1980).

Notes on Angels and Devils

John L. McKenzie

There is hardly any doubt man, up to quite recent times, has always and everywhere felt that he walked in a world populated by unseen beings endowed with hidden powers whose effects were indeed palpable, but whose operations were beyond human comprehension and control. These beings were usually personal, possessed of a superior intelligence. Yet they were at the same time pathetically feeble, controlled by incantations which are collections of nonsense syllables, valid only if they are recited correctly. Sometimes these unseen beings are identified with the spirits of the departed, who cannot rest because they have been denied decent burial. There is no doubt that in many places, the practices of burial and of cremation were intended not only to dispose of the remains of the deceased but also to put their spirits at rest.

These unseen beings could be either well-disposed or malicious; in either case, human beings who enjoyed the rare gift of communication with them and some degree of control over them were credited with supernatural power, always to be feared and sometimes to be annulled by such desperate means as the killing of the possessors of occult power. Many of these ancient beliefs and superstitions survive in the pranks and costumes of Halloween, the witches' sabbath. That the beliefs lie at a shallow depth below the surface of civilized rationalism is suggested by the recent success of the novel and the film, *The Exorcist.*

Even a superficial acquaintance with the demonology of the ancient Near East shows that the books of the Old and New Testaments were written in the same world of spirits in which their contemporaries in neighboring lands dwelt. Yet traditional Christianity has long regarded the existence of the world of spirits as an article of faith. Belief in the existence of demons was a primitive attempt to explain a number of evils of which no cause could be observed. Unless man in some way can control or at least hinder such demonic operations, life could not be tolerated. Evils of genuine catastrophic magnitude were not attributed to demons; these had to be the work of an angry and hostile deity. Demons might be responsible

---

This article appeared in PACE 13 (1982–1983).

for the souring of milk or a toothache, but a hurricane or an earthquake lay beyond their powers of wreaking evil. If ancient man were asked whether the universe were friendly, he would have answered, "Of course not; but we can handle it, unless we are compelled to resort to prayer." It was not their belief in demons which distinguished Israelites and Jews from the Gentiles; it was their belief in a different quality of deity. Superstition is essentially antireligious, but the human mind is such a marvel of inconsistency that the two can coexist in the same person.

In modern times, a more profound and a more extensive understanding of natural forces has made it unnecessary and even impossible to postulate the existence and operations of demons. The same knowledge does not so obviously make it impossible to postulate the existence of benevolent spirits or angels. Yet the fact that we do not experience the operations of angels makes it difficult to argue their existence on the basis of the Bible or traditional belief. The theologian now regards the ancient belief in angels and devils as on exactly the same level as the ancient belief in a flat earth about which the sun revolves, above which there lies heaven and beneath which there is hell. The observation of the ancients did not go as far as modern observation has gone. We should not stop with that rather arrogant remark. Like all mythologies, angels and demons were an attempt to face reality. It is not intellectual progress to deny that there is a reality to be faced.

I am aware that there is danger of a logical fallacy in making my experience the criterion of reality, and even the collective experience of many does not escape this fallacy. We all know (from experience!) how easily we, as a crowd, can convince ourselves collectively of things which are not so. The same century which saw the career of Isaac Newton saw also a firm, popular conviction of the reality of witchcraft. Hence, I say that I have never experienced angels or devils at work with the added caution that I do not know everything, nor have I ever met anyone who did. I can say that, like others, I have never made the existence of angels or devils a factor in my plans, nor have I known anyone who did.

I realize also that the convinced atheist may leap on this uncertainty and say that I also lack any experience of God. I can only respond that the existence of mankind and the world is an object of experience, and that neither is a sufficient explanation of its own reality. If they are, then they are God. If they are not, then I am not satisfied, as the atheist seems to be, with explaining chickens as the product of eggs and eggs as the product of chickens. I intend to convince or to refute no one, but simply to set forth in very summary from the shreds of logical discourse on which conviction of the reality of God is joined with some uncertainty about the reality of angels and devils. I am all but certain that the angels and devils of popular belief are mythological beings. This does not entitle me to say that the area of reality does not contain spiritual creatures of which I know nothing.

The Christian theologian who takes up this topic cannot and should not evade the fact that the Gospels exhibit a belief in the reality of angels and devils and that they present Jesus as sharing this belief. The exorcisms of the Gospels are just that, exorcisms—the expulsion of real personal beings who do real harm. The fact that these beings drown when the pigs which they inhabit are drowned should cause even the fundamentalist reader a second, or a third, thought; I know nothing about spirits, but I cannot find room in my mind for spirits which can be drowned. Contemporary interpreters assume that the Gospels sometimes relate events which never happened, and they seek the meaning of the text in some place other than literal, historical narrative. Perhaps they sometimes fail; they think their failures are preferable to accepting the drowning of two thousand personal spiritual beings.

But the evil wrought by devils in the New Testament is greater than the illnesses and other afflictions which can often be readily explained as diseases not recognized and not subject to treatment by ancient medicine. Satan appears in the Gospels and Epistles as the Tempter, the great inciter to evildoing. This figure of the Tempter appears only in some later books of the Old Testament and very frequently in the apocryphal books of Judaism in the later pre-Christian centuries. The New Testament Satan is clearly derived from this figure. He is a cosmic figure of evil, a true anti-God. He struggles with God on equal terms as long as God permits him; but, in Judaism and in early Christianity, this struggle must and will issue in the final and total defeat of the Tempter and the final and total reign of God. And it seems that this conception of the two cosmic kingdoms at war is reflected in the Epistles and was accepted by Jesus himself.

To this point several remarks may be made. The first is that the language of the New Testament, and of Jesus himself as reported, is the language of popular beliefs about God, man, and nature which modern man feels unable to take seriously. The men and women of New Testament times lived on a flat world of narrow dimensions. They thought of its age as not much greater than what we call historical memory; its origins, so to speak, lay just beyond the horizon. Man had always been historic man, physically and culturally unchanged as far back as human memory ran. People could not even think or speak of the world in terms other than those of experience. Jesus did not come to explain the circulation of the blood; but if he had, what terms intelligible to his contemporaries could he have used? I suppose one could put the difference between the ancient worldview and our worldview if one were to say that the ancients thought of the world as stable. In modern times we expect that world to change and to change beneath our eyes.

I have already noted that the people of this stable world had lived for several thousand years (the period of history) in a world populated by spirits. I do not know what words Jesus may have used about their existence; I am sure that those who remembered and reported his words could not have created a world in which there were no spirits. What could Jesus have said about angels and devils which would have been meaningful to his listeners? In his speech, angels are literary ornaments, as they were ornaments of religious symbolism in Christian art. About devils he said the only meaningful thing he could have said: Do not fear them, because they have no power over you. When a child fears the dark (I confess that I did), the fear is removed not by denying the existence of darkness, but by showing that the darkness is not dangerous. It is not for nothing that the devil was called the prince of darkness. If Christians had believed the words of Jesus about the power and will of God for good, they would have overcome the atavistic fear of demons and not have allowed the history of Christendom to be defaced by centuries of superstition, which issued in such episodes of panic as the burning of witches—some of whom pathetically seem to have believed in their own maleficent power.

This seems to sum up the teaching of Jesus in words he never used: Whether devils exist or not is unimportant; it is important to know that God communicates to you his power over them, and any fear of them is pathological. But the devil serves a useful purpose in human thought and culture, as I shall point out shortly; hence, the admonitions of Jesus to ignore him have rarely been heard, while even modern man clings to the thought patterns of a vanished culture. It would be worthwhile to dwell briefly upon these patterns which lie behind so much of the New Testament. The reign of evil is seen as a power hostile to the reign of God. This power is rendered concrete as the domain of personal beings, headed by Satan, the chieftain of the infernal kingdom. The reign of evil is hostile to man, for only through man can it attack God. Satan and his minions are the agents of all the evils which afflict mankind; they are not only the tempters to sin, but they are the agents of disease, especially diseases of the mind (hence *demoniacs*). They are the inciters of strife. Late Judaism identified demons with the gods of the Gentiles, a belief which Christians did not adopt; it is implicit in the temptation of Jesus according to Matthew, in which Satan offers Jesus all the kingdoms of the world. They are his to give. I mentioned that Satan is called the prince of darkness; he is also called the prince of this world. The celebrated Four Horsemen are demonic figures (Rev. 6:1–9): Pestilence, War, Famine, and Death. One may ask how Jesus could say or imply that these demons are powerless or how Paul could write that no power, even a spiritual or cosmic power, can separate us from the love of God (Rom. 8:38–39).

In Jesus, God begins to roll back the frontiers of the kingdom of evil. Every victory over sin, every healing of disease, every reconciliation, every relief of misery is a recovery of territory from Satan. The image implies that it is a long struggle, in which victory is achieved only by the recovery of individual persons from the reign of evil. It also views the reign of evil as more comprehensive than the reign of sin, although it never presents the evils of the human condition as detached from the basic evil, which is human wickedness. It also shows that no one is delivered from the reign of Satan unless he so chooses, unless he changes his allegiance.

Is this not mythology? I see no reason to call it anything else; but let us not forget that myth is an effort to come to terms with reality. If one does not think about reality mythologically, one will have to think about it in some other terms. One can easily poke holes in the myth; the existence of demons, especially of the prince of demons, demoniacs, possession, and some similar primitive views. The fact remains that the history of the twentieth century is as easily explained by the release of four horsemen or the opening of seven seals or seven vials as by some of the more sophisticated current interpretations which do not deal with reality. I do not think, to use some unexceptional examples, that Adolf Hitler or Charlie Manson were devils or possessed by devils. I think they did wicked things; to many of my contemporaries, human malice is as mythological as demons or demoniacs. But that is the hard core of reality which so many cannot swallow; there is much wrong with the human condition, but it cannot be human nature, because we are told that men and women are essentially good. And that is the countermyth.

I said above that the devil has long served useful purposes in human thought and culture. He has been a scapegoat for human wickedness. When people were unwilling to accept responsibility for what people had done, which was often, they hid behind the excuse of a cosmic evil. Did not Jesus himself speak of the tempter? So he did, but he also said that the invincible reign of God is here, in which the tempter has no power. He spoke of faith more frequently than he did of the tempter. Against the shabby excuse that "the devil made me do it," he said that faith the size of a grain of mustard seed could move mountains.

In modern times, when the myth of Satan has become obsolete and the realities with which it attempted to deal are still present, contemporary mankind has created other devils. By devils I mean any power for evil, great or small, which is thought to be beyond human control and for which mankind, collectively or personally, cannot be held responsible or blameworthy. Space does not permit me to recite examples; the thoughtful reader can think of some for himself or herself, and they might not be those which I would suggest. I think of things which modern science has revealed as maleficent factors in the human conditions which were unknown in earlier times. Man makes them a devil when he denies responsibility for them or denies that they can be controlled when all that is required is some massive changes in the civilized ways of life or the civilized standards of living. I think of things like war and lesser violence, of the exploitation of nature and of persons, of all those things which we say we do only because we have to do them—for what? To survive? No, but to maintain the quality of our state of life. These are devils, and to the degree to which we adore and serve them we are devil-worshippers.

We have reached the point where we may identify the Devil, or identify the cosmic principle, that anti-God who is the enemy. The Devil has been portrayed in literature, but in modern literature the horns and the cloven feet (the Devil is really a goat like the god Pan) do not appear. He appears as a handsome, young adult male (Lilith is out of fashion)—suave, debonair, articulate, athletic; something of a poet and a philosopher; possessed of many skills; a ready fluent speaker; an artist; a charming, attractive person who embodies the idea of a gentleman—all that we would like to be. He is all Dr. Jekyll and nothing of Mr. Hyde. He is ourselves, all that we are and all we would like to be. Humanity and human persons are the Devil, the cosmic principle of evil, the tempter, the destroyer. Human beings are the sole cause of all that is wrong with the human condition. When we worship ourselves and our achievements, we are devil-worshippers. Mankind is what Jesus came to save, and mankind is the only thing in all of God's creation that needs to be saved. The Reign of God moves against the Reign of Evil and attacks the very seat of its power, the human person. If there were a devil and he were intelligent, he would stay far away from people, because he would know that no one is safe in our company, not even ourselves. Why should the devil do dirty work which I and my kind are capable of doing for ourselves, even the ultimate work of self-destruction? I do not believe in the devil because I know that we do not need a cosmic principle of evil or a Great Tempter; we human beings are the cosmic principle of evil. We are not nice people with good hearts who can be counted on to do the right thing. If that were the case, Jesus lived and died for nothing.

I have not forgotten the angelic world. In fact the world of angelic spirits seems to have arisen in human belief as counterweight to the world of demonic spirits. In a universe so full of malevolent personal beings, it seemed only fair that there should be a balancing force of benevolent personal beings, to make the odds against mankind a little less overwhelming. The hostile host should be met by a friendly host. Just as the devils seem to be unnecessary as forces of evil, so the angels seem unnecessary as forces of good. If men and women can do all that devils do, I may risk the assertion that when men and women have decided not to play the role of devils, they can do all that the angels are expected to do. Anyone as old as

I am has experienced those human actions which make the angels unnecessary. I need not believe in people; I have experienced their goodness. Gloomy as the world may appear, I believe that it belongs to God, the sole and supreme power for good. To paraphrase St. Paul, no little people are big enough to overthrow the government.

*At the time of this writing, Rev. John L. McKenzie—
author of The Old Testament Without Illusion,
and The New Testament Without Illusion,
and many other works—was officially retired and
lived in Claremont, California.*

On Monkey Trials and Teilhard

Brennan R. Hill

No one would have suspected this several years ago, but creation is becoming one of the most hotly debated topics around today. The current shift to the right in this country has brought back the old creation-evolution debate in a way that reminds one of the Scope's "Monkey Trial" in the 1920s. Reagan promoted a fundamentalist view of creation in his campaign, and both Johnny Carson and Phil Donahue have featured the creation controversy on their talk shows. Court battles are going on in over a dozen states about creation, and forces have built up among scientists and fundamentalists who argue the topic of creation.

In this article, I would like to look over the landscape of this battle-field. I will discuss the fundamentalist position on "scientific creationism," look at what some of the evolutionists are saying, and then treat the Catholic position. It is my contention that the long-neglected approach of Teilhard de Chardin offers Catholics a response which also does justice to science and religion.

"Scientific Creationism"

Fundamentalists, who hold that the Bible must be taken literally, have been in the forefront of the recent controversy over creation. In San Diego, there is a Creation-Science Research Center with a six-figure budget dedicated to the promotion of "creationism," which teaches that creation took place exactly as it is described in the Bible. The thrust of this center is to publish texts which the proponents feel should be used in science classes at least along-side, if not replacing, texts on evolution.

In March 1981, the Creation-Science Research Center caught the national attention. The Seagraves family, who direct the center, sued the State Board of Education. They claimed that children were being forced to learn evolution, which they consider "a tenet of secular humanism." They demanded that the biblical account of creation be given equal time in

---

This article appeared in PACE 13 (1982–1983).

public school science classes. As it turned out, the "creationists," as they have come to be called, did not gain what they wished, but they did make inroads. The court decided that science teachers have to acknowledge the existence of other theories when they teach evolution.

At the same time as that trial, another legislative struggle over creation was going on in Arkansas. This event didn't get the publicity that the California trial did, but the outcome was much more dramatic. On March 19, 1981, Arkansas became the first state ever to require the teaching of "scientific creationism" in public schools. Four months later, its neighbor to the south, Louisiana, passed a similar law. These were major victories for the creationists, and they didn't intend to stop there.

In tandem with those who initiated court procedures and promote creationist textbooks, another California group, the Institute for Creation Research, has set out to discredit evolution. Led by Dr. Henry Morris, the author of many books "proving" that the biblical accounts of creation are scientifically correct, the institute has gathered a number of scholars and scientists to promote their position on "scientific creationism." These scholars are out to prove through scientific research that evolution is not tenable as a theory to explain the development of living things and, in particular, of humankind. As an alternative to evolution, many of these scholars propose that the biblical accounts of creation are accurate and scientifically verifiable.

Reaction from Scientists

The mainstream of scientists considers evolution to be a fact. Although they admit that there are serious gaps in fossil records and that much research must still be done, they claim that the evidence for evolution is too overwhelming to doubt its truth. Precisely *how* evolution has taken place in all its stages and the exact times of major breakthroughs like the appearance of human beings still lack data. Yet scientists, for the most part, teach that evolution has taken place through mutation and natural selection.

Many scientists simply hold their ground and are not eager to enter open debate with creationists. Some, however, like Stephen Jay Gould of Harvard and Carl Sagan have chosen to go public and take on the creationists. Gould has been promoting evolution in popular magazines and newspapers. Sagan made strong statements supporting evolution in his TV series *Cosmos*. He also agreed to appear as a witness for the American Civil Liberties Union in its effort to declare the Arkansas law on creationism unconstitutional. These efforts have, so far, been successful. The law mentioned above has been declared unconstitutional by the Arkansas State Supreme Court. At the time of writing, the case is being appealed.

Where Do Catholics Stand?

In many ways, it is easy for Catholics to know where the creationists are coming from. We have been there. Until fairly recently, Catholics took the Genesis accounts of creation literally and believed that God directly created each item in the universe at specific times in the not too distant past. I can recall learning in grammar school in the forties that the world was about five thousand years old. This figure was arrived at by simply adding up the centuries covered in both the Old and New Testaments. I would be willing to wager that many Catholics today still take the Genesis accounts of creation literally, because the majority of Catholics are still fundamentalists at heart.

In the nineteenth century, the Catholic Church—along with almost everybody else—was upset with the appearance of Darwin's position on evolution, which seemed to threaten the Church's teaching on creation and original sin. In 1909, the Roman Biblical Commission asserted that the literal sense of the creation stories in Genesis could not be questioned regarding "the creation of all things accomplished by God in the beginning of time, the special creation of man, the formation of the first woman from the first man, the unity of the human race, the original happiness of our first parents." Even as late as 1950, Pope Pius XII expressed the need for great caution on the part of those studying evolution and held that polygenism (the appearance of humanity in groups) was apparently irreconcilable with the Catholic teaching on original sin. The fundamentalist view of the Church at that time was reflected in the statement of Pius XII's encyclical *Humani Generis:* "Original sin is the result of a sin committed, in actual historical fact, by an individual man named Adam, and it is a quality native to all of us, only because it has been handed down by descent from him."

Biblical Criticism

Catholicism took its first steps away from fundamentalism in 1943 when the same Pius XII, through his historical encyclical *Divino Afflante Spiritu,* allowed Catholic scholars to use scientific methods to study the Bible. Once such freedom of biblical research was allowed, it was not long before Catholic exegetes abandoned a fundamentalist approach to both Old and New Testaments. As a result, the Genesis stories of creation are now viewed as myth carrying religious truth and not as the stuff of history or science. St. Augustine's statement of the fourth century that Scripture tells us "how to go to heaven and not how the heavens go" was now given new currency. The Church began to be less defensive about the findings of modern science and found a new compatibility between science and religion.

23

The Church and Science

Vatican Council II ushered in a new era of the Church's openness to science. The council defended science's rightful independence and stressed that science and faith are not mutually opposed. In the *Pastoral Constitution on the Church in the Modern World,* the council stated: "If methodical investigation is carried out in a genuinely scientific manner and in accord with the moral norms, it never truly conflicts with faith." Of course, the council was quick to add that created things do depend on God and that "without the Creator the creature would disappear." A clear distinction was made between science and religion, but the two areas were viewed as complementing each other. The faithful were therefore encouraged to integrate modern science with Christian morality and doctrine. Religious faith should keep pace with scientific knowledge and advancing technology. Consequently, Catholics are free to accept the findings of modern science regarding creation and, at the same time, to hold firm to their belief in God's creative role.

Pope John Paul II has continued to carry on this positive attitude toward science. His recent statement to German scholars during his visit to Cologne might well be applied to the conflict between creationism and evolution. He pointed out that in the past, science struggled for freedom against a Church which opposed progress. Now science's struggle has taken an ironic turn. Science finds itself under attack from political and religious leaders who are disillusioned with scientific progress. Today, science finds itself turning to the Church and asking it to defend the autonomy and freedom of research. The pope asserted that the Church is now entering a new partnership with science since both are jointly responsible for forming modern culture. He expressed regret that the Church in the past interfered in scientific affairs. The future will be different, because the current cultural crisis can be solved only "in renewed linking of scientific thought with man's power in faith to seek the truth." The pope frankly told scientists that "we need each other."

Teilhard de Chardin

Teilhard de Chardin's work offers Catholics a valuable approach to the current controversy over creation. At the beginning of this century, Teilhard saw that the Church's biblical fundamentalism ran contrary to the findings of modern science. As a geologist and paleontologist, he came to accept evolution and urged the Church to revise its teachings concerning the timing of creation and original sin. Unfortunately, the Church was not ready for Teilhard. He was rejected as a voice in the Church, literally exiled, forbidden to publish; and, even after his death, his work was discredited.

But in May, 1981, a rather amazing document was issued from the Vatican regarding Teilhard. Cardinal Casaroli, the Vatican Secretary of State, wrote a letter to the rector of the Catholic University of Paris on the occasion of Teilhard's one hundredth birthday. The letter was written on behalf of Pope John Paul II, and it contained some rather encouraging news. Rome was at long last paying tribute to Teilhard de Chardin! The letter points out that Teilhard's research, his personality, and the richness of his thought have "left a lasting mark on our age." Teilhard is praised for his "insight into the deep value of nature, a keen perception of the dynamism of creation, and wide view of the becoming of the world." It is pointed out that his synthesis indeed offers hope to so many today who are tormented by doubt.

It is my view, then, that Teilhard's approach to the integration of science and religion offers us a position from which to dialogue with creationists in a positive way. Teilhard was eager to face the fact that the universe, the earth, and, indeed, all living things were not directly created, but evolved over billions of years. He saw creation, not as a one-time event, but as a dynamic process which continues to go on. The genesis of all reality moves from the birth of the cosmos to the appearance of life, from the birth of the human spirit to the completion of all things in Christ. Teilhard sees creation moving gradually from simple units, such as electrons and atoms, to the most complex of all phenomena, the human spirit. Love is seen as the basic energy which can draw all of reality to an ultimate unity.

Teilhard did not resist the notion of an evolutionary process. Rather, he had great faith in such a process and in the participation of human beings in it. Moreover, he did not see matter as opposed to spirit or to the personal. He believed that spirit finds its source in matter and that spirit is the crowning achievement of matter's evolution.

Nor did evolution pose a threat to Teilhard's faith in the creative power of God. No matter what discoveries science made regarding our origins, Teilhard held firm that God's creative power and all embracing love were within the process, giving it meaning and direction. He believed that Jesus Christ is the model of all creation, the crowning point of human evolution, and the ultimate goal of all reality. This vision, presented throughout his works, can be found in simple form in Teilhard's *Hymn of the Universe.*

Where Do We Go from Here?

Today, Catholics are in a much better position than ever before to deal with the issue of creation. Biblical criticism has matured to the point where we can understand the literary forms of the Old Testament. We know now that Genesis is not teaching us history or science, but religious truth. At the same time, science has made major breakthroughs in the study of evolution and has both verified and corrected Teilhard's insights.

With the help of Teilhard's perspective, Catholics are in a position to face the question of creation intelligently. We need not side with scientists who—like Carl Sagan in *Cosmos*—rather flippantly trifle with the notion of a "Great Designer" and superficially describe the birth of the human spirit. Nor need we be intimidated by the Moral Majority and the other proponents of "scientific creationism." Indeed, we can believe that God is the Creator of all things, and yet we no longer need accept that creation was a onetime event as described in the Bible. We can accept the findings of evolutionists and still believe that God is the ultimate creative power.

At the time of this writing, Dr. Brennan R. Hill was a special consultant for the Office of Religious Education in the Diocese of Albany, New York.

Toward a Theology of Work:
Work As Co-Creation

Joe Holland

Machinists, taxi drivers, lawyers, clerk-typists, computer program-mers, flight attendants, teachers, doctors, trash collectors, parents, waitresses, orderlies . . . What do these have in common? They are all names for ways in which we humans work. What, then, is the theological meaning of work?

Although we are seldom told of its spiritual significance, work is intended by God to be one of the most profound ways of our experiencing the divine energy in the world. Work is the way in which we humans share in the maintenance and transformation of nature, as part of the emerging creation of the universe. Whether we advert to it or not, in its inner depth working is a religious experience—hence, the central role of a theology of work.

In exploring here a theology of work I will attempt three things: (1) to examine some of the distorted or reductionistic understandings of work that prevent us from realizing its religious significance; (2) to explore the profound spiritual meaning of human work as co-creation with nature and the Creator; and (3) to offer some fundamental criteria for distinguishing authentic work from degraded work. The theology of work sketched here is drawn heavily from Pope John Paul II's encyclical, *Laborem Exercens* and his attempt to recover the "subjective" dimension of work. This attempt, I believe, represents a whole new stage in Catholic social teaching.

Distorted and Reductionistic Interpretations of Work

Several common interpretations of work prevent us from realizing its religious significance. Unfortunately these distortions have often been communicated to us with the Christian tradition. But they are disfigurations of God's revelation and of our Christian tradition.

Religious Versus Secular Work: This distortion causes us to consider religious only those works done by priests, sisters, or brothers. Religious work is limited to work done in "religious" institutions. Other workplaces are called "secular."

Often we refer to people who do these "religious" works as having "vocations" from God, as if other forms of work were not also vocations

This article appeared in PACE 15 (1984–1985).

from God. Thus when we use the language of "praying for vocations," meaning these "religious" vocations, we fall into the trap of this first distortion of work.

Otherworldly Spirituality: A second distortion sees work as a distraction from spirituality. In this view, work is necessary because of our bodily or "earthly" nature. We have to work, but it would be better if we didn't. If we didn't, we could be busy with "heavenly" things. Here prayer and spirituality begin only when work ends. By setting up such a radical separation between work and prayer, we say that religious meaning is found only outside of our work in the world. Work becomes part of our exile, our vale of tears.

In this distortion, work gains status to the degree that it is removed from the material world. Thus jobs that get our hands dirty or require physical labor are seen as inferior to jobs that keep our hands clean and require only mental labor. Mental labor becomes more "heavenly," while manual labor remains "earthly." Our educational system reinforces this dichotomy. A more intense version of this distortion is to see work simply as a curse for original sin.

Earning a Living: In this distortion work is simply the activity by which we earn money in order to buy consumer goods. Work becomes primarily a way to get spending money. Such money may be spent for frivolous or necessary consumer items, but the focus is on the act of consumption, not the act of work. As I mentioned in the first essay, this can lead to the "rat race" of consumerism, which becomes a false religion.

This interpretation is not so much a distortion as a reduction of the meaning of work. Certainly many people have to work simply to keep themselves and their families alive. The error is not to assert this, but to stop there—for work is also something much more.

While this fourth distortion comes to us from secular sources, it may be the fruit of the longtime devaluing of human work within the religious tradition. If tendencies in our received religious tradition tended to isolate only certain works as religious, to view work as a distraction from spirituality, and to see work as a curse for sin, then it should be no wonder that our social world—a product of work—has become excessively secularized. Similarly it should be no wonder that our society forgets the inner religious meaning of work and focuses instead on consumerism. To heal the destructive effects of both the classical spiritual degradation of work and its modern secularization, we need to recover the religious depth of work itself.

The Spiritual Meaning of Work

As creation-centered spiritual writers like Matthew Fox and Thomas Berry have reminded us, the starting point for spirituality is the affirmation of creation. (See for example Matthew Fox, *Original Blessing: A Primer in Creation Spirituality* [Santa Fe, NM: Bear and Co., 1983].) Creation is the fundamental doctrine of theology. Without creation there is nothing to theologize about. It is in the context of continuing creation that we need to understand the spiritual meaning of human work.

The Process of Creation: According to Thomas Berry, the universe is a developmental process of ongoing creation, reaching deeper and deeper into the power of life. The first stage of its creativity was the formation of the galaxies (still unfinished), the second stage the emergence of life (from the simplest forms up to the mammals), the third stage the emergence of reflective consciousness. We see the third stage embodied in our own selves, for in human beings (and perhaps other rational creatures in other galaxies?) the universe beings to think.

Human consciousness is not simply the private property of human beings who are systemically distinct from and superior to the rest of the planet earth or the rest of the universe. No, human consciousness, as Teilhard de Chardin so mystically expressed it, is the evolutionary point at which planet earth, and perhaps the whole universe, begins its conscious phase.

Consciousness and Culture: The transforming process of human consciousness across time and space is what we call human culture. Culture is constantly reshaping the world in myriad ways, each reflecting the creativity of the human imagination. We humans are in turn reshaped by the cultures we create.

Berry suggests that human consciousness has now passed through three distinct stages of human culture and is presently entering into a fourth. The first stage we might call primal, referring to the tribal phase of human culture; the second the classical stage, referring to the high civilizations out of which the world religions were born; the third the modern stage, referring to the techno-industrial and secularizing tendencies of our present culture; and the fourth a post-modern or ecological-holistic stage of human culture. These four stages constitute the ongoing journey of human culture, and each stage is marked by a different view of work and spirituality.

Space does not allow me to review all these stages. Let me simply repeat that in the classical stage, "high" spirituality was uprooted from everyday life, including work, while in the modern stage the world began to be secularized and work degraded. It becomes our task in the post-modern stage of human culture to reroot spirituality in life and to relink it with the creativity of work.

In the post-modern framework, we are called to become explicitly conscious of the theological meaning of work. This means that we must rediscover the fact that work is the way in which we humans, as a particular expression of nature, become artistic co-creators with the divine Creator. We are the point (or a point) at which God's own creative drive comes to consciousness. Our work, if it is good work, is the artistic expression of that very creative drive.

Thus we encounter the Creator in and through the creativity of our work. The experience of this world as creation is the most profound basis for our meeting the Divine. The privileged place for experiencing this world as creation is through our own work of sustaining and transforming the world. For the Creator is present in every point and at every moment of the universe's creative drive, and especially in authentic human work. Such work thus becomes our share in the loving expression of the Creator's artistic creativity.

All Work As Religious: It should now be clear that all authentic work is profoundly religious, even if we are not conscious of the fact. Again, such work is nothing less than the cultural creation of human participation in the divine creativity that is expressed in the reality of the universe. Work is meant to be the cultural way in which we reveal God's actively creative love. Work is meant to be the cultural place where we come together with the Creator to continue the process of creation.

How absurd then to suggest that only certain works are religious. Or that work is a distraction from knowing God. Or that work is a curse from sin. Or that work is only a means for buying things. Such religious and secular distortions of work ultimately deny the religious significance of creation.

Work, then, is meant to be a fundamental religious act. It is a basic source of dynamic unity with the Creator. What we call "religious" in a narrow sense is only legitimately religious to the degree that it builds and reflects upon this basic religious experience. Work is thus the foundation of worship, and worship is real only when it grows out of work.

But, obviously, all work is not so clearly our participation in the divine creativity of the universe. The creativity of work may be blocked by structures that disfigure its meaning. Thus work may be reduced to oppression by slave labor or to drudgery by denial of human creativity, or work may be denied entirely to people through unemployment. So it becomes necessary to distinguish between authentic work and degraded work. I will describe authentic work as "holy" and degraded work as "evil."

Holy Work and Evil Work

Holy work opens the work process to the creativity of the human species, of the rest of the universe, and ultimately of the divine Creator. By contrast evil work blocks all three interrelated sources of creativity. When this threefold creativity of work (human, ecological, and divine) is blocked, work becomes destructive. Destructive work is anticreative and hence blasphemous.

Distinguishing holy work from evil work occurs at the personal and at the social levels. At the personal level, each of us wrestles with our own individual vocation—namely, how we will apply the energies of our work to sustain and expand this creativity. Similarly at the social level, large institutions, trade unions, corporations, governments, even the whole world community—all struggle over how work will be socially expressed. Both at the personal and social levels, we face the danger of allowing work to become evil. But we also have the opportunity to allow our personal work and the work of society to open themselves ever more to the creative power of the universe and their divine source.

These two dimensions—the personal and social—are not just set side by side. Rather they are interdependent. On the one hand, social work is the sum of all personal works in the society. On the other hand, personal works are limited or challenged by the range and style of opportunities presented by the society's institutions.

Of course, evil work may not be the fault of the actual workers who perform the work. It may not be their fault if a work situation stifles human creativity, injures the natural ecology, and shuts out the image of the divine Mystery. Such workers may be the victims of evil work, rather than the cause. The work may be imposed on them by a larger institution, much as slavery was imposed on slaves against their will.

Nonetheless, in the name of the religious vision of authentic work, workers have a divine obligation to struggle against such degrading structures of work and to transform them, much as slaves had an obligation to struggle against their own slavery. Of course, how and to what degree such struggle is possible or prudent becomes a matter of delicate discernment.

Yet much of our life is neither purely holy nor purely evil, but is rather somewhere in the middle ground of ambiguity. Nonetheless, even with ambiguous work, the call to holiness is a call to purify it of its ambiguity and to make it clearly holy.

Three ethical criteria seem particularly important today in judging the degree to which human work is holy. These criteria flow from the three dimensions that constitute work—again the human, the ecological, and the Divine. There is not space here to develop these criteria at length, nor to argue why they are critical for us today, so I will simply state them as proposals.

Conscious Participation: Since reflective consciousness distinguishes human work from the preconscious sectors of creation, then human work needs to be judged by the criterion of conscious participation. To the degree that workers are treated only as objects to be externally managed, without conscious participation in shaping their work, then their dignity and their work is disfigured. Their work becomes evil. But the evil is not their personal evil. It is rather the evil of the structures and the elites of these structures that treat them as unconscious instruments. By contrast, to the degree that workers are drawn into conscious participation, the work process becomes holy.

One way that institutional structures repress participation is by becoming too large and centralized. Participation becomes feasible only to the degree that the institutions of work reorganize themselves into networks of decentralized small-scale units. The late E. F. Schumacher argued this case in his famous book, *Small Is Beautiful: Economics As If People Mattered* (New York: Harper & Row, 1973).

Ecological Wholeness: Just as much contemporary work treats workers as objects to be controlled, so too it often treats the earth as an object to be plundered. As we now know, the end result is an ecological crisis. Work becomes evil when it treats the earth as something to be manipulated and used with no respect for its internal value. The historian of science, Carolyn Merchant, in her book *The Death of Nature: Women, Ecology, and the Scientific Revolution,* 1st ed. (San Francisco: Harper & Row, 1980), has investigated how the technological explosion of the modern world was in part founded on this disparagement of nature.

As mentioned earlier, the secularization of the earth, indirectly promoted by the high spiritualities of the classical period—which sought the holy outside this world—may have been a beginning of this abuse of the earth. Only when the world was religiously "secularized" could it then be plundered.

By contrast, holy work respects nature, cooperates with nature as a partner in the creative process, learns from nature, is careful never to abuse it, is conscious of itself as part of nature, and treats nature as sacred. Holy work is thus ecological work.

One dramatic way that modern work seems to violate nature is by losing a sense of cycles. All of nature's life (and we are part of nature) follows a cyclical rhythm. Yet modern work is predominately structured on a linear model of intensive drive and efficiency. In capitalism this efficiency is measured by profit. All other values are subordinated to this drive. It is this sense of drive without rhythm, or work without rest and play, which makes modern life seem like a rat race. Frantic work may become efficient but uncreative. Failing to give life, it begins to take it.

Another way the cyclical dimension needs to be honored relates to waste. Frequently tasks associated with waste (e.g., trash removal or sewage removal) are held in low esteem. Yet these are holy tasks in which a special aspect of God is revealed—namely, the way in which life appears to die yet provides the seed for its own renewal. The waste materials of life are as sacred as life itself. They are but the hidden moments of life, which reveal the hidden face of God. How important, therefore, that all workers conscientiously take into account the waste products of their work and attempt to recycle them creatively.

Religious Celebration: The final criterion for holy work is that it be self-consciously religious. To the degree that we consider most work secular, we deny its religious depth and block its creative energy. As I proposed several times earlier, if the economy has become morally secular and autonomous, it is perhaps in the long run due less to greedy capitalists then to spiritual theologians who blinded themselves to the spiritual meaning of the economy. If our spiritual leaders failed to perceive the religious mystery of the economy, can we blame the business world for echoing that failure?

How often do we hear in sermons on Sunday that the liturgy is the celebration of the religious depth of our work during the week? I have never heard such a sermon. In fact, Christianity as it is presently con-structed often functions as an institution lodged almost exclusively on the consumer side of life—relating greatly to home and personal life, but little to the other work of its believers. Many church ministers consider it important to visit the homes of their fellow Christians, but how many ever try to visit their workplaces?

Yet work is a foundation of liturgy. Fortunately the U.S. Catholic bishops, in the first draft of their pastoral letter on the U.S. economy, remembered this linkage of work and worship. But even there it appears an afterthought. The linkage is relegated to a section appended to the end of the document and is not woven throughout.

These criteria then—conscious participation, ecological wholeness, and religious celebration—are three of the norms by which we distinguish structures of holy work from structures of evil work. When they are present, the creativity of the universe continues its divine journey. When they are blocked, to some degree the divine journey of the universe is blocked. The religious and secular distortions of work are one source of this block. The healing transformation of these blockages requires a spirituality that understands the religious depth of all work as our partici-pation with the rest of the universe in God's creative love.

At the time of this writing, Joe Holland was on the staff of the Center of Concern in Washington, DC. With Peter Henriot, SJ, he co-authored the influential book, Social Analysis: Linking Faith and Justice (Maryknoll, NY: Orbis Books, 1983).

"The Word of the Lord: Thanks be to God"
"A Hard Service" (Job 7:1–7)

Walter Brueggemann

To refer to the Bible as "The Word of the Lord" may be theologically correct. The phrase asserts the profound authority of Scripture that is not doubted among us. But it is a very inexact way to describe the literature found there. Specifically, many parts of the Bible do not claim in any direct way to be the speech of God. They are rather quite clearly and unreservedly the speech or writing of human persons. This may include the love song of the Song of Songs, which is addressed by a lover to a beloved. It includes the book of Proverbs, much of which is teaching that the older generation applies to the younger generation. Much of the Book of Psalms is very human prayer—clearly the voice of a human agent—addressed to God. It is not at all obvious how or in what sense these pieces of the Bible can be claimed as "The Word of the Lord."

Job 7:1–7 As Revelatory

The text we consider here is such a text. It is a speech of Job (7:1–7) that is part of a larger speech, including all of chapters 6–7. The general structure of the greater poem of Job is that of a series of long monologues or soliloquies in which Job and four friends make statements that are more or less in dialogue with each other. If one reads carefully, one can draw the conclusion that such a generalized argument is not meant to be addressed to anyone in particular, but is a rather general intellectual reflection. In any case, this material is not at all presented as "The Word of the Lord." Indeed, except for some elements in chapters 1–2, God is silent in the book of Job until chapter 38. Chapters 3–37 are human speech. Moreover, the exchanges in the poetic speeches are part of a drama, so that Job is not a historical character but only an actor in this peculiar and sophisticated drama.

At best, what we have here are lines in the script of a play, uttered by a created dramatic character, authored by an unknown. Indeed, the lines

---

This article appeared in PACE 15 (1984–1985).

seem to have no historical anchorage at all. Clearly, when the Church calls this passage "The Word of the Lord," it means to say the passage functions in some way as revelatory. The formula is about authority and surely not a statement about the voice that is heard, because in no way could this text be taken as the voice of God.

In Hope and Yet in Despair

The longer section, chapters 6–7 of Job, in which our text is set, is a series of wisdom sayings that function as a lament or complaint. A number of speech forms, including rhetorical questions, are employed to articulate the sorry state in which Job finds himself. But the overall dramatic effect of the speech is complaint, saying that the life-world of this speaker is miserable. He does not like it; he cannot bear it.

The actual verses of our reading (7:1–7) are a statement of the difficult and burdensome destiny of a human person. The verses do not propose an argument that is developed to a conclusion. They seem to be rather a series of statements that might come in any sequence, but all of which tend to make the same point. The point made is under the metaphor of *a day laborer.* The speaker says that his life is like that of a company lackey who must work endlessly, is always exhausted, but has no hope of relief and can never get enough ahead of the game to break the vicious circle. The situation of the speaker is like a tobacco farmer on marginal land who is forever caught between the tobacco company's capricious price setting and the bank's harsh loan arrangements that always squeeze, but always stop short of complete bankruptcy. So one lives from day to day and from crop to crop in hope and yet in despair, for one knows that no matter how good the crop, the final tally will come up just slightly short. It is all prearranged that way and the speaker is helpless, for he has no access to the decision making.

1. The subject is *man*—a man, any man, every man. This is not a specific man, not an Israelite, not a believer. The passage is a reflection on the "human predicament" in which everyone is caught. The language is masculine, necessarily so in that culture, but the argument surely can be extended to every woman as well as to every man.

2. The metaphor is *economic.* The human person is a person of bondage. The characterization first of all refers to the economic process, but the horizon of the poem is much more inclusive. All of life is like that. The human person is a person trapped in endless effort, like a day laborer who gets nothing free, no paid vacation, no fringe benefits, but only what is earned, if all of that.

3. The servant wants nothing more than a place to rest in the shade from the hot sun (v.2). The hireling has a very simple yearning. He does *hope*. But his hope is limited to pay at the end of the day or the end of the week. Such an image is about the marginal who are too poor to save, too desperate to defer any need at all. Satisfactions are so rare that when one can be satisfied, one wants it now, which of course only contributes to the continuing bondage. There are those who quickly run to spend all that is earned and are immediately back at square one, dependent and hat in hand.

4. Verses 3–5 characterize the futility of such a life. There is little escape from the demands of work. It is all meaningless (empty). The nights are miserable, perhaps because of exhaustion, more likely because it is all so endless and one is so helpless. At night one has time to think about all of that. Neither the day nor the night is fulfilling. Life consists of going through the motions—in the night, waiting for the day; in the day, wishing for the night. Life becomes an empty routine that is devoid of every satisfaction.

   Verse 5 is difficult and more obscure. It seems to describe a diseased body. Verse 6 seems to change the picture slightly. In verses 3–4 it all seems unrelieved and intolerably slow, whereas in verse 6 the days tumble out one after the other. What had been hopelessly slow now speeds by. The second use of the word *hope* occurs in verse 6. In verse 2 the same word, *hope,* is translated "look for"; but in verse 6 it is, in fact, the word used—but of course there is a difference. At least in verse 2 there *was* the modest, restricted hope of wages. Verse 6 gives the real verdict. The slave in fact is *hopeless,* a victim of routine, despair, and resignation. The hope of verse 2 is only a slight intrusion in that. It is not at all hope for rescue or release, or for the breaking of the system generating despair. So the modest hope of verse 2, by verse 6, has become realistic and so has become *hopeless.* The system—theological or economic—is closed and there is no chance of anything else. One must function in that hopeless arena or one must die. Notice in verse 21 Job hints that he will choose death as the better option.

5. Verse 7 draws the conclusion that life is transitory and of little value. One such as him will never see *good,* never benefit, never enjoy blessings, never know prosperity.

This dismal picture is followed in verses 11–16 with a resolve to complain and a bitter attack on God for having given humankind such a destiny. Verses 17–18 assert that God oppresses and nags and burdens humankind. God's oppressive way with humankind is unnecessary and leads to no good.

No Hope for Relief

The picture presented is unrelieved. The poem is a *word of hopelessness*. Because the language is poetic and metaphorical, the precise intent of this scenario of hopelessness is not clear. The dominant view among interpreters is that this is a statement, both cosmic and personal, about the *absurdity* of all human life. It is such a comprehensive statement that it rejects the whole operation of creation. It is as personal as this voice of one individual, who has looked clearly and seen passionately and pitifully. The despair comes very close to that of Ecclesiastes who reaches the verdict that "life is vanity." That speaker had tried work, riches, leisure. Nothing satisfied him. Human fate is to live an unsatisfied life. It is as though one reaches for a kind of satisfaction, but does not even know what it is that is sought. The frustration is massive and inescapable and universal. It touches all of us.

Such a reading may be correct, or it may be too urbane and sophisticated. Perhaps the metaphor or the hireling should be kept closer to historical reality. Perhaps it is a metaphor not chosen at random, but chosen to make precisely an economic point. Then the poem could be the voice of one who is trapped and oppressed by the social system, one who is speaking about poverty and economic hopelessness. For such a voice, absurdity is too grandiose, and the poem is, in fact, a statement about injustice that seems ordained into the fabric of life.

Either way, with *absurdity* or with *injustice,* there is no hope. Perhaps whether one reads it more *existentially* or more *economically* depends upon one's social setting. The weight of scholarly opinion favors the former interpretation, but that may be a comment on the needs and location of the scholarly community. In any case, the theological point is the same. There seems no relief from the burdens of life, and the key figure in the poem has no hope for relief and no prospect for relief in the future.

Quitting Pretense Creates Hope

How could a text such as this be God's word to us—a word that would cause us to give thanks? Likely, we should be honest and say that such a text does not fit the theological claims or the liturgical formulas of Church faith, and we should not give thanks for it. But let us press the point to see what is possible:

1. This poem is an exercise in *self-awareness*. The gospel at least invites us to know ourselves fully and how it really is with us. The gift of the poet (God's word) is a disclosure of how it is with us. It may be a statement of our entrapment, our lack of self-sufficiency, and our inability to hope. The disclosure at least delivers us from romanticism about ourselves and our location in life. The truth of the matter is that for many, this is an accurate portrayal. It may be the truth not only for helpless peasants, but for people who seem to do better in the rat race but who still have to keep running with the rats. This text may be the truth and in some sense is God's truth about us.

2. The Bible, of course, is not simply about self-awareness. This passage is not simply a portrayal. Job's words are a *complaint*. Job does not like the way he finds life. He dares to address his complaint to God. In later verses (vv. 12–21) Job utters the divine "Thou," albeit in defiance. This is God's word in the sense that this hopeless human voice is given freedom and energy to protest, *to engage in lively combative conversation with God.* Now that is a very unusual notion of God's word. It is not a word *from* God, but a word addressed *in faith to God.* Perhaps we may with elasticity take the phrase "The Word of the Lord" to mean that it is a word addressed to God and a word that God needs to hear. When we give thanks for it, we give thanks that somebody finally had the courage to say it, and we give thanks that God would receive such a word. This God does not want only docility and submissiveness, but has invited his creatures to ask, to seek, to knock (Matt. 7:7). Here Job is asking and seeking and certainly "knocking." This complaint is an act of faith insofar as it carries the pain of human life to the ear of God. We may be glad for voices of faith that bring to speech the hurt that is common to all of us.

3. These first two notions are not very satisfying. We may do better to say this complaint is *a tutor* (Gal. 3:24) or *preparation* for God's word, which is yet to be spoken. The confession of hopelessness perhaps puts the speaker (and us) in a situation where God's responding word can be heard. The wonder of the book of Job is that God does indeed answer Job (38:1), and in the end God does transform Job's situation to one of well-being and satisfaction—the very satisfaction for which Job had wished, but no longer hoped (42:2–17). Read this way, our verses (7:1–7) should be taken only with the resolution of the

gospel that comes later. These first verses are important, for unless there had been such protest, the response may not have been made.

4. In the lectionary reading for the Fifth Sunday of the Year (cycle B), this text is grouped with Mark 1:29–39. Taken in such a combination, this text sets up the problem to which the gospel of Jesus of Nazareth is the response and resolution. The gospel reading is about the enormous healing power of Jesus who is moved by pity and who rights every human ailment. The proposal of this lectionary grouping is that the gospel is the resolution of the hurt and frustration of Job. This implies, of course, that the Gospel not only treats specific ailments, but transforms systems, because Job's complaint is not about a momentary hurt, but about the dysfunction of the entire system. By juxtaposition of these texts, the hopeless one receives the hope-filled action of Jesus. One can argue then that our text is not the word of the Lord, *unless it is accompanied by this gospel story.* But the reverse may also be claimed. The healing action of Jesus cannot be told unless it is told in the context of these texts of hopelessness.

I suspect this is the most that can be made of this text as God's live word. We must not permit the Good News too easily to nullify the pain and pathos of our text. The truth in this text is that human life is desperate; that in itself is an important truth, especially in a society that engages in self-deception, that does not notice, and that denies so much of the misery and inhumanity around it. This is God's word in that it is realistic and refuses every cover-up—theologically, politically, and economically. For starters, we confess that God's word does not lie about us and our situation. We may give thanks because when we know how it is with us, we may quit pretending and get on with the prayerful combat with God that creates hope and new possibility.

A Retrospect

We say, perhaps too easily, that *the Bible is the word of God.* In the four studies we have presented, we have seen that this formula has many different meanings, depending on the particular text. Indeed, our study indicates that the formula can have no single, enduring meaning, because no single meaning can accommodate the enormous variety of texts found in Scripture. In such case, with each text, we must ask *in what way* the particular text is the word of God. Our understanding of that claim will necessarily vary from text to text. To try to make all texts fit under one claim requires us to ignore the particularity of the text. Good Scripture study, however, concerns precisely the particularity of the text—something which cannot be ignored. This makes our work of interpretation more complicated. It makes our claim more delicate, and we must not say too boisterously that the text is the word of God, until we can say more exactly what we mean by that. Most who casually make that claim do so by a reductionism that forces everything into a set pattern. But the live word of God in the text will tolerate no such reduction and no set pattern. That is how we know it is a word of God.

In these four studies of different texts, we have considered different ways in which the text may be heard in the Church as the word of God.

1. Our first text (Neh. 8:1–8) presents to us *a summons to obedience.* It is not merely a recital of law. Rather it is a narrative that makes available to us a context of preached law. Thus the text alludes to much more of law than it makes explicit. It invites each new generation to stand in the public place of listening and there to be addressed again by the entire Torah, which has been entrusted to Israel.

   The community of faith, which heeds this text, joins the meeting and participates in the articulation, interpretation, and embrace of Torah. In this context of address, Israel (and we) are not given simply specific commands, but are called to recognize our entire life as one of obedience. The text then issues an invitation to a sustained conversation about the meaning and specificity of obedience in our situation, which is obviously very different from that of Nehemiah.

2. Our second text (Jer. 20:7–13) is a text that invites us to *communion with God in prayer.* The text enables us to overhear an ancient prayer of Jeremiah; in addition, it gives us an opportunity to participate with Jeremiah and his community in prayer. As in the first case, the text not only gives *words* for prayer, but provides a *context* within which prayer can be offered freshly and differently.

   This, then, is no conventional prayer of stereotyped, anemic piety. It is not an act of submission and docility. Rather the text is a permit for another kind of prayer—one that is candid and abrasive and calls God to accountability. As God's word, this text issues an invitation to a vigorous act of communion with a God so alive and so free that he does not flinch from a real prayer partner with a life and mind quite distinct from God's. This God does not want prayer to be simply an echo of an old theological settlement, but a probe for a new settlement that is bold and fresh.

This invitation is to a process of prayer that is dynamic and transformative. The process lets the speaker begin where he or she is—in anger and hostility. But the prayer does not permit staying there. The very act of prayer traces a transformative move so that vengeance is turned to thanksgiving and hostility becomes resolved in doxology. This text is an offer of community through which God meets us. But the meeting and its outcome are not the kind conventional prayer envisions. This is a live meeting holding surprise for both parties.

3. Our third text (Ezek. 2:1–10) is an experience of prophetic exchange. The text concerns the specificity of Ezekiel and one historical moment. But because this is God's word with continuing vitality, we are also addressed here. The text asserts to us *an alternative word of God's judgment and God's new possibility through grief.* As such, the text intends to intrude into and disrupt all of our settled historical explanations.

All of us have a propensity to want equilibrium. We arrange social power and social belief to justify and legitimize the way things are. We often do not notice any incongruities or the fact that things are not working as we claim them to be. We are often insensitive to the ways in which things have gone awry. We are greatly tempted to arrange our life so that we do not have to notice. If we could, we would fix things so that we are never abrasively addressed in ways that remind us of what we want to forget.

But a text like this interrupts such a life arrangement. It insists that we are addressed, and we are called to notice—even if we do not want to. Through prophetic speakers—whom we may dismiss as being "troublemakers, traitors, blasphemers"—we are called to hear another voice that intrudes in a sovereign way.

That other voice, which we sometimes hear as God's judgment, may announce that the end of our fabricated world is at hand. At other times we hear this unwelcome voice as a statement of

41

an alternative possibility God would give us—but only through loss, suffering, and displacement. Such a text as this reminds us that God's will and way with us have their say, even if we resist and ignore and reject. This is not a world in which we are unaddressed, and we can never finally make ourselves immune from this voice. We are addressed in ways that shatter, cause us to notice, cause us to grieve and then, perchance, to be made new.

4. Our fourth text (Job 7:1–7) is a dreary text of hopelessness. This sort of text is not obviously God's word, for we do not expect God's word to us to be one of despair. It may be best to take this text: *(a)* as an anticipation of God's life-giving power, *(b)* as a characterization of our own situation of distance from God, and *(c)* as a contrast between God's life-giving power and our own situation of despair and resourcelessness. Insofar as this is God's live word, it is a word of judgment and candor, exposing our true situation without God. Such a disclosure means an end to all human ingenuity and self-congratulation. It means a recognition that life on our terms, existential and economic, without the power of God is a lost life. Taken in the Bible as a whole, we suggest that a poetic discourse on human hopelessness (as we have here) creates an opening for the power of the hope of the gospel. Such a construct requires that we sort out the real focus of hope and possibility. Job speaks for all those who are caught empty-handed with idolatry in the form of self-constructs. The text then is an honest requirement of waiting. The text knows that there is no word of life we can generate, even as Job could not. Articulation of hopelessness may be surprisingly fertile ground for the intrusion of God's hope. But that is beyond this particular text and always at the eleventh hour.

These four texts are, of course, not the whole Bible. There are other texts, better known, which are much less abrasive and much easier to understand as God's word. But our assignment has been to consider some of the difficult texts, in order that we should not claim too much or be reductionist about the Bible. In any case, these four texts are examples of the way in which the Bible may be heard in the church as God's live word:

1. As a summons to *obedience,*
2. As an invitation to *community in prayer,*
3. As disclosure *of God's judgment and God's possibility* in grief,
4. As a cry of *hopelessness that waits* for the gift of hope.

Again, there is much more in the Bible than this. But mature faith permits the Church, without being docile, to receive these texts and after receiving them, to answer "Thanks be to God." Thanks be to God for obedience that identifies, for communion that transforms, for judgment that permits newness, for hopelessness that waits for hope. In each case, the text is under way as a vehicle for God's purpose with us.

At the time of this writing, Dr. Walter Brueggemann, author of many books including *Praying with the Psalms* (Winona, MN: St. Mary's Press), was Evangelical Professor of Biblical Interpretation at Eden Theological Seminary, St. Louis, MO.

Mary of Nazareth in Cross-Cultural Perspective

Marina Herrera

When the Ribbon Ceremony took place in Washington, DC, in August 1985, banners by the hundreds of thousands represented those people and things that in the minds of the creators it would be unthinkable to lose in a nuclear holocaust. Many banners depicted scenes of people and of nature with quotations from the Scriptures.

But the most clearly religious and Catholic was a banner, painstakingly embroidered and stenciled, that depicted Our Lady of Guadalupe with the caption "Virgen de Guadalupe, Ruega por la Paz del Mundo, Dodge City, Kansas." The banner was all the more striking because it was displayed next to one that said, "In memory of the world's best cat."

Created at a time when Marian devotions and religious manifestations that are openly celebrative of Mary are on the wane, and placed as it was among banners with more secular, sentimental, and individualistic themes, the banner depicting Our Lady of Guadalupe caused me to reflect on the significance of Latin-American Marian devotions and how they had affected and continue to affect my life. The reflection led to an examination of the contributions those insights may make to the life of my daughter and to the Church in this country of which we are now members. That banner, then, became the backdrop and the catalyst for this reflection on the relevance of Latin American Marian devotional practices for contemporary Catholic life in the United States.

Through this simple and lovingly prepared banner, some key characteristics of the meaning of Mary for Hispanics in this country today slowly emerged, much more clearly than through any of the scholarly works that I read in preparation for writing this article. The banner from Dodge City was unmistakably (1) feminine, (2) personal, (3) creative, and (4) spontaneous in its realization, although it clearly took many hours of embroidering.

Femininity, personalism, creativity, and spontaneity are the characteristics of Marian devotions in Latin America that I will highlight here. These characteristics offer North American religious educators the richest

---

This article appeared in PACE 16 (1985–1986).

avenues of thought for rediscovering the role of Marian devotions, both in education and in communal celebrations in this country.

Contrasting Femininity

Among many North Americans, Latin American women are seen as poor, passive, oppressed, uneducated, and apparently little more than reproductive machines and toys for men's sexual and power games. Like other stereotypical perceptions, those images are often born of the casual observation of Hispanic customs by outsiders and of public behavior by men and women, without reference to the more significant dynamics of family intimacy.

In describing themselves, however, Latin American women are likely not to consider important or primary those characteristics that refer to sociocultural variables and economic achievements or lack thereof, but only those characteristics that are born from the natural roles of daughter, wife, and mother.

In the view of Latin American women, femininity is not so much a quality that can be gained or shed at will at it is a natural outgrowth of being a woman and of the roles assigned to women by nature itself. To renounce those roles is seen as forfeiting women's most legitimate claims to an honorable place in the family and the society. Only if a woman fulfills her primary duties as daughter, wife, and mother will her other activities or careers be justified. When the characteristically male qualities of independence, entrepreneurship, and assertiveness are exhibited by Latin American women in the marketplace, they are acceptable and even expected only if that is what their familial roles demand.

The stereotypical image of an immigrant to the United States is that of a man looking for economic opportunity. But according to a recent study published by the U.S. Department of Labor's Bureau of International Labor Affairs, more Latin American women than men immigrate to this country. This show of independence, courage, and creativity is acceptable because in the United States, a woman, who is more easily employable than a man, can be the source of income for a husband, children, and parents or even grandparents who have little or no possibility of profitable employment in the home country.

The Marian-Christian Connection

At this point, religious faith and Marian devotions come into the picture. It is not uncommon to hear many of these immigrant Latin American women express with deep sincerity and faith their unshakable belief that the pain of exile and separation is the cross they have to bear. And, they add, it is a minor one compared to the one that Mary, their model, had to carry. It is rare to find Latin American women who do not consciously see their misfortunes or difficulties in light of the difficulties or pain endured by Mary as she tried to fulfill her maternal and familial duties.

Since they see themselves as following in the footsteps of Mary, under whatever title they honor her, these women strongly feel that Mary will accompany them in their journeys, make things easier, and allow them to find the means to improve the lives of their children because, like them, she knew the struggles of motherhood and even endured exile for the sake of her child. Mary's own exile is often cited by these women as the model for their exile. The often seen placid picture of the Holy Family's exile, with Mary seated on a donkey and Jesus on her lap followed and supported by Joseph, does not seem to have trivialized Latin American women's perceptions of the similarity between the pain of their own exile and that of Mary's.

Because in the fulfillment of their natural roles they so often must endure sacrifice, pain, and isolation, Latin American women are more at home in situations of struggle and of suffering than of prosperity and success. Theirs is, by and large, a stance of seeming dependence, power-lessness, and receptivity rather than one of independence, power, and assertiveness. They do not seem to attempt to eliminate or deny the cross in their lives. Jesus' words, "If you want to be a follower of mine, renounce yourself and take up your cross every day and follow me" (Luke 9:23), are present to these women, and their prayers focus on the fortitude to bear that cross.

Motherhood: Two Perspectives

While North American women may think that the past emphasis on women's natural roles is greatly to blame for the oppression and inequality that they suffer, it is not unusual for Latin American women to see their own oppression from a different perspective. In the Latin American view, the injustices women suffer result directly from men's envy of the centrality of women in the natural unfolding of life and from women's own inability to understand and value their unique and irreplaceable role.

Both perspectives—the Latin American and the North American—somewhat contradictory at first sight, are only different views of the same picture; but neither side recognizes in the other's view what it is accustomed to seeing in its own. These different views might be summarized in this way: The femininity of the Latin American woman rests on her natural roles as daughter, wife, and mother. But the femininity of the North American woman emphasizes the dignity of the person without any necessary relation to her utilitarian or natural functions. I believe that both notions of femininity are already contained, integrated, and made concrete in the Marian theology of the first Christian communities.

46

What Luke writes about the invitation Mary received to be the mother of Jesus represents a radical departure from the dynamics of male-female relationships in the Jewish tradition. Having children was the expected role of all women; there was no other choice if one was to be an honored member of the community. The degree of respect accorded to women was linked to their ability to bear healthy children who would ensure the continuation of the group.

But with the angel's invitation, a different dynamic comes into play. The Incarnation of God has to bring about many changes, and the first one in the new dispensation is the giving to women a direct voice in the decision-making process. (That was as radical then as it is now!) The angel's announcement points to new rules that allow women their freedom and uniqueness without distorting or diminishing the natural roles they have traditionally held. Both their freedom and value as persons, as well as their procreative abilities, are now placed at the very heart of the salvific plan of God. Because Mary *chose* the maternal role, she shall be called blessed!

The shortcomings of our cultural traditions have left both Latin American and North American women with a lopsided notion of femininity that is in need of adjustment and change. On the one hand, when women see themselves as totally subjected to their natural roles and dependent on the expectations of the family or the society, the result is that women endure rape, humiliation, and violence because they have little or no awareness of their dignity or their freedom and can be victimized easily by men, other women, and institutions.

On the other hand, when women are overly concerned with their freedom to choose and to seek fulfillment apart from the family or the community, they may lack respect or appreciation for the sacredness of their life-giving powers; the outcomes are abortion, child abuse and abandonment, prostitution, alienation, and all the other situations in which women become instruments of death or oppression.

A key task for the Church today and hence for religious educators is, then, to help children and adults, both male and female, regain a sense of the sacredness of the mothering and fathering roles and of the centrality of child rearing in the plan of salvation.

The present downplaying of the importance of women's roles as mothers, as well as the subtle ways in which the Church and the world try to isolate women engaged in this task, will have dire consequences for the vitality of the faith community of the future. Only a new understanding of the centrality of Mary and of her maternal role in the Christian dispensation can rescue modern women from the shortcomings of the materialistic and secularizing perspectives that stress the interchangeability of men and women in every role in the same way that we interchange machine parts or management systems. I firmly believe that each creature's role is an indispensable component for the ecological health of the entire system and that, in downplaying those roles that are innately feminine, we debilitate the natural preservation mechanisms of the system.

Personal and Lay

It is a widely known fact that Latin Americans are characterized by a warm, personal approach to relationships. They are, in Edward Hall's schema of styles of communication, a high context culture (*Beyond Culture* [Garden City, NY: Anchor Books, 1976]). For Latin Americans, how you say something is more important than what you say, and in order to understand the message being communicated you must know much about the internalized context of the speaker. A preacher can deliver a wonderful sermon couched in carefully chosen words, but if it is not accompanied by the right nonverbal clues that indicate a certain knowledge of and feel for the people, the sermon will have little meaning for its listeners.

This personalizing and contextualizing of relationship is seen even in the way Latin Americans relate to the divine and the saints. It is not uncommon to find Latin Americans referring to God as "Papa Dios" or the even more familiar form "Papacito Dios."

We find a similar approach in the ways that Latin Americans refer to Mary. In English, Catholics may refer to Mary as "the Blessed Mother," "Our Lady," or "the Virgin Mary" and write about the significance of certain Marian titles (e.g., Seat of Wisdom or Immaculate Conception). But Latin Americans prefer to use such familiar, diminutive forms as "*la Virgencita*," "*la Morenita*" (in reference to the brown color of Our Lady of Guadalupe), and "*mi Madrecita*." Or they may call Mary by the nickname associated with a specific title: "*Charito*," or Our Lady of Charity among the Cubans; "*Tatica*," for Our Lady of Altagracia among the Dominicans; and "*Provi*," for Our Lady of Providence among the Puerto Ricans. The degree of intimacy among a family's relatives and friends can be detected by outsiders through the kinds of nicknames used in their interactions. The same process is transferred to the interactions with God, Mary, and the saints.

Marian devotions in Latin America rest on the story of a favor granted by Mary to a family member, told in the family, as well as on the significance of given apparitions of Mary and the places where these have occurred. These devotions are not based on the biblical, theological, or historical meaning that the Church has elaborated in the course of its history. Latin Americans know very little about Marian dogmas or the biblical exegesis related to Mary's role in Church tradition. What matters to them is that they feel Mary's presence and her compassion because they have experienced in their lives—if not personally, at least through relatives or friends—some concrete moment in which Mary mediated a solution or gave a ray of hope.

The shortcomings of this personal but unbiblical or ahistorical approach are experienced by Hispanics in the United States when proselytizing fundamentalists attempt to show them that Catholic Marian devotions are diabolical and idolatrous. Hispanics have no way of counteracting such attacks and often feel so ashamed of their ignorance of the Scriptures that they succumb easily to the proselytizers.

The United States does not have a Marian devotion that is truly its own, and whatever devotions have survived in the last twenty years are a reflection of those born in other countries. The Shrine of the Immaculate Conception in Washington, DC, is a good example. A gigantic mosaic of a very male-looking Christ the King dominates the nave, and Mary is relegated to the side chapels where all the ethnic devotions that are alive in the country are commemorated. Although it does not have its own unique Marian devotions, this country, however, can boast of theologians, both male and female, who have tried to make Mary intelligible and relevant through significant biblical and historical studies.

Here too, North and South can learn from each other. Hispanics need to gain access to the Church's rich Marian, biblical, and historical theology. Only then will they link their personal devotions to the communal faith in which they share and thus have the means for defending that faith from its detractors. At the same time, non-Hispanics need to rediscover the personal dimension of Marian spirituality in ways that are not threatening to the gains made by women in their struggle for greater recognition of their dignity and equality before God. This rediscovery may lead them to the realization that they have in Mary the best ally in their search for a Church that is more responsive to women and to what women represent for the community of faith and for the world.

Simplicity, Creativity, and Spontaneity

Marian devotions in Latin America flow from the attitude of humility and simplicity characterizing the laity, an attitude that is in sharp contrast to the triumphalism and sophistication found in some clerical circles. It is laypeople who preserve and sustain many of the traditions and celebrations connected with the various feasts of Mary; the clergy too often take little or no real interest. Because laypeople feel a special closeness to Mary, they see no need for intermediaries or for the support of the clergy. The laity lead the committees that are responsible for the preparation of Marian feasts. Very often they are the leaders of novenas and other devotional practices that do not fit in the priest's schedule.

Since Marian devotions are not under the constant vigilance of the clergy, they are often characterized by spontaneity and creativity. The people freely enter into the celebrations, creating artistic contributions of banners, flower arrangements, songs, and poems. In some parts of Latin America and Spain there are rhyming contests aimed at the spontaneous creation of verses in honor of Mary or the patron saint of the city or town. This encourages the laity to express feelings and theological insights in ways that are nonexistent in the United States, where theological discourse has been relegated to journals to which only professional theologians and ministers have access.

To outsiders, Marian shrines in Latin America are disturbing because there is no recognizable pattern, no hierarchical ordering for handling visiting groups, nor is there a progressive and orderly unfolding of ritual. There is no such thing as making arrangements weeks or months in advance for groups to be ushered through a given shrine.

That is because, in Latin America, the need to visit a shrine comes from a personal experience and therefore requires an individual response. A family may come to the shrine because the mother promised such a visit if a favor was granted. Part of the promise may include staying in the shrine in prayer for a day or half-day while fasting. None of these activities could be carried out within the tight time restrictions of the tour group. These visits, connected as they are to particular promises or vows made to Mary, are occasions to exhibit each person's individuality and style of relating to Mary.

At these shrines, there is no such thing as a list of suggested offerings for the purpose of buying a little spot where a family may have its name engraved. Latin Americans present their offerings to the shrine, but they are in the form of symbolic representations of the favor received through the intercession of Mary. In most shrines there are walls covered from floor to ceiling by small silver pieces that represent the gratitude of thousands of believers acknowledging Mary's intercession on their behalf.

The free-flowing and spontaneous way in which women express their relationship to the holy has important consequences for the way in which they participate in the civic life of the community. Latin American women's protests against injustice and oppression through weekly appearances at the Plaza de Mayo in Argentina and in the pots-and-pans marches of Chile—two of the most famous protests—have become legendary and powerful models for women everywhere. The total significance of these protests may not be apparent or their effects too obvious. But in the final analysis, we Christians believe that the victory will not be ours but God's. The most important contribution we can make, then, is to persevere in our repudiation of injustice and oppression through our refusal to participate in it and through our unwavering hope in God's victory.

Here, too, there is a Marian dimension. Mary's Magnificat is the feminine song of liberation par excellence: Our own accomplishments are not what deserve praise, but how faithfully and willingly we have collaborated with those seeking the realization of a more just, peaceful, and loving world. Perseverance in our denunciations of injustice and faith that the mighty will be dethroned are the feminine responses.

Women in the North have internalized for themselves the rules of the technocracy of which they are a part—the need for new product lines and an impatience with anything that is not cost-effective. When these two criteria are used to determine modes of Christian action today, it is easy to be inconsistent, to violate Christian values themselves, and to forget the nonutilitarian dimensions of human life. Here the simplicity and humility of Latin American women may offer some inspiration and serve as a critique of much of the overtly defiant, bellicose, and aggressive behavior that some varieties of secular feminism urge on North American women who are trying to take a stance against injustice and oppression.

Conclusion

Finally, as a woman who has been fortunate enough to share in the spiritual and material goods of both North and South, I strongly believe that we cannot renounce our nurturing and supporting roles without seriously endangering the quality of life for this generation and those to come. But I also am convinced that this stance for life can be made freely and in strength when we appropriate for ourselves the compassion, the receptivity and the dedication to the well-being of others so clearly and simply made concrete in Mary of Nazareth.

At the time of this writing, Marina Herrera, Ph.D., lectured at the Washington Theological Union and was a writer and consultant on multicultural religious education.

Teaching Catholicism Today: The Challenge of Fundamentalism

Richard P. McBrien

There is no more serious problem confronting the religious educator today than the problem of fundamentalism. No longer confined to the Protestant churches, fundamentalism is at the root of much of the present malaise in the Catholic Church.

Many Catholics who complain about the erosion of orthodoxy, for example, are really fundamentalists who simply do not understand the nature of theology or even the most rudimentary principles of biblical interpretation.

This fundamentalist mentality has nothing to do with conservatism or respect for tradition. As Thomas O'Meara, OP, has pointed out in his unusually perceptive essay, "The Trouble with Seminaries," in *Church* (Spring 1985):

> *Rigid people do not intend to preserve the past; indeed, they are often too uneducated to distinguish the medieval from the baroque, the romanticism of the nineteenth century from the daring of the patristic period.*

> *The attraction to a golden age of faith (like the 1950s!). . . comes not from a real knowledge of the period or a real understanding of the theological questions asked and answered. (p. 19)*

The attitude, therefore, is not one of genuine conservatism, but of an intellectual laziness "in which thin beliefs and vague pieties replace theology" (p. 19).

I should argue, in fact, that fundamentalism is such a serious problem today that the US Catholic bishops might usefully consider writing a major pastoral letter on the subject, if for no other practical reason than that the Catholic Church is losing thousands of members to fundamentalist churches, prayer groups, and assorted movements. And it is ironic that

---

This article appeared in PACE 16 (1985–1986).

Protestant fundamentalists, once so bitterly anti-Catholic, now find common cause with Catholics on social issues such as abortion, tuition tax credits, and pornography.

Protestant fundamentalism has always been of a biblical kind, based on the premise that all Scripture is inspired (2 Tim. 3:16) and, therefore also infallible. Scripture alone, as interpreted by fundamentalist authorities, is the measure of truth and moral life.

The Catholic version of fundamentalism is primarily of a doctrinal, not biblical, kind. Catholic doctrinal fundamentalism is based on the premise that all official church teachings are supremely authoritative (if not "inspired"). As such, these official teachings alone, as interpreted by certain Catholic authorities, are the final measure of truth and moral life.

Both kinds of fundamentalism are really based on rational principles, not on the Word of God or on divine authority, as they often claim.

Biblical Fundamentalism

Biblical fundamentalism rests its case on 2 Timothy 3:16. "All scripture is inspired by God and profitable for teaching, for reproof, for correction, and for training in righteousness."

By a process of rational deduction, not by appeal to Scripture itself, the Protestant fundamentalist concludes that Scripture is infallible (inerrant) and is the exclusive source of divine Revelation. I say "by a process of rational deduction," because the Bible itself nowhere says that it is infallible or inerrant. One has to deduce the principle of inerrancy rationally from the principle of inspiration.

One also has to determine by a process of reasoning, not by an appeal to Scripture itself, which books are inspired and which are not, which are canonical (i.e., part of the official "list") and which are uncanonical. Nowhere in the entire Bible does it tell us how we know which books belong in the Bible and which do not.

Neither is there any place in the entire Bible where it says that everything written in the Bible is unfailingly accurate in every historical detail.

Nor does it say anywhere in the Bible that the Bible is central, or exclusively authoritative, for Christian faith and life. Second Timothy 3:16 says only that Scripture is "profitable" for teaching, and so on.

Nor is there any evidence in the Bible itself that Jesus ever sanctioned what has come to be called the New Testament, although his reverence for the Hebrew Scriptures is clear.

Indeed, there was no "New Testament" in the early Church, and yet there existed Christian faith and Christian life. The "New Testament" came after the Church, not before. The Church produced the Christian Scriptures, not vice versa.

53

For Protestant fundamentalism, principles ("fundamentals") are primary; people are secondary. And yet the parable of the sheep and the goats (Matt. 25) suggests that we will be judged, not by our adherence to principles, but by our behavior toward one another.

Catholic Fundamentalism

Catholic fundamentalism, of a doctrinal rather than of a biblical kind, labors under similar inconsistencies. Catholic fundamentalism, too, is rationalistic in the sense that its main principles, or fundamentals, are derived through reason, not through a direct appeal to doctrine itself.

Nowhere is there any official list of doctrines that the Church officially and infallibly requires every Catholic to accept. The Church doesn't even provide us with a list of dogmas, that is, a list of infallible teachings. We know of a few of these dogmas, but not all. We have to deduce them rationally, by a process of theological reflection.

Nowhere does the Church officially, much less infallibly, teach that Church doctrine alone is the source of truth for our faith and life. Nowhere does the Church officially and infallibly teach that doctrines are always the last word in any disputed matter.

Nowhere does Jesus himself refer to a set of doctrines as the core of the Gospel or as the final test of fidelity to his call to accept and practice the Gospel. Indeed, the early Church got along for centuries with no, or very few, doctrinal pronouncements. The Nicene Creed, for example, was first formulated in the year 325 and not finally accepted until 381.

My point here is not to suggest that the Bible is unimportant to Christian faith and life, or that doctrine is similarly insignificant. On the contrary, my concern is to underline the radical inconsistency of the fundamentalist positions, Protestant and Catholic alike. Both positions claim divine authority for their social, political, and ecclesiastical views. But, in fact, both rely on rationally deduced principles to support those views. Fundamentalism is, indeed, a form of rationalism. Its appeal to divine authority is superficially compelling, but ultimately without warrant.

The best treatment of the subject is by the British Protestant biblical scholar James Barr in his book *Fundamentalism* (Philadelphia: Westminster Press, 1978). A summary of this book's thesis is given in Barr's lecture "The Problem of Fundamentalism Today," reprinted as chapter 5 of his *Scope and Authority of the Bible* (Philadelphia: Westminster Press, 1981). As Barr describes it in the latter book:

> *The real fault in fundamentalism is not its lack of intellectual gifts but its way of looking on other people. Fundamentalism as a movement has no insight into ways in which it might live along with Christians who think quite differently, or live alongside people who are not Christians at all.*

Its only real positive message to people is that they must be converted to Christ, which in effect means that they must become fundamentalist Christians. (p. 76)

Barr continues, "On the personal level this means that the basic weakness of fundamentalism is its inability to *accept* other people for what they are" (p. 76).

What to Do About Doctrinal Fundamentalists

What to do about fundamentalism within the Catholic Church? First, recognize that it *is* present in the Catholic Church, both in its doctrinal and its biblical forms. The most practical defense against doctrinal fundamentalism is the citation of official doctrinal statements that contradict the hardened views the fundamentalists hold. The fundamentalists won't be convinced, but at least their arguments will be neutralized. What is more important, the counterargument will serve to reassure Catholics in the broad center of the Church who may have been momentarily disturbed by the fundamentalists' arguments and led to worry that these arguments might, in fact, be right.

Thus, against those who quote papal and conciliar documents out of context, one can cite the remarkable document *Mysterium Ecclesiae,* promulgated by the Congregation for the Doctrine of the Faith in 1973. Ironically, the document was intended to counter Hans Kung's views on infallibility. *Mysterium Ecclesiae* insists on the historicity of dogma:

Difficulties arise from the historical condition that affects the expression of Revelation.

With regard to this historical condition, it must first be observed that the meaning of the pronouncements of faith depends partly upon the expressive power of the language used at a certain point in time and in particular circumstances. Moreover, it sometimes happens that some dogmatic truth is first expressed incompletely (but not falsely), and at a later date, when considered in a broader context of faith or human knowledge, it receives a fuller and more perfect expression. In addition, when the Church makes new pronouncements she intends to confirm or clarify what is in some way contained in Sacred Scripture or in previous expressions of Tradition; at the same time she usually has the intention of solving certain questions or removing certain errors. All these things have to be taken into account in order that these pronouncements may be properly interpreted. Finally, even though the truths which the Church intends to teach through her dogmatic formulas are distinct from the changeable conceptions of a given epoch and can be expressed without them, nevertheless it can sometimes happen that these truths may be enunciated by the Sacred Magisterium in terms that bear traces of such conceptions.

What to Do About Biblical Fundamentalists

Against those who cite the Bible out of context, we can appeal to Pope Pius XII's *Divino Afflante Spiritu* (1943), often described as the Magna Charta of Catholic Biblical Scholarship, and to the Pontifical Biblical Commission's *Instruction on the Historical Truth of the Gospels* (1964). This is how the latter document puts it:

> In order to bring out with fullest clarity the enduring truth and authority of the Gospels (the Catholic exegete) must . . . make skillful use of the new aids to exegesis, especially those which the historical method, taken in the widest sense, has provided; that method, namely, which minutely investigates sources, determining their nature and bearing, and availing itself of the findings of textual criticism, literary criticism, and linguistic studies. . .

> Unless the exegete, then, pays attention to all those factors which have a bearing on the origin and the composition of the gospels and makes due use of the acceptable findings of modern research, he will fail in his duty of ascertaining what the intentions of the sacred writers were and what it is that they have actually said. The results of recent study have made it clear that the teachings and the life of Jesus were not simply recounted for the mere purpose of being kept in remembrance, but were "preached" in such a way as to furnish the Church with the foundation on which to build up faith and morals. It follows that the interpreter who subjects the testimony of the Evangelists to persevering scrutiny will be in a position to shed further light on the enduring theological value of the Gospels and to throw into clearest relief the vital importance of the Church's interpretation.

With the biblical fundamentalists, however, it is almost always a mistake to be drawn into an argument over a particular text, because your effort to make the proper distinctions will be no match for the direct-aim rifle shot of certitude you'll get in return. A more practical tactic is to distract the fundamentalist with a fundamentalist text of your own. Among my favorites are these two: "It is easier for a camel to go through the eye of a needle than for a rich man to enter the kingdom of God" (Mark 10:25, with a parallel in Matt. 19:24); and "Not every one who says to me, 'Lord, Lord,' shall enter the kingdom of heaven, but he who does the will of my Father who is in heaven" (Matt. 7:21). And there are many others.

If even that tactic shouldn't work, we can at least remind the Catholic fundamentalist that his or her Protestant fundamentalist bedfellows are committed anti-Catholics. We have only to ask them what they think of the papacy (not simply what they think of Pope John Paul II, but the very idea of the Petrine ministry), Mary, the ordained priesthood, the seven sacraments, and the Church's authority to interpret Sacred Scripture. Jimmy

Swaggart is one of the few, if not the only one, among the TV evangelists who has been open about his rejection of traditional Catholic teachings.

Catholic fundamentalists cannot have it both ways: They cannot have on the one hand alliances with Protestant fundamentalists on the interpretation of the Bible and in the formulation of a social and political agenda and, on the other hand, a stubborn attachment to the theology and the devotional life of a pre-Vatican II Catholicism that they can barely recall, if at all.

In summary, teaching Catholicism today is at once a challenge and an opportunity. Effective catechesis will indeed focus on "the basics" and will present them with catholic breadth and balance. But the temptation for the religious educator is to follow the easier path of *theology without tears,* that is, theology without study and effort. Fundamentalism therefore remains a constant problem. But no matter how it is dressed up, fundamentalism is still the most *unorthodox* way one could follow in teaching Catholicism today.

At the time of this writing, Rev. Richard P. McBrien was the Crowley-O'Brien-Walter Professor of Theology at the University of Notre Dame and the author of the widely-used study Catholicism (Winston Press).

Peace, Justice, and the Middle Class: The Middle Class and Social Justice

Gregory Baum

This essay on the middle class and social justice is written under the impact of John Paul II's visit to Canada in September, 1984. The pope offered a rather severe message on this topic. Because the Canadian Catholic bishops had published a series of radical social messages that caused conflict in the country and even in the Church, Canadians were wondering what the pope's reaction would be. John Paul II fully supported the bishops.[1]

Crisis of Capitalism

What was the controversial point made by the Canadian bishops? In their *Ethical Reflections on the Economic Crisis* (January, 1983), they had argued that capitalism was moving into a new phase, one associated with great suffering for a growing sector of the human community.[2] In their analysis the bishops leaned heavily on John Paul's own *Laborem Exercens* (1981).

The phase of capitalism that began with the New Deal in the United States created and distributed great wealth. The capitalists realized that they needed the support of the entire community. They made an unwritten contract with society in favor of full employment, welfare support, and respect for labor organizations. At the present time, however, because of several historical factors, capital is reorganizing itself around the giant transnational corporations. It no longer needs the support of society.

Since the internationalization of capital leads to de-industrialization in North America, since the growth of the corporations allows the important decisions to slip into the hands of fewer and fewer people, and since entry into high technology removes thousands upon thousands of jobs, an ever

This article appeared in PACE 16 (1985–1986).

wider sector of the population is being marginalized in Canada and the United States. Unemployment and poverty, the Canadian bishops claim— and they are seconded by the U.S. bishops in the draft of their pastoral on the U.S. economy—produces great human misery: first material want, then eventually, moral pain, despair, and spiritual decline. We live in a sinful situation.

The new orientation of capitalism in Canada and in the world, the Canadian bishops argue, must be stopped. What is needed is a growing movement of solidarity, embracing workers, employed and unemployed; all the disadvantaged; and all who love justice, of whatever social class. In our democratic countries, only a ground swell of this kind can alter the present economic orientation.

The Liberal and Conservative parties of Canada, representing middle-class interests and attitudes, were appalled by the bishops' statement. Yet upon arriving in Canada, John Paul II fully supported the bishops in their social analysis. At an ecumenical service in Saint Paul's Anglican Church in Toronto, the pope quoted a controversial sentence from the bishops' statement and added his own words:

> The needs of the poor must take priority over the desires of the rich; the rights of workers over the maximization of profits; the preservation of the environment over uncontrolled industrial expansion; and production to meet social needs over the production for military purposes. (14 September 1984)

At Edmonton, the pope went a step further than the Canadian bishops. Discussing the relations "between the increasingly wealthier North and the increasingly poorer South," the pope had this to say:

> The poor of the South shall sit in judgment on the rich North. And poor people and poor nations—poor in different ways, not only lacking food, but also deprived of freedom and other human rights—will sit in judgment on those people who take these goods away from them, amassing to themselves the imperialistic monopoly of economic and political supremacy at the expense of others. (17 September 1984)

Many Catholics were embarrassed by the bold teaching of the pope. Middle-class Catholics felt that in the past the Church had asked them to work hard, to improve their condition, to do well in society; and now that they had succeeded and were comfortably well-off, the Church was suddenly putting a question mark behind the present system. Yet the bold social teaching put forward by the bishops and the pope was welcomed in Canada by labor groups struggling against new odds; by the unemployed who try to organize themselves; by the native peoples and other marginalized groups; and by the New Democratic Party (the Canadian equivalent of the British Labour Party), which represents the interests of workers and the low-income sector in Canada.

Middle-Class Consciousness

John Paul II offered Canadians a critical analysis of middle-class consciousness. He seemed to be saying that while Third World countries suffer *economic* oppression and Soviet bloc countries undergo *political* oppression, the industrialized societies of the West are subject to *cultural* oppression.

Of course, people in the industrialized Western countries also suffer from economic hardship, but the real oppression touching the lives of their entire populations is cultural. The dominant culture has made people individualistic and utilitarian in their concern; they have lost the sense of social solidarity and joint political will. For these reasons they are now unable to solve the relatively simple problems of their rich economies. Western culture has made them—*us*—socially impotent.

The elements of John Paul's analysis were distributed throughout the speeches he gave in Canada. He had made the same points in previous pronouncements, including in his encyclicals. First, he strongly emphasized the dominance of the consumer mentality in our society. Our market culture makes us define ourselves as consumers. We evaluate ourselves and others in terms of what we own and what we consume. We make the important judgments in our lives in terms of utilitarian considerations. Utility becomes the overriding value. We have become individualists; we concentrate on our own desires; we lose the sense of community; we fail to discover in ourselves impulses to social solidarity; we no longer have access to a collective political will. As a society we have become powerless to correct the institutions that cause grave harm to more and more people.

In the draft of their pastoral letter on the U.S. economy, the U.S. bishops have picked up this theme.[3] They call North Americans to a new moral consensus, to the recovery of social solidarity, to a sense that they are jointly responsible for one another. Apart from a moral and cultural conversion, there is no solution for the present misery.

Second, John Paul spoke of the technological mentality that challenges the Gospel. What does he mean by this? The pope rejoices in the inventions of technology. He regards technology as a marvelous instrument destined to serve people in their societies. But he believes that in the present age, the excessive reliance on technology has created great temptations for society. Here are his own words:

*The temptation exists of pursuing technological development for its own
sake, as if it were an autonomous force with built-in imperatives for
expansion, instead of seeing it as a resource to be placed at the service of
the human family. A second temptation exists which would tie technological development to the logic of profit and constant economic expansion
without due regard for the rights of workers or the needs of the poor and
helpless. A third temptation is to link technological development to the
pursuit or maintenance of power instead of using it as an instrument of
freedom. (14 September 1984)*

Each of the temptations mentioned deserves lengthy commentary. Let
me briefly say that technology threatens to become the one reliable model
of truth and practice, the overriding metaphor of human existence. Society,
then, feels itself dispensed from ethical reflection on its political and
economic policies. Social problems are left to the experts, who look for
solutions that rely on value-free scientific research and appropriate
measures of social engineering.

In his analysis of middle-class consciousness, John Paul II goes one
step further. He suggests that social policies helpful in the past and the
entire system that brought us prosperity are being invested by us with great
trustworthiness and authority. We want to believe that they will again
provide the answer for the future. We cling to the inherited system, even if
we have an inkling that it is not working well anymore. We refuse to
question the received structures; we look away from the human suffering
they produce; we tend to make the system into an absolute. It becomes an
idol for us. Pope John Paul II thinks that the East-West conflict is essentially a clash between two ideologies, both claiming absolute and universal
truth.

How can this middle-class consciousness be overcome? What remedies
does John Paul II suggest? First and foremost for him is the "remedy" of
Christian faith. If we turn to Jesus Christ, in whom God's justice and
mercy are revealed to us, we are able to distance ourselves from the
dominant culture. We can escape the power of consumerism, technological
bias, and the idolatry of the system. More than that, in Jesus Christ we are
able to transcend our individualism, discover ourselves as part of a
community, and recognize that we are responsible for one another in
society. In Jesus Christ we discover what the Latin American, the Canadian, and the U.S. bishops have called 'the preferential option for the
poor.'

John Paul II thinks that the cultural roots of the West are still intact.
Social sources of communal values are still present in our societies. The
Christian Churches and other religious communities belong to them;
ethnic and national traditions often mediate a sense of social solidarity; the
labor movement also generates a sense of community and joint responsibil-

ity. Turning to these, the pope suggests, we may find the resources out of which to acquire a new consensus of social solidarity.

Who Are the Middle Class?

Who belongs to the middle class? In the United States and Canada it is not helpful to define *class* in terms of people's relationship to production, as we find it in Marxist sociology. Nor is it helpful to define *class* as the result of stratification according to income, as it is found in mainstream sociology. *Class* in North America has to do with people's economic situation but also with their self-understanding, mediated as it is by powerful cultural forces (John Paul II speaks here of a "culture industry"), including the mass media.[4]

In North America a wide sector of the population *thinks* of itself as middle-class. People with good incomes in business, government, and the professions belong to the middle class. White-collar workers and even a large segment of blue-collar workers think of themselves as middle-class. People in insecure jobs sometimes think of themselves in the same way: They hope for a better future tomorrow. Even the unemployed sometimes regard themselves as middle-class: Being without a job is perhaps just a brief episode.

Through a complex set of cultural symbols, our society successfully persuades masses of people that they belong in one way or another to the upwardly mobile middle class. They understand their lives as personal journeys, as struggles to do well and succeed, against the background of a society vaguely perceived in market terms. And if they themselves cannot move into the comfortable life of the great consumers, their children will.

During the period of economic expansion from World War II to the late sixties, there was a good deal of validity in this self-understanding for a very large sector of North American society, certainly for a majority of its white population. Since that time, however, a grouping sector of North Americans who think of themselves as reasonably secure in their jobs and upwardly mobile are suffering from an illusion. Their standard of living has already declined; they may lose their jobs in the persistent recession or the jobless recovery, and their children may never find permanent employment. At this time, the economic crisis is pushing many people who think of themselves as middle-class into poverty.

Besides the middle class, there are basically two other classes in North American society. First there is the power elite, consisting of the directors and managers of the large corporations and the high officials of government and military. This power elite controls the important decisions regarding the economy and has a disproportionate impact on the political policies of the nation. Many research studies have been done of this class.[5]

Then there is the lower sector of society, consisting of the people in unskilled, low-paying jobs—the people trapped in structural unemployment; the people wounded by society and now unemployable; in other words, the poor. The percentages of blacks, Hispanics, and women are disproportionately high among the poor. Michael Harrington has analyzed this sector in his earlier book *The Other America* (New York: Penguin Books, 1981) and in his more recent *The New American Poverty* (New York: Holt, Rinehart and Winston, 1984). For many white North Americans living in middle-class areas, the oppressed sector of society remains almost invisible, even though it is now growing at a considerable speed.

Crucial Choices for the Middle Class

The future of North America and—because of its economic ties to the Third World—the future of the world will depend upon the manner in which middle-class North Americans react to the present crisis. Will they ally themselves with the interests of the power elite? Or will they, following the invitation of the U.S. Catholic bishops, make an "option for the poor," entering into solidarity with the oppressed people at home and overseas? As the circle of prosperity shrinks, as more and more people who thought of themselves as middle-class are pushed into insecurity and material hardship, ordinary middle-class North Americans are becoming frightened. They are quite powerless. They have no influence on the controlling class. Their spontaneous reaction is to hope that if they do their best, they will not be expelled from the shrinking circle of prosperity and comfort. The middle-class consciousness, as analyzed by John Paul II, acts as the great shield that protects people from deeper political reflection and allows them to remain caught in the consumerist individualism they have absorbed from the culture.

There is, however, another possibility. The U.S. and the Canadian bishops call upon us, the middle class, to recognize the dangerous orientation of society and to stand in solidarity with the poor, both the poor at home and the struggling people in the Third World. While we are powerless by ourselves, we may at least yearn inwardly for a just society that does not crush so many people, for an economic system that demonstrates that we are one another's keepers. If we all loved justice, political action would enable us to transform the social order.

How can this message of justice be communicated to Catholics of the middle class? It would be wrong, I think, to make them feel guilty. Many of these Catholics have lived their lives dedicated to a high ideal as it was offered by the Church at an earlier period. They strove for the love of God and the love of neighbor. They were not told of the 'option for the poor.' And yet they helped those in need whenever they had a chance.

John Paul II did not analyze individuals' personal failures, but rather he examined the impact of structures on their consciousness. We are all caught in a self-understanding that we have not created but into which we have been socialized. Now we must ask people—and ourselves—to take a critical look. A feeling of shame and confusion that we are benefiting from our middle-class status should not prevent us from standing apart, taking a critical look, and joining in Jesus' own longing for justice.

"What can we do?" This is the first question our good people ask after they hear the new message. And there are no easy answers to this question. How can a few persons of good will turn around the orientation of society? Yet if all who are badly treated by the system and all who love justice (though not so badly treated) joined in solidarity, then society could be transformed. Still, there are two responses that middle-class Catholics can make right now.

In the Present: Conversion and Action

For some Catholics it begins with conversion—a new sense of discipleship, a longing for God's approaching reign. The "option for the poor" is here the entry into a spiritual way. We shift loyalties; we look upon the world from the perspective of the victims; we find it existentially impossible to be reconciled to a society that structures people into misery.

The second response is that of action—opposing or resisting oppression. For some Catholics this follows the spiritual conversion. For others, on the contrary, action is the starting point that leads to conversion. For many Catholics action means joining a group, possibly a church group, that struggles along with oppressed people for greater justice. Such action strengthens the countervailing movements in society and lays the foundation for future change. Today there is a growing network of social justice groups in the Churches. Christians also join secular organizations wrestling in similar ways against the forces of injustice.

This action—both in church groups and in secular settings—in turn intensifies the spiritual lives of these Christians. They gain a greater sense of being disciples of Jesus—merciful, at odds with the world, identified with those who suffer, mourning over those caught in misery, hungering after justice, and acting as peacemakers. Even though they still belong to the middle class and reap some of its benefits, in their hearts they have already transcended their class to become brothers and sisters of Jesus.

Endnotes

1. Pope John Paul II's messages in Canada are collected in *The Canadian Catholic Review* 2 (October 1984). For an analysis of these messages, see G. Baum, "Labor Pope in Canada," *The Ecumenist* 23 (January–February 1985): 17–23.

2. For the social messages of the Canadian bishops and two commentaries, see G. Baum and D. Cameron, *Ethics and Economics* (Toronto: James Lorimer and Co., 1984).

3. "First Draft of the U.S. Bishops' Pastoral Letter on Catholic Social Teaching and the U.S. Economy," *Origins* 14 (15 November 1984): nos. 82–84.

4. For the distinctions among classes employed in this essay, see A. Portes and J. Walton, *Labor, Class, and the International System* (New York: Academic Press, 1981), pp. 173–180. See also A Chicago Reflection Group, "Exploring the Meaning of Liberation," in *Theology in the Americas,* ed. S. Torres and J. Eagleson (Maryknoll, NY: Orbis Books, 1976), especially pp. 226–227.

5. For examples, see G. W. Domhoff, *Who Rules America?* (Englewood Cliffs, NJ: Prentice-Hall, 1983) and W. Clement, *The Canadian Corporate Elite* (Toronto: McLelland and Steward, 1975).

At the time of this writing, Dr. Gregory Baum was
a member of the faculty of
religious studies and sociology at
Saint Michael's College, University of Toronto.
He is the author of many books on religion and society,
including the paperback *The Priority of Labor,*
published by Paulist Press.

Three Mystics for Our Times:
III. Teresa of Ávila

Gloria Durka

Teresa of Ávila (1515–1582), a Spanish Carmelite nun, is generally remembered as a religious reformer and a mystic. Those familiar with the details of her life are often impressed by her character as well as her mysticism. She is depicted as shrewd, determined, intelligent, and feisty.

For example, William James called Teresa "typical of shrewdom;" Walter T. Stace called her "lacking in intellectual power;" Pere Hahn pointed out her physical indications of "hysteria." Kate O'Brien, a sympathetic biographer, comfortably calls her a "saint . . . alarming . . . deluded . . . if you like, mad."[1] Yet the Catholic Church canonized Teresa, and in 1970 she was declared a Doctor of the Church, a status previously reserved for men.

How can we reconcile a mad shrew who lacks intellectual power with this woman who is called "mystical doctor" and saint—and who, in the last half of her life, not only traveled the length of Spain creating a new religious order but also wrote a great mystical treatise, *Interior Castle?* Has a patriarchal psychology misunderstood the psychospiritual journey of Teresa of Ávila? *Can contemporary psychology understand a female at all?* After all, feminists remind us, no truly feminist psychoanalysis or therapy presently exists. What can be learned from Teresa from the perspective of Christian feminism?

Teresa as Woman of Power: Another Look

Teresa may be more relevant to contemporary women than is apparent at first glance. Recent work in the importance of the social imagination and the impact of culture and political climate makes it easier for us to understand Teresa in the light of the complex historical context in which she lived.

Teresa grew up in a patriarchal culture, where males and activities viewed as masculine were considered superior. Women's roles were limited and narrow, leaving most women with the choice of either marriage or

---

This article appeared in PACE 17 (1986–1987).

convent, the latter offering greater opportunities for leadership roles. Teresa chose the convent and entered at age twenty-one.

But even as a child, Teresa exhibited what some have termed her "masculine turn" of mind. In her large family of two sisters and nine brothers, Teresa was a leader, even of her older brothers. She longed for adventure and fed her mind on the romantic novels supplied by her mother. Her world was full of soldiering and new worlds to conquer. The action was masculine; the values were masculine.

Behavioral scientists have documented that, because of being ignored or stereotyped as a class, women themselves have internalized a poor self-concept. They "breathe in" the notion that men are more intelligent, capable, independent, and powerful than women. So it is not surprising to read Teresa's account of her need for male approval. About the establishment of her first convent in secret, she wrote:

> *I did nothing without asking the opinion of learned men lest in any way whatever I should act against obedience. As they saw what bene-fits . . . were being conferred upon the whole Order, they told me I might do what I did, although it was being done in secret, and I was keeping it from my superior's knowledge. Had they told me that there was the slightest imperfection in this, I think I would have given up a thousand convents, let alone a single one.[2]*

So important was male approval to Teresa! Although Teresa's actions challenged the model of the submissive and docile woman-nun, her resistance to such stereotyping was indirect. She simply chose advisers she believed would counsel her to do as she intended!

Today, resistance to sexism is being directed to the public ritual life of the Catholic Church. Teresa was limited in her ability to imagine liturgical reform, to challenge what was and should not have been. Christian feminists will look in vain at Teresa's life for a reform agenda concerning the public ritual life of the Church. But they can find a model of a woman whose personal life and public life were congruent with her most highly held values.

In 1561, at the age of forty-six or forty-seven, Teresa received divine permission to refuse obedience to her superiors:

> *"As for what the Queen of Angels said concerning obedience, it per-tained to the fact that it distressed me not to give obedience to the Order, but the Lord had told me it wasn't suitable to give it to my superiors. He gave me reasons why it would in no way be fitting that I do so"* (Kavanaugh, p. 226). *Instead, he told her she should petition Rome. Clearly her ego, dressed in divine clouds, had regained control in her life.[3]*

After she received a command from her Lord to strive with all her power to establish a new monastery (thus disobeying her convent superiors), Teresa's life and letters reflect a woman who is constantly receiving special commands "from the top" to get out there and be herself.

Teresa's reform, the founding of strict and enclosed monasteries, satisfied her longing to be a leader in an active life. She once more had to deal with worldly concerns, religious and divine authorities, critics, and disciples. She was in a leadership position, healthy enough to ride back and forth over country roads on the back of a mule in all kinds of weather. And since her reform was not finally released from the jurisdiction of the Observance until 1581, she was often doing her work in disobedience and contumacy.

After the conversion experience from which Teresa derived divine permission to go ahead with her reform, her growth as a new active person can be discerned. Her self-confidence, her problem-oriented nature, her creativity, and her sense of humor define her as an assertive, self-actualizing person who provides present-day women with a splendid role model for intelligent leadership.

Teresa's journeys and exhausting efforts at establishing the reform of the Carmelite order challenged the limits of "women's place." Though she endured physical trials that were formidable, the psychological pressures were most draining. When she set out from Ávila in 1568 to establish other convents, many of the townspeople thought she was mad. She had already heard herself denounced from the pulpit.

Ten years later Teresa was still being denounced. The papal nuncio at Madrid called her a "restless, contumacious gadabout." Her gutsy spirit was undaunted, however, and she continued to travel and speak the words of reform until her death, always joyful, so that she could exclaim even on her deathbed, "Lord, I am a daughter of the Church!"

Teresa as Liberator and Transformer: Refining Our Focus

While much of Teresa's experience was acceptable in terms of her culture, women today must question some of its validity in terms of their own experience. Nevertheless, Teresa's initiatives in the public realm give clues about women's potential as leaders. Her "mysterious illness" and her subsequent dialogues with Christ gave her a path to power in a culture decidedly closed to feminine autonomy.

Teresa was well aware of the limitations that her culture placed on women. She envied missionaries who could devote themselves to the salvation of souls while she had to content herself with the work that was within her reach—the following of the evangelical counsels in a life of prayer and penance. Commenting on this restriction, she wrote:

68

As if I could do anything, or were anything, I wept and besought Our Lord that He might find a remedy for so great an evil (as the loss of souls) . . . and I realized that I was a woman and thus prevented from carrying out what I wanted to do for the service of the Lord.[4]

Yet, with the power of the Spirit, Teresa did overcome in herself, and eventually in the Church, those prejudices against women that were prevalent in her day:

1. **Restrictions on the interpersonal and societal life of nuns:** Teresa's concept of religious life included a new form of relationship, not only among the sisters themselves, but also between the sister and the "outside world." She did not enclose herself psychologically within convent walls, shutting out humanity. Her letters—and in those letters more than anywhere else her real personality is revealed—are full of expressions of solicitude, affection, and love. If she sometimes blamed herself for a lack of detachment, at no stage in her life did she seem to have cut herself off from affection for either friends or relatives. To have to cut herself off from others would have been a betrayal of charity in her eyes. Moreover, she wanted affection in return.

2. **Restrictions of social prejudice:** Teresa also overcame social prejudices and discriminatory situations and circumstances, especially those of her Jewish ancestry. Teresa's paternal grandfather was a Jew forced into Christianity by the Inquisition, a fact deliberately ignored and obfuscated by subsequent generations of Carmelites obsessed with "blood purity" as a requirement for entry into religious life. Teresa's opposition to discrimination of this kind was radical. The repeated occurrence in Teresa's writings of the theme of true and false honor and the need for poverty in the face of worldly honors and distinctions is completely consistent with her particular experience of liberation from the fetishes of her society.

3. **Restrictions on women's spirituality:** In the area of spirituality, it was presumed that women would be content with vocal and external devotions and should not venture forth into the path of mysticism. Teresa boldly challenged this limitation when she wrote:

> *Now I turn to those who wish to follow this road, that is, until*
> *they attain a drink of this water of life. . . . It is important and*
> *even essential to take a firm resolve not to stop before we reach*
> *the font . . . come what may, happen what may . . . murmur who*
> *will. . . . As frequently happens the world will tire itself*
> *repeating . . . "It is not for women, who are given to illusions;"*
> *"better that they should sew;" "they have no need of these*
> *refinements;" "the Pater Noster and Ave Maria are enough for*
> *them."* [5]

For Teresa, God existed not outside the self, but deeply within, constantly beckoning and enticing individuals into relationships of quiet union. But this desire for a personal, experiential encounter with God was daring and dangerous in sixteenth-century Castile. The climate of suspicion in which Teresa worked identified mysticism with Lutheranism; thus the climate was basically hostile to the desire for personal, experiential encounters with God such as Teresa advocated.

Even more important than the kind of prayer advocated by Teresa were the odds against which she had to struggle for a woman's right to such a prayer experience. Her efforts cannot be appreciated apart from this context, and the revolutionary understandings and struggles for women's rights to have direct experiential encounters with God cannot be properly understood when her life and work are wrapped up in pious generalities.[6]

The story of Teresa of Ávila is evidence of the need for a revisionist history of the Christian tradition and a reconstruction of women's spirituality in the light of contemporary experience. Such revision and reconstruction, by giving us a richer, more complex understanding of where we have come from, could enable us to move with greater freedom and hope in the future.

Such work has begun. Beside the now well-documented, classical Christian stereotype of the female—as misbegotten male; daughter of Eve; temptress; insatiable harlot; and nagging, unfaithful, garrulous wife—we have found it possible to set *another persona*—Teresa, the seeker after God, the model of human holiness and divine action, wholly equal with her brothers in the pursuit of Christian perfection. While her life does not necessarily provide an exact model for our future, it does generate questions and challenges for us.

Legacy for Religious Educators

All three mystics focused on in this series—Hildegard of Bingen, Julian of Norwich, and Teresa of Avila—have given us a rich inheritance that includes these dimensions:

An Integrated Spirituality

Not only did Hildegard, Julian, and Teresa reject the dualism of body and soul, they cherished and cared for their physical bodies as integral to their spiritual well-being. They survived serious illness and lived long lives, especially for their times (Hildegard, eighty-one; Julian, seventy-five or more; Teresa, sixty-seven). Their reverence for physical life and their sensitivity to the needs of their psyches can teach us much about the traps of overwork and stress.

A Worldly Spirituality

These mystics' understandings of the world were not naive; they were based on firsthand experiences through travel (Hildegard and Teresa) and from constantly receiving travelers (Julian). It is their *realism* that today we find so attractive. These women can be a source of optimism for us in the face of the progressive rape of the environment and the threat of nuclear holocaust.

The spirituality of these mystics was obviously informed by their place or home: Hildegard, the lushness of the Rhine Valley; Julian, the social intercourse of a center of commerce; Teresa, the external, ostentatiously religious environment of sixteenth-century Spain. They prompt us to ask ourselves what the unique characteristics of our own place might be and what could be our appropriate response to them in our spirituality.

A Transformative Spirituality

These mystics can still remind us of the relationship between personal liberation and social liberation, the value of simple living in the building of a more just society, the awareness of a God who is both liberated from the limitations that people put on the way God functions in human life and a God who is capable of liberating. For women they offer a theological use of imagination that provides us with alternatives to the stereotyped images of women. They offer images of women
- as persons who delight God;
- as persons who constantly receive God's love;
- as persons whose faithfulness does not require weak subservience to God, institutions, or individuals; and
- as persons who can be agents for just deeds.

Companionhood for the Second Half of Life

All three mystics modeled for us that there is life after mid-life, that mid-life itself need not be merely a culmination of the unreflective life of youth but instead, the culmination of a long gestation period that can flower fully at last. These women heeded in their own times what Jung cautioned against centuries later when he wrote:

The afternoon of human life must also have significance of its own and cannot be merely a pitiful appendage to life's morning. . . . Whoever carries over into the afternoon the law of the morning . . . must pay for so doing with damage to [one's] soul.[7]

Each of these mystics experienced healing and empowerment during her mid-life. The act of writing—that is, of making public their insights into the life of the spirit—was the occasion of owning and claiming their own self-esteem.

Conclusion

These three compassionate mystics have presented us with a view of spirituality that is not only compelling but attainable by everyday people. They have shown that contemplation is *a part of* our common vocation, not something *apart from* daily life. We can drink from the wells of their wisdom and be filled with hope and courage for the future.

I am convinced that as women examine their religious tradition with a deeper historical awareness and a more genuine feminist perspective, women mystics such as Hildegard, Julian, and Teresa become more than just impressive spiritual leaders or reformers. When their leadership and reform abilities are seen in combination with their power to affirm their unique spiritualities and their determination to defy narrow cultural and religious norms in pursuit of their own visions, then they can be seen as midwives to the birth of a new vision of Christian community.

Endnotes

1. Quoted in Romano, "A Psycho-Spiritual History," p. 274.
2. *The Book of Her Life,* chap. 33.
3. Romano, "A Psycho-Spiritual History," p. 284. Romano's extract includes a quotation from the Kavanaugh translation of Teresa's autobiography.
4. *The Way of Perfection,* chap. 1.
5. Ibid., chap. 21.
6. See Weaver, *New Catholic Women,* pp. 193–194.
7. Jung, *Modern Man,* p. 109.

Sources

Burrows, Ruth. *Fire Upon Earth: The Interior Castle Explored*. Denville, NJ: Dimension Books, 1981.

Clissold, Stephen. *St. Teresa of Ávila*. Minneapolis: Seabury Press, 1982.

Durka, Gloria. "The Religious Journey of Women: The Education Task," *Religious Education* 77, no. 2 (March-April 1982): 163–178.

Egidio, Teofanes. "The Historical Setting of St. Teresa's Life." In *Carmelite Studies: Spiritual Direction*. Ed. John Sullivan. Washington, DC: Institute of Carmelite Studies Publications, 1980, pp. 122–182.

Galilea, Segundo. *The Future of Our Past: The Spanish Mystics Speak to Contemporary Spirituality*. Notre Dame, IN: Ave Maria Press, 1985.

Jung, Carl. *Modern Man in Search of a Soul*. New York: Harvest, 1933.

Romano, Catherine. "A Psycho-Spiritual History of Teresa of Ávila: A Woman's Perspective." In *Western Spirituality*. Ed. Matthew Fox. Notre Dame, IN: Fides, 1979.

Teresa of Ávila. *The Book of her Life* and *The Way of Perfection*. Selections from *The Collected Works of St. Teresa of Ávila*. Trans. O. Rodriguez and K. Kavanaugh. Washington, DC: Institute of Carmelite Studies, 1980.

Weaver, Mary Jo. *New Catholic Women*. New York: Harper and Row, 1986.

At the time of this writing, Gloria Durka was a professor of religious education at Fordham University. She had authored or edited six books and lectured on women and spirituality in the United States, Canada, and Europe.

Holiness and Finitude:
Creaturely Spirituality

Michael J. Himes

God and creation are not in competition. That, if anything, we should have learned from the doctrine of the Incarnation. Our knowledge and awareness of God are in direct proportion to creation's fulfillment; i.e., God is more fully and perfectly seen to be God as creation is more fully and perfectly realized as creation.

God is not glorified in the abasing of creatures. "The glory of God is humanity fully alive," Irenaeus wrote toward the end of the second century. This claim is grounded in the Incarnation, expressed powerfully in Philippians 2:6–11, "Though (Christ) was in the form of God, (he) did not regard equality with God something to be grasped. Rather, he emptied himself, taking the form of a slave, coming in human likeness" (vv. 6–7). That is probably the most extraordinary statement regarding the dignity of humanity and consequently of creation which has ever been made: God has chosen to be a creature!

The roots of this breath-taking assertion lie deep in Scripture. In the "priestly source" of the first chapter of Genesis, God creates human beings as the climax of creation, the masterpiece on the sixth day. For this *chef d'oeuvre*, God is depicted as not creating simply by decree as in the earlier works: Let there be light; Let there be a firmament; Let the waters come together and the dry land emerge, etc. Now God deliberates before this last and greatest creation: "Let us make [human beings] in our image, after our likeness" (v. 26). For this ultimate creation God uses a blueprint—God's self. Thus, in the first chapter of Genesis, the claim is already present that in creation God has expressed God's self. The "Yahwist source" makes the same claim in chapter two, although in different imagery. There the order of creation is reversed. Instead of humanity being created last, after all else is prepared, the human being is the first act of God and everything else is brought into existence in answer to human needs. In this account, the culminating act of God is the creation of genuinely human community when the first human can say of another, "This one, at last, is bone of my bones and flesh of my flesh" (v. 23). In this second creation story Yahweh,

This article appeared in PACE 19 (1988–1989).

having fashioned the human being from the soil of the earth, blows the breath of life into it (v. 7). Thus, the breath which enlivens humanity is the very breath of Yahweh. The images are different, but the point is the same in both creation stories: The culmination of creation is God's self-expression.

The refrain which punctuates each day's work in the "priestly" account is the divine judgment: God looked at what he had made and saw that it was good. Again and again this first judgment is announced. The goodness of creatureliness is a major theme of the creation stories in Genesis, a theme which must be emphasized constantly if one is to be true to the tradition of Scripture. To weaken that proclamation of creaturely goodness is to destroy the relationship between God and everything which exists. Indeed, to deny or dismiss the rightness of finitude may be the very root of evil. In the Yahwist source's account of the entry of evil into creation, the familiar story of the Fall in the third chapter of Genesis, the primal temptation is to be like God. That is the incentive which the serpent holds out to the human being. But in the "priestly" creation story which begins the book of Genesis as we now have it, we are told that the human being is created in the likeness of God. The serpent's invitation assumes that likeness to the divine must be achieved by human initiative, that it must, in fact, be wrested from God who has jealously tried to prohibit creatures from attaining any likeness to God's self. For the temptation to be persuasive, the human being must regard creatureliness as inherently "unlike God," unsatisfactory and undesirable. The primal temptation is precisely a call to reject the first judgment: Whatever God may have declared when God looked at what God had made, we have examined it ourselves and have concluded, "Not good at all." The first sin, the introduction of evil, is the denial by creatures of the goodness of creation.

The differences among three of the greatest works of Christian literary imagination may illustrate the point. Opera-lovers have long remarked that, when the devil appears as a character in an opera, he gets all the best tunes. In *Paradise Lost* he gets all the best lines. Milton may have intended to "assert eternal providence, And justify the ways of God to men," but poetry assigned to God has a stateliness which borders dangerously close to dullness, whereas Satan's speeches are dazzling. This is not simply due to the fact that Satan's actions are the mainspring of the plot of the great epic. The problem lies in Milton's notion of sin and its relation to creatureliness. He accepted the position that the root of all sin is pride. And so the Satan of *Paradise Lost* is a monster of pride. Pride is indeed a vice. But, it is also an attribute of tragic heroes. Milton's "lost archangel," newly flung to hell, bids farewell to the "happy fields/Where joy forever dwells," and thunders,

Here at least
We shall be free; the almighty hath not built
Here for his envy, will not drive us hence:
Here we may reign secure, and in my choice
To reign is worth ambition though in hell:
Better to reign in hell than serve in heaven.
(Bk. 1, 11. 258–263)

The poet may have intended us to respond with horror, but I suspect that most readers get a thrill, perhaps of horror, but a thrill nonetheless. This may be evil, but it is majestic. The third chapter of Genesis sees evil as rooted in the denial of one's own majesty as a creature.

By contrast, Satan in *The Divine Comedy* neither speaks nor acts. When in the last canto of the Inferno section of his great poem Dante comes to Lucifer, the devil is locked in ice formed by his tears frozen by the endlessly useless flapping of his wings (Canto 34, 11. 49–54).

Dante's devil is not a monster of pride. Rather, he is personified despair, incapable of speech or action. Here there is horror and no thrill, no shred of heroism, no hint of tragic grandeur. For Dante knew that carved on the gate of hell is, from Canto 3, 1.9, "Abandon hope, all you who enter." The entry to hell is not pride; it is despair. At the heart of evil is the absolute denial of the goodness of creaturely existence.

And it is despair that leads Faust to form his pact with the devil in Goethe's magnificent poetic drama. Disgust with the world and with himself, both of which are too limited, has brought Faust to deny the goodness of finite being: "Existence is such a burden to me that death is desirable, life hateful to me" (Pt. 1, 11. 1570–1571). And the devil, Mephistopheles, whom Faust conjures up, defines himself, in what may be the most chilling description of evil ever written, as the negation of the value of creatureliness:

I am the spirit who says 'no!' And rightly so for everything which exists
deserves to be destroyed. Better would it have been that nothing had ever
come into being. (Pt. 1, 11. 1338–1341).

Here the demon is the one who wills non-being. Everything is finite, limited, and so ought not to exist. Indeed, Goethe's devil, far from hating God, thinks that only God ought to be; whatever is not God, including Mephistopheles himself, should not be at all. He is the spirit who negates, who denies the value of everything, who says 'no.'

Any reading of the Christian tradition, any form of asceticism, any kind of spirituality which denies the goodness, dignity and glory of creation, including the human person, is fundamentally distorted. It may, in fact, be demonic, in the sense of Goethe's demon, the spirit of negation.

76

That such a destructive asceticism, one motivated by fear or hatred of creatureliness, has been a possibility within Christianity is tragically true. There have been forms of spirituality which sought infinite being by trying to obliterate finite being, which so terribly misunderstood the incarnational principle in Christianity that people were taught to find God by escaping humanity. These styles of spirituality must be criticized both by the central beliefs of the Christian tradition they contradict and by the damage they have wreaked on humanity and on nature. And in light of such criticism, our tradition must be explored to make richer and healthier forms of the spiritual life available to men and women in our time.

In subsequent articles in this series, I intend to treat three issues which should be taken into account in any discussion of forms of spirituality in our situation as late twentieth-century English-speaking North Americans. The first is the need for Christian spirituality to incorporate the tragic in human life. The second is the loss of the incarnational principle because of the terror inspired by the passage of time. The third is the need to reappropriate Trinitarian theology.

The movement within this country called *creation spirituality* provides a convenient context in which to consider these issues, for it attempts to do the work both of criticism and of construction. Creation spirituality quite correctly recognizes the urgency of the task of giving shape to a spirituality which promotes global consciousness, avoids destructive introspection, weds growth in the life of the spirit to passionate action for justice, and reinvigorates both religion and art. Its primary exponent, Matthew Fox, has written in the best and fullest statement of creation spirituality that all theological studies have to return to a whole and let go of their Newtonian, specialized parts mentalities. This is why the term "spirituality" is not even found in solid theological thinkers of the Middle Ages, such as Thomas Aquinas: The whole theological enterprise was one of finding one's place in the universe.[1]

I share Fox's concern to avoid the splintering of theology into discrete compartments; although, if theology is to be genuinely public discourse in David Tracy's sense (i.e., Tracy's insistence that "each theologian must attempt to articulate and defend an explicit method of inquiry and use that method to interpret the symbols and tests of our common life and of Christianity"[2]), theology must entail some division of labor into fields of specialization. "Spiritual theology," however, is not such a field of specialization; it is one way of casting the whole of theology. Fox's concern to anchor spirituality in a reappraisal of the whole Christian tradition is necessary if spirituality is to avoid becoming esoteric and privatized. He writes that "what distinguishes a spirituality from a cult is precisely tradition."[3]

To reappraise and reappropriate a tradition, especially a tradition of the depth and richness of Christianity, requires extraordinary balance and inclusivity. Though there must be no hesitation to exclude that which distorts or corrupts the tradition, great care must be taken in evaluating the contributions, historical influence, and present utility of elements within the tradition. If we have learned anything from biblical and historical studies, we should be aware of the pluralism of theologies and spiritualities which Christians have used to express their experience of God's work in the world and in their lives. And if the Church is really becoming catholic for the first time,[4] we must be sensitive to the question of pluralism in spirituality and theology at present. Fox notes this several times in *Original Blessing* when he distinguishes creation spirituality from what he calls "fall/redemption spirituality."[5]

Yet Fox concludes his "primer" by writing: "This entire book and its journey into creation-centered spirituality also leads to a letting go of certain forms of religion, those based on fall/redemption theologies, structures, and spiritualities."[6] His description of his book is a just one: It is a call to turn to one way of casting some elements of the Christian tradition and to turn from another way of casting other elements in that tradition. Although Fox several times warns against dichotomization, against "either-or" ways of thinking, he is quite explicit in his introduction to *Original Blessing* that his warning does not apply when it comes to fall/ redemption spirituality.

Some people will object that to contrast fall/redemption spirituality and creation spirituality is to create a dualism of either/or instead of living out a dialectic of both/and. But when it comes to human concepts, there are either/or choices that we must make—a psychology that says, "The soul makes war with the body," (fall/redemption, Augustine) and one that says, "The soul loves the body," (creation spirituality, Eckhart) are not saying the same thing. Only a mushy and basically sentimental mind would say that they are of equal value. We must choose. A spirituality is a way, a path. We do not come to two paths in a road and say, out of timidity and fear to make a decision, "I will go down both roads at once."[7]

I think that Matthew Fox is quite wrong here and badly serves his own purpose. It would take far too long to rehearse at length the tendentious reading of history which pits some figures from the tradition against others in a fashion so overstated that he can actually write: "The abysmal, theologically one-sided dominance of Augustine over Jesus and the prophets must cease."[8] It is true that he denies that *Original Blessing* is "a polemic against Augustine or the fall/redemption model for religion,"[9] but when he explains the importance of the notion of original sin in some strands of the Christian tradition by claiming that it "plays kindly into the hands of empire builders, slave masters, and patriarchal society in general,"[10] it is difficult not to describe the statement as polemical.

Creation spirituality plays a vital and necessary role in its expression of certain core elements of the Christian tradition and is especially illuminative of particular aspects of our human experience. What Matthew Fox names fall/redemption spirituality has given expression to other central elements of the Christian tradition and has, in William James's phrase, "yielded religious comfort to a class of minds" in responding to other equally real and pressing aspects of human experience. In his classic *The Varieties of Religious Experience,* James employed a distinction between two "classes of minds": "The once born" and "the twice born," or, as he also termed them, those who responded to "the religion of healthy-mindedness" and those who resonated to "the religion of the sick soul."[11] He readily acknowledged that these two types of religious sensibilities seldom exist in their pure forms.

In their extreme forms, of pure naturalism and pure salvationism, the two types are violently contrasted; though here as in most other current classifications, the radical extremes are somewhat ideal abstractions, and the concrete human beings whom we most often meet are intermediate mixtures. Practically, however, you all recognize the difference: You understand, for example, the disdain of the Methodist convert for the mere sky-blue healthy-minded moralist; and you likewise enter into the aversion of the latter to what seems to him the diseased subjectivism of the Methodist, dying to live, as he calls it, and making of paradox and the inversion of natural appearances the essence of God's truth.[12]

James's categories are rough and ready, no doubt, but they serve to make one very important point: Various styles of religious experience, various spiritualities, develop from real but different personalities. One cannot dismiss any spiritual tradition, particularly one which has fruitfully formed many men and women over the course of centuries, without simultaneously dismissing the religious experience of those men and women. That other men and women have found that particular tradition fruitless or burdensome does not mean that it is a destructive and distorted form of spirituality. Rather, it is another evidence that no single form of spirituality answers the needs of every woman or man. One can no more dismiss Augustine's experience than Eckhart's (although the two have far more in common than Matthew Fox ever admits). A Catholic spirituality should be catholic; it should recognize that various spiritualities may be of equal value for different persons—or for the same person at different moments in his or her life.

There is no single spirituality, as there is no single theology, which deals with the whole tradition with perfect fidelity or grapples with all human experience with full success. Pluralism, here as everywhere, is the name of the game, and complementarity is the first rule. With what aspects of the tradition and with what issues in living today do different spiritualities deal best—ah, that is for another article.

Endotes

1. Matthew Fox, O.P., *Original Blessing: A Primer in Creation Spirituality* (Santa Fe, New Mexico: Bear and Co., 1983), p. 21.
2. David Tracy, *Blessed Rage for Order: The New Pluralism in Theology* (New York: Seabury Press, 1975), p 3.
3. Fox, p. 21.
4. Karl Rahner, "Basic Theological Interpretation of the Second Vatican Council," *Concern for the Church, Theological Investigations* 20 (New York: Crossroad, 1981), pp. 77–89. Note: Rahner suggested the Catholic Church became a world church only after centuries of being Hebraic, then Hellenistic, then European and European-derived.
5. Fox, see esp. pp. 210–219.
6. Fox, p. 305.
7. Fox, p. 28.
8. Fox, p. 22.
9. Fox, p. 26.
10. Fox, p. 54.
11. William James, *The Varieties of Religious Experience: A Study in Human Nature. Being the Gifford Lecturers on Natural Religion Delivered at Edinburgh in 1901–1902. The Works of William James 13* (Cambridge, Massachusetts: Harvard University Press, 1985), see esp. pp. 71–138. James took the phrases "once born" and "twice born" from the British writer Francis W. Newman; see the latter's *The Soul, Its Sorrows and Its Aspirations: An Essay towards the Natural History of the Soul, as the True Basis of Theology.* 3rd ed. (London: John Chapman, 1852), pp. 81 and 89.
12. James, *The Varieties of Religious Experience.* pp. 139f.

At the time of this writing, Michael J. Himes was associate professor of theology at the University of Notre Dame. Department of Theology, University of Notre Dame, Notre Dame, IN 46556.

Martyrs From Polycarp to Romero: Archetypes of Christian Witness

Berard L. Marthaler

Almost from the beginning the Church has recognized the need to have heroes—role models—for the community to imitate and emulate. Early Christians would have been bewildered by the jargon of moral imperatives, but they readily understood the life and death demands of faith and commitment. The martyrs provided both inspiration and instruction, or, what we might call today the affective and cognitive dimensions of moral action. Martyrdom came to be regarded as the summit and crown of Christian spirituality.

The aged bishop of Antioch, Ignatius, on his way to Rome to be devoured by wild beasts, composed several letters in which he reflected on the fate that was to befall him. Ignatius saw the martyr as the most perfect imitator of Christ: A person is a true disciple of Christ only if he/she dies for Christ's sake. Anyone who does not accept death willingly, with eyes fixed on Christ's passion, does not have the life of Christ within. As the persecutions intensified toward the end of the second century, the "exhortation to martyrdom" became a steady theme in Christian preaching and literature.

The local churches copied and circulated the *Acta,* records of official proceedings that told of the trials of their martyrs. The Church at Smyrna wrote a letter to the Christian community at Philomelium giving an eyewitness account of the heroic death of St. Polycarp. *The Passion of Perpetua and Felicitas,* said to have been edited by Tertullian, is based on Perpetua's own diary. The *Acta* and the *Passiones* belong more to the genre of biography than to the genre of hagiography, which became popular in the middle ages and which included romanticized legends of the martyrs and the lives of the monks and bishops.

Biography pulls the reader into a world of action populated by people with real names, family ties, and street addresses. The heroes are figures with emotions, loves and hates, noble ideals and petty jealousies; they are

This article appeared in PACE 19 (1988–1989).

torn between past memories and dreams of the future; some are simple people with great insight; some are educated but insensitive. In describing real-life situations, biographers confront us with conflicting demands of personal ambition versus social responsibility; choices between goods or, as seems more often the case, between lesser evils. From Plutarch's *Parallel Lives* to John F. Kennedy's *Profiles in Courage,* writers have used biography as a means to teach moral values by holding up individuals whose characters and achievements make them deserving of imitation and emulation.

As in the stories of the martyrs, moral courage requires a good deal of physical courage as well. Despite the fact that the early Christians saw martyrdom as the best way of becoming partners in the sufferings and death of Jesus, they discouraged anyone from volunteering for the honor. Death was not to be an escape. In the account of Polycarp's martyrdom, the conduct of the aged bishop is contrasted with the bravado of one Quintus. Quintus gave himself up to the authorities and persuaded others to make public avowal of their faith. When faced with torture and death, however, his will weakened; Quintus repudiated Christ and offered incense to the statue of the emperor. On the other hand, Polycarp, warned that the imperial authorities were looking for him, went into hiding but did not flee the city. He chose to remain with his people. Finally, when apprehended, Polycarp was fearless. The proconsul offered him a chance of freedom: "Swear, and I release you; curse Christ." Polycarp replied, "For six and eighty years I have been serving Him, and He has done no wrong to me; how, then, dare I blaspheme my King who saved me!"

One might have expected an eighty-six-year-old bishop, leader in the Christian community and set in his ways, to have defied the imperial authorities. The case of the twenty-two-year-old catechumen, Vivia Perpetua, is another matter. She was well-born, educated, married and nursing an infant son when she was apprehended along with her pregnant maid-servant Felicitas and three male catechumens in North Africa. The account of Perpetua's ordeal was intended to strengthen the resolve of Christians, but it offers no solace to today's parents who resort to deprogramming in their efforts to persuade their daughters and sons to abandon deeply held convictions. Her gray-haired father repeatedly entreated Perpetua to change her mind, citing the ruin that it would bring upon the family and appealing to her maternal instincts for the well-being of her child. At the time of her sentencing, Perpetua watched helplessly as the soldiers clubbed her father because he could not dissuade her to abandon her faith.

In today's world, where torture has become a refined science, Perpetua and her friends would have been isolated from one another. The six—one died in prison—were arrested, thrown into the dungeon, tried, and executed together. Perpetua was the most prominent of the group, but Saturus was the apparent leader. Absent when the arrest warrant was served, he surrendered to the authorities to be with the group. Through the long ordeal, they supported, encouraged, and consoled one another. Visits by deacons and other members of the Christian community assured them of the Church's prayers and backing. (This persecution under Septimius Severus, A.D. 202, was intended primarily to intimidate potential converts.)

The martyr is the archetype of the Christian witness. In the pagan world (and, according to some, in America today) where cynics derided noble ideals and altruism, the martyr was recognized by Christians and pagans alike as a symbol of a new culture aborning. Martyrs honored by the Church are men and women of the Church. They are at once witnesses to Christ and representatives of the Christian community and, as such, represent a threat to totalitarianism in all its forms. From the earliest times, Christians were persecuted on political grounds. The Sanhedrin forgot the sage advice of Gamaliel (Acts 5:34–39); they perceived the likes of Stephen as a threat to their own authority. Stephen's martyrdom (Acts 6:8–7:60) was intended to intimidate the community. The Church did not set out to overthrow the Roman emperors, but its values and ideals undermined them. Christian witness is a political act; martyrdom is the ultimate defiance of oppressive regimes and earthly despots who appropriated to Caesar the things that are God's.

The accounts of martyrdom are not simply isolated stories of heroic individuals; they are owned by the Church and stored in her living memory. They are part and parcel of the Christian ethos in that they project an image of a people who believe in Someone, something worth living and dying for. The stories of the early martyrs, and even the fictionalized legends of a later time, captured the imagination of generation after generation. Saints begot saints. Ignatius of Loyola, Teresa of Ávila and Therese of Lisieux are a few who confess to having been captivated by them.

In the sixteenth century, John Fox compiled a *Book of Martyrs* that was clearly intended to steel the resolve of Protestants in the face of persecution, legitimize the Reformation, and present the Roman Church and Catholic sovereigns in a bad light. Fox depicted the victims of the Inquisition, the "brave Waldenses," John Hus, Jerome of Prague, Willima Tyndale, and other champions of reform as latter day descendants of the early martyrs. It has been said that after the Bible itself, no book so influenced early Protestant sentiment as John Fox's *Book of Martyrs*. And in England and Wales, Catholics had their lists of martyrs as well. The Protestants and Catholics were at odds over many issues, but true believers all, they were one in their determination to die for their convictions.

The Age of Persecutions did not end with Constantine. Martyrs follow inevitably in the wake of missionaries, and often the missionaries themselves are among the first to give witness with their lives, as was the case of St. Boniface in Germany and Isaac Jogues and John de Brebeuf in North America. Wherever the Gospel is preached, there is a record of martyrs. The Church calendar commemorates Paul Miki and his companions, who were crucified in Nagasaki, Japan (February 6) and Charles Lwanga and the Ugandan martyrs, executed in the nineteenth century (June 3). In 1984 Pope John Paul II canonized a hundred Korean martyrs who had witnessed to Christ.

Christians continue to pay a heavy price for their convictions and, to complicate matters, their persecutors are themselves often Christians. One thinks of Thomas Becket and Thomas More in England., both of whom ran afoul of their sovereigns. The issues may not have been as clear-cut as when Christians were asked to deny Christ, but for them it was still a matter of conscience and fidelity. And there is the case of Joan of Arc; though not officially listed as a martyr, she was forced to choose between her inner voices and the dictates of realpolitik in fifteenth century France. Saints all. Their lives do not belong to that "genre of pat little stories in school readers," that Lawrence Kohlberg spoke of, "in which virtue always triumphs." They continue to speak as modern men and women caught in the web of conflicting responsibilities.

The lives of the saints have provided the plots for drama, but, as moving as the plays and movies are, theater has not done well in dealing with the source of their strength and drive, their personal faith. Nor is faith a dimension that fell in Kohlberg's ken. His interest centered on the process and stages of moral development; the lives of the saints focus on commitment, love and a vision that sees beyond death.

A list of twentieth century martyrs has yet to be compiled (though it is the kind of a project that a high school class could undertake). The Roman calendar already commemorates Maria Goretti (July 6) and Maximillian Kolbe (August 14), whose witness reflect conditions of the time. Time is needed to learn the names of the heroic women and men in the Third World, in eastern Europe, the Near and Far East, who died with their eyes fixed on the passion of Christ. Many in Latin America whose Christian witness challenged the rich and powerful are no less martyrs because they disappeared without trace. The fate that met Maura Clarke, Jean Donovan, Ita Ford, and Dorothy Kazel in El Salvador and Stanley Rother in Guatemala is, thanks to the intervention of the U.S. government, well enough known, but it will take the services of agencies like Amnesty International to learn of the many others whose very lives are a challenge to despotism.

When the martyrology of twentieth century Christians who have died in the struggle against contemporary forms of idolatry is compiled, the name of Oscar Romero will be high on the list. A worthy successor to St. Polycarp, Archbishop Romero anticipated the fate that awaited him because he would not be intimidated by the imperialistic demands of the El Salvadoran government. He preached the kingdom of God, a kingdom of justice and peace. He championed the cause of the poor and disadvantaged, denouncing oppression and exploitation in all its forms. Those who feared the message stilled the voice of the messenger with a bullet while he preached. But Archbishop Romero lives on. His story, like the stories of thousands of martyrs before him, will be told and retold to challenge new generations of Christians. These new witnesses, strengthened in the Spirit, will confess their faith before God and the world. The martyr continues to embody the archetype of the Christian witness, the symbol that reminds us that there are values and ideals worth fighting and dying for.

Further Readings

George Bernard Shaw, *Saint Joan* (1923).
T.S. Eliot, *Murder in the Cathedral* [Thomas Becket] (1935).
Robert Bolt, *A Man for All Seasons* [Thomas More] (1960).

At the time of this writing, Berard L. Marthaler, OFMConv., was professor of religion and religious education at the Catholic University of America.
Father Marthaler also edited *The Living Light*, a quarterly review for professional religious educators.

Death, Resurrection, and Responsibility in El Salvador

Robert McAfee Brown

I have stood on holy ground. Two days ago, as I write this, I was on the spot in the University of Central America in San Salvador where six Jesuits, their housekeeper, and her daughter were allegedly murdered by units of the Salvadoran military.

I have been to shrines before and to the sites of martyrdoms, but I have never been at a place where the results of human destruction were still so vividly apparent and unchanged—from shattered glass lying all over the floors, to walls pock-marked from hundreds of bullets, to part of the roof buckled by heavy military bombardment, to chaos in bedrooms with furniture still upended, and to bloodstains still present on walls, floors, and the ground outside where bodies were dragged. The sense of immediacy of being at the site of such acts of human ugliness (on the part of the murderers) and human sacrifice (on the part of the victims) was awesome.

Three days earlier, in the United States, Jon Sobrino, who escaped death simply because he was out of the country at the time of the shooting, was in our home, giving me letters to take to El Salvador for his friends. That, too, created a sense of the immediacy of the crime. And at the site itself, it suddenly became very important for me to link the two immediacies by asking to see his room. Like the other rooms, it remained as it was on the morning after the murders, pending the completion of a judicial investigation. It is even now not fully clear to me who was occupying Father Sobrino's room that night, but the circumstances described by the Jesuit who accompanied me are staggeringly clear. When the body of the man who had been shot was dragged across the room by the assassins, their movement dislodged one of the books in the bookcase, which fell to the floor and became saturated with the martyr's blood. The book, crying out a poignant message, was Jurgen Moltmann's *The Crucified God.*

It will be a long time before I have succeeded in putting together all the implications of that extraordinary juxtaposition.

The details of the killings are surely clear to readers and need not be recapitulated here. I report only that the mood engendered by all of these

---

This article appeared in <u>PACE</u> 20 (1991).

immediate brushes with the infinite was one of sadness and anger that lives had been destroyed and that others might be rendered fearful of a similar fate. So, they temper their words and lives accordingly. A perfectly natural question arises in such a situation: How can brutal destructiveness fail to overwhelm the fragile bulwarks we raise against it?

But that was not the need of the visitation. For after standing at the grisly shrine that was once the home of a family of priests, we went to a memorial ecumenical service in the chapel of the university, only a few yards away from the site of the killing. If the colors of the Jesuit residence are somber, the colors in the chapel are brilliant beyond description. Huge banners depicting the story of salvation, the heavenly city, and the principalities and powers it will finally conquer, are rendered in a contemporary medium splashed with vivid reds and greens and purples and oranges and blues. The cloths on the altar and lectern reflect the mood.

On the left side of the chapel are the freshly constructed tombs of the six martyrs, identified by simple, strong wall plagues, all of them flanked overhead by a large oil portrait of Archbishop Oscar Romero, who paid the price of martyrdom for his own faith almost a full decade ago.

That in itself is a somber but still triumphant architectural statement, since, as Archbishop Romero had said shortly before his death, "If they kill me, I will rise in the hearts of the Salvadoran people." Despite the fact that the rear wall of the chapel contains excruciatingly vivid charcoal drawings of various forms of modern torture, the ugliness does not engulf the beauty; for the most central symbol in the whole chapel is, of course, a huge crucifix that depicts the universal form of ancient torture—crucifixion. And the assurance that has sustained the Church for two thousand years is that crucifixion is not the last word as it is followed (no matter how long the delay) by resurrection.

But architecture alone would not have provided a clear enough reassurance to me on that particular day that the power of the gunmen can be overcome by another kind of power. It took the presence of the people of God in the chapel to do that, many of whom had been underground during the recent fighting, or had left the country and were surreptitiously beginning to return, or who knew they were on death squad lists. The service had been proposed, and was led, by the Lutheran Bishop of El Salvador, Medardo Gomez, who had himself returned to El Salvador "from outside" only the day before, in order to celebrate Epiphany with his people. He had already received two death threats earlier that day during the morning service at his church. The presence of Bishop Gomez stamped the occasion as one in which any songs of hope would have to be defiantly forged out of the crucible of death.

And songs there were, in abundance, led by young musicians, along with Scripture lessons and brief homilies on each one—a suffering Servant passage, the story of the three kings and the threat posed for Herod by the birth of a baby, and the twenty-first chapter of the Apocalypse with its vision of a new heaven and a new earth. Each of these signals of hope has, of course, a downside, but it was the signals of hope that carried the day and nourished the people who have known more about the downside of life for a full decade than most of us could learn in a dozen decades.

And then it was testimony time. No printed words can capture the flavor of that moment, as individual after individual came forward to affirm the possibility and necessity of courage and hope—of resurrection. I made an important discovery: The logic of Christian people caught in desperate situations is not, "The Jesuits have been murdered, therefore, we must be careful or we will be murdered too." It is, "The Jesuits have been murdered, therefore, we must take their place." As one young woman from Bishop Gomez' own church put it, "Do not weep for the martyrs; imitate them." (By the time this appears in print, Jon Sobrino will have gone to Spain to recruit a new faculty to replace those who were killed.)

Latin American liturgical events, such as the one being described, often conclude with a dramatic interchange in which the leader recites the name of someone who has been killed, and the people respond, "Presente!" meaning by that, "He or she is present in me and in all of us, and we will carry on the work." But there have been few exercises of this litany more powerful than the one on this occasion in which eight names were declared (the six Jesuits and two women), only yards from the site of their execution and only feet from the freshly made graves. With the reciting of each name, the intensity of the volume increased. If there were informers from the government present, as there surely must have been, they could scarcely have failed to realize that they were in the presence of a power no number of their own gunmen can totally erase.

That evening, President Cristiani went on television at 9 p.m. to announce that members of the armed forces, not yet identified, had been involved in the murders. This was not exactly world-shaking information. As the new rector of the university said the next morning, "He told us nothing we did not already know." The announcement, which surely resulted from White House pressure in order to make stronger the case for ongoing military aid to El Salvador, actually weakens rather than strengthens the hand of the White House. For Mr. Bush to suggest that this minimal announcement means that we should continue to finance the killing is only a further desecration of the six Jesuits and two women, not to mention the 70,000 Salvadorans who have preceded them in violent death. That the army is responsible for the deaths is a reason to *terminate* military aid, not to extend it, since we now have clear proof of how it is used.

Anyone who has stood on the site of the killings will realize that complicity in the multiple shootings must include high-ranking army officers. The entire area was surrounded by military units, one which had actually commandeered space on the campus. There is a huge army barracks within a stone's throw of the campus. The fact that three groups of ten men each could converge on the Jesuit lodging at 3 a.m. from different directions, that they could carry out their mission—fire hundreds of rifle shots and larger artillery—and that they could then escape without a single military finger being lifted to stop them, indicates that many people in high places had engaged in coordinating the action. And about the best case scenario we can hope for will be a rerun of the judicial farce in the aftermath of the murder and rape of the Roman Catholic sisters and lay worker a decade ago, when low ranking individuals were convicted and those with authority got off scot-free.

Either the Salvadoran government gives the army its orders, or it is powerless to prevent the army from doing whatever it pleases. To continue military aid in the face of such a reality is to say, "Now that everybody acknowledges how evil you are, we will reward you with more money to continue doing evil."

If we are to be faithful to the Jesuits, the women who died with them, and countless more, we must press a different kind of logic: If we ever had any doubts about the complicity of the army in the deaths of thousands of civilians, those doubts are laid to rest. We know the armed forces are guilty of heinous crimes. Therefore we must stop the military aid, so that the heinous crimes will stop. To do otherwise is to ensure that the blood—not only of Jesuits, but of many more Salvadorans—will continue to shed, as it has been shed for over a decade.

And we will be guilty.

Robert McAfee Brown is one of the United States' most distinguished Christian theologians. He wrote these reflections shortly after returning from El Salvador at the time of the murders.

Consider Jesus:
The Humanity of God With Us

Elizabeth A. Johnson

Introduction: A Living Tradition

A seed grows into a flowering tree. Lovers discover ever greater depths in each other and develop new language to communicate their affection, words which never fully capture their love. A new interpretation of a law brings to light unsuspected depths: All black persons and white women are included in the "all men" who are created equal. Each of these experiences has been used to illumine the development of doctrine, the changed expression of the Christian heritage that happens when the community of believers in Jesus Christ ponder their faith in new cultural situations.

Through prayer and thought in the context of fresh actions, insight into the mystery of God's ways ripens. Different ways of expressing the meaning of faith emerge in accord with cultural variations. Doctrine develops. Whether the image is taken from the world of nature, from human psychology or the social order, the analogies of the tree, the lovers, and the law suggest something alive in the history of belief. They point to a vital community of faith nourishing a tradition which is not a dead weight, like a millstone tied around the neck, but a genuine living tradition.

The Living Tradition of Jesus Christ

Since the time of Jesus, his disciples have been asked to answer a crucial question:

> *And Jesus went on with his disciples to the village of Caesarea Philippi; and on the way he asked his disciples, "Who do people say that I am?" and they told him, "Some say John the Baptist, and others say Elijah, and still others say one of the prophets." And he asked them, "But who do you say that I am?" (Mk 8:27–29).*

Through the centuries, the answer to this question has changed its shape: From Peter's "You are the Christ" (Mk 8:29) and Martha's "You are

This article appeared in PACE 20 (1991).

the Christ, the Son of God, the one who is coming into the world" (Jn 11:27); to the answer of the fourth and fifth century councils "You are one in being with the Father; truly God and truly human in one person;" to the medieval philosophical idea of Christ's human nature was hypostatic in the person of the Logos; to Luther's existentially powerful insight that Jesus Christ is our Savior who graces us before we deserve it; to the nineteenth century answer that Jesus is the lover of our souls whose Sacred Heart ignites the fire of our own love—from these answers and so many more then and now—it is clear that the Church's answer to the christological question is part of a truly living tradition.

The question "Who do you say that I am?" is not academic but arises from the experience of salvation. Something exceedingly good happens to people in their encounter with Jesus Christ. Fundamentally they are put right with God. Consequently they are reconciled within themselves, restored to inner integrity, healed in body and spirit. Relationships with other persons, with social structures, and with the earth are also set right; peace becomes a real possibility. People experience a new lease on life pervaded with hope in the future, even if it be hope against hope. Among those who have been thus graced by the Spirit of Christ, community forms. Given the profound impact of Jesus Christ on their lives, the question arises—who is he? The experience of salvation coming from God in Jesus makes him fundamentally interesting.

Since the middle of the twentieth century, Catholic theology has experienced a burst of energy regarding this question. Nourished in innovative ways by what has gone before and responding to the particular challenges of this century, it has been developing new insights into who Jesus is and the difference this makes. It is the purpose of this and three subsequent articles to explore some of the new answers in this still living tradition about Jesus Christ.

Jesus Christ, Genuinely Human: The Problem

It has always been more difficult to believe in the genuine humanity of the Word made flesh than in his true godliness, as the batch of early Christian heresies against Jesus Christ's humanity shows. More so than Protestant thought and piety, Catholic understanding has tended in this direction too, stressing the godliness of Christ to such an extent that the truth that he is one of us has slipped from view. All unawares, the Catholic approach has promoted the fourth century heresy promoted by Bishop Apollinaris. Christ incarnate did not have a real human soul, he argued, and therefore no real human psychology. Instead the divine Word substituted for the human soul. This means that while Jesus' body was real flesh, his interior life was the very life of God. He looks human on the outside, but is really God on the inside. As Karl Rahner has commented, the ghost of Apollinaris haunts the Catholic Church.

And yet it is crucial to our salvation that Jesus Christ be genuinely human. For in the Christian view of things, God does not save by a word or decision in a distant heaven. Rather, salvation happens by God's personal engagement with the world, entering fully into its joy and pain, its temptations and choices, knowing the life of the flesh, the rhythm of day and night, and the power of love and rejection. The world is saved not from above but from within. So radical is the importance of genuine incarnation for our salvation that early Christian theologians developed an axiom: What is not assumed is not redeemed. If anything essential to human nature is left out of the incarnation, then it is not blessed by this connection with Emmanuel and is left out of the promise sown in history by God's blessed nearness.

Suspicion and distrust of humanity in general, uncomfortableness with our own real humanness, led Catholic thought and piety to ignore and even be suspicious of the genuine humanity of Jesus the Christ. It seemed somehow not worthy that God-with-us should be assailed by temptation, limited by ignorance, surprisingly troubled by difficult disciples, pressed to make free choices about his fidelity to ministry, agonized by the experience of abandonment by God. However, for all its seeming inappropriateness, the confession of true humanity is part of the ancient dogma. Jesus Christ is "truly God and truly human; one in being with the Father as to his divinity, and one in being with us as to his humanity . . .", as the Council of Chalcedon in 451 confessed. The first wave of renewal of christology in this century came when Karl Rahner and other theologians celebrated the 1500th anniversary of this council (1951) by taking another look at the old doctrine. What they discovered anew was the confession of the genuine humanity of Jesus Christ as dogma and its importance for a world seeking for the meaning of being human amidst war and crises.

Theological Underpinnings

To reclaim the ancient confession that Jesus Christ is truly human is one thing. To make it seriously imaginable for people today is another. For we come to the doctrine with a sense of the opposition between the divine and the human. What is presumed, sometimes unconsciously, is an either-or situation, so that if Jesus is truly God-with-us then he could not possibly have real passions, limited knowledge, genuine freedom of choice. His divinity overshadows his humanity to such an extent that his humanity is swallowed up in the blaze of divine glory. If his identity is so profoundly rooted in God then he cannot be one of us.

To deal with this block, Karl Rahner and many other Catholic theologians today challenge this basic either-or presupposition. In place of a competitive model of the God-human relationship, only a cooperative model will do justice to the incarnation. What characterizes a truly mature relationship between human beings and the mystery of God? Surely not the diminishment of human beings whom God has created out of love, but their flourishing. Developing this basic insight in the field of Christian anthropology gives us a tool with which to rethink Jesus Christ anew.

A. Human. Human beings are a restless bunch. Catch us in the act of asking a question; receiving the answer just sets up the possibility of asking a new question. See us loving, and watch our desire and capacity for love grow ever stronger. Ponder us imprisoned, suffering, or thwarted, and note how our imagination can envision new possibilities and our hope push against the pain. Tracing human experiences such as these, Karl Rahner concludes that at our most characteristic, we human beings betray that our spirit is a dynamic thirst for truth, for love, for life. Indeed, we desire as much of these as we can get, and even more, all the way to infinite truth, love, life, which Christians call God. We are so made that we are dynamically structured toward the infinite and will only be satisfied by the infinite God. We are not a closed off, limited reality, but human mystery which opens into depth which is the mystery of God's own self. Augustine expressed this well in his lovely observation, "You have made us for yourself, O God, and our hearts are restless until they rest in Thee." Christians say that it is no accident that we are made this way. God graciously made us this way precisely in order to be our fulfillment.

B. Divine. If human nature is a deep mystery with a questing capacity for the infinite, divine nature is an even more incomprehensible mystery of self-giving love. God creates and redeems the world out of love, and out of love destines creation for the day when there will be no more death or crying out. And even more than the human spirit quests for God, the overflowing love of God seeks for human beings. What then, glorifies God? Not the diminishment of the beloved creature but our enhancement and growth. The more truly human we become, the more God's love succeeds. As the second-century Bishop Irenaeus exclaimed, "The glory of God is the human being fully alive!"

The underlying truth here can best be seen by the analogy of human love. Parents' love for their children does not diminish the children's personhood but is actually creative of these little ones' mature human selves. Good married love transforms the partners into their true selves the more united they become in their love. The love of friendship has a similar effect, enabling friends to flourish as human beings.

Could anything less be true of God who is Love? Given the way God has created and redeemed us, we are not in competition with God but rather made for God and completely human only in nearness of divine mystery. God's drawing near is creative of mature, genuine humanity, not

93

destructive of it. The closer we become to God, the more fully our own true selves we become, not less ourselves. Rahner sums up this insight in a mind-bending proverb worth pondering: "Nearness to God and genuine human autonomy grow in direct and not inverse proportion."

C. Unity of human with divine mystery. In the case of Jesus of Nazareth, we are dealing with someone who was more profoundly united to God than anyone else we know of. Doctrine guards this intuition with its language of "hypostatic union," a union at the metaphysical level of the person. If his humanity is united to God in this most profound way, what are we to say about him as a human being? The logic of the non-competitive model of divine-human relationships leads to the realization that he is profoundly human in a way more human, more free, more alive than any of us because his union with God is more profound. Rather than the confession of his divinity diminishing his humanity in our imagination, it releases him to be a genuine human being. Because of the incarnation he does not become less human but the most genuinely human of us all.

One can go to the Scriptures and see sign after sign of this: Like us in all things, tempted in every way that we are yet without sin (Heb 4:15–5:3), from divine glory Jesus Christ "emptied himself" and was counted among sinners, learning from what he suffered (Phil 2:6–11). Understanding human nature as capable of bearing God without being violated, the ancient dogma is now being read differently. We do not say, "Jesus is God and in addition human as well." Rather, we start at the other end and say, "As this human being, Jesus is the Son of God. Precisely as this human being he is Emmanuel: fully personal, genuinely free, God-with-us who has self-emptied into our history." The non-competitive model of relationship between God and creation restores to our consciousness a way of envisioning Jesus to be genuinely human at the same time that the confession of his genuine divinity does not slip from view. Vatican II gave this recovery of Jesus' humanity a ringing affirmation, stating in one beautiful passage:

> *Human nature as he assumed it was not annulled. . . . He worked with human hands, he thought with a human mind, he acted by human choice, and loved with a human heart. Born of the Virgin Mary, he has truly been made one of us, like us in all things except sin.*
> —*The Church in the Modern World*
> *Gaudium et Spes, 22*

Religious Results

Realization of Jesus' humanity is entering our conversation again in the Church and is having ramifications in many areas. It leads to reevaluation of the humanness of all of us in a very positive direction. Religious education, preaching, spiritual direction, formation programs in religious communities—all begin to communicate a sense that each of us as human is a gift of God, filled with potency for God; a sense that human nature itself is created in movement toward God. A new asceticism of cherishing and promoting humanity is growing. The dignity of every human person precisely as human, and therefore the rightness of the claims to human rights and justice take on new prominence. The Church's social teaching is grounded on a deep christological motif: Because of the incarnation, every human being is traced with a dignity beyond compare. Therefore whatever disfigures or damages a human being is an insult to God and must be resisted. In a poetic way Rahner envisions that because of the Word of God in our history, each of us is a little word of God. The one Word of God in our midst reveals to us our own beauty, our own power to spell out together a great parable to the glory of God: "Human nature is the grammar of God's self-utterance." Our human nature is so made that God can speak in and through us. All of this flows out of the incarnation, which is real and not a pretense on God's part. That Emmanuel is actually one of us leads to valuing all human beings as gifted with a tremendous dignity precisely as human.

For Further Reading

Karl Rahner's recovery of the humanity of Jesus Christ is carefully set out in *Foundations of Christian Faith* (New York: Seabury, 1978). It is a tough read but rewards close scrutiny. A key to Rahner's approach is provided by Leo O'Donovan, ed., *A World of Grace* (New York: Seabury, 1980), which describes Rahner's christology in a readable way.

At the time of this writing,
Elizabeth A. Johnson, CSJ, was
associate professor of theology at
Catholic University of America, Washington, DC, and
author of Consider Jesus: Waves of Renewal in Christology
(Crossroads, 1990).

Forms of Jewish Spirituality

Sherry H. Blumberg

Jewish spirituality has many different forms of expression. Jewish spirituality can include general piety, a devout life, an interior life of prayer and meditation, and the way in which a person understands the ethical or religious obligations of being a Jewish human being.

Spirituality in this context is defined as ". . . that form of religious (Jewish) expression which the believer considers indispensable. It is the ultimate focus of his religious energy, that dimension on which he places supreme emphasis. It defines the authentic believer at his best" (Gillman 5–18).

In this article I will introduce several paths of Jewish spirituality. Each of these expressions may be found in the different movements of Jewish life—Orthodox, Conservative, Reform, Reconstructionist, Secularists—but some are more characteristic in one movement than in another. Then I will describe briefly my own liberal Jewish path that combines several of these forms to demonstrate how there is flexibility for the individual.

Spirituality of Deeds: The Mitzvot or Commandments

For some Jews, the encounter or experience of God is found in fulfillment of the mitzvot or commandments. This is a spirituality of deeds. It includes both ritual deeds and ethical deeds. It is a spirituality that pays attention to the details of one's life. This path is born of the belief that God wants Jews to perform the mitzvot, to fulfill the required actions with both Keva (regularity) and Kavanah (correct feeling and intention).

For example, a Jew is supposed to say 100 B'rachot (blessings) each day. Saying a B'racha is a way of both praising and thanking God. Rabbi Hanina B. Papa said: "Whoever enjoys anything in this world without offering a benediction, it is as though he has robbed the Holy One, praised be the Eternal" (Talmud, Berachot 35a, Epstein 220).

There can be a problem with this spiritual path if the performance of the mitzvot becomes perfunctory. For this reason, Abraham Joshua Heschel defines a mitzvah as "a prayer in the form of a deed" (Heschel 69) and

This article appeared in PACE 22 (1992).

suggests that the blessing reminds us of the wonder of the thing that we bless. This sense of wonder leads us to a radical amazement about being alive and being able to do the actions of the commandments.

Spirituality of Study: Talmud Torah

For many Jews there is a spirituality found in study—especially in the study of Torah, Talmud, and Jewish sacred texts. Sparks of divine light are supposed to be hidden amongst the letters and interpretations of the texts. For the mystics, the text was seen as a "ladder by which a person might reach the higher goal of cleaving to God" (Ben Zion Bokser).

Study in this context is for its own sake (called *Torah L'shma).* The spirituality of the study is found in the acts of interpretation that seek to find the whole "truth" of the text. One uncovers the meanings in the texts by finding the plain meaning of the words and the inner meanings—the metaphoric or allegorical meanings, and the mystical meanings. Searching out these meanings, struggling with the texts, studying to learn more and thereby to be able to study more is one way of finding God.

A problem inherent in this path arises when a person uses study as a way to prove how intelligent or knowledgeable the student has become. If the study of Torah leads to arrogance or if it absorbs people so much that they neglect the other aspects of their lives, then the spiritual path is lost.

To maintain the contact with the spirituality of study, it is important for the Jew to have an awareness that "to learn" and "to teach" come from the same root word. One must study in order to uncover what God wants from human beings, and then one must share that with others and teach them.

Spirituality of the Pursuit of Justice and Social Action

"Justice, justice you shall pursue." (Deuteronomy 16:20)

For many Jews, especially those of the Reform movement, the quest for an ethical world is the essence of Judaism (baeck). As a result, many Jews find their religious identity by working for causes such as world peace, fair housing, civil rights, ecological rights, food for all, and universal education. There is a spiritual demand that leads to doing deeds of loving kindness and taking stands on social and ethical issues.

This spiritual path is defined by the concept "Tikkun olam," translated as repair of the world. Each individual is seen as a "fixer," a person who can help to bring the messianic age by restoring the small sparks of holiness buried in our world. These sparks are uncovered by doing acts of social justice. For the Orthodox Jew and the Hasidic Jew, Tikkun Olam also includes the performance of the ritual mitzvot. For the Reform and Secular Jew, the path of "tikkun olam" is the passion for social justice, and it gives meaning to their spiritual lives.

Spirituality of Jewish Peoplehood

While other civilizations have come and gone, Jewish life has survived; insuring its survival becomes a spiritual path of great and transcendent power. Mordecai Kaplan, the founder of the Reconstructionist movement, said that "the significance of peoplehood is the universal message of Judaism" (Kaplan 138). For some Jews, it is their primary path to a spiritual life. For these Jews, the miraculous existence of the Jewish people, despite all of the persecutions and trials, is a source of strength and a communal religious experience.

For some Jews, the power of peoplehood is translated into a spirituality that is directed toward the nation of Israel. This spiritual path, often called *Zionism,* is appealing especially to secular Jews who feel their Judaism as a cultural and ethnic expression of life. There is a miraculous quality for these Jews about the survival of the people, the return to the land of Israel after over 2000 years and making the desert bloom once again.

Mystical Paths

It is also important to mention that, while the preceding are often the most common or mainstream forms of Jewish spirituality, they are not the only spiritual paths in Jewish life. There is another path—the way of the mystic—that has gained in popularity during this last part of the twentieth century.

The mystical paths are also numerous, and this article will mention only two of them. While there are ascetic streams within the tradition which include "Yihuddim" (acts of ritual piety and penitence such as contemplation of the divine name), most Jewish mystical traditions are nominal rather than anti-nominal. In these expressions of Jewish life, great attention to the details of Jewish living is a key towards mystical union with God.

Lurianic mysticism explores the ways in which God is known through the emanation of God in the ten s'firot. These s'firot include: Keter (crown), Hochmah (wisdom), Binah (understanding), T'fereth (beauty, harmony and balance), G'vurah (strength with justice), G'dolah (nurturing power with mercy), Hod (majesty), Yesod (foundation with Tzedek, righteousness), Netzach (endurance), and Malchut (kingdom). The emanations are arranged in a mystical diagram which relates each of the emanations to each other and to the parts of the body as well. Contemplation and meditation upon these emanations are a way toward mystical union with God.

The early Hasidic movement stressed joy in the little daily tasks and placed an emphasis on prayer with singing and dancing. The text "Raise a shout to the Eternal, all the earth, break into joyous songs of praise," from Psalm 98:4, is characteristic of the spirit of Hasidism. The Hasidic sects are led by a Tzaddik, a leader thought to have special connection to God. Hasidism places more emphasis on a form of Jewish meditation called "Hitbodut" and on D'vekut, the act of cleaving to God rather than scholarship and acts of social justice.

A Spiritual Path for a Liberal Jewish Woman

My own spiritual path is one that combines several of the expressions mentioned above. I try to recognize and cherish the sacred possibility of each moment, finding religious meaning in the mundane and ordinary as well as the sacred and special. My path is one in which the tensions and paradoxes of living provide the possibility of encountering God.

While not accepting all of Halacha (Jewish Law) as binding, especially since as a modern woman I find it patriarchal, it has been important for me to explore the mitzvot (commandments) and to choose the ones that are communally and personally meaningful. For me, this has meant that the ethical mitzvot become binding, and the ritual mitzvot are open for interpretation. I try to live in today's world while also trying to act as much as possible in harmony with the Covenant (Brit) of God with our ancestors and with us.

I am committed to study, both learning and teaching, and make it a regular part of my life. I am committed to living "b'tzelem eloheem" (in the image of God) as human being and as Jewish woman. This often means finding the beauty in each person, living between the tension of justice on one hand and mercy and compassion on the other. I am committed to sensing God's presence in nature, in the world, and in both the joy and sorrow of living. I try to sing and pray with my whole heart, living open to God's presence, and sometimes to God's call.

In conclusion, I have tried to mention several of the major spiritual expressions of today's Jewish community. There are many other forms of spirituality, and many Jews combine their paths in unique ways. For all Jews, while the paths to God may be different and varied, God is One.

References

Baeck, Leo. *The Essence of Judaism,* Revised Edition. Victor
   Grubenwieser and Irving Howe, translators. New York: Schocken
   Books, 1948.

Ben Zion Bokser. *Jewish Mystical Tradition.* New York: Pilgrim Press,
   1981.

Epstein, Rabbi Dr. I., editor. *The Babylonian Talmud, Seder Zera'im.*
   London: Soncino Press, 1945.

Gillman, Neil. "Judaism and the Search for Spirituality," *Conservative
   Judaism,* 38.2 (Winter 1985–86).

Heschel, Abraham. *The Quest for God: Studies in Prayer and Symbolism.* New York: Scribners, 1954.

Kaplan, Mordecai. *The Meaning of God in Modern Jewish Religion.* New
   York: Berhman's Jewish Book House, 1937.

*At the time of this writing, Sherry Blumberg was
assistant professor of Jewish education at
Hebrew Union College–Jewish Institute of Religion in
New York City.*

Grace Amid Paradigm Shifts: Rahner's Retrieval of "Grace" for Postmoderns

Robert A. Ludwig

In her book, *States of Grace: The Recovery of Meaning in the Post-Modern Age,* Charlene Spretnak discusses the relevance of the wisdom traditions to our times:

> *As the assumptions of modernity unravel around us and we race the clock against the momentum of destructiveness, we are challenged to create new possibilities and haunted by failures of immense proportion. . . . Because it is now apparent that modernity has failed to fulfill its promises of a "better life" in many of the deepest senses, we are compelled to search for new, or perhaps recovered, modes of understanding . . . . As the cultural grip of modernity weakens, the insights of spiritual teachings can be shared once again (Spretnak 10, 12, 27).*

No single Catholic thinker has done more to retrieve the insights of Christian spiritual teaching for our time than Karl Rahner, the German Jesuit who persisted in integrating the insights from his experience of "The Spiritual Exercises" into a coherent revising of fundamental Catholic theology. Rahner's theology of grace, a major presupposition in many of the Second Vatican Council's documents, yet largely hidden from the popular Church three decades later, needs a new hearing in the light of today's cultural crisis and new spiritual quest. Rahner's theology can properly be called "constructive or revisionary postmodernism." He seeks to overcome the modern worldview by constructing a postmodern worldview through revision of modern premises and traditional concepts (see Greiffin, Introduction, xii).

That such a revising is sorely needed today is evidenced by the results of a recent Gallup Poll on "The Spiritual Needs of Americans" done by Princeton University: 70 percent of the respondents identified "meaning and purpose" as their number-one concern, and 66 percent believed the Churches and synagogues were failing to address this need. Indeed, the Catholic Church in the U.S. is reeling under its declining credibility in

This article appeared in PACE 23 (1994).

spiritual and ethical concerns, especially among young people. They see the Church's attachment to patriarchy and hierarchy, its self-understanding as a broker of grace, its inability to deal consistently and positively with human sexuality without reference to "the procreative function," and its preoccupation with lawsuits, real estate, and money, as obstacles to any persuasive role in today's search for spiritual meaning. Spiritually eager young people are today more interested in Buddhism and Native American spirituality than they are in Catholicism's "new" universal catechism or even participation in the great Easter Triduum.

The fact is, however, that the majority of them have never been offered an understanding of Catholic Christianity that is described in nondualistic categories and grounded in universal human experience. Most have no understanding of gracious Mystery immersed in their own bodypersons' quest for fulfillment and revealed in the **humanity** of Jesus of Nazareth and his social revolution.[1] They have never been given access to the blending of cosmology and mysticism in creation theology's rich reflections on divinity's immanence in nature. Most have experienced only the dry abstractions of Catholic doctrine unrelated to experience or, worse yet, "Catholic propaganda"—an ideological presentation of the tradition in dualistic and exclusivistic terms in the context of a controlling, authoritarian patriarchy.

For most young people today, "grace" and "sin" have never been described in terms of the dynamics of the self, relationality, the experiences of alienation/oppression and reconciliation/liberation, or the role freedom plays in our interconnectedness with all creation. But today's postmodern critique and the popular experience of the loss of meaning in personal and cultural life open up new opportunities to revisit the wisdom tradition we call "Christianity" in dialogue with the quest for meaning and purpose.

Enter Karl Rahner—obviously, with the help of the translator.

Rahner's Starting Point: Experience and Questions

The starting point in Rahner's thought is our shared human existence and the curiosity and wonder which attention to it prompts. Rahner begins with **experience**. *God* cannot be the starting point, nor can *Jesus* or the *Bible*. These hold no immediate credibility; the modern world has, in fact, come to understand them as part of the problem. No, the starting point must be experience, fundamental and universal human experience, what Rahner calls "unthematic knowledge." Such knowledge emerges from our immediate experience before it has been "thematized'" in concepts and language. This is knowledge acquired not from without, but from within, "original knowledge," because it wells up from the origins of our own selves in our lived interaction with the world.

This knowledge seeks expression in concepts and words, but our efforts at expression never completely capture the experience itself. We try to thematize our experience, which is what "appropriating our experience" and "communication" are all about, seeking to understand it ourselves and to share it with others. But we continually recognize the limitations involved in this process, using terms like "you really had to be there" or "I can't put it into words—it was just incredible!" Thus, there is a continual interplay between our raw experience ("unthematic knowledge") and our efforts to understand and communicate it ("thematic knowledge").

In this way, Rahner moves initial human knowing back beyond rational concepts and language, beyond Descartes's starting point ("I think, therefore I am"). Here, Rahner finds a universal human experience of wonder and mystery: We are swimming in a sea of unappropriated encounters and have no words, **yet,** to name what we "know."

This is where Rahner begins to build his postmodern understanding of the human person and our encounter with God: God giving God's self to us, not in concepts of words but in the immediate experience of gracious mystery that is fundamental to our "original knowledge." Rahner says we always carry this experience with us—it's always there, not only as backdrop from our past, but as an ongoing encounter in the present. We may try to ignore it, deny it, bury it under piles of concepts and words. In fact, we all do attempt to flee from this raw experience, because within it we are vulnerable and dependent and not in control. Yet we never really escape it. Further, this "original knowledge" emerges again and again into consciousness, becoming the source of our freedom, our transcendence, and our questions. We know ourselves to be immersed in mystery—a context of continual wonder and frightening dependency.

This is the context, then, for our hearing of the Gospel. It is a story about Jesus of Nazareth that comes to us from our historical tradition through our Scriptures, and yet it is **first** a story about our own experience, a story we already know "unthematically." Jesus' liberating "yes" to God and his "no" to temptation, his radical trust in "Abba" and his reconciling compassion for others, his death and resurrection—this is the story form of our own "original knowledge." And if it is our story, it is the story of all the earth—a universal story about gracious mystery as our source and destiny and the need to live by courage and trust. Yet this story is not "an answer" to our questions, as the fundamentalists would have it. Rather, the gospel is the thematization of our experience of mystery, helping us make peace with our deepest questions by our acceptance of incompleteness, vulnerability, emptiness.

The Mystery We Call God

One of the great pieces of twentieth-century theological writing is Rahner's meditation on the word *God* in his *Foundations of Christian Faith* (see 44ff). *God* is different from other words, which have clear referents in human experience. *God* doesn't point to anything concrete like *tree* or *table* do. The word *God* is so much without contour: "It says nothing about what it means, nor can it simply function like an index finger that points to something encountered immediately." But for this very reason, because its referent is so liquid and diffuse, "it is obviously quite appropriate for what it refers to" (Rahner 46).

For Rahner, "God" is "the nameless one . . . the silent one." "God" does not enter into the realm of our existence through an **active** process: "We should not think that, because the phonetic sound of the word 'God' is always dependent on us, therefore the word 'God' is our creation." No, we hear and receive the word *God*. It comes to us in the history of language and in the story of humankind and through our own story. It is "our opening to the incomprehensible mystery" (Rahner 50–51). This is the meaning of grace—that "God," the incomprehensible mystery which is both source and destiny, gives us its very self at the level of our unthematic experience.

We don't know God as an object "out there," nor is God simply the product of our imagination "in here." This is the Enlightenment's dualism (Kant). Our knowledge of God is not through empirical observation, nor through rational deduction—the **only** ways of knowing in modernity. Rather, God emerges in the relationship between our questioning selves and the unexplainability of things. Our minds are driven toward coherence and meaning, and yet the focus of our thinking (the concrete, material world of things and persons) does not and cannot finally provide coherence and meaning—precisely the point! We are driven beyond the things in themselves to the mystery which they intimate. As Michael Buckley observes, "God is given as the orientation of the mind when it moves through nature in its drive for truth . . . moves toward reality and finds it is finally and radically mystery" (Buckley 35).

God is not "a supreme being," whom we come to know like the person down the street or our office colleague. Nor do we come to know God by reading the Bible or studying theology. We come to know God, not by undertaking the task directly (trying to know God), but experientially in our search for meaning and coherence in history and the world. We don't know God by turning away from the world (in "otherworldly" pursuits), but precisely by turning to the world. God is not another **thing,** even a very big and powerful thing. God is first and always what we come to know by questioning things all the way, by wondering how they finally make sense, by pursuing the truth freely. When we simply ask the question "Why?" we are caught up in a process which leads ultimately to Mystery, which is the ground and context for everything.

Grace as God's Self-Communication

Grace, then, is seen as God's self-communication to us: Absolute Mystery's coming into self-donating relationship with human persons. The first movement of grace is that we are created as capacity for this gift; we have an incompleteness, an unfinishedness, an emptiness at the very center of our self. We are radically open to Mystery, driven there by our search for fulfillment. This is the great paradox: that our greatest gift is the hunger, the thirst, the desire, the persistent search for "more" and "beyond." This hunger can be "satisfied" only by our "yes" to Mystery. What makes us capable of receiving the divine into our very selves is the incompleteness that is integral to being human.

I like to describe the human person in Rahner's theology as a donut, an emptiness at our center. Just as there are no donuts without holes. there are no human beings who are not empty (and thus open). We find this emptiness unsettling, to put it mildly. We would be complete **now** and seek quick and easy fulfillment in finite realities. We will see in the third article in this series that there is no satisfying this spirit-hunger with "things." That this is the way of addiction: the more we feed our emptiness with things, the more ferocious our hunger becomes. In order to be "satisfied," we must make peace with our incompleteness and be open to Mystery. This is the way of grace.

Grace and Human Freedom: Our Lived Decisions

We are created incomplete and unfinished, internally driven toward the "more." But this doesn't mean that there's no role for human freedom in the dynamics of grace. Quite the contrary! Grace is also a decision. We can say "no" to Mystery's self-gift, stuff our emptiness with idolatrous spirit-substitutes, and seek to flee our radical incompleteness and dependency. We are created with a potential for God's self-gift, but this potential needs freedom's "yes" to be realized.

Perhaps the most insightful piece of Rahner's theology of grace is this: Our decisions about grace happen unthematically, too. We don't sit down and thoughtfully choose to be open to Mystery's amazing self-gift, nor dispassionately say "no" to grace in favor of an alternative. Our choices are happening in the living of life, as we go about the normal processes of human activity. Here we encounter Mystery in thinking, loving, creating, hoping. Our "yes" to grace is in our relationships, our work, our leisure, our politics. Our "no" to God's self-gift comes as we shut down transcendence. We demand absolute control in seeking power, absolute security in pursuing wealth, and absolute certainty in creating and clinging to ideology. Making peace with our emptiness and living with openness before Mystery is challenging—particularly as we face this challenge every day and every hour, in interaction with self, others, social structures, nature, economic and political realities.

Now we can understand Vatican II's new approach to other Christian denominations, other religions, to atheistic and agnostic persons. Grace is universal as a possibility, built-into the fabric of our humanity, and receives our free response quite apart from Church membership or religious affiliation. Our "yes" or "no" to grace is in life. That is why not all those who cry "Lord, Lord," are saying "yes" to grace, nor are those who claim to be atheist or agnostic saying "no" to God's self-gift. Our openness to Mystery's self-disclosure and self-donation is embedded in the fabric of our lives and the processes that make them up—in our self-understanding, relationality, generativity, and integrity.

Redefining Church in the Light of Rahner's Thought

Vatican II's call for a renewed and reformed Church seems clear in the light of Rahner's theology of grace. Nothing short of a revolution in pastoral practice will do! The Church is not the broker for grace. Rather, it is the people who come together to confess and to celebrate the deepest meanings of their lives by reference to Jesus Christ and the Gospel. The Church is the context for thematizing the unthematic—for bringing to consciousness and then to expression the dynamics of God's offer of grace and our freedom. The Church is a support group for our everyday "yes" to Absolute Mystery's self-gift. As a community, it is a laboratory for learning to make peace with emptiness and openness to grace, a situation in which we are mutually involved in learning the practice of transcendence and freedom. Church is where we gather to scheme together about global transcendence—the going beyond ideology and socio-economic structures which deny human dignity or attempt to prevent access to human fulfillment. The Church is an instrument of personal and communal liberation and reconciliation, where we together remember Jesus' "yes" to grace and encourage one another and the world to live in solidarity with that "yes."

The interplay of personal self-understanding, interpersonal relationships, our mutual interdependence and responsibility before nature and society—these are at the very heart of being Church. Retrieving "grace" in a postmodern world demands the radical redefining of Church. In today's paradigm shift, something old is collapsing, but something new is coming to be. The continuity is deep and profound, nonetheless. We are simply rediscovering ancient truths and finding new language to describe what goes on in the adventure of human life—amazing grace!

Endnote

1. John Dominic Crossan's research on the historical Jesus presents a picture of Jesus that is both credible and compelling to today's young people. In *The Historical Jesus: The Life of a Mediterranean Jewish Peasant* and in his forthcoming popular version, *Jesus: An Historical Portrait,* Crossan's theology becomes clear: literal reading of Jesus' socio-economic teachings, spiritually symbolic reading of the resurrection and miracle traditions, issuing in a program of "radical egalitarianism."

References

Buckley, Michael. "Within the Holy Mystery." *A World of Grace.* New York: Seabury, 1980.

Crossan, John Dominic. *The Historical Jesus: The Life of a Mediterranean Jewish Peasant.* HarperSanFrancisco, 1991.

_____. *Jesus: An Historical Portrait.* HarperSanFrancisco, 1993.

Griffin, David Ray. "Introduction to SUNY Series in Constructive Postmodern Thought," in Varieties of *Postmodern Theology.* Albany, NY: SUNY Press, 1989.

Rahner, Karl. *Foundations of Christian Faith.* New York: Crossroad, 1982.

Spretnak, Charlene. *States of Grace: The Recovery of Meaning in the Postmodern Age.* HarperSanFrancisco, 1991.

Additional Reading

Carpenter, James A. *Nature and Grace: Toward an Integral Perspective.* New York: Crossroad, 1988. Especially his chapter, "Rahner or Nature and Grace and Related Issues," pages 57–75.

Cote, Richard. *Universal Grace: Myth or Reality?* Maryknoll, NY: Orbis, 1977.

Dreyer, Elizabeth. *Manifestations of Grace.* Collegeville, MN: Michael Glazier, 1990.

Griffin, David Ray. *God and Religion in the Postmodern World.* Albany, NY: SUNY Press, 1989.

_____, ed. *Varieties of Postmodern Theology.* Albany, NY: SUNY Press, 1989.

Haight, Roger. *The Experience and Language of Grace.* Mahwah, NJ: Paulist, 1979. Especially his chapter on Rahner.

Huebsch, Bill. *A Spirituality of Wholeness: A New Look at Grace.* Mystic, CT: Twenty-third, 1988.

O'Donovan, Leo, ed. *A World of Grace.* New York: Seabury, 1980.

Rahner, Karl. *Foundations of Christian Faith.* New York: Crossroad, 1982.

At the time of this writing, Robert A. Ludwig was director of university ministry and instructor of religious studies at DePaul University in Chicago.

Issues

Keep That Salt-Shaker Handy!

Mary Perkins Ryan

This coming summer the majority of PACE subscribers will probably be involved in courses, seminars, workshops, etc., in which they will encounter some new and perhaps exciting ideas, theories, and methodologies. But before we plunge into such summer activities, it might be prudent to consider the appropriateness of the old expression, "Take it with a grain of salt," to the religious educator's situation today. Salt both heals ("gargle with salt and water") and flavors, and so the Baptismal Rite uses salt as a symbol of wisdom. (In fact, the Latin word for wisdom, *sapientia,* comes from a root meaning "taste.") Wisdom, according to Webster's *New World Dictionary,* is the "power of judging rightly . . . based on knowledge, experience, understanding, etc.;" Christian wisdom is, therefore, this power enlightened by faith. "Take it with a grain of salt," then, can be understood to mean that when we are presented with a new idea or theory or way of doing things, we would do well to apply some Christian wisdom to it before allowing it into our mental-emotional digestive processes.

Of course, there was a time when a great many Catholics felt that it was their duty not to accept or even examine any new ideas that might "hurt their faith" as they understood it. Happily, most of us have since come to see that this siege mentality does not nourish a living faith, that we must instead continually engage in what will often be a painful dialogue between what we believe as Christians and the new facts, ideas, and theories that are influencing other people and our society. But this does not mean that we have to swallow any of them whole without the seasoning of Christian wisdom.

For example, take "process theology." Probably a number of PACE subscribers read the two-page interview with Fr. James Empereur, entitled "an Introduction to Process Theology," in the *National Catholic Reporter* for February 1 this year. If you hadn't happened to wrestle with this kind of thinking before, you may well have felt that all your certainties about God were being dissolved. Here is one paragraph:

This article appeared in PACE 4 (1973).

111

God is that about the whole process of reality which gives it direction but saves all that is of value. Nothing that is good is lost. The purpose of creation and of human life is to become part of God. We do not become God, but we become part of God and we enrich God's life. When we enrich God's life, God can become more God. He surpasses himself in his whole reality.

The salt which needs to be applied to this (or any) kind of theologizing, it seems to me, is the basic Christian conviction that God is beyond all our formulating, all our images, all our thinking. He wants us to think about him, since he reveals himself to us "in many ways and diverse manners" and uniquely in Christ, and has commanded us to love him with our whole *mind,* as well as our heart and soul and strength. And yet our thinking can never encompass him.

Process theologians are trying to find a systematic, philosophical way of describing God which will be compatible with the God of Judaeo-Christian revelation who is concerned with, involved in, human history and is therefore in some sense "changeable," whereas classic theology worked with the Greek idea that change means imperfection and therefore God, who is perfect, cannot change. Or as Fr. Empereur put it, "Classical theology was interested in studying being, whereas process thought is interested in studying becoming." This effort is, obviously, a legitimate and fascinating enterprise which will surely, in time, fructify Christian thinking about God. But anyone who tries to follow process theology needs to keep firmly in mind that God is ultimately beyond all our categorizing—beyond both "being" and "becoming" as we understand them.

It is a pity that process theologians themselves don't always preface their works with this proviso and thus save many readers spiritual and mental anguish. A priest friend of ours, reading Gregory Baum's *Man Becoming* late at night, was so disturbed that he called a friend whom he thought to be more "with" modern theology than himself, to come over right away at two o'clock in the morning and help him. One of the friend's suggestions was that maybe Baum had not yet found the right vocabulary in which to express his insights. Perhaps this suggestion is another kind of salt to apply to some theologians' works. (Incidentally, for any readers who want to study process theology in a manageable form, the paperback, *Process Theology,* edited by Ewart H. Cousins, Newman Press, 1971, is an excellent introduction.)

Again, many Scripture scholars and theologians have done away with both good and evil angels, explaining that these are simply personifications of tendencies within human nature and creation. I remember how suddenly lonesome and disoriented I felt when I first read a convincing statement of this theory. Are we human beings all alone up there as the "spearhead of the evolutionary process"? This is a pretty scary idea, especially when you look at the world today. But while statements of this theory can be eloquent and persuasive, what about all the evidence, from flying saucers to poltergeists, that, as Shakespeare put it in *Hamlet,* "there are more things in heaven and earth than are dreamed of in your philosophy"? What about the conviction of many astronomers that there are intelligent beings—perhaps far more intelligent than man—somewhere in the universe? Or what about the reality described by Michael Novak in his article, "Never Exorcised at All" in *Commonweal* (February 22, 1974)?

> *"I do not try to imagine the Devil as a person. I do not try to imagine him at all. Does not the very notion 'spirit' warn that the imagination has no purchase here. . . . To speak of the Devil is to remind ourselves that the world of our experience exceeds the dreams of modernity. Evil is greater, more mysterious, more persistent than we."*

Maybe the kind of salt needed here is an open-mindedness to the possibility of "spirits" combined with loving trust in the Holy Spirit.

The same kind of open-mindedness, it seems to me, can be applied to the conclusions of Scripture scholars about, say, the Infancy Narratives. Maybe Matthew and Luke were writing theology in the form of stories, but maybe too there was some basis for these stories in real events.

Obviously this "take it with a grain of salt" attitude toward new approaches in theology and Scripture study poses difficulties for parents and catechists of young children. We don't want to teach them anything they will have to unlearn later. Process theology poses no problem, since it is the "God and Father of Our Lord, Jesus Christ" to whom we are trying to introduce young children, not the God of philosophers and theologians. As they grow up, young people need to learn to "theologize" according to their abilities, and to become acquainted with the main Christian theological traditions and trends, so as to mature in their understanding of God and to be able to "give a reason for the hope that is in them." If their early religious training has been sound, we can hope that the intuition-conviction of God's Otherness-and-Nearness would be so deeply rooted in their minds and hearts that they could cope with whatever theological systems and approaches they might meet.

But what about angels and devils, who appear in the Gospels with such embarrassing frequency? Or what about the Infancy Narratives, which parents and catechists can hardly avoid at Christmas time? It seems to me that if children are given a great variety of stories—the great legends of different cultures and times, and good modern stories of different kinds, from C.S. Lewis's Narnia series to more or less factual accounts of life in different situations—they will develop a pretty good sense of literary "forms." Then it will not be any great shock to them when they are older to learn explicitly that parts of Scripture are "stories" rather than "histories" (of course, the creation stories should be presented as such from the outset) and that nobody knows for sure about some other parts. And if they ask questions about angels or devils, the possibility of different explanations could be given them in a way suited to their stage of development—which would help them begin to cultivate that open-mindedness toward such questions which we should be cultivating ourselves.

In any case, no such problems arise about the liberal application of the salt of wisdom to the latest trends, emphases, and methods. Consider briefly two areas: the present stress on "family-centered" education, and the growing passion for "evaluation."

Family-centered education is certainly an advance over rigidly segregated age-grouping; helping family members discover how they can learn from each other is much better than convincing them all that they can only learn from priests and qualified catechists. Such education is still better when it brings families together in "clusters" to learn with and from other families—clusters which, one might hope, would develop into communities of sharing and caring and become the "open circles" described by Mrs. Newland in her article in this issue. But family-centered education can't be the *only* kind of education a parish stresses. What about the innumerable people, from sixteen or so on up to "senior citizens" who are not members of parishes? And nobody in a family wants to be considered *only* as a family member—in relation to religious education or anything else.

The kind of salt needed here, it seems, is a concern for the *whole* Christian community, and for finding ways to help more and more of its members become involved in educating one another in many forms of teaching-and-learning and interaction.

And finally, take the current preoccupation with "evaluation." Of course, program designers and coordinators and teachers want to discover the degree to which they have accomplished what they set out to do, so as to improve their programs. And those to whom they are responsible— pastors, the parish council, the whole parish membership—want to know this too. The need is all the more acute since the whole field of religious education is in such a state of flux and everybody feels the need for reassurance that something constructive is really going on. So in answer to this need, many variations have been developed on the same cycle of operations: Establish long-term goals and then immediate objectives—that is, steps toward these goals which can be objectively measured—and set up yardsticks of measurement; then work out programs to achieve these objectives; carry out the programs; use the yardsticks to evaluate the programs; and with the aid of the information and experience thus obtained, start the whole cycle all over again.

Taking these steps certainly makes good sense, and it is a pity that the basic rationale of the process is so often concealed in one or another form of managerial or educational jargon. But the kind of salt we need to apply here, it seems to me, is an acceptance of the fact that some of the most valuable effects of truly religious education just cannot be measured "objectively." Some can be evaluated "subjectively"—that is, the participants can give their opinions about what has happened. But some effects cannot be evaluated at all: How can you evaluate your own or someone else's growth in faith, hope, and charity as a result of a given program? And if we don't keep in mind the impossibility of measuring in any way some of the most important results we would like to achieve, we will yield to the temptation of designing only programs that can achieve measurable results—which would mean a useless and sterile kind of religious education.

These are only some areas in which "take it with a grain of salt" seems like sound advice. Readers will think of many more. All of us have had embarrassing experiences of going all out for some new idea or method, only to find that we had to modify it in the light of other old or new ideas or considerations. All of us have probably, at one time or another, inflicted our latest enthusiasm on other people and caused confusion and damage because we did not properly digest it first with the aid of the salt of wisdom. So, from now on, let's try to keep the salt-shaker handy.

At the time of this writing,
Mary Perkins Ryan was editor of PACE.

115

The Christian Experience of Prayer

Robley Edward Whitson

The central personal action in religion is prayer. This is true of all the world's religious traditions and of all their systems of spiritual discipline. But when we look closely at this centrality of prayer, we quickly discover that prayer is defined in many different ways (even within a single tradition) and can include an often perplexing variety of elements. The Jewish, Christian, and Muslim traditions of the West seem to be in basic agreement that prayer is a specific focus of consciousness in which we affirm our relationship with God. But for Buddhism, prayer is essentially a meditative process of enlightenment-awakening which at least does not seem to orient subjective consciousness beyond itself. Or again, for Confucianism, prayer is ritual; each form of which affirms a dimension of the inherent Harmony which is the source and destiny of all together—man, the universe, and heaven. These contrasts are drawn very simply, but they illustrate the very real differences in the meanings of prayer—differences which are multiplied within each tradition by division of sect and schools of spirituality.

But there are common factors in the prayer process. First of all, it is consciousness, and as such it reflects the persons who pray. It is *consciousness* turned upon their most value-charged meanings and so has a *substance*—that which actual people perceive as defining life. It has *forms,* taking shape from the language and culture and from subjective needs and capacities as these vary from moment to moment in an individual or groups. Perhaps the single most important factor in prayer, however, is *expectation:* a personal action in consciousness presupposes we have already perceived "something" and, having decided to pursue "it," seek to pray in a particular way. Even more than differing substances and forms, important though these are, the very profound differences in prayer expectation determine the inner dynamism of prayer.

What do Christians do when they pray? We can answer this question by specifying substance and form; for example, a prayer might be an act of

This article appeared in PACE 4 (1973).

trustful reliance by a creature humbly affirming the providence of the Transcendent Creator. What do Christians expect to be doing when they pray? This is a subtly different question, moving far beyond matters of substance and form and reaching to the roots of the experience of what truly constitutes being *of Christ.* The expectation at the center of our consciousness as we begin to pray reveals what is at the core of our faith-experience.

The first disciples were the followers of a holy man, Jesus of Nazareth. At the beginning, of course, they had to *decide* exactly who he was—a great rabbi, a prophet, the Messianic prophet, perhaps the Messiah himself. But whatever their judgment as to his identity and role, he was clearly a holy man and as such was attractive to religious seekers. Throughout Israel's history there were many holy men, but few of these were prophets. To progress in a life of holiness one sought out a holy man who became a spiritual master precisely because the disciple discovered in him the achievement of inner holiness and the ability to guide others in that path. Some who met Jesus became disciples to learn how to follow his way—"to walk as he walked." As would be true of the disciples of any holy man, they observed *how he prayed* and wanted to learn to pray *his way.*

> *"And once he was in a certain place praying; when he had finished one of his disciples said: 'Master, teach us to pray even as John taught his disciples'" (Lk 11:1)*

There is a specific expectation implied here. They have seen Jesus praying *in his way,* and this evidently differs from the way of John the Baptist (and presumably of others as well). Whatever it is that Jesus does when he prays, that is what they want to learn to do.

> *"And he said to them: 'When you pray, say: Father, may Your Name be proclaimed Holy; may Your Kingdom come. . . .'"(v.2).*

It is here that we can locate Christ's revolution in consciousness, embodying one of the essential dimensions of what is the uniqueness of Christianity. He perceives God to be his own Father, and the disciples are taught that this must be their own expectation in consciousness whenever they pray. We have grown so accustomed to hearing "God is my Father" and "God is our Father" and to praying "Our Father . . ." that we no longer *feel* the revolution in this way of prayer.

The disciples heard Jesus praying to *God as his Father.* This was not to be expected within the tradition of Israel. However much the sense of Covenant drew people to faithfulness to God, it was to the awesome God of Sinai who gave the Torah, the jealous Lord, the Judge, the wrathful Avenger, the compassionate and all good Creator, the just Restorer, and all the other

117

revealing images which clearly proclaimed the absolute gulf separating all creation from the Transcendent. The most powerful focus of religious consciousness, the Temple of God's Presence, insisted on the ultimate *distance.* The ritual space of the Temple reinforced the sense of separation: The uncircumcised remaining in the outermost precincts, then the women stopping before the men's court, the Levites and Priests drawing closer to the building itself, a priest each day entering the Holy Place to offer incense, and once a year the High Priest entering the Holy of Holies alone with the blood of the atonement sacrifice. Yet even the Holy of Holies was not the actual "location" of God but the "place" where God's Power-Presence was to be felt, symbolized in the Ark as the "footstool" of God enthroned in Heaven. It is true that on occasion in the Scriptures the prophets use very human images of God—as a Father to the king, as a Husband to Israel—but these are clearly poetic images. To suggest that literally God is somehow truly the Father of any man must be blasphemy. God was seen as personal to man—involved and concerned with his creatures—but was also clearly Transcendent, before whom all were but dust. The faithful rejoiced in this dual recognition of the Personal-Transcendent Lord, and this was at the core of their expectation in prayer.

When we consider Jesus' address to God as his own Father, we realize that the use of the Father-image and its Trinitarian implications are complex. All the substance and form of prayer among Christians reflect this, and thus any serious consideration of prayer from those dimensions would inevitably be subtle and complicated. The expectation dimension of prayer, however, allows us to approach the core significance through our own faith experience. We know the disciples heard Jesus praying to *God as his Father;* instead of attempting a substance/form analysis of what it meant for him to say "My Father" or "Our Father," let us explore what such words indicate that *we should expect to be experiencing* as we pray *that* way.

We can ask ourselves a set of diagnostic questions. When Jesus prayed to God as his Father (as the disciples heard him and recorded their reactions, and as we find ourselves now in community with them), do we think of Jesus praying with a sense of separation in his consciousness, dividing himself from his Father? Do we think of him as seeing himself "over here" addressing God "over there"? Is his personal prayer to "Somebody else," who must be *contacted* however near or far away he might be at any moment? Or put directly, Does Jesus pray to God *outside* himself or does he pray *with* God *within?* The kind of answer we give to this pattern of probes demonstrates what actually is the expectation in prayer experience which is essential to the Christian faith experience.

In the tradition of Israel the disciples expected him to pray *to* God. However present to man God might be, God and man remained ultimately *not in interior union.* We cannot begin to appreciate the shock that took place as they realized: Jesus prays *with* God, he prays *from within* and not outwardly towards "another." That the shock was positive we know from the fact that they wanted to learn to pray as he prayed. This can all seem obvious until we remind ourselves that typically we do not pray *with* God but *to* God. We are always reaching out to contact God who is, therefore, not seen by us as *within*. In prayer, we find ourselves speaking to Someone Else rather than conscious of ourselves *in interior union with* the One in whom we live. The disciples asked Jesus to pray the new way they observed in him, and he did. Our problem in prayer is simple: We do not pray *that way*. We have changed our expectation, so that when we pray we expect to be addressing Someone Else—however loving and close—nevertheless *distanced* as an object to which we attempt to relate as subjects.

"Say this when you pray: Father. . . ." In the Matthean parallel to this passage, we find the teaching on prayer transformed into an actual form of prayer, most probably used antiphonally in the earliest Liturgy. In that form the expectation of praying *within* God is reinforced in the opening affirmation: "Our Father . . ." If they really meant *Our* Father, this had to be blasphemy; the violent reaction of their fellow Jews in those first years of the Church in Palestine tells us clearly what the disciples communicated by their words. Jesus had been condemned because he had made God his own Father, and the disciples were also condemned for insisting God indeed is his Father and their own as well.

Apart from using the one word "Father" alone, only the modifiers "My" or "Our" can be used without changing the essential expectation of this way of praying. Any other word or image creates a sense of distance. "Almighty Father" or even "Our Almighty Father" insists on a consciousness of separation: He may well be Father to me (us) in some way, *but* He is Might-Power-Creator while I simply am not! We can observe this change in consciousness in the evolution of liturgical prayer forms. The oldest addresses to God *through* Christ reintroduce distance, even though (and this is most important) as little distance as possible—it is possible to "move across" this distance by remembering we are One in union in Christ, and so prayer *through* him can "take us with him." But the further development in liturgical forms draws resolutely away from this sensitivity, and distance is firmly reestablished in prayer expectation. God is prayed *to*; the Trinitarian formulas put Christ as Son psychologically on the "other side," the intercessory saints of the *koinonia* also gradually shift to that "other side." The same psychological pattern affects all: We "here below" pray to and through them "above in Heaven," ultimately to God Father-Son-Spirit, who has become *in expectation* as separated from us as the image of the Lord God of the Torah. The revolution in prayer consciousness is now theologically postponed: In the eschatological future, when we dwell post mortem in God and He dwells in us, then we will "see him as he really is."

There are many factors at the root of the early drift away from the prayer from-within-with-God to prayer outwards-towards God. In terms of prayer traditions, all the prayer of Israel is necessarily outwards-towards, and so the use of the Scriptural prayers, especially the Psalter, continually reasserts the not-from-within. The psalms simply do not and cannot have this expectation and so in their tangible form must run counter to and ultimately undermine the revolution. (We can see this on a large scale in the present revisions of the Liturgy with the impact of the Responsorial Psalm.)

The Matthean "Lord's Prayer" form introduced another problem in the ambiguous meaning of "heaven" and the dialogue effect achieved in the antiphonal shape. "Heaven" can be an image of separation if it is used in a cosmological theology, especially as this affects the folk-level of religion. But again, in the radical change of expectation experienced in Christ, the disciples were taught a new meaning no longer cosmological but intensely personal-communal: Heaven is within, in each and in the midst of all gathered together as One. In that meaning, "Our Father in Heaven" dramatically reinforces the sense of prayer from within—the now inherent unity in consciousness of man-with-God. The coming of the Kingdom is then no mere aspiration for some day in the future, but another deepening of the sense of from-within, since the revolution of expectation extends to the Messianic Kingdom which is not to be an external rule by God imposed from on high, but is to come from within and be within the new form of life begun in the Christ-Union.

The great problem of prayer from-within rests with us as we are, regardless of the expectations molded by traditions. The plain fact is that the development of a life of prayer from-within-with God is extraordinarily difficult. It embodies the most basic *conversion,* a constitutional change, or in the classic terms of spirituality, a true *metanoia.* It is clearly easier to see oneself as a mere creature dutifully *approaching* God—who therefore remains safely "outside." We can thus avoid the self-responsibility inevitable in truly participating in the fullness of all God is. We really prefer to postpone this wonderful destiny for some later phase of our existence. It is easier and surer to take only the responsibility of *responding to* God, and not enter into co-creativity.

Once again, this is exemplified in the parallel passages of Luke and Matthew on the significance of prayer. Prayer is always "answered," as Matthew (7:11) gives Christ's teaching: "If therefore you who are evil know how to give good gifts to your children, how much more will your Father in Heaven give good things to those who ask him?" But Luke (11:13) understands Christ's teaching with a very different expectation: "How much more will your Father in Heaven give the Holy Spirit to those who ask him?" We are not promised "good things" but the very Power of God, the Spirit who transforms us into the new Christ-Life in which we are member-for-member Christ living in his bodily Resurrection.

Unquestionably this is an inspiring and attractive vision, but on second thought we really would prefer to have "good things" than the Power within us to create for ourselves. It is easier to be faithful/obedient by waiting to receive *from* God outside us; it requires a less developed sense of responsibility ("I'm only carrying out orders from above"). God "out there" need not be the more primitive sense and image of a multi-storeyed world with a heaven-place at a distance from our world and daily life. The "out there" can be less than a "metaphysical inch" away—God present, yes, but safely not from-within.

Although we cannot consider it at length, we should at least point to what is perhaps the most neglected element in Christ's way of prayer, captured in the phrase "May your Name be proclaimed Holy." This is the all-important center of consciousness in Hebrew spirituality, "Kiddush Ha-Shem." In the Rabbinic tradition, with its seemingly endless interpretations and applications of the Law of Moses, the Torah is seen as containing over six hundred *mitzvoth* or precepts, both positive and negative. All are believed to be contained in one summary, as found in Leviticus 22:31–33.

"You must observe my commands and put them into practice. I am YHWH. You must not profane my Holy Name, so that I may be proclaimed Holy among the sons of Israel. I YHWH make you Holy. I brought you from the land of Egypt to be your God. I am YHWH."

God is proclaimed Holy by our own living of lives of Holiness. The unknowable God can be known reflectively in our own experience if our way of life follows the pattern set down in Torah—as we become Holy by enacting the Law-pattern, we can begin to realize something of what it means to say *God is Holy.* We make Holy the Name/Presence of God by living in the way which brings to perfection the human being as actually constituted by the Creator. To "walk in the Law of the Lord" is to live in ultimate realism as a human. This deepmost meaning of *Kiddush Ha-Shem* is celebrated throughout the Psalter, the Wisdom books, and all the prophetic understanding of convenantal history.

Jesus proclaims a New Covenant, not external to man, but reconstituting man in internal Union in God. And so for Christians there is a New Torah, the new life pattern of this reconstitution. "May Your Name be proclaimed Holy—*Kiddush Ha-Shem*" is thus the prayerful experience of faith actually lived:

"No man has ever seen God. If we love one another God dwells in us and his Love is perfected in us. By this we know that we dwell in him and he in us: because he has given us His Spirit" (1 Jn 4:12–13).

121

The expectation we bring to prayer involves us in an existential choice. Do I seek to pray from-within-with-God: Father, Holiness, Kingdom? In that Spirit of rebirth Who slaps us into our first cry of New Life, I answer, "Abba—Father!"

*At the time of this writing,
Rev. Robley Edward Whitson was
director of The United Institute in Bethlehem, Connecticut.
His most recent book was
The Coming Convergence of World Religions
(New York: Newman Press).*

The Church (and the Parent) in the Modern World

Dolores Curran

Working with parents has been a terribly comfortable apostolate in the past but, like many other apostolates in our Church, I'm afraid the age of discomfort has set in. Recently, after I had presented to a group of enthusiastic young parents ideas on enhancing family prayer and liturgies, an older mother stood up. Here is what she said.

"This isn't a personal attack on you, but I think this evening is just one more example of how parents are cheated in our Church. I and lots of other parents my age reared our children by Mary Reed Newland. We did all those things you are suggesting and more.

"We went to daily Mass with our big families during Lent—every Lent. We didn't just shove our kids off to Catholic schools and colleges. We prayed with them, worshipped with them, and furnished the kind of Catholic home you encourage.

"And what happened? Out of my seven children, one is a nominal Catholic. The rest string out from agnosticism in New York to an ashram in New Mexico. The children of our friends are the same.

"I came here tonight to see if the Church is finally going to touch the real issues facing today's parents—cynicism, alienation, guilt, affluence, media, the women's movement, and such, or just go on giving these young parents the same false hopes it gave us. And the inevitable guilt. No wonder I feel cheated."

She looked at the stunned faces around her and her voice softened, "Do all these things if you like. They'll give your family some pleasure, but don't count on them to produce the kind of children the Church says they will."

Although her candor dismayed the host pastor and Director of Religious Education, I was refreshed by it and said so. I have been hearing that kind of comment from parents almost as long as I have been writing and speaking, but it is just now beginning to filter out to the Church at large. If I

This article appeared in PACE 5 (1974).

had been free to do so, I would have turned the evening over to a discussion of parental fear, frustrations, and resentments, but the hour was late and the session wasn't mine.

I've given her words a lot of thought since that memorable workshop. Are we cheating young parents by promising something that has proven futile in the past? Are we giving them Advent wreaths when they need each other? Catechetical clusters when they need hope? And Right To Life Committees when they need family help?

Surely one of the ironies of the abortion controversy lies in the fact that neither the pro-abortion nor the pro-life advocates are very pro-parent. While the former eliminates the problem by eliminating the fetus, the latter ignores it by focusing on the immorality of abortion rather than the needs of today's family.

Both groups have managed to evade the question central to the issue: Why are people choosing to have few children in the first place? Is it that they are more selfish than their parents? Are they seeking different rewards from life? Are they afraid they will fail as parents?

In seeking some answers to these questions, I did a good deal of research culminating in an article which appeared in the February, 1974, issue of *U.S. Catholic,* "Why Are People Afraid to Have Children?" The article—plus the response to it from parents the country over—triggered the editors of PACE to ask me how the Church, as one of the institutions I indicted for failure to help parents, might better become a partnering institution in the parenting process.

It's a fair request. Any time an institution is criticized for failure, the critic should have some alternative actions and behaviors to offer. I do, but before I extend the discussion to how the Church can help parents, let me recap the basic ideas in the original article. Here are five assumptions that grew out of my research:

1. *Yesterday's parents were not as good as they were cracked up to be.* Studies show that children from large families do not tend to have large families themselves. Also, child density, or the ratio of children to years of marriage, plays a significant role in marital satisfaction. As the density of children increases, marital satisfaction decreases.

2. *Five don't eat as cheaply as two.* Today's parents, in direct contrast to yesterday's, are conditioned to furnish more for and ask less of their children. Straight teeth, college educations, and lessons of all sorts are expected to be furnished by parents, while old age assistance is not expected to be furnished by children.

124

3. *Motherhood is no longer enough.* It is the woman who stays home today parenting who apologizes for "doing nothing," while her neighbor who holds a position in a former male stronghold has become the model for the brightest teenage girls.

4. *Children constitute the major uncontrollable factor in the adult's quest for happiness.* "Hassle," not happiness, is the word parents frequently use in describing their role in the home. Sociologist E.E. LeMasters puts it this way, "It is impossible to interview modern parents without concluding that large numbers of them are confused, frustrated, and discouraged. They have been robbed of the traditional ways of rearing children without having an adequate substitute; they feel they cannot achieve what they are expected to achieve; the standards for child rearing are too high; the authority of parents has been undermined by mass media, school officials, social workers, and the adolescent peer group."

5. *Parents serve as the universal scapegoat for society's ills.* Parents suffer from abandonment by institutions. Potentially helpful institutions—church, government, schools—have taken on the role of critic rather than helper. Yet when these institutions are called upon to explain their failures, they reach for the facile and self-serving reason, "If the parents did their job, we could do ours."

So much for the original article. Response to it, while varying in intensity on a particular point, punctuated my general thrust that parents today are discouraged, resentful, and frustrated at being thrust into parenting under such different circumstances, pressures, and times then the generations before them.

A California mother echoes many of the letter-writing parents: "I personally have felt abandoned by institutions around me and I have fears about it, for I feel that parents cannot raise their children without outside help. Perhaps it is our fault for not speaking out. But I believe the time has come when we must demand support."

This brings me back to the older mother who faced the young parents at a parish workshop. At risk of censure and ridicule, she told them to demand more help from their Church, real help, not just paraliturgies. We can expect more parents to do more demanding in the future. If the sixties were the years of clergy and religious awareness, surely the seventies are showing signs of lay awareness.

How can we, as educators and catechists within our institutional Church, give parents more support in their complex role of rearing children in our Future Shock culture?

We must help parents to feel less alone in their role. This means turning family life efforts back to family life. Let's stop using "family life" as a euphemism for anti-abortion. Fighting abortion isn't helping today's families. By all means, let's continue the fight, but let's stop using the monies and personnel supposedly dedicated to enhancing family life for lobbying against abortions.

We need strong family life efforts from chanceries on down to the smallest parish. We need specialists ready to step in and help harassed and uncertain parents to gain confidence in their role. Parents should demand such help from their Church.

We need to get parents together to share ideas, fears, hopes, and strengths, weaknesses, and yes, resentments. Parents have these feelings, and they express them to close friends rather than to those in institutions who might be able to help them.

Let's take the problem of parents trying to rear children in our sex-laden society. One of the topics frequently discussed by "good Christian mothers" concerns loose sexual attitudes bound to be confronted by their adolescent offspring. "How do we deal with sexual permissiveness?" parents ask. "How can we teach our daughters to handle the inevitable situation of being expected to sleep together on the second date when we spent whole retreats on the morality of French kissing?"

Giving parents vague theological reasons to pass on to their skeptical children isn't going to help much, but there *are* ways we can help one another. My daughter might not respond to my insights on purity (being "mother" and therefore suspect) as readily as she would to a younger friend of mine who is closer in age and in tune with the times. But this same friend's son might respond more eagerly to our family's kind of social action involvement because our sons are older than he is and as such, respected by him.

We all need neighborhood models, and most of us can serve as models. Our parish can become a coordinating force in creating extended family structures. On a practical level, this means foregoing the geographical family clusters in favor of compatible family groupings which would include single people also, of different ages. Encouraging such small groups of "families" to cluster, not just for religious education purposes but for supportive family life purposes, could ultimately give us the kind of results we aren't getting in strictly "religious ed" efforts with nuclear families.

We have to broaden our religious course of studies for parents. Is television violence a religious subject? What about child psychology? Government corruption? Vandalism?

We aren't going to give parents a wider view of religion until we adopt one ourselves. How many parishes offer courses in parenting alone? A precious few. More often, parents are brought in as adjuncts at sacramental times or to shore up a sagging "adult ed" program. Yet I envision good parental interest in courses touching on family psychology: Interaction between parents and children; What is a good parent?; How children understand at various levels; Why people are afraid to have children.

Some of our most successful parish family programs have little to do with catechetical ideas but concern themselves with courses like Dr. Gordon's *Parent Effectiveness Training,* Dreikur's *Children, the Challenge,* Harris' *I'm OK, You're OK,* and the like. When individual parents will pay $100 for Parent Effectiveness Training from a local night school, the parish should study the appeal of such a course.

This isn't to say that strictly religious courses are not valuable to parents. They are, but it's a bit foolish to bombard parents with basic theological concepts when they're worrying about how to deal with alienated pre-teens or how to improve family communication. First worries first, as we say in the kitchen.

One of the most reasonable and readable books I've read for parents is Sidney Callahan's *Parenting.* A parent discussion group would be attracted by the chapter titles alone and could use them well for weekly or monthly discussion starters. What parent could resist these sessions: "Who Are We as American Parents?" "What Does a Good Parent Do?" "How to Read How-to Parent Books," "Parent-Child Politics," "Are Parents Born or Made?" "Future Parenthood"?

We must allow parents to educate non-parents in the Church. We keep hearing the charge that our Church is family-oriented, but the preparation of our clergy and religious doesn't provide an understanding of parenthood. Why isn't there a course on the Psychology of Parents in every seminary, taught by parents and preferably attended (and attested to) by parents along with seminarians?

Frequently, the outspoken parents in our Church are written off as disrespectful and disruptive. Yet they are the ones who must teach us how to help them and their peers. My husband has a cynical formula for evaluating parent discontent within public education. "One phone call from a parent on an issue is a crank call," he says. "Two show a trend, and three are a mandate."

We have successfully staved off the mandate in our Church because parents have been conditioned to equate criticism with disrespect, but if the mandate has been stifled, the discontent remains.

Few of us are rearing our children the way we said we would. Why the change? Because of cultural influences we didn't anticipate. It is these influences that are frequently ignored or misunderstood by those in leadership positions. Let's have a panel of parents discuss the effects of television on family life before the Family Life Commission. Or a group of alienated teenagers address the bishops' synod with the same reasoning they use with their parents about religion and Sunday Mass. Or a group of mothers evaluate religious education as *they* perceive it for the benefit of their local pastoral institute.

Why should this be so shocking? The Second Vatican Council's *Constitution on the Church in the Modern World* states explicitly, ". . . let it be recognized that all faithful, clerical and lay, possess a lawful freedom of inquiry and of thought and the freedom to express their minds humbly and courageously about these matters in which they enjoy competence."

Thousands of Catholic parents enjoy competence, not only in their homes but in disciplines and professions which could be extremely useful to others in their Church. Educators, psychologists, pediatricians, behavioralists, therapists, and other family specialists are largely untapped by our own Church. Is it because they are unknown or suspect?

The leadership can't be blamed alone for this void in its education. Often we find competent parents who lack either the courage to tell what family life is like today to those spiritual leaders who have taught it should be otherwise or who lack the energy to get involved. Either way, their fellow parents lose and so do their spiritual leaders.

We must help lift the sense of failure and guilt from parents' shoulders. Rarely do institutions realize how readily they indict individuals for their own failures. Once they are aware of this temptation, though, they can eliminate it as quickly as they have eliminated derogatory ethnic slurs. By keeping a close check on their willingness to intensify the parental scapegoat complex, they can consciously minimize the use of phrases like, "If parents only did their job . . ." "What the parent does can't be undone," and "If a child doesn't learn love by age five, he will never learn to love." (What does this say to a parent with four children over ten?)

We have allowed parenthood to become product oriented, i.e., the end result is proof of effective or ineffective parenting. In kitchen language, this points to a "successful offspring." What is a successful offspring? A well-educated one? A rich one? A happy hobo? A Catholic? A Christian?

Parenthood is simultaneously an adventure and a risk. In the words of Clayton Barbeau, "We are what we are, parents." That's the wider more helpful view we can give parents of their role. If we can help them accept that they are not responsible for a product but rather nurturers of some of God's unique creations during some important years, parents can relax and enjoy parenting more. They won't feel called upon to be super-moms and super-dads, experts in all disciplines at all times.

They won't have to scourge themselves with guilt if they haven't produced a priest or have produced a guru, as long as they have done their best with what God has sent them.

Specifically, this affects pastors and religious educators in that we must encourage parents to make the decision to choose or ignore our programs without loading them down with guilt if their children end up rejecting their religious values. We've done that in the past by stressing the value of our CCD and parochial programs, a value that parents questioned among themselves. If parents rejected substandard CCD classes and their children later rejected their beliefs, we've been tempted to say or imply, "Well, it's your fault, parents. We had the programs for you."

Some homilies and adult group sessions about parent power—the extent of it—and parent guilt could be invaluable today, particularly for those many Catholic parents who still have to hear it from "Father" to believe it.

Finally, we can help parents become institutionally responsible. One widely quoted paragraph from my *U.S. Catholic* article was, "How can parents rear good children in a bad environment, and whose job is it to furnish a good environment? Isn't that the basic purpose of the institution?"

One respondent wisely pointed out that institutions are, after all, made up of people and that we can't blame the Church for allowing a bad environment without blaming ourselves. I presumed that was implied but, on further reflection, I realize he may have articulated the most basic problem: separation of parent and institution. Are we each waiting for the other to solve our own problems while indicting each other for failure to do so? Does not that put us in an adversary rather than a partnership position? Is this creating the abandonment that parents feel from the institution and the apathy that leaders associate with parents?

When I mentioned environment, I was including such diverse areas as corruption in government, racism, questionable patriotism, just or unjust warring, pornography, sexual exploitation, profitable pollution, acceptable vandalism, hypocrisy in leadership, and so on.

We tend to leave those issues up to church and government, preferring not to get involved as laymen. Involving ourselves directly with our institution to improve our national and local environments could serve two fine purposes. It would help us feel directly responsible for the environment as individuals operating within an institution, and it would put us in partnership with our institution in creating a better environment in which to rear our children.

Our Church needs to offer us more outlets for actually improving our environment. I envision parish- and diocesan-sponsored groups, set up along the lines of anti-abortion groups, to monitor television violence, to help parents with sex education in a permissive society, to involve parents in the decision-making processes in their schools, and to encourage parent involvement in local politics and boards.

Of course, this means getting involved, which means risk. Just like parenthood. Only it wouldn't seem so lonely. We would be risking together... finally.

*At the time of this writing,
Dolores Curran, mother of three, wrote
a weekly column for the NC News Service.
Author of four books, she served as the
only mother in the American delegation to Rome for the
First International Catechetical Congress
in 1971.*

Why Read the Bible?
The Possibility of a
Fresh Perspective

Walter Brueggemann

It is strange that the Bible is our most treasured book, and yet it seems so difficult that we don't find it very helpful. Perhaps we have expected the wrong things of it; we have asked of it what it cannot do. We have expected the Bible to keep promises that it has never made to us. The Bible cannot be a good luck piece to bring God's blessing. Nor can it be an answer book to solve our problems or to give us right belief. So the first question about reading the Bible is what we can indeed expect of it.

I suggest that the Bible is precious to us because it offers us a way of understanding the world in a fresh perspective, a perspective that leads to life, joy, and wholeness. It offers us a model, a pattern, through which we may think about, perceive, and live life differently. Each of us has adopted one or more models for living our lives, even though we didn't do it consciously. We learned a certain perspective by living in certain contexts and listening to certain voices. They gripped our lives and shaped our experience, and we didn't know it was happening. Yet over a period of time they came to have great power over us and finally define our identity and destiny for us.

The model which I regard as central to the Bible, and which I will present here, is what I call a **covenantal-historical** way of understanding our life and faith: By "covenantal" I mean an enduring commitment by God and his people based on mutual vows of loyalty and mutual obligation through which both parties have their lives radically affected and boldly empowered. By "historical" I mean that these covenant partners, God and his people, have a vast deposit of precious memories of decisive interactions; these interactions, which run the gamut of love and hate, affirm to us that our whole existence depends on staying seriously and riskily involved with the covenant partner.

This article appeared in PACE 6 (1975).

To bring out the uniqueness of this model, I will first sketch out several alternative ways of understanding life which are shaping people in our society. In some respects, they have points of contact with the model here proposed and are reflected in the Bible. But on the whole it is clear, as I will try to show, that the biblical view is quite distinctive from the others. Thus reading the Bible can mean changing the models through which we understand life.

One powerful model today is what we might call the **modern-industrial-scientific** perspective on life. This view has emerged in the last several centuries and has been of decisive importance in shaping our public institutions. It includes the notion that knowledge is power, and therefore that life consists of acquiring enough knowledge to control and predict our world, and thereby to secure our own lives against very danger and threat.

It also includes the notion that life is built on a reliable scheme of performance and reward. Put in traditional language, "good people prosper, evil people suffer." Put in more contemporary language, it means that all things and all people are valued for their usefulness. This means that life is governed by a firm arrangement of effectiveness and pay-offs, whether in the marketplace, the home, or the church. All relations are a **quid pro quo** pattern of scratching each others' backs. Such an understanding of reality places a high value on competence and achieving, on success and getting ahead. Such a view yields a notion of personhood which says, "I have value for what I can **do**," or in its more decadent form, "I have value for what I **have**." The human community consists of people getting what they earn and deserve. Those who earn little and therefore deserve little, do not figure; in fact, they do not for any practical reason even exist. Obviously, such a view favors those who succeed and are competent. It tends to be the case that those who have, get more, and those who don't, get less or nothing.

As a result, this view puts a premium on what is knowable, manageable, and predictable. Obviously, it does not appreciate graciousness. It is not open to mystery and hardly has a place for transcendence. While much of our modern world is organized this way, and many of us are deeply into it when we least know it, nonetheless, such a model of reality is quite at variance with that of the Bible.

A second influential model of life today goes under the name of **existentialism.** This perspective was originally articulated to present an alternative to a coldly objective and rational world of control and mastery. While a cold, objective rationalism may be more dominant in modern society, existentialism is congenial to a counter-culture posture.

Existentialism holds that meaning exists only in, and derives from, the decisions made by the individual in the present moment. It is thus a protest, and an important one, against a static view of reality which regards everything as fixed and closed and insists on keeping things that way. Conversely, this model of reality tends to be community-denying, locating meaning only in terms of the solitary decision-maker who must make decisions alone and live with the consequences alone. And, along with such uncompromising individualism, this model also tends to devalue the historical process as it moves from event to event. There is no value in the sweep of history nor in the continuities of the process because meaning is located only in the **now** of the present decision. While this view does appreciate the full power of the present moment, it tends to leave the individual in a vacuum because, by definition, memories and hopes are not matters of significance for the identity or destiny of the individual.

This means that existentialism posits the human decision-maker as the sole agent of meaning. Not only can meanings not be appropriated from others but there is no possibility of transcendent meaning in experience. There are no meanings given to or prior to the individual in the moment. While existentialism intends to be a statement of radical freedom and radical responsibility, it also holds the likely prospect of weariness and despair. While the promise is great, if my world depends solely on me, that is more than I can bear.

A third alternative view of reality we may designate as **transcendentalism.** By this, I mean a view of the world which imagines that the give-and-take of our experience which is always ambiguous, if not contradictory, is not the source or locus of real and significant meaning. Enduring meaning is immune from the incongruities and discontinuities of historical experience and may be located beyond historical experience in an abiding and enduring state of eternity.

Such a history-denying view of life has a variety of manifestations. It may be expressed as cold reason, which is logical in the extreme and regards only logic as providing relevant data. Conversely, it may be mystical meditation which seeks to negate historical experience, to be emptied of such sensitivities for the sake of other once-removed meanings. Such a quest for non-historical reality may be pursued by a mystical pilgrimage to deny historical consciousness, by meditative reflection after the manner of Eastern religions or, more broadly, in religious celebrations which serve to escape the realities of daily life.

Transcendentalism tends to eschew suffering and to seek serenity beyond the reaches of historical hurt. Implicit in such a view is that historical experience—and, indeed, historical personality—are not essential embodiments of fundamental meaning. It will be evident that such a view of religion is in conflict with a religion of incarnation, i.e., of historical embodiment of decisive meaning, and tends to deny the exigencies of historical risk and hurt.

Distinct from all these perspectives, the Bible is a primary source of an alternative model of reality which may be described as covenantal-historical.

This view may be contrasted at important points with the faith options we have already reviewed:

A. Distinct from the **modern-industrial-scientific world view,** this model insists that human existence does not consist primarily in the capacity to know and control and manage. Against a **quid pro quo** world based on success and competence, it asserts that reality consists in risking commitments, in powerful memories and compelling visions, none of which can be reduced to **techne.**

B. **Distinct from existentialism,** the convenantal-historical perspective asserts that meanings are never private but always communal, never in an isolated "now," but always in an ongoing process of trust and betrayal, and never with us as the only actors. It insists that life consists in a dialogue with a powerful, compelling Other who bestows mercy and compels accountability.

C. **Distinct from transcendentalism,** the biblical frame of reference denies that meaning can be immune from the incongruities and discontinuities of history; it asserts that decisive meanings are located in and derived precisely from historical hurts and historical amazements which judge and heal and call to repentance.

When we read the Bible, then, we need to learn to pay attention to the understandings of reality which permeate the text. Unless we do this, we may fail to discern what in fact is present to the text and to the Church. For the believing community is always confronted by the text as summoning it to make a new decision about perspective.

Thus the reason why we read Scripture is to keep ourselves from settling easily for any other notion of life, from forgetting who we are, and the understanding of life we have confessed and embraced. Informed by the Bible, we can live fully and faithfully according to the model of reality which is peculiar to our faith tradition and provides us with a context for living quite different from the reigning alternatives. In other words, one of the most important gifts the Bible can give us is a frame of reference for our lives. Given that frame of reference, we are still left with major decisions to make about our world, our freedom, and our responsibility. But Scripture reading can provide us with resources and images enabling us to understand, embrace, and respond to life in all its richness. For the Bible presents human life in terms of the vitality of being in history with a covenantal Partner who speaks newness in a world which always seems fatigued and exhausted.

That is what is most deeply characteristic about this view of reality: **We are in covenant with One who speaks newness, who dismantles what is old in our lives and who calls us to welcome and live toward his newness.** Here are some other characteristics of this view that matter to us as we shape our human future.

1. This way of talking about reality never proposes religion in general; it is **intensely particular.** It is precisely identity in a particular people (Israel, the Church) which energizes and authorizes a clear identity and a bold mission. This Church, i.e., the people consciously in covenant with Yahweh, the God of the Bible, bound to him in love and loyalty, is a locatable community. This is crucial in a culture in which many people experience displacement.

2. Covenantal-historical perspectives help people to link themselves to a rootage in a **precise historical memory.** We do not live in an abstract realm of ideas, but in a people which has a particular memory that gives power to us. This memory, as it is expressed in biblical faith, is a memory of liberation (Exodus) and empowerment (David), of passionate, caring-suffering (crucifixion), and the surprise of new life (resurrection). This rootage tells us something about God, that he is not a remote agent who is for himself, but he is for us characteristically involved on behalf of his creatures. Our life is not about success, or about private decisions, or about private escapes. It is about liberation and empowerment, about self-giving for others and about being surprised by new life when we thought it not possible. Our identity is secured in the places of cost and joy in which we have been involved. It is this very particular memory to which we are heirs and of which we are bearers.

3. A fresh perspective of a covenantal-historical kind transmits to us a **special expectation for the future** and a **dynamic which lets that promised future come among us.** The shape of our expectation is quite concrete even though it tends to be expressed in poetic imagery. We live toward and await a community of justice and righteousness, in which the last ones will be first (Luke 13:30), in which the humbled ones will be exalted (Luke 14:11), in which the hungry ones will be fed (Luke 1:53), and the ones who mourn will be comforted (Matt. 5:4). Our expected future which God has promised in the Bible has many points of commonality with the best of civil religion and the substance of the American

135

Dream. But the texture of this future is expressed in the staggering inversions of life which contains not only new gifts but also harsh judgments against those who resist the vision or seek to have a piece of it on their own terms. This vision requires an abandonment of present arrangements for the sake of what is promised. Moreover, this future, while it has its utopian aspects, offers the dynamic of a Promise-Maker and a Promise-Keeper, God himself. That is what is covenantal about this tradition. We are not in covenant with a good idea which is simply there or with our best intentions which depend on us. But we are in covenant with an active, caring, intervening God who keeps his promise. The future here envisioned is not a withdrawal from history but a renewal of humanness in history.

4. A covenantal-historical perspective **defines human existence in terms of vocation,** i.e., not in the sense of an occupation, but in terms of being called by our Covenant Partner to live our lives in ways consistent with this relationship. The One who has called the world into covenant with him (creation) is the same one who calls us to a relationship of responsibility. Our life is not for self-indulgence, nor for desperate coping, nor for frantic, empty surviving. It is life lived after the manner of this very God who empties himself to obedience in the life of Jesus. But it is not emptying as a simple spiritual discipline. It is rather emptying for the sake of healing, caring, and bringing newness. Vocation is then not simply what we do with our lives, but it is in fact the very shape of our lives.

Thus the Bible provides us with an alternative identity, an alternative way of understanding ourselves, an alternative way of relating to the world. It invites us to join in and participate in the ongoing pilgrimage of those who live in the shattering of history, caring in ways which matter, secured by the covenanting God who likewise pilgrims in history. This way of understanding our lives lets us be open to hurts (crucifixions) but also to healing surprises (resurrections) which emerge in our common life. It lets us embrace our own experience as important and the life of our brother and sister as part of our own. Most of all, it tells the story of this One who has committed his life to us, who promised in every hurting and rejoicing place in life to be there with us (Matt. 28:20). While other perspectives promise other things, this perspective finally promises that the Lord of Glory, the One hidden and yet known, is there with us in all the hurting and healing of historical existence.

In our time, as perhaps in every time, the Bible provides standing ground against other attractive and seductive alternatives which we judge to be not so compelling for us:

1. Against a modern-industrial-scientific view of reality, the Bible asserts that we live in a world where healing mysteries surge among us. We are not called to be successful or secure but only faithful, to learn that in our risky caring, gifts of life are indeed given which sustain us.

2. Against existentialism, the Bible insists that life consists in communities of meaning. We not only invent meaning but it comes to us from outside ourselves. Meanings are entrusted to us in the structures and institutions of common life but also in the flow of memory and vision between the generations.

3. Against transcendentalism, the Bible affirms that life's issues and ultimate meanings are situationed precisely in the give-and-take of history. It denies that there is another realm of meaning to which we may appeal or withdraw.

This way of living our lives lets us take God with real seriousness, to face his sovereignty over us and his freedom from us but also his strange poverty among us which heals. It also lets us take ourselves and our lives seriously, knowing we are about something important. We can be serious about living our lives but also buoyant about them because of our faithful Covenant Partner. Finally, this fresh perspective assures us with all our mothers and fathers in faith before us, that we belong to our faithful God who is at work among us for our well-being which is his will for us.

All of this makes the Bible no easier to read. It is still strange because it does not accommodate our conventional language, images, or presupposi-tions. But it makes the point that in the Bible is rooted a perspective on life which is of urgent importance for our common life. That fresh perspective concerns not just the Church as a separate believing community but as a vision of a new humanity in his new creation. The Bible is keenly pertinent to our contemporary "crisis of the human spirit." The Bible provides hints of an alternative notion of what our humanness is, human in **history,** human in **covenant.**

At the time of this writing, Walter Brueggemann was dean of academic affairs and professor of Old Testament at Eden Seminary in St. Louis, Missouri.

If You Are Pro-Life . . .

Sidney Callahan

Christians should be leading the way in support *for* the Equal Rights Amendment and *against* abortion "on demand" for identical reasons. The roots of the struggle for the rights of women and the rights of the fetus are the same. A Christian understanding of life and of our duty to be just and principled in our dealings with one another can only lead to seeing these two causes as complementary and to working for them both. That they have too often been made to seem opposed to each other is a tragic shame. But let me argue the point.

Both the movement for women's equal rights and the movement for the rights of the fetus rest upon a view of human life as being full of meaning. It's no absurd accident that we are all here in the universe milling around and striving to exist and grow. We believe that not a sparrow falls without the knowledge of God, and all human beings created out of God's love for life are destined for eternal life. Important to this good news, and revolutionary news indeed, is the word that God does not judge as the world judges. All human life is sacred; the poor beggar covered with sores is equal to the beautiful rich young man. The dying child or ill widow is as beloved as the powerful centurion. God is no respecter of, and does not judge by, the worldly standards of health, power, productivity, I.Q., class, or race.

More to the point, God does not discriminate by sex or degree of human development, either. For generations the powerful world has accorded full human rights only to white, middle-class adult males; this has been the image and standard of what counts as a human being. The others have only presented social "problems:" i.e., the poor, the old, the sick, the handicapped, the Indians, the Blacks, and finally women, children, and life in the womb. We know that "In Christ there is no male or female, slave nor free, Jew nor Greek," but in the world, wealthy white males have called the tune and have ground the others down.

Women and children have been assured of rights only if they were able to become allied with powerful males who would then protect them. But the price of family protection was a form of ownership and bondage. In a world

This article appeared in PACE 7 (1976).

ruled by force, the only real rights are those that can be protected by power and influence in the present. A reliance on instant power keeps people from having empathy with the powerless and from being able to envision their future potential, much less to affirm human life which may seem "different." Feminine life, immature life, has been seen as so different from that of adult males that too great an act of imagination was needed to accord such lives fully human status.

But one measure of the advance of a civilization is the distribution of fundamental human rights irrespective of power and privilege. When women have been accorded equal rights before the law, then children, infants, and others who are powerless to defend themselves can also hope to be recognized as fully human. Nor, in our long tradition of seeking impartial justice for all, have we ever—in theory at least—allowed the powerful to judge their own case in a conflict of interest with the powerless. It's an elementary principle of justice that you never hand over the lamb to the lion for judgment. Consequently women should not be subject to the discretionary power of men, nor offspring totally in the power of their parents.

Women need the fullest protection and guarantees of the law of the land given in a public symbolic affirmation, i.e., the ERA. Immature human life in the womb needs the protection and guarantee of the law of the land given in public symbolic affirmation, i.e., a new Supreme Court ruling or some form of constitutional amendment. Christians should be leaders in the effort to educate, persuade, and lobby for these guarantees. The role of law and the rule of law can effect righteousness only when laws equalize the rights of those who are dependent and those upon whom they are dependent. Dependency is not, as some cults of individualism would suggest, a crime punishable by the loss of all rights.

Moreover, human rights are not to be granted only when the more powerful parties "want" or desire the dependents. Why should a woman have to be wanted, desired, and so protected by male relatives in order to have full legal rights? Through our laws we have struggled to ensure that women cannot be arbitrarily repudiated by their fathers and husbands and so lose their rights. When we go further and complete that struggle with the Equal Rights Amendment, each woman will be guaranteed legal redress and equal access to all important civil and economic rights whether she is "wanted" or not. Giving in to the prejudices, wants, and emotions of the privileged and powerful is the death of justice.

In the same way, letting parents decide that they can extinguish an "unwanted" new human life is to give in to unjust control of the helpless by the strong. Morally speaking, immature human life does not exist on the sufferance of others, upon their emotional desires to keep that life alive. Nor are human dependents and the weak to be killed when they do not measure up to the standards and desires of the powerful. In classical times, fathers used to have the right and power to kill any newborn (often unwanted female infants), and there is little progress when this principle of arbitrary paternal power is transferred to women and extended to an earlier stage of human development. What real difference is there between infanticide and a late abortion on demand? Absolutely none. Especially when an infant is aborted alive and is allowed to die on parental orders. We should not be surprised that public arguments in favor of infanticide are now increasing. Infanticide has a long hidden history in Western culture, like child abuse and the exploitation of women; all are based upon the rule of might, not right; expediency, not principle.

Rules of privacy added to a spirit of false pragmatism have sustained the abuse of fundamental human rights. Privacy, which is also related to "privation" (as in "deprivation"), has a negative side as well as a positive one. Evil done in secret, without public scrutiny, was always private or privileged. In the name of privacy and privilege, those without advocates and without power have been suppressed. What cruelty, for instance, has taken place in the privacy of the home behind locked doors, cruelty mostly directed at women and children with no place else to go. The old idea that God and the law should only reach down to the woman as subordinated to the man in the sacred family unit, or to children subordinated to both parents, has been a fountain of abuse. Women must have direct access to the community and the law outside the family structure, and children have to be given rights of their own. No male can own a woman, and no woman can own a child; all human life receives its dignity directly from God.

Of course, the institution of the family should be supported, and dependents have to be cared for, but unless each individual is individually granted equality and rights by the whole society, his or her protection within the family can be endangered. If women do not have full legal equality outside the home, they will get less protection within marriage, for second-class citizenship invites victimization in private. If children are not considered the responsibility of all of the community under the law, then parental rights and power can be seen to justify child abuse. Abortion, and soon infanticide, will be claimed as part of the parental right to privacy and a necessary bulwark of family life.

Consequently, society as a whole has to set limits to privacy and family discretion when family interests overrule the rights of an individual life. But at the same time society has to be committed to help those in need. If we forbid abortion and yet as a society offer no parent any help in the enormous burdens and expenses of child care, we are hypocritical indeed. If handicapped children are stigmatized and have no rights to special education and public help, then how hollow pro-life arguments will be. If young, unmarried pregnant women are forced to leave school and given no help, then those who support the life of the fetus must also support the rights of such women for help. If there is no justification for killing inconvenient dependents, then it can hardly be justified to allow anyone with dependents to suffer severe penalties. When women are abandoned, they will have difficulty not abandoning their own unborn children. Women have to be strong to resist abortion when it is easily obtained and legally sanctioned. But as long as adequate aid to women with children is withheld, it is no wonder that many women conclude that our society really doesn't care a fig about life—so why should they?

This is why, as the November elections approach, voters need to consider the *whole* record and mind-set of each candidate. If he or she is "pro-life" only on the issue of abortion and not on issues such as reforming the welfare system adequately to take care of people's basic needs, then he or she isn't realistically pro-life at all. And it even might be that a candidate who does not appear to be strongly opposed to the existing abortion laws might be so strongly pro-life in other ways as to be the better choice over a single issue anti-abortion candidate with a poor record on issues of social justice.

Proponents of abortion also try to equate abortion with contraception, which is a far different thing. Most forms of contraception are means of control over one's own body *before* conception, *before* a new human life is present in the womb. Abortion has been called the only act in which killing and self-mutilation can be combined. It seems indeed to exemplify a very aggressive (male?) method of solving some difficulty: Root it out, search and destroy, cut it away with a technological attack with no thought for the whole context of the problems or the interrelationships of the many factors involved.

But women who have been suppressed tend to identify with the aggressor. The weak are tempted both to pass on any aggression received and to take it out on themselves. Only those women with great feminine pride and strength can see creative alternatives and take risks for life. It's no accident that the rise of feminine pride coincides with the rise of the incidence of single young women keeping their babies. Unfortunately, the abortion rate is rising also, and one, at least, of the many factors involved is that women have been conditioned to see their bodies and reproductive capacities much as males do theirs. The whole socioeconomic system has been structured so that only male bodies existing without encumbrances can work easily and gain society's rewards. Thus many women are persuaded that male sexuality is superior and that they must gain a masculine type of control over their sexuality as the price for advancement, or even survival, in the man's world. Only when women's equal rights, and especially economic equality, have been gained will women be able to "own their own bodies" as the female bodies they are.

141

When women gain equal rights, equal education, and equal economic opportunities, they can appropriate the final completion of feminism: self-love, self-pride, and altruistic protection of growing human life, in and out of the womb. Women have already begun to assert themselves to improve pregnancy and the birth process. Childbirth today is far more human and safe than a few decades ago when women were instructed to be simply passive patients submitting to male professionals.

When women are no longer treated as objects and second-class citizens, they can refuse to treat their own bodies and their own young as objects without rights. When women are given equal responsibility in social life, they will be able to respond to the challenge of unexpected and difficult pregnancy. Altruism comes from strength. Hope also springs from optimism and a trust gained from past experience. All adherence to principle, defined as not giving in to instant expediency, requires a strong sense of self-worth, especially if most of those around you disagree. Parents, boyfriends, husbands, and friends insist upon abortions. Stress, isolation, and worry about the future always tempt a woman to take the quick and easy way out. Self-confidence, hope, and social support from others can encourage women to accept a pro-life position. The support of other women and their example and encouragement is particularly good for the self-image of women. Those to whom much has been given can give more easily. The insecure are tempted to keep every shred of security and safety they can manage.

Great women and the struggle of feminists to liberate women will help women be strong. Sisterhood is powerful. Despite some dissension, women working for a feminist goal such as the passing of the Equal Rights Amendment strengthen all women's sense of their own potential. Recognize women's potential, and they can recognize the potential life of the fetus with imagination, empathy, and courage. Liberty, equality, and maternity. If you are pro-life, support the ERA.

Dr. Sidney Callahan is a professor of psychology at Mercy College, Dobbs Ferry, NY. She has written eight books, the latest being Parents Forever: You and Your Adult Children *(New York: Crossroads, 1992).*

The Ambiguity of Professionalization

Gabriel Moran

Who wishes to be called "unprofessional"? Very few people, I would guess, judging from the extensive literature on professionalization. The desire to be a professional seems especially strong these days among parish religious educators in the Roman Catholic Church. I have no intention of opposing either the general movement or any of the particular steps advocated in this journal and elsewhere. In this article, nonetheless, I will raise this question: (1) What is the historical background of this somewhat mysterious concept of "professional"?

My main hope is to stimulate the reader to investigate some of the books listed at the end of this article. I hope to show that the history of professionalism is of practical importance to anyone trying to professionalize parish religious education.

Historical Introduction

The recent study, *A National Inventory of Parish Catechetical Programs* (USCC, 1978), could be depressing to anyone advocating professionalization. Two examples of the study's data will indicate why: (1) Only 7 percent of parish directors earn $10,000 or more; 49 percent are unpaid. (2) One-third of directors do not have a college degree. The *Inventory* makes a most unfortunate choice in describing as DRE "anyone who was in charge of parish education." There is no logic to this terminology, given the fact that only 32 percent described themselves this way. Fifty-one percent of the people surveyed called themselves "coordinator" and 9 percent called themselves "the pastor." The result is that "DRE"—the most likely term to indicate some specific professional development—is swallowed by its indiscriminate application.

The picture gained from the *Inventory* can look so bleak that one is forced to ask: Is the Catholic Church on some path other than that of modern professionalization, and, if so, is that all bad? The question is not meant to

---

This article appeared in PACE 9 (1978).

143

excuse low salaries and incompetent work in the Church but to probe whether the modern meaning of professional is an unambiguous good. Possibly some of what is assumed to be a weakness of the Church can, from another perspective, be a strength. What is called "underprofessionalization" might actually be a pre-modern form of professionalization.

Pre-Modern Meaning

The last statement implies that there has been a considerable shift over the centuries in the meaning of professional. On this point the evidence is clear: In many ways the meaning of professional is the reverse of what it once was. There has also been continuity, of course, but the shedding of the pre-modern meaning is what interests me here. Is the modern meaning preferable in all ways to the pre-modern? If some of the pre-modern meaning is desirable, we may want to retain that which may still exist in the Catholic Church.

A simple, dramatic contrast between the pre-modern and modern understanding of professional can be made with these three points: (1) In the pre-modern form, the professional lived in the community and served it on a permanent basis. In the modern meaning, there is a "professional community" which supplies individuals to local communities on a temporary basis. (2) In the pre-modern meaning, a professional was willing to sacrifice money because the work itself was so valuable. The modern professional is the person who expects to get higher pay. (3) In pre-modern times the professional accepted his/her knowledge as a grace to be shared; the community granted "license" to this person's challenging the community. In its modern form the professional's knowledge and license give one a protected status: The community is not allowed to intrude. Robert Jay Lifton summarizes the shift in this way: It was from advocacy based on faith to possession of technique devoid of advocacy.

The pre-modern meaning of professional has its roots in the Catholic religious order. A person professed vows, or, more exactly, one was professed in vows. The vowed person stepped before the community to *confess* what he or she was *pro-fessed in.* A lawyer or doctor was supposed to have a comparable dedication to higher values and a loyalty to some chosen community. Obviously, the ideal was often violated, but the ideal was nevertheless clear.

Modern Meaning

The change to a modern meaning of professional occurred over a period of centuries during which the very concept of "modern" was born. Individualism, rational science, technology, and international trade helped to bring about the modern world and to define the meaning of modernity. The modernizing of the professional was already advanced in England by the seventeenth century. There were more professionals existing in increasingly narrow specializations while achieving money and status.

An interesting sidelight is that conditions in the North American colonies delayed the process. The minister (who in the eighteenth century was likely to spend his entire professional life in one local church) might also function as doctor or lawyer. Until 1765 there was no medical school in the colonies. There were few lawyers or, stated differently, nearly everyone functioned as his or her own lawyer. Women, it should be noted, played a larger role then than they would in modern professions which are inherently sex-biased. In the nineteenth century, women were allowed into medicine and education as a sub-professional class. They could be nurses and teachers (the paradigm for professional educator was the male administrator), and to this day 95 percent of "professional women" are either teachers or nurses.

When the United States became professionalized in modern form, it did a thorough job. All kinds of groups from engineers to undertakers seized the concept and its modern meaning. In 1850 a leading educator, Jonathan Turner, had pronounced that 5 percent of any population are the professional class; the other 95 percent of society are fit to be the industrial class. The twentieth century seemed to democratize the concept, but there may be a flaw in supposing that the nineteenth century's sex- and class-biased meaning of professional can simply be spread to everyone. When everyone is a professional, who are the clients or consumers? The answer is: all of us. The other side of professionalism, the consumerist culture, is causing increased frustration. A society made up of innumerable niches of expensive and esoteric services is not really what anyone had in mind, but it is what we have increasingly become.

Post-Modern Meaning

Thirty years ago no one talked about a crisis in the professions. We may have had too few doctors or engineers, but the solution was clear: more recruitment, higher pay, and better working conditions. What we have today is an attack upon the professions themselves, and the attack is by no means confined to a weird fringe. In one week this year, the President of the United States delivered stinging attacks on both the medical and legal professions. Malpractice insurance rates are a symptom of our society's distrust of doctors, the same people who by nearly all criteria are the top profession. Some people seem to pine for the pre-modern world, a sentiment I do not share at all. Anyone familiar with the fourteenth century will not look to it as the golden age of medicine. Nonetheless, we might have to reappropriate some of the pre-modern meaning of professional.

It would be tragic if those of us in Church education were fighting today to get into the nineteenth century. Doctors, lawyers, soldiers, engineers, and athletes are experiencing a breakdown in the modern meaning of professional. We cannot assume that the meaning of professional is sitting there waiting for our adoption. The world is looking for a "post-modern" meaning of professional that may have resemblances to the pre-modern meaning. The person working at the intersection of Church and education is one of the people to demonstrate a new meaning of professional which is also an old meaning. Every professional in the post-modern era will have to relearn something about religious devotion and on-the-job training. A Church educator has something to learn from modern professionals but also something to teach them.

Given the strengths and weaknesses of the Roman Catholic Church, an educator there has no choice but to be creative and imaginative. A new meaning of professional can and must be created. Central to this meaning is a rethinking of the professional's relation to community (which will allow some different thinking about money). Becoming professional is certainly going to remain highly desirable. In contemporary speech everyone wants to be professional because the opposite of professional is ignorant, unskilled, and incompetent. However, the opposite of our modern professionalist/consumerist culture is not necessarily a culture of ignorance and incompetence. There could be a society in which communities or persons possess a variety of skills with a variety of degrees of training.

Some Helpful Books:

Bledstein, Burton. *The Culture of Professionalism.* New York: Norton, 1976. (The nineteenth century and the university's role.)

Boorstin, Daniel. *The Americans: The Colonial Experience.* New York: Random House, 1958, pp. 185–239. (The eighteenth century and professionals.)

Calhoun, Daniel. *Professional Lives in America.* Cambridge, MA: Harvard, 1965, pp. 88–177. (Church transition in eighteenth and nineteenth centuries.)

Furnish, Dorothy Jean. *DRE/DCE: The History of a Profession.* Nashville, TN: United Methodist, 1976. (Twentieth century Protestantism.)

Gaylin, Willard, ed. *Doing Good: The Limits of Benevolence.* New York: Pantheon, 1978. (Historical essays on the welfare state and professionals.)

Hall, David. *The Faithful Shepherd.* Chapel Hill, NC: University of North Carolina, 1972. (New England ministry in the seventeenth century.)

Haskell, Thomas. *The Emergence of Professional Social Science.* Urbana, IL: University of Illinois, 1977. (Late nineteenth and twentieth centuries.)

Lasch, Christopher. *Haven in a Heartless World.* New York: Basic, 1977. (Influence of professionals on the family in the twentieth century.)

Lifton, Robert Jay. *The Life of the Self.* New York: Simon and Schuster, 1976. (A different paradigm for the professional therapist.)

Mattingly, Paul. *The Classless Profession.* New York: New York University, 1977. (Education in the nineteenth century.)

Scott, Donald. *From Office to Profession.* Philadelphia: University of Pennsylvania, 1978. (The early nineteenth century change in Church profession.)

Wirth, Arthur. *Education in the Technological Society.* San Francisco: Intext, 1972. (Early twentieth century split of professional class and vocational education.)

At the time of this writing, Paulist Press was about to publish Brother Gabriel Moran's book, Education Towards Adulthood: Religion and Lifelong Learning.

Signs of Hope:
8. Religious Education

Thomas H. Groome

For Catholic religious educators, the 1970s are frequently described as a time of confusion, crisis, and lostness. Be that evaluation true or false, I am convinced that there are signs of a new life and fresh hope in these first years of the 1980s and enough evidence to warrant that our hope is not in vain.

As in previous essays on other topics, to appreciate and understand the present signs of hope, we will begin by situating the present state of the discipline within a brief historical overview.

High Points from History

The first Christians clearly understood that Christianity is a "way of life." They fashioned their educational efforts to bring people to such a lifestyle: to live the Gospel of Jesus Christ. (See for example, the *Didache.)* In the Catechumenate that emerged at the end of the second century, there was still a strong awareness that Christian faith is a lifestyle that engages the whole person. Now, however, the role of the total Christian community in bringing people to such formation and transformation is more clearly understood. In the formation of Christian identity, the socializing influence of the Christian faith community was seen as indispensable. When the Good News was proclaimed through the catechumenal process, the mode of communicating it was to tell the story of salvation history (see for example, St. Augustine's *De Catechizandis Rudibus,* written about A.D. 400) and to celebrate this story in liturgies.

After the invasion of the Western Roman Empire by the tribes affectionately known to history as "the barbarians," there followed the Dark Ages when much of formal learning was obliterated. But even in those dark times, the Faith continued to be handed down, especially at a grassroots level—a sign to us of the resilience of our enterprise. Scholarship and Christian learning survived in Ireland and Britain, and the influence of the Celtic

---

This article appeared in PACE 12 (1981–1982).

monastic system bore fruit in the Carolingian Renaissance of the ninth century and in the Cathedral Schools.

The great Cathedral Schools of the late Middle Ages grew to become the first universities. There the beginnings of scholasticism soon flowered in such great scholars as Peter Lombard, Albertus Magnus, and Thomas Aquinas. The scholastics had a profound impact on the Church's educational ministry, leaving us the rich legacy of a firm commitment to reasoned inquiry in the enterprise of "faith knowing." There was also, however, an undue emphasis on the orthodox formulation of Christian beliefs.

This concern for orthodox teaching (formulated most often in Greek metaphysical terms) was augmented further in the Reformation and Counter Reformation eras. The success of Luther's *Small Catechism* (A.D. 1529) prompted the Catholic Church to follow suit. There emerged the great catechisms of Canisius (A.D. 1556), Trent (A.D. 1566), and Bellarmine (A.D. 1598). Thereafter, and for most of the next four hundred years, the primary mode of intentional religious education in the Catholic Church was by the catechism.[1]

The first significant shift away from an exclusively catechism approach to Catholic religious education came with the Munich Method in the early 1900s. With its emphasis on preparation (activities, experiences, etc.), presentation, explanation, and application—the Munich Method heralded the advent of modern pedagogical principles into Catholic religious education.

Josef Jungmann in the 1930s appreciated the pedagogical principles of the Munich Method but charged that the content being taught was a dry and fragmented doctrinal summary and not the Good News of Jesus Christ. Jungmann gave birth to the kerygmatic approach (in North America usually called the "salvation history" approach) with its emphasis on proclaiming the Good News of salvation. Jungmann claimed that there are three other sources of catechesis besides doctrine, namely, Scripture, liturgy, and Christian witness.[2]

In the 1960s, a critique of the kerygmatic approach emerged.[3] The names of Nebreda, Van Caster, and Babin heralded the advent of a more life-centered and experiential approach to catechesis. The presence of a strong political consciousness at the Catechetical Study Week of Medellin (1968) brought a new awareness to Catholic religious educators of the political implications of our work.[4]

Salient Convictions in Our Present Situation

In the light of this past history, Catholic religious educators today seem to have reached consensus on four important convictions.

1. There seems to be a conviction that the source for "coming to know God" is not Bible/Tradition alone nor contemporary experience alone, but both sources together and in dialogue with each other.

2. There is an expanded and more complete understanding of what it means to live the Christian faith. Over our history, and especially since Trent, Catholics have had a tendency to define faith as belief in a rather intellectualist sense, while Protestants have tended to define faith as trust in a fiducial sense. In the years since Vatican II, we have returned to seeing faith as having an affective (trust) as well as a cognitive (belief) dimension, and we have become more convinced of the necessity of the behavioral (praxis) expression of lived Christian faith. Regarding the form that Christian praxis must take, the rediscovery of the centrality of the Kingdom in the preaching of Jesus has brought a stronger awareness of our intra-historical responsibility to live now for the values of the Kingdom as Jesus preached it.

3. Recovering the example of the early Church, there is a strong conviction that formation in Christian faith requires the context of a Christian faith community. Such socialization calls not simply for better pedagogical techniques or curricula for classrooms, but for the building of faith communities capable of forming people in authentic Christian identity.

4. There is now a solid conviction that lived Christian faith is a lifelong journey, a process instead of a point of arrival. Thus, faith education must attend to a whole life passage.

Signs of Hope in the Present

These four convictions find expression in many concrete ways in our present North American context. I see these as signs of hope.

1. In response to our awareness that *both the faith handed down and contemporary experience must be honored and held in dialogue* if we are to come "to know God in Jesus Christ" (see John 17:3), we find the following:

   • In attempting to honor the activity of God in the contemporary world and in people's own experience, people are being invited in the catechetical context to speak their own word, to name their own reality, to come to their own "faith knowing." They are being invited to reflect upon their own experiences and to do so critically. In essence, this is a shift away from simply telling people what to think and a shift toward inviting them to think for themselves: to come to do theology rather than having it done for them.

- There is a renewed sense of loyalty to "the faith handed down," causing Catholics to reclaim and prize the richness of our Tradition. There is a kind of regrouping from the apparent confusion in the aftermath of the Council toward the redefining of Catholic identity with the inclusiveness and openness that epitomizes the Catholic tradition at its best.

- And there are signs that Catholic religious educators are not taking an either/or approach to the above two sources. Instead, we are attempting to honor both the "faith knowing" that comes from contemporary experience and the knowing that comes from the people of faith before us, and to hold the two sources in a critical correlation, in a fruitful dialogue with each other. Padraic O'Hare writes insightfully that now "we know enough about the ineffectiveness of exclusively didactic approaches to education and the vacuity of certain stripes of experiential education to give us some hope that we may approach a correlative practice of religious education in the eighties."[5]

2. In response to our conviction that *Catholic faith lived according to Jesus' preaching of the Kingdom entails our heads, hearts, and lifestyles,* we find the following:

- Catholic religious education has always had a strong commitment to teaching the content of the Faith. Now, however, the emphasis on faith as trust is leading to a renewed emphasis on spiritual formation. Many of the contemporary curricula materials have a strong liturgical catechesis; there is an emphasis on forming people as "pray-ers" rather than simply teaching them the standard prayer formulas.

- The good works required of people in Christian faith, lived in light of the Kingdom, now more obviously include the task of living and helping to build a world of peace and justice. That Catholic educators are to intentionally educate for these values is clearly stated in Church catechetical documents. The *National Catechetical Directory* and *Catechesi Tradendae* of Pope John Paul II make it clear that we must educate for the faith that does justice.[6]

3. In response to the conviction that *formation in lived Christian faith requires the socializing influence of a Christian community,* we find the following:

   - The centrality of the family in Christian faith formation is now a key emphasis in many parish programs and curricula series. The family is more clearly seen as "the first school" in Christian faith identity.[7] There is a greatly increased emphasis on intentionally engaging the whole family in the work of catechesis.

   - Catholic religious educators are making valiant attempts to establish integrated and total catechetical programs which take the faith life of the parish as a whole as the primary curriculum. The use of the Rite of Christian Initiation of Adults (RCIA) is adding fuel to the fire of this movement.

   - Catholic schools, in rapid decline only a few years ago, are now showing amazing resilience and vitality. Many schools are taking on the challenge to build a community where the total environment, and not just the "religion class," can be harnessed to promote the formation in Christian faith of their students, faculty, and staff.

4. In response to the conviction that *faith is a lifelong journey,* we find the following:

   - There is now a concerted effort to make Catholic religious education "adult centered." This is a phrase that Gabriel Moran first introduced into the field more than ten years ago, but he was often misunderstood. In advocating adult-centered religious education, Moran was not saying that children should not be catechized, but that all of our religious education should be education "toward adulthood."[8] The developmentalists lend weight to Moran's insight. There is now a far greater openness than ten years ago to see the journey toward maturity of faith as just that, as constant *journey*, for everyone of every age, and never a point of arrival.

• Closely allied with the previous sign of hope is the realization that the ongoingness of the faith journey requires a constant process of conversion. Another way of stating this is to say that Catholic religious educators are now more aware of their task to promote an ongoing critical consciousness, a critical consciousness that will empower people to engage in the world on behalf of the values of the Kingdom. By causing people to think for themselves and to think critically about the social, political, and economic structures of our society and world, Catholic religious educators are realizing their political task and are becoming agents of transformation in the Church and in our society as well.

Conclusion

These are the signs of hope for Catholic religious education which occur to me, and I'm sure there are many more besides. But perhaps the greatest sign of hope is that we Catholic religious educators are coming to a renewed appreciation of our ministry and an expanded understanding of our own identity in the Christian community. We have our own unique way of sharing in the threefold ministry of Jesus as it has been traditionally categorized—priest, prophet, and politician (king).[9] Our ministry is "to make present the Story" (priestly), "to propose the Vision" (prophetic), and to sponsor people to a lived Christian faith that is in solidarity with and emancipatory for all God's people (political).[10] There are many signs that we Catholic religious educators will continue, and grow in fulfillment of, this noble ministry in the years ahead.

Endnotes

1. For overviews and key documents in the history of the Church's educational ministry see the following: Kendig O. Cully, ed., *Basic Writings in Christian Education* (Philadelphia: Westminster Press, 1960); T.F. Kinlock, *Pioneers in Religious Education* (Freeport, NY: Libraries Press, 1939); Adolf Meyer, *Grandmasters of Educational Thought* (New York: McGraw Hill, 1975); Elmer Towns, ed., *A History of Religious Educators* (Grand Rapids, MI: Barker Book House, 1975); Robert Ulich, *A History of Religious Education* (New York: N.Y.U. Press, 1968); and John Westerhoff and O.C. Edwards, eds., *A Faithful Church* (Wilton, CT: Morehouse-Barlow, 1981).

2. For an excellent history of the rise and fall of the "salvation history" approach, see Mary C. Boys, *Biblical Interpretation in Religious Education* (Birmingham: Religious Education Press, 1980).

3. See Alfonso, Nebreda, *Kerygma in Crisis* (Chicago: Loyola University Press, 1965).

4. For a fine summary of the shift to the "experiential" (or what he calls the "anthropomorphic" approach), see Luis Erdozain, "The Evolution of Catechetics," *Lumen Vitae* 25, no. 1: 7–31. This is also a good overview of the six International Catechetical Study Weeks.

5. Padraic O'Hare, "Giving an Account of Our Hope: Religious Education in the Eighties," *New Catholic World* 224, no. 1339 (January/February 1981): 16.

6. See *Sharing the Light of Faith: The National Catechetical Directory* (Washington, DC: USCC, 1978), p. 95ff; and Pope John Paul II, "*Catechesi Tradendae,*" *Origins* 9, no. 21 (8 November 1979): 337, etc.

7. See "Declaration of Christian Education," in *The Documents of Vatican II,* ed. Walter M. Abbott (New York: American Press, 1966), p. 641.

8. See Gabriel Moran, *Education Toward Adulthood: Religion and Lifelong Learning* (New York: Paulist Press, 1979).

9. For an excellent summary of the priestly, prophetic, and political dimensions of the task of the religious educator, see Maria Harris, "Political Ministry and the Claim to Power," *New Catholic World 224,* no. 1339 (January/February 1981): 25–28.

10. See my *Christian Religious Education: Sharing Our Story and Vision* (San Francisco: Harper & Row, 1980), chap. 12.

At the time of this writing, Thomas H. Groome, author of the widely acclaimed book <u>Christian Religious Education</u> (Harper and Row), was associate professor of theology and religious education at Boston College.

154

Doing Justice to Justice

Daniel C. Maguire

G.K. Chesterton said that it is not that Christianity has failed, but that it simply has never been tried. Philosopher Soren Kierkegaard, unlike Luther who had ninety-five theses, had only one—that Christianity has not been made a reality. Both gentlemen were correct in the main thrust of their assertions: A failure of nerve leads to a failure of vision. We sense the challenge of Christianity, and then we shy from it and distort it.

Let us take, for example, the biblical notion of justice. The Hebrew and Christian Scriptures (terms I prefer to Old Testament, New Testament) give us one of the richest notions of justice ever to grace this good earth, and we miss the message almost completely. Small wonder! To take the Bible seriously on justice would lead to a nonviolent but upsetting revolution in our private lives and in society.

An advance warning is in order before we look at biblical justice. Such justice is not easily understood. Indeed, it is almost unintelligible to the likes of us. To understand this justice, we must, in effect, be "born again." That often misunderstood term means here that the vision of God which shines forth in the biblical message is so alien to our way of thinking and behaving, that symbolically we must start all over and be reborn into a new way of thinking. The opening cry of the Gospel is *metanoeite*—a verb usually translated "repent" (Mark 1:15). It means more than that. It refers to a whole new way of thinking. Literally it means to turn your mind inside-out. Let a new mind be in you such as was in Christ Jesus. To do this, you have to set the axe to the root of your current thinking. Every mountain in your little mindset must be leveled and every valley filled with newness. Nothing will be the same if you will be baptized into this new vision, this new and good news.

First of all, the Bible presents justice as God's primary and consuming passion. The Psalmist describes God quite simply as "a lover of justice" (Psalm 99:4). Jeremiah speaks of the God who brings justice to the world and who finds in justice his delight (Jer. 9:23). Isaiah asks in what sense God is holy, and his answer is that God's holiness is shown by God's justice (Isa.

This article appeared in PACE 12 (1981–1982).

5:16). As Abraham Heschel said, justice is not just a value in Scripture; it is nothing less than God's stake in history.

Justice is also our contact point with God, the prime sacrament of encounter with God. Deuteronomy says that "the decision of justice belongs to God" (Deut. 1:17). This means that the individual is the channel for God's justice. Doing justice is communion with God. There is no other holiness. If indeed you are bringing your gift to the altar at liturgy and become aware that you have not done the reconciling the work of justice, you are to leave the church, attend to the work of justice, and then you are qualified to return to worship. Liturgy without a lived pattern of justice is not even worship.

But what then precisely is this justice upon which God puts so high a stake? For one thing, it is utterly un-American in its concept. The United States' concept of justice is that of the blindfolded lady holding a scale which is perfectly balanced. The Bible would have none of that. Biblical justice would rip off that blindfold and check to see who is dickering with the scale. And sure enough, it would be quickly discovered that the scales do not balance, that there is a different measure if you are white, rich, male, or other. The Bible, in a word, is not naive. It does not reduce justice to the mathematics of a balanced scale, and it does not ignore the sinfulness of humankind.

The biblical image of justice is much more powerful than the American image. According to the prophet Amos, justice is like a mighty mountain stream tumbling down a ravine with enormous power, taking all that it touches with it (Amos 5:23). Clearly this is more dynamic than a dubiously balanced scale.

But what is the direction of this thundering torrent that God wants justice to be? Quite simply, it is the utter elimination of poverty and oppression from this earth. The mandate of God is simple and straightforward: "There shall be no poor among you!" (Deut. 15:4). Notice, there is no biblical distinction between deserving poor and undeserving poor, between the needy and the "truly needy" as we hear the term used today. Poverty as such is totally repugnant in the eyes of our justice-loving God. Why? Because "the poverty of the poor is their ruin" (Prov. 10:15). And precious in the sight of God is the blood and the flesh of the poor (Psalm 71:12–14). Such flesh must not be blighted with poverty, oppression, or insult. This signals the mission of justice.

To achieve that mission, biblical justice proceeds with a shockingly undisguised bias and partiality. Here is the passionate center of biblical justice—*its burning bias in favor of the poor.* With disconcerting imbalance, our God looks at the destitute in our society, the failures, the convicted prisoners, the dropouts, those Dickens called "the unsoaped," and to them says: "Blessed are you!" Then the divine gaze goes to the likes of most of us, the securely well-off, the disciplined, respectable, law-and-order type, the kind you would hope your daughter or son would marry, and to such God says: "Woe to you! It would be easier to get a camel through the eye of a needle than to get you to understand that justice which is to be the mark of the reign of God!" (Matt. 19:24; Luke 6:20–26).

What does this seemingly preposterous message mean? Are we all to be poor? Didn't we just say that God is against poverty which is the ruin of the poor? Of course. We are not called to poverty. We are called to justice which would sweep poverty away with the roar of a gushing stream. *But we are unequivocally called to view reality through the eyes of the poor, to think out of the plight of the poor, to judge all issues with an eye to the perishing, insulted poor that we have always with us.* Biblical justice commands us to take on the cause of those who are weak and helpless in their own defense. To be just is to become a father and mother to the poor and to search out the cause of strangers whom we do not even know. (See Job 29:12–16.) In the Bible, the burden of proof is not on the poor to explain their condition, but on the rich for permitting and profiting from poverty. Those who are secure will always justify the way things are. These are "the rich" against whom Jesus and the prophets railed.

But there is yet another strong point in the realistic, down-to-earth notion of justice the Bible gives us. It stems from a clear-cut recognition that private, one-to-one care of the poor won't suffice. The Bible is concerned with the structures, also—privileges and systems of the political and economic order that keep people poor. (Jesus would not have been cruci-fied—a political punishment—if there were not important political implica-tions to his teaching.) In biblical perspective, it is not enough to bring a poor man a turkey on Thanksgiving, for the systems that keep him poor will leave him in need of another turkey next Thanksgiving Day. It is the systems which keep poverty a permanent fact of life that must be changed. Involve-ment in the political and economic order is not optional in the Bible's view, for it is precisely in these orders, in contrast to the private and interpersonal world, that most decisions are made about who shall eat and be poly-saturated, and who shall starve and die. The Bible knows that God's justice demands not just changes in our private lifestyle, but in the social order which up to now in human history has never reflected the compassion or the justice-hopes of our God. At the very least this means that Christians should become more politically active and join groups such as Bread for the World (32 Union Square East, New York, NY 10003), Public Citizen (P.O. Box 19404, Washington, DC 20036), and Common Cause (2030 M St., N.W., Washington DC 20036) to find out in particular and practical terms what each of us can do.

To see how serious the Bible is about changing the structures of society, look to the Year of the Jubilees which occurred every fifty years in ancient Israel (Lev. 25). Here we find a whole system of redistribution built into the law. Put simply, it amounted to this: Suppose that I were a farmer, a lazy farmer and a bit of a drunkard and ne'er-do-well, who had squandered my way into great debt. So I sold my farm to a neighbor, a good person who gave me much more than my farm was worth, in hopes that the windfall would redeem me from my wasteful ways. Come the Jubilee Year, according to law, guess what happens! I get my farm back and the neighbor loses his claim to it! Why? Because "There shall be no poor among you." Even "undeserving," wasteful poor are precious in the sight of our God, and their flesh is too sacred to be ruined by poverty.

The Jubilee Year was not always observed in all its prescriptions any more than our Constitution and Declaration of Independence have been. But the message enshrined in the Jubilee Year was social justice and the need for systematic redistribution to keep justice intact. The scriptural writers, in a word, would agree with the ancient Thales, who said that whenever there is immoderate wealth *and* immoderate poverty, justice does not obtain. The Hebrews, of whom we Christians are the insufficiently grateful heirs, knew that one way or the other it was precisely that unjust state of affairs which would result unless we took steps against it. Some people were going to get immoderately rich and others would be left in numbing poverty. Wealth does not simply distribute itself fairly; some people are luckier or pluckier or smarter than others. (Luck is, of course, the major cause of personal wealth.) Some, try as they might, will fall victims to the power of existing monopolies, social arrangements, or prejudices. So every fifty years, the Hebrews decided to scrunch things back together in a way that was suitable to their agrarian economy. No one should be without his piece of the land, for that would make you, in that time, literally "dirt poor" and helpless.

Do not miss the spirit of Jubilee's justice. It is not enough that you do not cheat people, or that you care for your near and dear. You must seek out the cause of the despised and helpless whom you do not even know. "If your brother becomes poor and his power slips, you shall make him strong" (Lev. 25:35). Scriptural scholars tell us that the basic word for justice in the Hebrew Scriptures means "showing mercy to the poor." The poverty of the poor is our business. "On you the unfortunate man depends; of the fatherless you are the helper" (Psalm 9:14). "He shall deliver the needy when he cries out and the poor that has no helper" (Psalm 71:12). Such responsiveness to the poor is the mark of God and of those who would be one with God.

We live in a world where more than a billion dollars a day are poured into the making of weapons. As one writer said, we have created the end of the world and stored it in our silos—and every day we add to that store of death while a quarter of the world's children starve. Where is that mighty stream of justice? Every week a million people are added to the world's population. Ninety percent of these are born into desperate poverty, poverty of the sort that most of us have never seen, where women gather dried dung for fuel and children pick in fresh dung in the hopes of finding there some undigested grains.

To a black child born in almost any of our United States cities today, we Americans send this message: "Your mother is three times more likely to die in childbirth than the average white mother. You are twice as likely as a white child to die in your first year of life. If you live, no matter what you do, you are five times more likely to be murdered and three times more likely to be unemployed than a white; and you are twice as likely to get no further than high school. At least by age eight, you will understand that the impressive, dominant white society thinks you are not just down on your luck, but inferior, and your gentle center of self-confidence will be raped. Welcome, little child of God, to the nation that thinks itself a Christian and goodly people."

No, Chesterton's and Kierkegaard's quotes given at the outset were none too cynical. In the image of theologian Paul Ramsey, we have avoided the mighty stream of justice and settled for a gentle spray. We have declined the invitation of God "to do justice and love mercy" (Mic. 6:8). Since fear is the beginning of wisdom, we would do well to ponder if the most terrifying words of the God in the Bible are directed toward us in our mean-spirited contentment: "I have never known you. Depart from me" (Matt. 7:23).

And yet hope must have the last word. Any people who believe as Christians do that resurrection, not death, is the final destiny of life are a hopeful people. God's vision of justice could catch on. Christians could be Christianized. The hour is late for that, but hopefully not too late.

At the time of this writing, Dr. Daniel C. Maguire taught ethics in the theology department of Marquette University. His most recent book was *A New American Justice: Ending the White Male Monopolies* (Doubleday).

Slaves, Harlots, and Pagans

Joanmarie Smith

L etty Russell, a noted theologian and feminist, speaks of the "search for a usable past." She elaborates: "Human beings need to find identity and strength from the images of past history which can help to guide them in shaping their present and future."[1] Joann Wolski Conn takes a similar tack when she writes of "reconstructing a tradition to support women's spirituality."[2] I hope to contribute to that search and that reconstruction.[3] Women and other oppressed groups have been denied strong images. Studying the Scriptures for models with whom we can identify and from whom we can draw strength can be a painful experience. The double-bind figure of the virgin-mother is hardly imitable.[4] Nor do other prominent women, who separate into the unappealing categories of slave-servant or repentant harlot, provide figures that can nurture a contemporary spirituality for women. In fact, some feminists have found the Judeo-Christian Scriptures "irredeemably sexist."[5] I prefer to stay as long as possible in the camp of those who think that when the overlay of male supremacy is removed from the translations and interpretations, a usable past may emerge. In this article I search out and attempt to reconstruct an Egyptian slave, a reputed harlot, and a quasi pagan. But first I would like to demonstrate the existence of the patriarchal overlay.

Internalizing Patriarchy

More and more we understand that we do not have "raw" sensations. Sensations are filtered through interpretive schemes, molds, models.[6] We do not know the sensation; we only know our interpretations of the sensation. And it is to that interpretation we respond. For example, what do you see below?

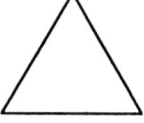

This article appeared in __PACE__ 13 (1982–1983).

Most of us would say, "a triangle." But, I would remind you, "triangle" is a very sophisticated mathematical concept. Perhaps you would say, "Well, I see lines." And I would say that they are hardly less sophisticated than triangles. You might then want to say, "Ink on a page." But even as you spoke you would undoubtedly have recognized that "ink" and "page" are ideas, interpretations—not what you *see*. Our experience bears out the insight: All data is theory laden.[7]

Where do these theories or interpretations come from? We seem to accumulate them in our acculturation. *Sesame Street* takes great pains to help children as young as three and four distinguish triangles from squares, circles, and other plane figures. In geometry we accumulate more information about triangles; and, finally, in philosophy class we are taught that triangles do not exist in the concrete; they are mental constructs—composed in our mind and only approximated in the real world.

But, of course, our concern here is not triangles. Their discussion was a prelude to the thesis that for over four thousand years the prevailing cultures have been dominated by an interpretive scheme in which the male was the model of what it was to be human. Females were something less. Those who still take exception to the use of "humankind" for "mankind," as well as inclusive substitutions for related terms, must not appreciate the fact that the inability of women to inherit, to vote, and to retain their own names is directly traceable to this equation of "human" with "male."

Vestiges of this patriarchal interpretation still abound. To prove it to yourself, just compare the connotations distinguishing the male referent from its female counterpart. "Wizard" is not so bad, but "witch"? And while it is all right for a girl to be a "tom boy," for a boy to be a "sissy" is some kind of unforgivable offense. Similarly, "bachelor" connotes an enviable lifestyle; "spinster" does not. The double standard does not apply only to sexual activity. It permeates all our interpretations.

Nowhere is it more evident than in religions and in the Scriptures which ground those religions. Certainly the Bible, which we now recognize to be historically conditioned, seemed for centuries to have canonized the patriarchal system it pictured. And even when it did not, the filter through which these Scriptures were read prevented our seeing the exceptions. Almost all the women in the Bible owe their presence there to the relationship they had with a man. They are most often cited because they are the mother, wife, or whore of some prominent male figure. Yet, even when this is the case, some startling revelations can be discovered—and a usable past can emerge.

Hagar

Hagar is remembered as Sarah's slave, Abraham's concubine, and Ishmael's mother. But study the following passage:

The angel of Yahweh met her near a spring in the wilderness, the spring that is on the road to Shur. He said, "Hagar, slave-girl of Sarai, where have you come from, and where are you going?" "I am running away from my mistress Sarai," she replied. The angel of Yahweh said to her, "Go back to your mistress and submit to her." The angel of Yahweh said to her, "I will make your descendants too numerous to be counted." Then the angel of Yahweh said to her:

"Now you have conceived, and you will bear a son, and you shall name him Ishmael, for Yahweh has heard your cries of distress. A wild-ass of a man he will be, against every man, and every man against him, setting himself to defy all his brothers."

Hagar gave a name to Yahweh who had spoken to her: "You are El Roi," for, she said, "Surely this is a place where I, in my turn, have seen the one who sees me." (Gen. 16:7–13)[8]

Notice just three quite remarkable events in this scene.[9] First, Hagar names God. "You are El Roi (the God who sees)." Who else names God in the Scriptures? In fact, Moses is rebuffed when he asks God's name (Exod. 3:14).

Second, a case can be made that she names herself too. "I am the one who has seen the one who sees me." Compare this to Abraham's conversation with Yahweh in the very next chapter. Here Yahweh appears and says, "I am El Shaddai" (Gen. 17:1). And it is Yahweh who changes Abram's name to Abraham (Gen. 17:5). In any case, Hagar's words emphasize that she has looked on God and lived—a rare phenomenon as Yahweh suggests to Moses. "You cannot see my face, . . . for man cannot see me and live" (Exod. 33:20).[10]

Finally, the formula with which Abraham is set up as a patriarch is all but identical to the words spoken to Hagar. To Abraham: "Look up to heaven and count the stars if you can. Such will be your descendants" (Gen. 15:5). To Hagar: "I will make your descendants too numerous to be counted" (Gen. 16:10).

There is also an intriguing parallel between the testing of Hagar in Gen. 21:14–21 and that of Abraham (Gen. 22:1–19). Unlike Abraham, Hagar will not cooperate in what appears to be the imminent death of her son. Having used up the little water with which she was sent into the desert, Hagar places Ishmael in the shade of a bush and sits at a distance saying to herself, "I cannot see the child die" (Gen. 21:16). Yahweh intervenes, as is done with Abraham. "Come, pick up the boy and hold him safe, for I will

162

make him into a great nation" (Gen. 21:18). Instead of a ram, God provides a well for Hagar and Ishmael.

> *God was with the boy. He grew up and made his home in the wilderness, and he became a bowman. He made his home in the wilderness of Paran, and his mother chose him a wife from the land of Egypt (Gen. 21:20–21).*

Certainly, Hagar is nothing less than a matriarch in this story, yet the significance of her role has been overlooked for centuries. And, although there may be some bias here, I definitely prefer Hagar to Abraham as the model of a test-taker.

Mary Magdalene

The name "Mary Magdalene" commonly conjures up the idea of a harlot. In fact, however, while she is specifically mentioned in four roles in the Gospels, not one of them is that of a sinner. She is described as traveling with and ministering to Jesus with Joanna, Suzanna, and others (Luke 8:2). All four Gospels represent her as standing at the cross. In Matthew and John, the Risen Jesus appears first to Mary; and, again, in all four Gospels she is commissioned to tell the apostles of the resurrection. How could someone with such credentials appear in the popular imagination as the prototype of a reformed sinner? The history of that image turns on the interpretation of a phrase in Luke 8:2 and in the appendix to Mark (16:9). "Mary surnamed the Magdalene, *from whom seven demons had gone out. . .*" (italics added).

Carroll Stuhlmueller remarks in the *Jerome Biblical Commentary,* "Such possession can indicate only a very serious illness,"[11] which, in fact, it does in almost every other allusion to possession by devils in the New Testament. The peculiar "sinful" interpretation of Luke 8:2 has been coupled with an identification of Mary Magdalene as the sinful woman who washes Jesus' feet with her tears in Luke 7:37–38. However, no scriptural scholar would hold that there is any reason to make this identification. Raymond Brown sees the identification as reinforced by the liturgy. Since the time of Gregory the Great (d. 604), the Western Church at the feast of St. Mary Magdalene has celebrated the confusion in the readings of the Mass. "Not without demur," he notes in his 1966 book on the Gospel of John.[12]

The demur has been low-key though; and, I would suggest, it has still not been heard by the people in the pews, while everyone seems to be aware of St. Christopher's changed status. The data of Mary Magdalene seems not simply theory laden but actually distorted to fit a patriarchal predisposition to see any woman who played such a stunning role in the Gospel as having to be raised to this exalted state from a position even lower than that of most women.

The Samaritan Woman

A similar theory seems to be acting in the story of the Samaritan Woman. The item everyone seems to remember is precisely that—an item.[13] She had five husbands, and the person she is currently living with is not her husband (John 4:16–18). The fact that the term *ba'al* (master, lord) also named a pagan deity and that the Samaritans were reputed to have had five gods and that their present *ba'al* was not the pure Yahwism of the Jews (John 4:22) is made little of. Funny, because when the passage is read in this last light it makes much more sense. It quickly parallels the profound theological discussion of Jesus and Nicodemus in the previous chapter.

Moreover, unlike the cautious Nicodemus, this woman quickly evangelized her community, moving the people to meet Jesus on the strength of her word (John 4:39). How likely is it that the townspeople would have so rallied to the theological speculations of a great sinner? Has the data been distorted again to conform to a prevailing image of women? As Regina Coll notes with regard to the Samaritan woman: "Her history is a model for the lives of many women: What is important is what is known or guessed about their sexuality; what is lost is the good they have done in their lives."[14]

So, instead of a concubine, we can have a matriarch in our tradition. Instead of a harlot, an apostle to the apostles, and instead of a quasi pagan, a budding theologian. Such models provide the usable past with which we can shape the present and future for ourselves, our daughters—and our sons.

Endnotes

1. *Human Liberation in a Feminist Perspective—A Theology* (Philadelphia: Westminster Press, 1974), pp. 72–103.
2. "Women's Spirituality: Restriction and Reconstruction," *Cross Currents,* Fall 1980, p. 299.
3. I am a "Joannie come lately" to the feminist movement. In fact, almost all the ideas in this essay are the result of conversations with my friends Regina Coll and Maria Harris. Instead of suing me for plagiarism, however, they encouraged me to write and critiqued this paper. Ah, sisterhood!
4. Marian Warner, *Alone of All Her Sex* (New York: Alfred A. Knopf, 1976), p. 336.
5. Ann Patrick Ware, "Starting on a New Track," Inter-Faith Consultation Union of American Hebrew Congregations (New York, 6 March 1980).
6. The points in this paragraph are developed at greater length in *Modeling God,* by Gloria Durka and Joanmarie Smith (New York: Paulist Press, 1976).

7. Norwood Hanson, the philosopher of science, coined this pithy phrase in *Patterns of Discovery* (Cambridge: The University Press, 1958), p. 18. By examining the method of scientists in this book, he demonstrated that, whereas scientific study claimed to use only objective observation, there was no such thing.

8. "In the most ancient texts the angel of Yahweh . . . is not a created being distinct from God, . . . but God himself in a form visible to men" *(Jerusalem Bible,* footnote to Gen. 16:7).

9. Professor Winsome Munro of Dubuque Theological Seminary brought out these points about Hagar at the annual convention of the Association of Professors and Researchers in Religious Education, East Lansing, Michigan, November 1981.

10. See also Deut. 4:33 and Judg. 6:22–23; 13:22.

11. Carroll Stuhlmueller, "The Gospel According to Luke," in *Jerome Biblical Commentary,* ed. Raymond Brown, Joseph Fitzmyer, and Roland Murphy (Englewood Cliffs, NJ: Prentice Hall, 1968), p. 138.

12. Raymond Brown, *The Anchor Bible, The Gospel According to John* (Garden City, NY: Doubleday & Co., 1966), p. 452.

13. In another instance where Jesus cites the past of a person (John 1:48)—Nathaniel, "I saw you under the fig tree"—the allusion is ambiguous enough but has never been equated in the popular imagination with sin.

14. Regina Coll, "Paulo Freire and the Transformation of Consciousness of Women in Religious Congregations" (Ed.D. diss., Teachers College, Columbia University, 1982).

At the time of this writing,
Dr. Joanmarie Smith, CSJ, was
associate professor of Christian education at
Methodist Theological School in Ohio.
Her most recent book was
Morality Made Simple (But Not Easy),
published by Argus.

Peace, Politics, Parishes

David O'Brien

In the current discussion among the United States bishops regarding
nuclear weapons, several things are clear. First, the use or threatened use
of strategic nuclear weapons cannot be justified in Christian terms. Second,
all Christians have the absolute obligation to face the horrible truth of the
arms race and the danger it poses to the human community and to find
means by which they can act to reduce the danger of war and move toward
the eventual elimination of weapons of mass destruction. Third, Catholics
and other Christians are divided regarding the wisdom and morality of
maintaining a nuclear arsenal as part of a policy of deterrence, and they are
even more divided in their assessment of the political realities which provide
the context of the arms debate.

As Catholics debate these matters, two equally compelling arguments
are heard. On the one hand, there are those of a more or less evangelical
persuasion who measure the existing reality against the clear words of the
New Testament and conclude that no follower of Jesus can have anything to
do with the arms race. Individual Christians and the Church must denounce
the arms themselves, refuse to pay taxes or serve in the military, and stand
forth boldly in prophetic resistance to "the political economy of death."

On the other hand, there are those who examine the Scriptures, the long
tradition of the Church, its contemporary teaching and experience, and
conclude that, while traditional just-war categories cannot justify nuclear
war and, in fact, require the abolition of nuclear weapons, the process of
disarmament must be set in the larger context of international relations.
Building a just world order, marked by economic equity, personal and
national security, and mechanisms for resolving international disputes must
all be part of the peacemaking process. This being so, one must face the
realities of international life as they are, the existence of power hungry
states, the facts of international competition for resources and economic
advantage, the frustration of national and human aspirations, and the
bitterness of national, economic, racial, and religious differences. It is a
dangerous world, such realists argue, and the moral person must move

---

This article appeared in PACE 13 (1982–1983).

carefully toward the goal of peace, not risking war through careless or irresponsible actions. In this context they are prepared to argue that nuclear arms, while they cannot be used, can continue to be possessed and developed, provided the nation in question is sincerely committed to avoiding war and is working honestly for disarmament.

As the bishops confront these difficult matters, they face as well a number of problems within the Church—problems, in part, of their own making. Not only are Catholics divided, but the sources of divisions often have less to do with the fine points of theological analysis or political judgment than with ignorance, prejudice, and emotion. Most Catholics, in fact, have never heard the Gospel preached in a way that spoke directly to such issues. The only political sermons they have heard came on occasions like Thanksgiving, Memorial Day, or the day the Iranian hostages were released; and so common has it been to combine national self-congratulation and thanks to God that they hardly recognize that such sermons are political. In most pulpit oratory, the Beatitudes add up to little more than "being a nice person." The culture at large and our own history as Catholics generally combine to make religion a private matter, brought into public only to celebrate and affirm the nation. That the Church in fact has a long, sophisticated, and highly developed teaching on matters of politics and peace is even less well known than that Jesus had something to say about such problems.

Equally significant is the fact that Catholics are pretty much like other Americans: They are generally very uninformed about public matters, especially matters of foreign policy and international relations. Only at moments of crisis do we focus much on other countries or problems beyond our borders, partly because of our education, partly because of our media, but mostly because we are busy with our personal lives. Anyone who has met secondary school or college students from other countries will acknowledge the fact that they are almost always far more informed about us and our nation than we are about them and theirs. Our generally held view that we are a peaceful people who only become involved in wars or foreign interventions when forced to do so by the actions of others is comfortable and seemingly plausible but has almost nothing to do with reality. That others might fear us, or hate us, seems to show how unreasonable or ill intentioned they are; it hardly enters our mind that they might have reason. So, when Catholics hear their bishops speaking about our responsibility in the arms race, those words are filtered through a set of images and stereotypes that have little to do with the realities the bishops are belatedly examining. The pastoral task on these matters is thus twofold. On the one hand, the Gospel must be preached and, on the other, the world must be examined; the former could be called the evangelical task, the latter the work of Christian civics. Neither will be easy.

Preaching the Gospel means something more than repeating the words of Jesus or offering pious comments aimed at helping people be good to each other in their families and relationships. It means probing the deepest meaning of the Gospel and relating it to the realities of our lives, personal and social. It means recognizing that the imperatives of love go beyond hand holding and hugging, to our involvement with one another through politics and business, production and consumption, education, law and medicine, food, clothing, and shelter. All our lives, every aspect of them, are bound up with our world and its systems; we are already involved, like it or not. Whether the form of our involvement expresses and advances love and human dignity or represses people and builds injustice and hatred, are matters to be examined in light of Christ's life and mission and our sharing in that life through the Church. So, preaching is more than sermons and testimony; it is trying to read the Word and allow the Word to read us, making ourselves the kind of community where we can talk to each other about the meaning of the message for ourselves and one another, ask each other what we are doing with our lives and why we are doing things the way we are, challenging and supporting each other, trying to be ever more fully human and freely committed to our world and its people. Sermons, postsermon conversations, adult discussion groups, prayer, and Bible study sessions—all should be occasions for such growth and for the development of a proclamation and witness of behalf of peace.

Christian civics is even tougher. The method best known in the Catholic world is that summarized as "see, judge, act." How do we figure out what's really going on? What judgments do we make about it? What actions can we take to make things better? Seeing may be the hardest: What are the facts? Who has the power? Why are things done the way they are? What do policies mean for people? Newspapers, TV, even schools mystify as often as they clarify, ignoring some facts while emphasizing others, filtering all facts through layers of distorting images. Rarely do we see the people behind the statistics, face the consequences of public actions, especially for those who have no resources and no power. The Church must educate itself about what's happening and why, and few of us want to do that. Pacifists and nationalists have it easy: The one need only say that love is the answer, the other that the nation is the answer, the neither need be bothered much by facts. The rest of us have to try to make our values work in the real world, not the world as we would like it to be, because the victims of war and injustice live here, not there.

For religious educators, then, there are three important consequences of the current discussion. First, we must enable each other to understand the relationship between the Scriptures and everyday life, to become knowledgeable about God's Word and skilled in relating it to all our experiences, public as well as private. It is not enough any longer to simply tell people "the Church teaches . . ."; each of us must become learner and teacher, able to relate faith and our own lives, able to explore the relationship of faith to our common life. Still, few of us can do it alone; so we need to learn to talk to each other, learn from each other, be challenged and affirmed by each other, drawn beyond ourselves by the living God, alive in his Church, so that liturgy, prayer, and community remain central.

Second, we have to bring the world into the church, into our worship, prayer, and community life. Too often we move from Church affairs, conducted as if nothing outside the Church mattered, to programs featuring such global and immense problems as world hunger and nuclear war. To get from one to the other there is a neglected area—that of each person's own public life. Education, housing, medical care, transportation, taxation, in fact, most of what all of us do each day is public; yet only our sexuality, our "relationships," and our specifically "religious" lives seem to find their way into church. Economic life, for example, how we earn our living, make consumption decisions, and deal with financial problems, probably has a great deal to do with how we think and feel about ourselves, other people, the world, even God. Yet rarely do such economic experiences find their way into our lives as Christians, or the reverse. Similarly, such American symbols as success, opportunity, democracy, and due process probably shape our political attitudes more powerfully than do such Christian symbols as incarnation, crucifixion, resurrection, or the Eucharist. Yet how often have we done anything about our Americanness in church beyond ritual, lifeless self-congratulation? We have to help each other bring our daily experiences of the world into our Christian lives, and we must do so as intelligently and with as much reflection as we expend on sex, relationships, and faith itself.

Third, we have to retain, or recover, a sense of our Catholicity. Our Church, for all its historical ambiguity, has consistently refused to accept the alternatives of self-righteous, churchy isolation, or meek surrender to things as they are. Instead, it has always insisted that both the Church and the world demand our commitment: We are to be loyal and faithful Catholics *and* dedicated, responsible citizens, workers, artists, and neighbors. To know the Catholic Church, in imperial Rome, in medieval France, in today's Poland, Chile, or Nigeria is to know something special about religion and about politics. The parishioner whose self-understanding of Catholicism embraces his or her parish and the local Catholic Worker house, the nearby monastery, the local Christian women's center, the charismatic movement, perhaps the mayor, the inner-city neighborhood leader, and the crusading district attorney, already has a sense of the interaction of faith and real life. If, along the way, the parishioner expands a sense of fellowship to include Lech Walesa, Mother Teresa, Alexander Haig, Philip Berrigan, and Pope John Paul II, the conversation about Christianity and the arms race has a basis to begin.

A large agenda, to be sure. But perhaps it suggests an orientation, a direction, and a way to get started. The orientation is toward and not away from "the world," secular life; the direction is toward a Church in which serious conversation about public life is possible; the way to get started is to look around. "To look around" means that those of us who care about issues like peace had best become ourselves people of our age, informed and sophisticated about what's going on in our own communities, in city hall as well as in Washington, down the street as well as in Geneva. If we are informed, alert, and hopeful, if we believe God is alive in our history, we can be examples of what we hope all can become; if we are not, then we can forget about implementing the latest bishops' statement or starting a new justice and peace program. Politics, like charity, begins at home.

Some Concrete Suggestions for Religious Educators

1. Examine curriculum and materials to ensure that all programs promote a positive sense of responsibility for the world beyond the Church.
2. Form a committee to examine the many materials on Christian peace and justice education available from Pax Christi, The Catholic Peace Fellowship, Bread for the World, Maryknoll, Sojourners, and local and regional justice and peace centers.
3. Have a public affairs bulletin board with newspaper clippings on current events and encourage discussion about how a Christian citizen might understand and respond.
4. Reread and think about reintroducing lives of the saints, so many of whom were public persons responding to pressing problems of poverty, war, and injustice.
5. Form a representative group to explore creative ways of marking national holidays, both in the parish and in the wider community.
6. Become informed about the life of your own people, especially working and housing conditions, intergroup relations, and, especially, problems in and around the public schools.
7. Commemorate All Saints' Day as a moment to reflect on the worldwide community of the Church and our special people whose lives symbolize proper Christian presence in the world.

At the time of this writing, David O'Brien was a professor of history at Holy Cross College in Worchester, Massachusetts. He served as a consultant to the Bishops' Commission for the bicentennial Call to Action.

The Black Family: Its Faith and Spirituality

Nathan W. Jones

Once I visited an abandoned cemetery in Virginia which, I was told, had been the burial ground for the city's black folk. I can vividly remember my surprise and anger upon seeing the neglect of the cemetery by the present generation. Hungry and untamed weeds grew everywhere. Many tombstones had either fallen or toppled over. There was a pervasive feeling of abandonment. I wondered how my generation, which talked so much about reclaiming its ancestral roots, could permit this hallowed burial ground, "this black earth," to be forsaken. I could almost hear the spirits of my unknown and unsung ancestors calling out. And I wanted to reply, "Speak to me of what you've seen, of how you've lived. Tell me about your journey. Tell me the story of my blood so that I might pass it on."

My family easily could be compared to the beautiful house in which I was weaned and nurtured. Because it was lived in, this house wasn't always neat and tidy. It even had broken windows, a sagging porch, and rusting pipes. But this house was built with love, and I knew it was mine. From my family and people I have received the breath of life. They taught me to question my world and to possess a passion for truth. These lessons have remained close to me ever since.

What do we as black folk of faith believe about the experience of family? Is familyhood and the survival and stabilization of the family truly significant for us? What have been our personal experiences of family? Who or what constitutes family for me today? When the poet Nikki Giovanni lifts her voice, singing, "Black love is Black wealth," what is the human experience she draws upon? Each of us carries assumptions, hidden or revealed, about these questions. Our theology and ministries, our articulation and communication of the faith reflect these assumptions about family.

This article is aimed toward enabling us together to explore the cultural richness of the black family in the United States and the multiple shapes it takes. In addition, it explores some of the myths, problems, and contemporary issues facing today's black family within the context of Christian faith

This article appeared in PACE 14 (1983-1984).

and spirituality. The task before us is now to creatively enable persons in our various faith communities to build up, sustain, and transform the family.

A Biblical Perspective on Family

Whenever we refer to a religious perspective on the black experience, it is vital that we identify God's word as operative and intimately bound up with the black story. God's story and the black story have become one. We must continuously ask ourselves: "How has God acted and moved in the pilgrimage of his African people wherever we might be?"

The biblical term for family is closely related to our English word *household*. Biblically speaking, *household* is a much broader term than what the nuclear family model implies—parents and children. When the biblical tradition speaks of household it is including everyone who lives together in one place or under one roof. Therefore, a household could include grandparents, in-laws, aunts, uncles, cousins, nieces, nephews, and even pets! Single persons, older couples, widows or widowers living alone, two lovers—each of these also comprises a household, a family.

Drawing upon the insights of our biblical tradition, as well as contemporary black sociology, a family is composed of any persons who live in relationship (usually in one household, under one roof). Using this broader definition, a family is any kind of household unity, covenant community, or familial grouping. Families will include one-parent households with children, three-generation families, couples without children, and blended families of two adults with children from past marriages who have chosen to become a third family unit. Also, families will include single persons living alone, gay persons, families with foster children, retarded or handicapped members, and aging persons.

Of all the symbols of the Church, that of the "family" or, more biblically accurate, the household, is the most attractive for a people seeking the togetherness denied by the external forces of racism. The New Testament Church as *koinonia* becomes a model of family life. The sharing, fellowship, intimacy, covenant relationships, compassion, and network of care, which are so characteristic of Gospel living, are the foundational principles of wholesome family life even for us today. No matter what shape a family takes, these qualities of life together are at the root of meaningful relationships, with a view toward personal, collective growth and the transformation of society. No longer can we rely on the Adam-and-Eve image of family as functional for the contemporary black Christian household. Rather, we must rediscover the biblical message and uncover its relevance for us, as our ancestors have taught through words and deeds.

Myths About the Black Family

Few human tragedies, not even the Jewish holocaust, equal the psychic destruction of a people as happened during the Middle Passage, the African slave-trade experience. More than two hundred and fifty million men, women, and children were killed. The trade in slaves crippled the black race, and it was meant that we should never rise again. Our very soul, the spirit of our ancestors, the meaning of our existence, and the very purpose of our lives were eaten from us like skin from an antelope caught by a lion.

Therefore, when we reflect on ministry to the black family in America, we must be prepared to encounter the strain and frustration, the racial, social, economic, political, and cultural repression that black people and black families deal with daily in our relationships with one another and our world. The destruction of a civilization lies in the ability of an alien people to disrupt the family. And it is not unreasonable to add that had not the redeeming action of God been present in our lives, enabling us to adapt and somehow overcome, any remnant of the black family would have been totally destroyed as would have a total people.

The present-day black family has inherited the legacy of our earliest days on these shores. One only needs to look at the number of black men in prisons, the number of fatherless black children and husbandless black women, the unemployed black men, to see that our family structure is at best precarious. In 1979 alone, 62 percent of the black babies born in Chicago were of unmarried black women. In 1978, half of all black children born in the United States were of single black women. We are up against a new phenomenon with untold implications for ministry.

Two tendencies have surrounded scholarship on the black family. These are: (1) that the cultural retention of the African world-view was radically destroyed by the slave trade and/or years of bondage, and (2) that the horrors of the American experience have ultimately determined the nature of the development of black families. In other words, scholarship has looked at the black family only in comparison to the American standard, the conceptual family, the white family. The black family was conceived as only a "dark-skinned white family," an illegitimate white family. What resulted is the depiction of the black family as disorganized, pathological, and almost nonexistent. Most of the research to which you may be exposed points out the following themes: (1) Black families do not match the standard, conceptual white family model; (2) The original cultural and philosophical heritage of African people was destroyed; and (3) Black families are "made in America."

Current research by black psychologists and sociologists (such as Robert Staples, Andrew Billingsley, and Wade Nobles) rejects these assumptions and conclusions. To the contrary, it has been recognized that if black people are to be truly free, we must begin to conceive of ourselves based upon *our own frame of reference, our own positives* rather than being defined and reacting to someone else's negatives. Therefore, the black family can only be fully understood when it is conceived of as a unit or system deriving its primary characteristics, forms, and definition from its African nature. This implies not simply one vision of family, but many possibilities of how the family unit might take shape, as well as a cultural continuity with African roots.

Strengths of the Black Family and Implications for Ministry

Despite the many deathlike forces that have worked against the family, there stand forth many significant strengths which we must build on, as well as judge and transform. I will identify four of these strengths.

Love

The first strength is *black love.* It was love which enabled us to "look out for one another" and to take seriously the saying "Blood is thicker than water." Most black people can recall the special warmth that characterized their households, and most of us can say that our success and survival in life has depended in large measure on our family roots of love. Truly our greatest natural resource has been one another.

The most important area of family ministry in the black church is the development and enhancement of self-worth, identity, purpose, and direction for life. This feeling about ourselves, and those like us, is the foundation block for the individual, family, and larger society.

As black Catholics we must ask ourselves some critical questions. For instance: Can I identify four key black lay leaders in my Church? What are the criteria I use to determine these leaders? What qualities do I look for in leaders in my Church? How am I facilitating the leadership development of the people in the life of the Church? Where in my Church is significant black male and female leadership evident in decision-making roles? How is this leadership recognized in the community and honored? Are the black leaders in my Church accountable to black people or only to the white ministers? Is there a conscious effort on my part to identify and support emerging new leaders while opening new paths for old leaders? Do the black male and female leaders see their roles as complementary or as competitive?

Capacity to Extend

A second strength of the black family is its *capacity to extend itself,* to include and affirm rather than exclude and deny. The extended family is that human involvement of families with families, where no child is without a mother or a father, and no grandparent is without a son or daughter, where all is shared and we take care of each other. The extended family solves many problems. It is secure. When one eats, all eat. If one has a house to live in, all have a house to live in. Most of the needs of the members of the family are met by the family, such as care of the aged and seeing that all children have a parent. Single parenting is acceptable nowadays. White researchers once spoke of "illegitimacy" and "fatherless children." But how quickly the rules of the game change, especially when somebody else writes the rules!

Our catechetical ministries must begin to consider a model of catechesis based on households, the extended family, and all generations. This model could be termed "community-as-educator" and is based on the fact that everyone in one's household or within one's circle of significant others has a primary role in one's growth in faith. When we speak of family ministry in the black community we must refer to *all* those relationships in the lives of persons which are significant and formative: home, community institutions, the streets, the Church.

Adaptability

A third strength of the black family is its *adaptability,* its versatility, especially in regards to family roles. My mamma could play a leading role in our family and still be a woman. This kind of adaptability must affect every aspect of our Church life, its worship styles, leadership, exercise of authority, and service.

Spirituality

A fourth strength is the *spirituality* of the black family. How many times have our parents' prayers traveled with us along life's way? Family was the place where traditionally the values that lie at the heart of African-Americans were learned and practiced. Vatican II referred to the household as the "domestic church." I believe that basic communities of adults, young people, and children—celebrating, learning, and serving—are at the core of the life of the Church. Small, visible units within which the Gospel can be proclaimed and practiced are central to the Church. Black households must relearn the value of family prayer. We must consecrate family Bibles, bless homes with incense and water made fragrant with spices, meet in homes for prayer led by the head of each household.

As catechists and family ministers, we must provide opportunities in the life of our churches to celebrate a child's naming, engagements, and healings; to offer support in times of family crisis (whether marital or economic); to recognize and support young people as they move from adolescence to provisional adulthood; to welcome those moving into a new parish; to honor graduates, retirees, and the elders of our churches. We must teach persons to value conversation and family mealtimes rather than the bombardment by the commercial media in our homes. We must seek to

175

enable families to search out new "sacraments" that emerge out of their life-experiences together, and we must not be afraid to canonize these sacred moments.

The Association of Black Psychologists recently concluded in a study of black mental health in the urban community that most black people will go to their local churches and clergy persons for guidance, direction, and counsel more readily than they will go to their neighborhood mental health facilities. It is reasoned that the Church environment has traditionally been a place where Blacks have felt at home, nonthreatened. The black church has been a place of nurturance in times of crisis. Therefore, I can think of no better place to begin our ministries toward black family enrichment than in our churches themselves.

I believe in hope. Black people have survived the slave trade, the buffalo, and racism. As dim as the sun's rays are, the will remains to conquer this oppressive and impersonal world. Sound, life-giving, loving relationships rooted in a confession of faith in Christ Jesus are the foundation upon which rests the ultimate liberation of the race.

At the time of this writing, Dr. Nathan W. Jones was consultant on Black Church Education and Pastoral Ministry as well as consulting editor for Ethnic Communications Outlet, 5342 South University Avenue, Chicago, IL 60615.

On Spirituality and Religious Education

Francine Cardman

L ately, spirituality has become a trendy term. It is used to designate a
broad range of concerns about human living. Further, it is used by
almost everybody, religious or not, in almost any context, to convey a value-
laden message about the importance of these concerns and the laudability of
their pursuit.

When the word *spirituality* is used by Christians, its content and
context are almost as far-reaching as in more general parlance. Sometimes it
is meant to refer to exclusively "spiritual" things—prayer, especially, or
experiences like speaking in tongues or various sorts of liturgical highs.
Sometimes it is intended to convey a sense of the depth and significance of
"earthly" or even "earthy" things—trees, sunsets, sex, to name a few.
Occasionally, it is applied to the efforts of peacemaking or to the work of
social justice. In all these usages, Christian and other, it can connote the
superiority of those who are seekers of this elusive entity, "spirituality."

Is there an understanding of the word *spirituality* and the experiences it
symbolizes that can help religious educators, and other Christians as well,
thread their way through this labyrinth of possibilities, avoiding both the
dead end of judgmentalism and the comfortable cul-de-sac of parochialism? I
think there is, and in this article I would like to try to sketch out one such
understanding and some of its implications for religious education on behalf
of spirituality.

Spirituality As Our Stance Toward Life

As I have thought about the subject of spirituality and mused on the
phenomenon of its recent and rapidly growing popularity—even joining the
movement by teaching courses in the history of spirituality—I have come to
rely on a working definition of the term that is rather broad in the sweep of
its gaze but nevertheless looks at what it beholds through particular lenses.
The definition goes something like this: Spirituality is our way of being in
the world, as bodied selves, with others, in response to God's word and call.

This article appeared in PACE 14 (1983–1984).

Or, more aphoristically, spirituality is the shape of Christian life in the matrix of the world. To say this is to affirm that Christian spirituality is as much about politics as about prayer, about body as about spirit, about world as about Church.

Developed in Response to the Christian Story

Just like Moliere's *bourgeois gentilhomme,* who was surprised to learn he'd been speaking prose all his life, many people might well be surprised to learn that they have been living a spirituality. That is, they—we all—take a basic stance toward life, an attitude toward ourselves and the world, that is reflected in all our being and doing. When that stance has been developed, at least in part, in response to the Christian story, it is fair to identify it as a form of Christian spirituality. The gaze or scope of Christian spirituality, then, extends to all of life, while the lens through which it is focused and thereby takes form is the particular optic of the Christian story.

By Nurturing the Spirit of Limitless Love

To think and speak of spirituality in this way is not yet to raise the question of reflexive awareness or critical intentionality. Rather, it simply suggests something of the dimensions and possible significance of the term. Understanding Christian spirituality in this way also leads to the insistence that all Christians, by virtue of their Baptism, already *have* a spirituality. The Spirit of God dwells within us, bearing witness with our spirit that we are children of God and co-heirs with Christ (cf. Rom. 8:9–17). There is no need—and really no possibility—of "finding" or "earning" some other or additional spirituality. There is only the possibility of nurturing the Spirit already within us, of plumbing the depths and extending the breadth of the love that reaches out to love.

The Role of Religious Education

Spirituality and religious education intersect at this point—helping persons create an ever-more hospitable dwelling place for the Spirit so that less and less of the world is strange to us as we befriend those who were once "strangers." For this process of welcome and embrace to be a process of religious education, I would suggest (following the lead of many others) that it must be both conscious and critical. That is, it must foster both reflective awareness and critical intentionality. Without trying to be exhaustive or presuming to detail how these suggestions might be translated into practice, I propose to look at some of the things involved in assisting people to cultivate awareness and intentionality in their spirituality.

Cultivating Awareness, Especially of Relationships

Awareness involves reflective consciousness, the exercise of the understanding of experience, both personal and communal, both immediate and historical. It means becoming aware of one's own story, articulating that story, and then relating it to the stories of others, as well as to the Christian story. Awareness of this sort involves recognizing the persons, choices, and other factors that have shaped our lives, and acknowledging our connection to the lives of others, past and present, and even those to come. Because spirituality is profoundly relational, education on behalf of spirituality needs especially to cultivate the awareness of relationality. A crucial element of religious education as it touches on spirituality, therefore, has to do with enabling persons to come to greater consciousness about their relationship to self, to others, and to God. Telling stories, both great myths and small, and recounting journeys are some ways of encouraging this sense of relatedness; so, too, are practices such as scriptural sharing, small group prayer, and group spiritual direction.

Appreciating the Christian Past

Another aspect of religious education on behalf of spirituality is coming to know the stories of distant others, entering into their experience, and thereby extending the reach of one's own experience across time and space. I am thinking here particularly about learning something of the history of spirituality. Reading the "classics," studying the lives of saints and teachers, and becoming acquainted with the styles and schools of Christian living across the centuries help prevent the dwelling places we are fashioning from becoming too narrow and unwelcoming. An appreciation of the Christian past allows us to choose solid foundations on which to build, rather than having to start from scratch on unsure ground. This is not to say that everything in the tradition is of equal value, but it does recognize that there is much of real value. Similarly, theology can help nurture the process of welcome and embrace when it is done contextually, drawing on people's experience, evoking the longings of the heart, and weaving them together with the memories and hopes of the Christian community. Liturgy, too, is a place of this sort of religious education, where word, gesture, and symbol make manifest the presence of the Spirit of God within and among us.

Growing in awareness of our spirituality is not well served, it seems to me, by encouraging the development of many particularist spiritualities—the spirituality of singleness, for instance, or of marriage and family life, or even of directors of religious education. Rather, persons are freed to develop in the many different directions in which the Spirit leads and yet remain connected to other sojourners when they recognize that the various accents or keys of Christian spirituality, its many shapes and forms, are all essentially rooted in the same mystery. The mystery is God's love for us in creation,

God's continual care for us in Jesus Christ, and God's nurture of us by the life-giving breath of the Spirit. The mystery is paschal: Its direction is from death to life; its movement is toward all life.

Discovering the Dimensions of the Human and Christian Community

Awareness thus reaches toward intentionality. Intentionality involves not only the practice of attending to that of which one has become aware, but also the development of a critical dimension to one's awareness and action. By attending to the process of welcome and embrace, we gradually come to see who or what is not drawn into it, and to ask why. The critical consciousness that emerges from such attention soon comes to focus on the neglected or excluded side of the apparent dichotomies I mentioned earlier—prayer/politics, body/spirit, Church/world—and seeks deliberately to include and account for these and other absent aspects of human and Christian experience. By doing so, we develop an ear for the hitherto missing voices and the lost chapters of the story.

Religious educators have a particular responsibility in this regard to help persons discover the true dimensions of the human and Christian community. Attending to the feminist critique of the Christian tradition's failure to take seriously the experience of women is one instance of this responsibility. Unless women's experience is consciously and critically included and valued, it will become increasingly difficult for women to locate their stories, their lives, their spirituality within the compass of Christian spirituality. So, too, with the poor and disenfranchised. Awareness and intentionality need to extend to the social structures and processes by which their voices and stories have been and continue to be excluded or forgotten, their experience valued at nothing. In this context of expanding awareness and deepening intentionality, solidarity with people of distant places and very different cultures can be fostered as our spirits open to and bond with sisters and brothers around the globe.

This is perhaps the most important step in the process of religious education on behalf of spirituality—the step from the personal to the social. Once taken, social transformation becomes as much the hope of Christians as is the desire for personal transformation. A friend of mine puts it well: Our "living with" God enables us to "live for" all women and men. From there it is possible for the vistas of cosmic redemption to open out before us as they once did for Paul: "Creation itself will be set free from its bondage to decay and obtain the glorious liberty of the children of God" (Rom. 8:21).

Throughout the venture of religious education on behalf of spirituality, religious educators need to remember that they, too, need nurture and education in awareness and intentionality. More often than not, such befriending can come from the women and men with and for whom they work, if the venture is undertaken in the mutuality of partnership. For it is only out of the groaning of their own spirits that religious educators can bear witness to the groanings of others, so that together they may bring to birth the new creation that is already growing among us.

A Word About Resources

The suggestions below may not seem immediately relevant to either spirituality or religious education. They are neither "devotional" nor "practical." But they do contribute to developing the kind of approach to spirituality that I have tried to sketch out above.

Callahan, William R. *Noisy Contemplation.* Hyattsville, MD: Quixote Center, 1983.

Conn, Joann Wolski. "Women's Spirituality: Restriction and Reconstruction." *Cross Currents* (Fall 1980): 293–308.

Fox, Matthew. "Hermeneutic and Hagiography." *Spirituality Today* 30, no. 3 (1978): 263–269.

Harris, Maria. "Prayer and Vision." *PACE* 10 (1979–1980): Directions—A.

Leckey, Dolores. *The Ordinary Way: A Family Spirituality.* New York: Crossroad, 1982.

Meehan, Francis X. *A Contemporary Social Spirituality.* Maryknoll, NY: Orbis Books, 1982.

Russell, Letty M. *Growth in Partnership.* Philadelphia: Westminster Press, 1981.

Williams, Rowan. *Christian Spirituality: A Theological History from the New Testament to Luther and St. John of the Cross.* Atlanta: John Knox Press, 1979. (Note: British edition is titled *The Wound of Knowledge.*)

At the time of this writing, Dr. Francine Cardman was associate professor of historical theology at Weston School of Theology in Cambridge, Massachusetts.

Political Saints: Dorothy Day

David O'Brien

A t least one U.S. Catholic layperson enjoys a status equivalent to
sainthood today. When Dorothy Day died in December, 1980, she was
just as radical as, and perhaps even more cantankerous than, she had always
been, but somehow her public reputation had changed—again. In her early
years as a prominent Catholic, following the founding of the Catholic
Workers movement in 1933, Miss Day was widely regarded as a truly great
U.S. Catholic. Subscriptions to the monthly newspaper, *Catholic Worker,*
rose to over one hundred thousand; houses of hospitality sprang up around
the country; and clergy fell over themselves showing their appreciation for
the work of providing food, clothing, and shelter to the depression poor.

All that changed at the end of the decade. Day and the *Catholic Worker*
opposed the dominant ecclesiastical support of Franco during the Spanish
Civil War; they challenged the anti-Semitism of Fr. Charles E. Coughlin, the
radio priest of Royal Oak, Michigan; and they backed strikes by some
militant unions. Worst of all, the Catholic Worker movement persisted in its
seemingly eccentric pacifism even after Pearl Harbor. Opposition to war and
the military draft was one thing when U.S. Catholics were isolationists
opposed to involvement in World War II; it was quite another thing when
the United States joined the war and "our boys" were putting their lives on
the line. From 1942 until the 1970s, the once saintly Miss Day was widely
regarded as a crank at best, a communist at worst.

Still, if you live long enough in the United States, radicalism becomes
familiar enough to seem harmless. In the 1970s, Miss Day was still defending
pacifism, opposing war and weapons, and refusing to pay taxes or to accept
tainted money; she was even jailed for support of Cesar Chavez and his farm
workers. But by the 1970s, the Church itself had changed; it now expressed
at least a theoretical support for the poor and a general "concern" about
peace. So this aged woman, with her frequent references to Christ and her
obvious love for the Church, once again seemed one of us. Elevating her to
sainthood, as she well knew, was a convenient way to marginalize her

This article appeared in PACE 14 (1983–1984).

challenge while avoiding the embarrassment of community with her; she was one of those persons specially called by God to an extraordinary life; fortunately, the rest of us are called elsewhere.

At first glance, Dorothy Day does not fit our model of worldly Catholicism. As a young woman she was, to be honest, very wild; she lived among Bohemians, was jailed with the suffragists, and had associated with radicals and anarchists. Her one short-lived, common-law marriage failed, and she raised her daughter with the help of her sister and friends. Her conversion to Catholicism was an experience of grace difficult to understand. It separated her from her lover and many of her friends, and brought her into a Church that had little of her passionate commitment to justice.

In 1932, she met Peter Maurin, who instructed her in Church history, Catholic social teaching, and the possibility of a "green revolution," which would restore the harmony, solidarity, and community of the pre-industrial world. When they launched the Catholic Worker movement in 1933, they wanted to provide the workers with an alternative to communism in a movement that preached and practiced personalism.

In roundtable discussions, workers and scholars would explore a third way, one that would repudiate the materialism of both capitalism and communism in favor of a spiritual renewal centered on the value of the human person. In houses of hospitality, Catholics would practice voluntary poverty and devote their goods and their lives to the service of the poor, while in farming communes they would begin to construct the "new society in the shell of the old." On the farms, all would share in work on the land and in handicraft production. And, in the process, they would rediscover their relationship with God and one another, and would express it in liturgy and in the fruits of their common labor. Meanwhile, the *Catholic Worker,* which sold at a penny a copy, would broadcast the good news that life could be different, that the Church had a social message that answered the questions of the day and that pointed toward a more human, more spiritual, way of life.

In their call for voluntary poverty, for hospitality, for the practice of the spiritual and corporal works of mercy, and, later, in their insistence on nonviolence, the Catholic Workers were summoning U.S. Catholics away from their habitual preoccupation with "making it." The Catholic Worker movement held forth as an alternative not just the almost monastic asceticism of the house of hospitality but also the apparently reactionary model of peasant agriculture and handicraft production. The Catholic Workers sharply attacked conventional reliance upon the state as the agency for achieving social justice; it was too easy to pass off personal responsibility for one another to the impersonal hands of "Holy Mother the State."

While some Catholic Workers actively supported unions and strikes, Maurin and, in the final analysis, Miss Day, regarded unions as temporary means of self-defense. In the long run, it was better to reject the wage system altogether, for one should not sell one's labor. Rather, work should be regarded as the means whereby each contributes to the common good. Similarly, technology too often separated people from the products of their labor and, therefore, ultimately from their ability to live in the world. Isolated, alienated, and alone, people became prey to mass movements, to irrational symbols, and to demagogues. Middle-class U.S. workers and farmers might well hear such a message as a call to repudiate the world they and their parents had made and to seek an otherworldly utopia, on the land or in the slums.

Maurin was a thinker of great power who drew upon our pre-industrial heritage to level a scathing indictment of industrial society, one whose echoes are heard in the now quite faddish writings of E.F. Shumacher. Maurin's constructive position was flawed by the limitations of his experience, but it is all too easy for us to think that our modern technological society has presented an alternative that is better and more humane than Maurin's pre-industrial model. No influential school of thought has yet come to terms with Maurin's basic argument that industrial society is ultimately dehumanizing and destructive; one need only think of nuclear power in all its forms and of the terrifying scenarios of environmental disaster to appreciate the problem with which Maurin wrestled. He believed that directing technology toward human ends required the widest possible participation, the most modest human goals and aspirations, and the subordination of the material to the spiritual, a subordination requiring a rediscovery of the supernatural dimensions of human experience. To believe that this could be accomplished by a worldly Christianity comfortably at home in the bourgeois world was wishful thinking; against that delusion, Dorothy Day directed all her powers as a writer of grace and power and as a person of unmatched courage.

Similarly, the *Catholic Worker's* suspicion of state provision for the poor reflected insights more evident today than a half century ago. How long have U.S. citizens believed that poverty could be eliminated by simply expanding the quantity of goods and services through economic growth, taking care of the weak and handicapped by sharing with them the surplus produced by such expansion? How long have the costs of that growth been ignored? How long have we lived with the assumption that we could make more and more things and never ask for whom and for what they were intended? In an age of economic dislocation like our own, when we paper over the collapse of treasured assumptions with huge government and corporate debts, we might begin to understand better the message Miss Day preached: If we wish to have justice, we will have to be just; and if we wish to be just, we will have to practice charity, at a personal sacrifice, and we will only do that if we learn to love one another. Love is the answer, that is what

Christ preached. The message of love led Jesus to the cross; taking it seriously will require sacrifice and suffering. There is no easy way out.

But the *Catholic Worker's* message was never negative, and Dorothy Day was as far as one can be from what we today call "alienation." She loved the world and the people in it, not an abstract world of the imagination but the concrete world that she saw each day, not the people of a class or party but the real human beings—good and bad—that she met in the streets and the houses, on buses and college campuses. These people she loved with a passion that makes her simple words and sentences almost burn on the pages of her newspaper. Love in action is harsh and dreadful; this she knew. But love in action is also affirming, hopeful, and alive to human possibility; this she also knew.

In 1954, Dorothy Day reflected on the Catholic Worker's record, concluding that the movement had generally failed to implement Peter Maurin's program. The farming communes had failed; the work of hospitality was still carried on alone; the poor were more numerous than ever; and people had not developed a real philosophy of work. Indeed, Dorothy wrote, "Our failure is so continuous that we never think of it; we just go on working without judging ourselves, as Saint Paul tells us to do." She was still extremely happy that God had entrusted her with a particular mission and work, but she was concerned that somehow they had failed to communicate the importance of a positive attitude toward work. Perhaps nothing had been more misunderstood about Miss Day and the *Catholic Worker* than this: Peter Maurin's message had been positive, not negative, more prohuman than anti-industrial, more prowork than anticapitalist. The worst aspect of industrial society was not that it financially exploited the worker but that it deprived the worker of the satisfaction of completing a task and product and of seeing the results of his or her labor in goods and services that met the needs of other people and of society.

In that 1954 article, Dorothy complained of receiving "too many letters of pessimistic gloom from back-to-the-landers," which she contrasted with a letter received by Ammon Hennacy from a quite successful Kansas farmer whose simple language expressed joy in that hard, difficult labor of raising crops. If one's work led to pessimism, gloom, and alienation, Dorothy suggested, one should find other work. The Catholic Worker ideologue who was miserable on the land simply "wasn't cut out to be a farmer. He should find a trade, run a store, teach in a school, go in for village life. . . . Causade says that we know our vocation by our delight in it." Surely nothing is more important than this for laypersons to understand: We must enter the secular tasks of life with joy and delight, knowing that we are called to those tasks and that they are ways of sharing our gifts with others and, as Dorothy put it, of "making an honest living." Most of all, we must have a positive, hopeful philosophy of work.

If Dorothy was a saint, she was a secular saint. True, she was extremely conservative on sexual matters after her youthful escapades. But she was a woman of the city who delighted in the stubborn heroism of neighborhood families. She saw God in homemade clothes and in a well-prepared meal, in small flower gardens and in the urban cityscape. Her spirituality at times was almost Jansenistic, but always her love of the material world and the people who lived in it broke through. Where others grew depressed at the crowding and dirt, the gaudy consumerist display, and the inhuman mechanical power of the city and the factory, Dorothy always noted the human skills and ingenuity behind it all, which, if shaped by a positive philosophy or work, could make a better world, a new society within the shell of the old. She knew in her heart what so many of us always have to relearn: This world, with all its evil revealed in the events of the twentieth century, is after all our world, in which we have been called and in which God is always present. It is a world that we have made, and in its making, we have revealed both our sinfulness and our almost incredible potential. Every one of us, if we choose, can turn around and begin directing our gifts and talents toward human ends. To know the cross is to know the reality of sin, the presence of suffering, and the harsh and dreadful demands of love. To know the resurrection is to know that through the power of love—shining forth in our attitude toward God, the world, and one another—we can enter the work of creation and salvation and make the world fit for human habitation.

We are not to retreat from the world because it is too corrupt, nor are we to simply sit and wait in our home-made monastery for the return of the risen Lord. No, we are to enter life fully and without reservation. To the radical, otherworldly sectarian who would say, "Forget your desire for work and family and human love because they will cost you your integrity," Dorothy had a clear response: "Practically speaking," she wrote, "should none get married, none have children, until we prepare, plan, save, perfect ourselves to fit ourselves for our vocation? What nonsense!" No, to live now as best we can, with all our failures, with the confidence that we are about what God intends for us, is in itself the work of divine redemption. What Dorothy Day said of the Catholic Worker is true of all those secular saints trying to live as God intends in the very heart of normal, ordinary human life.

In twenty years we seem to have accomplished little. The same long breadlines continue at our houses. Throughout the land many a Catholic Worker family struggles and seems to get nowhere. But, meanwhile, the children are born and are fed and are launched into life with a more vital sense, let us pray, of God and their place in the Body of Christ.

Many of us hear that message in church, and leave it there; the witness of Dorothy Day is one that calls us to bring that good news into the heart of our everyday life. Only in that way, as Peter Maurin would say, will we ever explode the "dynamite of the Gospel" and lead a depressed and defeated humanity to say of us not "see how they pass the buck" but "see how they love one another."

Further Reading

Catholic Worker. 36 East First Street, New York, NY 10003. Subscription, twenty-five cents per year. Monthly.

Day, Dorothy. *Loaves and Fishes.* New York: Harper & Row, 1963.

_____. *The Long Loneliness: The Autobiography of Dorothy Day.* New York: Harper & Row, 1952.

Miller, William D. *Dorothy Day: A Biography.* San Francisco: Harper & Row, 1982.

At the time of this writing, David O'Brien was a professor of history at Holy Cross College in Worcester, Massachusetts.

Persistence and Peace

Gordon C. Zahn

One of the mixed blessings of longevity is the tendency of newer generations to turn to their elders for advice and counsel. It is gratifying to have experience acknowledged, of course, but the answers are not always easy and are sometimes impossible to provide. I am often asked, for instance, how I managed to avoid the bitter disillusionment that causes so many to leave the peace movement in despair of ever accomplishing anything. In this case the answer is easy: I haven't. In the forty years and more that I have been engaged in what many see as a futile pursuit of an unattainable goal, disillusionment has been an all-too-familiar state of mind. This leads, then, to a much more difficult question. How does one deal with disillusionment, or—more personally—what formula worked for me so that I never reached the point of "calling it quits"? This is an extremely important question at a time when the world is rushing headlong toward extinction and no one seems ready to consider, much less accept, the pacifist's alternative to war.

In my own case the answer has been a matter of perspective coupled with what some might regard as a "personality flaw." The perspective might be dismissed as a product of that longevity except for the fact that it is not much different today from what it was twenty or thirty years ago. It is optimistic as far as the Church is concerned, and the optimism is confirmed by comparing what the Catholic posture on war and peace is now with what it was when I served as a conscientious objector to World War II. Few would deny that a dramatic, perhaps revolutionary, shift of emphasis has taken place. A commitment to pacifism and nonviolence—something viewed as near heresy then—is now officially acknowledged as a legitimate, even praiseworthy, option for the Catholic. Although unusual today, a young man still might encounter priests here and there who advise that "no Catholic can be a conscientious objector"—but he would have no trouble finding a bishop willing to correct such misguided counsel. In my day, though, that counsel would have been accepted by most as "the mind of the Church."

This article appeared in PACE 15 (1984–1985).

(And, of course, far fewer would have thought of raising the issue of conscientious objection in the first place.)

In the above context, the personality flaw I mentioned earlier proved helpful—probably indispensable. That is, to be a pacifist in such a setting may have required the prophetic vision one is sometimes credited with today, but what really kept me going was a certain "perversity of spirit" that drew satisfaction from the obvious displeasure (and often worse) to be encountered from others. This was not, I hasten to add, a pious anticipation of spiritual rewards for suffering indignities in Jesus' name. Instead the pleasure came in knowing that notice had been taken and a reaction, no matter how uncomplimentary, provoked. The hopes of winning converts to the cause of pacifism were so slim that even a negative reaction was viewed as a gain. I am not sure such a stance or attitude can (or should) be cultivated, but when things look hopeless it can provide a psychological cushion against the "slings and arrows" that might otherwise seem too great a burden to bear.

Today's Catholic pacifists have less need for such perverse reinforcement. Pacifism may not be "mainstream" yet, as some make bold to claim, but there are encouraging signs that it represents "the wave of the future." Much as pacifists of my generation would love to claim credit for the change, full credit must be given instead to the changing nature of modern war itself, along with its weapons and strategies of annihilation. These have dramatized the inadequacy and irrelevance of traditional "just-war" teachings, forcing bishops and popes alike to seek that "entirely new attitude" toward war called for by Vatican II. Unfortunately, although lessons have been learned, attempts to make corrective applications fall short. John Paul II may tell the world that "the scale and the horror of modern warfare—whether nuclear or not—makes it totally unacceptable as a means of settling differences between nations," but the words fall on deaf ears. The arms race goes on, with little or no real hope of reversing the slide to the war that is forbidden.

It is no wonder, then, that today's generation of Catholic pacifists operate from a different, a more pessimistic, perspective. Instead of taking comfort in marking how far the Church has come, they see how far there is yet to go and how slow the progress is. For them Thomas Merton's urgent warning sets the agenda: "Every individual Christian has a grave responsibility to protest clearly and forcibly against trends that lead inevitably to crimes which the Church deplores and condemns. Ambiguity, hesitation, and compromise are no longer permissible. . . . We have still time to do something about it, but the time is rapidly running out." To make matters worse, the fact that much more time has already "run out" since Merton's warning was given adds a further note of desperation to the situation.

In a very real sense, disillusionment is a thoroughly rational, perhaps the only rational, response. Public opinion polls and massive demonstrations have little or no impact upon the foreign and military policies of unresponsive government leaders obsessed with delusions of a "national security" based on the threat of world annihilation. Even the brief flash of hope provided by the U.S. Catholic bishops' pastoral on war and peace—*The Challenge of Peace: God's Promise and Our Response*—has faded as the bishops demonstrate their reluctance to follow through with the moral leadership it promised to provide. One waits in vain for the nationwide educational program that was to make Catholic parishes and schools vital centers of activity for peace. What purpose was served by carefully spelling out those conditions of a "just war" if their flagrant violation—in the invasion of Grenada, the mining of Nicaraguan harbors, the continued support for the murderers and torturers in "friendly" authoritarian regimes—is passed over in silence?

Disillusionment as such, then, is not the problem. How one deals with it can be. Too many suffer burnout or quietly give up. The temptation to stop banging one's head against a stone wall and instead concentrate time and effort upon career, family, and other personal concerns is not easily overcome. After all, much as we may prefer not to admit it, there can be something pathetic about the diehard who refuses to come to terms with reality; who, again if the truth be known, often becomes an insufferable bore with an unending cycle of meetings and rallies to attend and an inexhaustible supply of leaflets to be read and petitions to be signed. As disillusionment turns to hopelessness, a prudent surrender begins to make sense. The tragedy in this response, of course, is that each additional defection from the ranks is really a double blow. Not only does it weaken the total effort by that much, but it undermines the morale and threatens the lasting power of those who remain.

The opposite response—in some respects no less a danger—is progressive escalation of protest activity until confrontational civil disobedience becomes the approved norm. This is not to criticize those who, after careful and mature deliberation, choose direct nonviolent resistance, even imprisonment, as a witness to their faith. Too often, however, the choice seems to be the product of frustration, an almost desperate reaction to accumulated disappointment. It is true that experience demonstrates the futility of most of the "normal" channels of protest—letters, vigils, demonstrations, and so on—especially when directed against a government determined to ignore them.

It is also true that (for a time at least) imaginative actions of civil disobedience along with a mounting number of arrests will draw the attention of the media and may even receive a generous hearing in the courts before the almost inevitable sentence is handed down. In the final analysis, though, they too have a limited and diminishing impact upon public opinion and apparently none at all upon the Reagan administration and its policies. Too often such actions develop a romanticized means of appeal for the disillusioned, and more attention is given to the actions themselves than what they are intended to express.

Even so, civil disobedience is certainly a response preferable to simply dropping out. Yet there are further negatives that should not be overlooked. Imprisonment, if that is the price to be paid, can be a heroic personal sacrifice and deserves to be honored as such. However, from the perspective of the larger movement, it removes valuable leadership from the scene at a time when it is sorely needed, and the further need for legal funds and supportive demonstrations can represent a serious drain on already limited resources. Under the circumstances, it is important to make certain that civil disobedience and the prison witness are preceded by a careful calculation of all the pluses and minuses and are not the testimony to frustration they can so easily become.

The problem still remains: How does one deal with the disillusionment that arises when all our best energies seem wasted in fruitless efforts to deliver a message few want to hear? In the face of destructive trends and policies that seem to develop an almost diabolical dynamic of their own, what means do we have to "stick to" an active commitment to peacemaking—especially when we, too, are sometimes tempted to see the cause as hopeless? The only answer I have to offer is persistence—stubborn, bullheaded, single-minded persistence.

It can be done. If we master the art of concentrating on long-run objectives and place every short-run action or possibility in that larger context, it will be possible to maximize the most minor gains and to ride out the disappointment and discouragement of even serious setbacks. Such an approach would take into consideration the effect our efforts have on the uncommitted, tempering our actions and appeals so as to avoid alienating prospective converts. The exercise of strategic restraint may require foregoing rhetorical display that, however much it may stir the pacifist heart, is all-too-often counterproductive.

This restraint does not mean we must "trim our sails" to the point of becoming ineffective, however. The extra care put into identifying our "target audiences" and addressing them in terms they understand and might accept will help us make sure the message has priority over the delivery. Some might feel this approach is overly cautious and perhaps a touch opportunistic. I would insist it is entirely in keeping with the pacifist ideal to choose reasoned persuasion over dramatic confrontation whenever possible.

It all depends, of course, on whether we can count on a "long run" with the world in its present state. For this we require an affirmation of faith, I suppose. Anyone involved in school and parish programs has a special opportunity (and responsibility!) in this respect. The leadership provided by the bishops in their pastoral on war and peace can be made fully effective only when response occurs on the local scale. If, as many fear, the pastoral is already losing its force, much of the failure lies in the halfhearted and largely ineffective efforts to promote the educational programs that were envisioned when the pastoral was adopted in Chicago in 1983.

These weak efforts, in turn, are a reality because local school and parish educators have not always committed themselves to the task set forth by the bishops—namely, "to creatively rise to the challenge of peace." An illustration might be in order here. At the 1984 convention of the National Catholic Education Association in Boston, Pax Christi sponsored a booth promoting educational materials prepared to help meet the challenge highlighted by the U.S. bishops. The level of interest in these materials, to put it mildly, fell considerably below our hopes and expectations. Nor did it help to witness the far greater notice given the neighboring booth with its assortment of novelties—particularly a child's telephone in the shape of a frog, which croaked instead of rang. Over the convention's four-day span that single item received more attention and comment than our entire display.

One cannot deny the obstacles encountered at the parish level. Overly cautious pastors, hyperpatriotic parents, even a less-than-enthusiastic bishop sometimes make it difficult to take up that "challenge of peace" and see it through. But at least the effort must be made. Again, a stubborn streak will help, and that "perversity of spirit" which measures success in the amount and intensity of the reaction (favorable or unfavorable) one provokes might help even more. On a more positive note, what will help most is the resource we *know* is always available for the asking: a deep and abiding religious commitment that, when things really get tough, provides the strengthening assurance that Someone is listening and ready to give the support and help we may need.

At the time of this writing, Gordon C. Zahn was director of the Pax Christi USA Center on Conscience and War, and professor emeritus, University of Massachusetts—Boston.

On Staying at the Table: A Spirituality of Christian Community

Parker J. Palmer

God calls us to community, to a mutually supportive, empowering, and accountable life together. We know that from the Bible, we know it from Christian tradition, and we know it from the yearnings of our own hearts. Today, the heart's call to community is amplified by the practical necessity for community in our lives. In this time of dwindling resources, we need to learn to share; in this time of increasingly dangerous human tensions, we need to learn to cooperate and celebrate.

But what, exactly, does "community" mean to us? What is it that we are called to and looking for? If we cannot answer those questions we are in trouble. If we fail to explore our ideas and images of life together, we may settle for something that falls far short of community. Or we may not recognize true community when we are in the midst of it—ignoring or even denying the gift when it comes.

So what does "community" mean? As a sociologist I could answer that question in a highly rational, objective way, listing the attributes of community in strict conformity to the best sociological theory. But I shall try to honor W.H. Auden's version of the eleventh commandment, "Thou shalt not commit a social science," for the simple reason that our everyday dealings with community have little to do with reason and objectivity. Our yearnings and our behaviors are shaped not by theories we carry in our minds but by images we carry in our hearts. If we look deeply enough within ourselves, I think we can locate and articulate the images that shape our hopes for the community we call the Church. If we find (as I think we will) that these images are romantic, unrealistic, and doomed to defeat, we can look for other images that will help us stay open to the community that God continually offers us.

I believe there are two images of community that are rooted so deeply in our psyches that they might be called archetypes. As such they have a very

This article appeared in PACE 15 (1984–1985).

powerful impact on our lives, our attitudes, our behavior. Both of them are to be found in the Bible—not surprising when one recalls that the Bible is full of archetypal material, so profoundly does it reach into human experience.

The first image of community is found in Genesis. This is the image of "the garden." Here community is portrayed as a harmonious, organic unity of all things. That is the way God created us before sin intervened—humans, beasts, vegetable and mineral life existing in oneness, in unity, in an ecology of grace. And there are words in Genesis that describe the human experience in this communal garden: "They were naked and unashamed." The image of the garden and the possibility of living naked and unashamed—these resonate deep in the human soul and draw us toward the dream of community.

Somewhere in each of us, as we come into community (whether that community be friendship or marriage or the Church), there is the hope that we will find a harmony that is not available in the larger world. And somewhere in each of us there is the hope that in community we can, at last, be naked—open and vulnerable about all the pains and failings of our lives—without ever having the feel shame about who and how we are. This image from Genesis, I suggest, is one that exerts a powerful influence on our expectations of what community is and can be. At least, that is true in my own experience and the experience of many people I know.

The second archetypal image of community is found in Revelations. This is the image of "the new Jerusalem," the city of God purified of all sin and sadness, made clean and holy by the action of grace. Here, too, the text offers key words to describe the personal meaning of this image for us: "And every tear shall be wiped away." The image of a holy city and the hope that our sorrows will meet with solace—these, too, resonate deep in the human soul and draw us toward the dream of community.

Or so it has been with me and with many people I know. We came into community hoping to find a safer and more sacred city than the ones we had known. We came into community hoping that our sadness and struggle might be lifted, that the kingdom of God might arrive. This image of the new Jerusalem, like the image of the garden, has a profound, if unconscious, impact on our hopes for community and our experience once we get there.

Of course, our experience of community is nothing like the garden or the new Jerusalem. Not, at least, after the first few weeks! For many people there is an initial experience of euphoria with the new marriage or the new friends or the new church. But soon "the honeymoon is over." Euphoria fades and dies, and we realize that all is not harmonious here; that it is not entirely safe to be naked with each other; that the kingdom has not arrived; that even if old tears are being wiped away new ones are being wept.

As the euphoria dies, as our images of community crumble, several options open up to us. For some people the option is simply to abandon their hopes for community altogether and to return to whatever form of isolation and individualism they lived in before. But they go back to that condition with an added burden of disillusionment and cynicism; the community that once existed for them as a hope and a dream no longer exists at all. For other people the option is to stay in community—sort of—but to withdraw their hopes and enthusiasms and energies, to help create the kind of church that the Bible calls "lukewarm." This is the condition of many of our churches, I think. People have dealt with their disillusionment by "sort of" staying in community with each other, but not at any depth of involvement or risk.

Then there is a third option we might take following the death of euphoria, the crumbling of our communal images. That is to keep on keeping on; to press deeper into the experience of disillusionment to see what it has to teach; to abandon our romantic images of community and look for new images that have the power to explain what is happening and to help us deal with it.

As I have attempted to take this third option, I have realized something crucial about the images of the garden and the new Jerusalem. Both of them are images from *outside* of history. The image of the garden comes before history begins. The image of the new Jerusalem comes after history ends. This does not mean that they are irrelevant to me (as I hope to show later). But since I live *in* history, it means that I must find an image of community that comes from the context in which I live.

Once again, the Bible provides an image. For between the garden and the new Jerusalem there is the story of God's action in history, of God's entry into history in the person of Jesus Christ, and of Christ gathering people into community—a story that reaches one of its high points in the experience of the Last Supper. So let us look to the Last Supper as an image of community in history. Let us see what that image has to teach us about the true nature of community. Let us see what we can learn from the Last Supper about how to keep on keeping on.

I said that the story of Christ gathering his people into community reaches one of its high points in the Last Supper; perhaps I should have said "low points." Here is Jesus who has been pouring out his life for the people around the table. Now he has gathered them in the universal symbol of friendship, family, hospitality—breaking bread together and passing the cup. And what do these people do? First, in response to Jesus' claim that one of them will betray him, they deny that any such thing is possible: "Not us, Lord, not here, not in this spiritual community." Having taken care of that little matter they quickly move along to an argument about who is the greatest among them! Blind to their own capacity for betrayal and obsessed with power struggles, the disciples around the table act out two of the issues that make community life so painfully difficult, so unlike the garden or

195

the new Jerusalem. As someone has suggested, they probably went on the quibble over who would pay the bill!

And what does Jesus do in the midst of all of this? Being fully human, he must have been tempted to get up and leave—just as you and I are when our romantic images of community fail. But Jesus does not leave. Instead, he keeps breaking the bread and passing the cup. Both here and in the rest of his story Jesus has the faith and the patience to stay at the table.

If we are to follow Jesus Christ, we must learn to stay at the table with our own communities, in our own churches. This does not mean that there never come times when relationships must be judged failures, when healing seems so distant a hope that we must make the agonizing decision to break up and move on. But we tend to make those decisions far too quickly and easily, with too little provocation. We must learn that betrayal and conflict— and all the other demons that emerge when real community happens—are not terminal ills but provide openings into deeper reaches of the spiritual life, into deeper relationship with one another and with God. That was true for the disciples as they journeyed on with Jesus, and that shall be true for us— if we will learn to stay at the table.

And how did Jesus manage to stay at the table? What was his "secret"? It was simple, really, and it was the same "secret" that Jesus taught through-out his ministry: Rely not on yourself or on others but on God alone, and God will provide. Jesus was not shocked or undermined or done in by the dissolution of the community that shared the Last Supper. He knew human nature, he knew our sinfulness; and the disciples only demonstrated what he already knew. But he knew something more—that there is a God who is with us more fully than we are with each other, a God who will keep us together if we will only place our trust in God and not in community.

To put it as sharply as I know how, community is not so much a demonstration of the kingdom as it is a *via negativa* to God. We will be disillusioned by community, but in the spiritual life, disillusionment is a good thing: it means losing our illusions about ourselves and each other. As those illusions fall away we will be able to see reality and truth more clearly. And the truth is that we can rely on God to make community among us even— and especially—when our own efforts fail. By being willing to suffer the failings of community, we give ourselves the chance to draw closer to God. By entering and staying with community, we enroll in a school of the Spirit where we will learn how life together is sustained.

For here is the paradox: As we become disillusioned with community and more dependent on God, we also become more available for true community with each other. But now it is different. Our eyes have been opened, and we have no more romantic illusions. Seeing ourselves and each other clearly, yet seeing God's continual healing presence among us, we can begin to experience the fruits of the Spirit with each other—love, joy, peace, patience, kindness, goodness, and gentleness. The community we have yearned for is among us, in exactly the measure that we are able to discern God's presence in our midst.

If the Last Supper is the image of community in history, what is the role of those two images from beyond history—the garden and the new Jerusalem? Their role is crucial. I will even dare to say that Jesus had these images in mind as he sat at the Last Supper and that they helped him stay at the table.

The garden is an image that has to do with memory, one of the basic spiritual disciplines. The memory of the garden is a memory of the fact that God created us in community, one and whole. It is from that ancient memory that our great yearning for community arises, the yearning to return to our created condition before sin intervened. If we want to live in and for community, we must cultivate this sacred memory of our God-given original state.

The new Jerusalem, at the other end of history, is an image that has to do with hope, another of the basic spiritual disciplines. Our hope is not in our own good works, as important as they are, but in the fact that God is always working toward the building of the kingdom. God does this work in the midst of our brokenness, and nowhere is our brokenness more evident than in our frail and failed attempts to create community. So let us live in community with the memory of the garden and the hope of the new Jerusalem—but also with the knowledge that we are joining in the Last Supper. And let us live in community, knowing that what God made whole and is bringing back together no man or woman can ultimately put asunder.

At the time of this writing, Parker J. Palmer was teacher and writer-in-residence at Pendle Hill, a Quaker spiritual community and adult study center near Philadelphia. His writings include The Company of Strangers and To Know as We Are Known: A Spirituality of Education.

197

Peace, Justice, and the Middle Class: Educating Scrooge—Hearts of Flesh for Hearts of Stone

Leander S. Harding

I cannot pretend to write as an expert on educating the middle class for peace and justice. I have not gone nearly far enough in placing God's Shalom in the center of my own heart, and I know more about what doesn't help others to make this important conversion than I do about effective education for peace and justice. Furthermore, my central pastoral experience has been with the middle class of a rural town in a remote area—a long way indeed from the staggering affluence of beltway suburbia.

But I have learned something. I do know that there are some approaches that are definitely counterproductive. I know too that if I am going to gain any ground on this front of educating for peace and justice, I need a guide to help me understand how I might, myself, take the issues of peace and justice more seriously and how I might cause others to do the same.

During the Christmas season, I realized that I had an old friend who knew a great deal about sensitizing the middle-class heart to the mandate for justice. He promised to be quite a canny guide, for he didn't appear to make the same mistakes that I did, and his pedagogical strategy seemed wise in the ways of the human heart. The guide is Charles Dickens. In his famous story *A Christmas Carol,* he lays out a pedagogical strategy that always gets this Scrooge thinking new thoughts, feeling new depths, and ready for new commitments. In this essay, I will try to tease some advice for religious educators out of Dickens's education of Scrooge.

Scrooge and the Middle Class

I think Scrooge is a very good symbol for the natural mentality of most middle-class people, including myself. However he may look from the outside, Scrooge sees himself as a paragon of virtue—hardworking, earnest,

---

This article appeared in PACE 16 (1985–1986).

thrifty, practical, and realistic. He is relentless in his pursuit of classical middle-class virtues, and he feels justifiably proud of the disciplined life that he lives. In fact, his values are a bit more noble than those of many modern inhabitants of suburbia; indeed he would be morally shocked at the conspicuous consumption of essentially valueless items that is so much a part of our contemporary scene.

But Scrooge shares with most of us in the middle class the conviction that we have worked hard for what we have; that many, including many so-called poor, do not work as hard; and that in the general scheme of things, we are more often abused and taken advantage of than treated fairly. It is ironic—but I believe true—that for many middle-class persons, the most vivid experience of justice they have is their sense of the injustice of their own situation. It is a mistake to ask people who think they have already given too much to give more. It is a mistake to ask people who think of themselves as victims to think of themselves instead as victimizers. Rather than feeling enlightened, they will feel, for the most part, misunderstood and will quickly tune you out.

Dickens doesn't make this mistake with Scrooge. He begins in a different place and at the right moment. He knows that something dramatic must happen to break Scrooge's shell. An impassioned description of the suffering of others is not the first thing called for. Instead, first must come a vivid experience of his own mortality and a sense of judgment in the face of death.

Confronting Death

Dickens begins his story of the education of Scrooge at a sensitive point. Death has come close to Scrooge. Scrooge, of course, takes it all in his relentlessly practical stride, and for seven years he suppresses this intimate knowledge. But Dickens finds a way to pierce this defense, to get to the fear and anxiety that are the natural part of any true intuition of the end of life. The instrument Dickens uses is the vision of Marley's Ghost. Marley comes to Scrooge and reminds him that he too will die. He confronts Scrooge with a graphic representation of Marley's own hellish spiritual state and with a frank threat of misery beyond the grave.

> *"I wear the chain I forged in life . . . I made it link by link, and yard by yard; I girded it on of my own free will and of my own free will I wore it. . . .*
>
> *"Or would you know . . . the weight and length of the strong coil you bear yourself? It was full as heavy and as long as this, seven Christmas Eves ago. You have laboured on it, since. It is a ponderous chain!"[1]*

199

The first guideline for educating the middle class about peace and justice that is suggested by this story will be difficult to take to heart, and it may even seem to some a return to a more private and primitive religion. Nonetheless, Dickens's approach with Scrooge suggests that education for peace and justice does not start with a presentation of the case for a renewed lifestyle. It starts instead with an attack on everything that protects us from the fact that we are going to die and on all that insulates us from the terrible possibility that God may allow us the misery of rebelling against God's will forever. A preacher who protects himself or herself from this knowledge has little chance of communicating it to others.

To put the advice clearly: Contemplate your own death; lead others to contemplate theirs. Know the hell you are in; lead others to recognize their own hell and to ask the question, Why should death alter this? People are unlikely to change directions as long as they believe their actions ultimately have no consequences for their own fate.

But the functional universalism of a great deal of modern preaching and teaching undermines the demand for this radical conversion in favor of God's Shalom. At some point—probably right at the beginning—it is necessary to point out the "bad news" to which the "Good News" is an answer. This is Dickens's advice, and it fits well with my own pastoral experience.

Dickens begins his pedagogy of Scrooge by bringing death close and thus makes an opening to the emotional and affective dimension of Scrooge's life, which Scrooge is normally able to keep safely sealed off. Having gotten his listener's attention, it would be tempting for Dickens to begin to make the case and to sketch out, as he could so masterfully do, the sufferings of the poor and the deprived. Dickens is wiser than that. He knows something that it took me a long time to learn. He knows that you cannot understand the suffering of others if you do not understand your own suffering, that you cannot feel the weight of others' hurt if you cannot feel your own hurt.

Discovering One's Own Hurt

After Marley's Spirit departs, the first visitor to haunt Scrooge is the Ghost of his own past. This Ghost carefully leads Scrooge to those places in the man's past where his needs for love, justice, and kindness were frustrated because he had covered over his own wounded need with the hard armor of striving and self-sufficiency.

Under the pedagogy of Marley's Ghost, Scrooge discovered his profound fear and anxiety in the face of death. But under the pedagogy of the Ghost of Christmas Past, Scrooge discovers his own loneliness, hurt, and suffering. He develops an empathy for himself, a nostalgia for his past, and a sense of remorse. As Scrooge begins to repossess the world of feeling he abandoned so long ago, an indispensable foundation is being laid for the moral conversion to which he finally comes.

> *"The school is not quite deserted," said the Ghost. "A solitary child, neglected by his friends, is left there still."*
>
> *Scrooge said he knew it. And he sobbed. . . . Then, with a rapidity of transition very foreign to his usual character, he said, in pity for his former self, "Poor boy!" and cried again.*[2]

Immediately following this recovery of the poignancy of his own childhood, Scrooge has his first compassionate feeling since the beginning of the story: He feels remorse for missing the chance to befriend a young Christmas caroler who comes to his door. It is a small beginning and pathetically myopic, given the misery that Scrooge has caused his family and his employee for years. It is also a long way yet from the serious contemplation of the individual's responsibility for the poor and for the evils of the social system. The Ghost smiles at all this, but unlike many fervent social activists, he says nothing and passes on, respecting this first tender feeling—the beginning of Scrooge's moral development.

Once when I was a farmer, I fell through a rotten hayloft floor and broke some ribs. I wasn't really sure what was wrong with me. I went to the doctor. He listened carefully and without hesitation touched me and found the place where it hurt. Initially, I was not sure of this doctor, though I wanted to trust him. But when he unerringly found the place where it hurt, I knew he could heal. I knew he knew his business.

The same skill is demanded of religious educators and pastors. The authority to confront people with the part they play in the suffering of the masses will be granted to the teacher who can, with a gentle hand, cause people to feel again their own pain. Such exact knowledge of the anatomy of suffering begins with a profound self-knowledge.

Being Grateful

The Ghost of Christmas Past not only leads Scrooge to the painful moments in his personal history, he also reminds Scrooge of the love and kindness he has experienced. Scrooge begins to get a sense of the bounty he was wasted. He feels the contrast between the love of his sister and the kindness of his former employer on the one hand and the way he treats his own family and workers on the other. A chink appears in Scrooge's philosophy of scarcity and self-sufficiency. Because he has unlocked the pain of Scrooge's past, the Spirit has also unlocked the truly consoling moments. The heart that can bear pain can feel joy and gratitude.

At this point in Scrooge's development (and ours), thanksgiving and hence Christianity are possible. It is time to preach and teach about the riches of God's love toward us. It is time to count blessings and realize the riches that we have and are offered daily by God through others. A tender heart and a growing sense of bounty make it possible to endure a round of deeper judgment.

Repenting

Scrooge is thus brought carefully to the point where he can look upon his failure to give himself to the one chance for love that came in his life. He is able to see the moment when he sacrificed his own true life and that of his loved one to the idol of security. Through the agency of the Spirit, Scrooge's knowledge of the depth of his personal hell becomes intimate. Having been built up, Scrooge is able to find the place in his past where the road forked and to count the cost of the wrong choice. It is a devastating moment, but it causes repentance. Scrooge is heartily sorry for sins against those close to him. His sense of sorrow about social evil is still to come, but when it does, it will be built upon this first knowledge.

Dickens has an uncanny sense of the limits and rhythms of self-disclosure. He gives Scrooge (and us) about as much as can be borne at any one moment and then provides a space in which the dark knowledge can be digested. Theologically, judgment and grace always come together. Dickens understands this. As Scrooge becomes more capable of honest self-evaluation, he also becomes more capable of enjoying himself. The Ghost of Christmas Past sensitizes Scrooge and opens to him again the world of feeling by helping him recover moments of pain, loss, and tenderness in his childhood.

After this haunting, Scrooge is far more human and likable than the miserly figure we met at the beginning of the story. We begin to think there may be some hope for him, and for ourselves as well. But a new Spirit is required to move beyond this point—the Ghost of Christmas Present.

Enjoying

The Ghost of Christmas Present represents a robust and earthy enjoyment of life. He knows how to enjoy food and drink, how to celebrate, how to party. A spirit of enjoyment has been absent from Scrooge's grim and driven life. Preoccupied with his need for success, Scrooge has forgotten how to laugh and enjoy life. Dickens understands so well that concrete acts of love proceed out of a sense of the fullness and bounty of life. Scrooge needs to be strengthened by this Spirit before he can look at the darker realities Dickens would have him see.

In the same way, parties, potlucks, and moments of fun together in parish life are not distractions from the serious business of being religious. They are a reassertion of the goodness and value of creation in ways that subvert the relentless and soul-deadening practicality of the middle class.

Moments of real celebration break down our sense of scarcity and deprivation, of being overworked and underappreciated, and this sense is our best
defense against the suffering of others. Rather than being celebratory,
though, not a few contemporary liturgies have the character of moral
nagging: "O Lord, let us not forget that . . . ."

Let us not forget instead to enjoy the simple and wholesome pleasures
of the good earth and our life together, and we might even feel we really
have something to share. This is the lesson of Christmas Present, and
without it Scrooge goes no further.

Appreciating Simplicity

Under the tutelage of this happy Spirit, Scrooge's moral sensitivity
begins to widen. He learns a subtle lesson as he is led to see the happiness
and gratefulness of people far less privileged than he. He sees people who
are poor, lonely, and in hard circumstances finding a way to enjoy and savor
their Christmas.

When the Ghost at last brings him to the Cratchit home, Scrooge is most
affected by the dignity and simple pleasure of their feast. This realization of
the goodness of life, even life lived in tightened circumstances, gives
Scrooge the ability to see the shadows that fall on his employee and the
man's family because of Scrooge's neglect.

Responding in Charity

Scrooge is becoming aware of possibilities in life beyond success and
respectability. He is beginning to see that small things matter and that it will
not cost him much to make a big difference in the life of at least this one
family. Having experienced the remorse of knowing how he has hurt those
close to him, Scrooge is given by this homely Spirit an intimation of the joy
and satisfaction he might get from helping those close at hand. Scrooge
realizes that simple things can count. The Spirit does not miss the chance to
present Scrooge with individual and particular cases of need. Responding to
these needs builds up in Scrooge a desire and a capacity for concrete acts of
charity.

> *Much they saw, and far they went, and many homes they visited, but always
> with a happy end. The Spirit stood beside sick-beds, and they were
> cheerful; on foreign lands, and they were close at home; by struggling men,
> and they were patient in their greater hope; by poverty, and it was rich. In
> almshouse, hospital and jail . . . he left his blessing, and taught Scrooge his
> precepts.*[3]

If our response to poverty is only and always at the level of charity,
justice will be frustrated. But charity has its place. Sometimes it is important

to be presented with a chance to take food across the street before being asked to take food downtown. Perhaps it's important to meet the hungry people downtown and have a chance to respond to them before being asked to understand the role of overconsumption in world poverty. Being presented with concrete opportunities both to give and receive help in small but noticeable ways and can lead people to begin asking the hard questions about the systemic causes of suffering.

One of the happier developments in my own community recently is the movement to establish companion diocesan and companion congregational relationships with churches in Third-World countries. This encourages people-to-people contacts and exchanges. Those in this country who are involved in these programs are often very motivated by the chance to take on particular concrete projects that can make a substantial difference to recipients in the Third World. Often they are overwhelmed by the richness of the spiritual witness of the visitors from these new churches. Such contacts have the converting power that Scrooge experienced. As we begin to care about particular people in circumstances different from ours, and as we experience that they care about us, it becomes more possible to see the world from others' perspectives.

Facing the World's Injustice

The Spirit has taught Scrooge about the richness of life and the possibilities of enjoying homely and simple things; he has given Scrooge some knowledge of the concrete charitable acts that lay close at hand and suggested even the joy Scrooge might receive from such good work. Now the Spirit presents Scrooge with the most terrible vision of the night. Scrooge thinks he sees something odd beneath the Ghost's robe. The Spirit throws open his robe to reveal two children.

> *They were a boy and girl. Yellow, meager, ragged, scowling, wolfish; but prostrate, too, in their humility. Where graceful youth should have filled their features out and touched them with its freshest tints, a stale and shriveled hand, like that of age, had pinched and twisted them and pulled them into shreds. Where angels might have sat enthroned, devils lurked and glared out menacing. No change, no degradation, no perversion of humanity, in any grade, through all the mysteries of wonderful creation, has monsters half so horrible and dread.*

> *"Spirit! are they yours?" Scrooge could say no more.*

> *"They are Man's," said the Spirit, looking down upon them. "And they cling to me, appealing from their fathers. This boy is Ignorance. This girl is Want. Beware them both, and all of their degree, but most of all beware this boy, for on his brow I see that written which is Doom, unless the writing be erased."*

"Have they no refuge or resource?" cried Scrooge.

"Are there no prisons?" said the Spirit, turning on him for the last time with his own words. "Are there no workhouses?"[4]

After a long pedagogy, Dickens, by means of the Spirit of the Present, causes Scrooge to look not upon particular cases, but upon the enormity of the suffering of the poor. He pushes him to face the tawdriness of conventional analyses and palliatives. Now Scrooge is strong enough to take it, though it is hard. The blindness of self-congratulation that was in his original perspective is completely broken, and Scrooge has learned to see that world in a very different way, one that will push him toward a more thorough conversion. But the night is not over yet. There is one ghost left.

Tasting Mortality

The Ghost of Christmas Future is the phantom of death and, once again, Scrooge is compelled to contemplate mortality. This Spirit shows Scrooge his death at the end of an unchanged life. In this vision, time has run out. It is too late. Nothing has changed, and the Ghost leads Scrooge to taste the baleful consequences. Scrooge is tortured by the fear that he will not have a chance to do the things he knows need doing if the vision is not to become his destiny.

"Good Spirit . . . Assure me that I yet may change these shadows you have shown me, by an altered life! . . .

"I will honour Christmas in my heart, and try to keep it all the year. I will live in the Past, the Present, and the Future. The Spirits of all Three shall strive within me. I will not shut out the lessons that they teach. Oh, tell me I may sponge away the writing on this stone!"[5]

The possibility that it may be too late torments Scrooge.

Dickens's last piece of advice brings us back to the beginning—the anxiety over death. I do not see how the biblical sense of crisis and the need for decision, commitment, and action can be regained without our finding a way to speak of death and judgment. It would be a terrible irony to make into opposites the ministry of preparing people for death and the ministry of promoting moral conversion. Each of these ministries is impossible without the other.

A Joyful and Just Life

Well, we know the ending of the story. Scrooge awakens and finds he does have time left and, unlike too many converts to the cause of social justice, he sets out with a heart full of thanksgiving to take advantage of the opportunities God places in his path.

What I most like about the story is that Scrooge becomes both more *just* and more *happy*. Scrooge's more responsible and caring life is also a more joyous life. The Spirits unlocked the place where painful memories, tender feelings, and thorough self-evaluation all grow together. Joy grows there too. People need to know that, also, and to see it, in us.

And it was always said of him, that he knew how to keep Christmas well, if any man alive possessed the knowledge. May that be truly said of us, and all of us! And so, as Tiny Tim observed, "God bless us, every one."[6]

Notes

1. Dickens, Charles. *The Annotated Christmas Carol,* notes by Michael Hearn (New York: Crown Pubs., 1976), p. 78.
2. Dickens, p. 93.
3. Dickens, p. 139.
4. Dickens, p. 142.
5. Dickens, p. 160.
6. Dickens, p. 172.

At the time of this writing, Rev. Leander S. Harding, an Episcopal priest, was a doctoral student in religious education at Boston College's Institute of Religious Education and Pastoral Ministry. He served as the rector of the Church of Our Savior in Arlington, Massachusetts.

Holy Water and Candles: Catholic Piety and Religious Education

Maria Harris

If I was pressed to name the reason why I am a Catholic or, put in a slightly different way, what about being a Catholic is most important to me, I'm fairly certain my response would be *the sacramental sense.* Perhaps even more accurately, I'd rest at the point of *the sacramental imagination.*

I find my life has been permanently shaped and formed by the conviction (or to use Nathan Scott's phrase, the "persistently central assumption") that everything that exists—stones and wood and earth and fire, song and dance and sculpture and poetry, touch and smell and hearing and sight, and most of all *people*—are revelatory of the presence of holiness. There is no place, no thing, no person that is off limits for a sudden discovery of the presence of God.

Once upon a not-so-long-ago-time, we Catholics were taught and we learned that besides having the sacraments, those great Major Meeting Places, we also had an attitude toward the world of creation that enabled us to call mundane realities *sacramentals.* The word *mundane* makes sense here, since the realities so called were bound to earth, worldly, from the Latin *mundus* or *world* (it was a time of reverence for Latin, too). But somewhere along the line, the notion of sacramentals got lost, or if not lost, muted.

It is time to revive that sacramental sense, however, and to bring it back into the center of religious education. In this article I will attempt that, by asking us to look at the power of the forms we use in our teaching that might be called *earth forms.* It's not a matter of starting from scratch; it is a matter of celebrating and reclaiming what's been there all the time.

Earth Forms

We are human knowers and learners not only through verbal forms— the teaching we do through our doctrines, our theology, and our creeds—or the ideas and concepts that are put into words. We know in addition, and perhaps more deeply, through the world itself—through concrete sensible

This article appeared in PACE 16 (1985–1986).

realities such as fire and water, wood and incense. In using the term *earth forms* here, I want to draw attention to those forms offered us by the world, the planet, the universe itself; by the earth, which is our mother and our home, and to which the God of earth came in taking flesh.

Earth forms teach in and through materiality, which makes a kind of first-level and mutual claim on us through our *own* materiality, that is, our bodies and our sense of touch, taste, smell, hearing, and sight. Our bodily persons are of course central in knowing, although here I want to draw attention not to our human learning capacities, but to the power of the earth to teach us about the presence of the Holy.

Wise men and women of all earthly tribes—mythmakers and shamans, gurus and rabbis, storytellers and sculptors, artists and liturgists, and most recently ecologists—have always taught through the stuff of the world itself. They know that our senses are geared to learning from the world. Don Juan, the Yaqui Indian from whom Carlos Castaneda learned so much, is a modern representative of such wise persons, while Castaneda is closer to many of us twentieth-century, sophisticated know-it-alls.

> *We were talking about my interest in knowledge; but as usual, we were on two different tracks. I [Castaneda] was referring to academic knowledge that transcends experience, while he [Don Juan] was talking about direct knowledge of the world.*
>
> *"Do you know anything about the world around you?" he asked.*
>
> *"I know all kinds of things," I said.*
>
> *"I mean, do you ever feel the world around you?"*
>
> *"I feel as much of the world around me as I can."*
>
> *"That's not enough. You must feel everything, otherwise the world loses its sense."[1]*

Don Juan is right. What might be added from a Catholic perspective is that unless we "feel everything," we lose not only the sense of the world, we also lose the *sacramental* sense.

I suspect that the implications of this understanding for religious education are fairly apparent. Although prestige is generally given to thinking and learning through the conceptual forms offered to us by theology, our human organisms persist in learning through the material that earth itself presents.

If we make earth forms our companions in our teaching and learning, therefore, our religious lives are immeasurably enriched. We come to realize, once again, that the stuff of earth has its own life. We come to a deeper reverence and respect for earth as it is in itself—a teacher who would assist us in learning what it is to dwell in communion with all that is. To know grass and glass, wind and smoke, stone and sound, wood and wine as our teachers is to begin to engage in repairing broken relationships—relationships hurt by the false notion that our primary relationship to earth is as its dominator, and that whatever is, is there for us alone.

Water

Four elements are essential in the religious educator's attitude toward earth forms. The first is water, and concentrating on it leads to the recognition that *all* water is holy water, not just the "blessed" water saved in a small container, though that ought not be necessarily excluded. Any source of water will do.

This can mean water at the ocean coast, the sea, or the lakeshore. It can mean rain, gentle mist, violent hurricane, sudden thunderstorm. It can mean the water we use any time we are washing—hands before meals, the body as the day begins or when the evening ends. It can mean the extraordinarily sacramental activity of washing the bodies of the very old, the very young. It can mean the water of human tears.

Earth

Earth itself is the next sacramental element. Earth in all its manifestations: dirt, clay, mud, ground, soil, desert, rocks, hills, valleys, mountains. Earth in all its sheltering of us as well: the ground on which we stand, the burial place of our foremothers and forefathers, the spinning planet groaning, as is all creation, in expectation of what we are to do and to be. Earth, the planet we share with four and one-half (soon five) billion other human persons. Earth, the religious educator holding us as we sleep and receiving us when we wake. Earth, which we have failed so often, but which has not as yet failed us.

The North American natives, who have given so much to us in the way of sacramental spirituality, have never been without this sense of earth, eloquently expressed in the 1854 address of Chief Seattle to an assembly of tribes preparing to sign treaties:

> *Every part of this earth is sacred to my people. Every shining pine needle, every sandy shore, every mist in the dark woods, every clearing and humming insect is holy in the memory and experience of my people.*[2]

For him the teaching to be done out of this conviction was clear:

> *You must teach your children that the ground beneath their feet is the ashes of our ancestors. So that they will respect the land, tell your children that the earth is rich with the lives of our kin. Teach your children what we have*

209

taught our children, that the earth is our mother. Whatever befalls the earth befalls the children of the earth. To spit upon the ground is to spit upon themselves. This we know. The earth does not belong to the people; the people belong to the earth. This we know. All things are connected like blood which unites one family.[3]

If we would engage in a renewal and a recovery of Catholic sacramental piety, we must do no less: We must teach our children that the earth is rich with the lives of our kin; that the earth does not belong to the people, but that we belong to the earth; that we are connected with it and with the past through the blood and body that unites us.

Fire

Candles have always been a central feature of Catholic sacramental life; they remind us of the third earth form to incorporate into our religious educating—fire. For most of the inhabitants of earth, fire is necessary if food is to be cooked, a truth we sometimes forget in a world of gas and electric stoves and microwave ovens.

Ritual religious services have always drawn on the power and mystery of fire. Lighting the candles before Mass and extinguishing them at the end is a way of saying, "Remember, you are on holy ground." It might be beneficial to light a candle as we begin any teaching situation as well, not only to symbolize the intention of teaching toward the enlightenment of the minds and the spirits of others, but more importantly to symbolize, "Here *too* we are on holy ground."

Air

Then there is wind, or breath, or spirit, the earth form without which we could not speak, the earth form that is one of the Names of God. The physical, personal aspect of teaching religion demands that we use speech, that we draw breath in the presence of one another. Oxygen, in amounts tolerable to the human organism, is essential if we hope to learn.

Indeed a practice of schoolteachers at the elementary level is to draw attention to the need for air, oxygen, and breath through physical exercises: "Class stand! Hands on shoulders—one, two, three, four. . . ." I am aware that this practice is quite common with the young, but I know of only one teacher of adults, a graduate school professor of theology, who leads such exercises regularly at the start of class.

However, I do know that in many classes, teachers and students are still and silent for a moment before learning sessions. In this way, they not only call on the One in whom we live and move and have our being and breathe, but they also incorporate air as companion, ally, and friend in the activity of religious education.

Meaning for Us as Religious Educators

The importance of these sacramentals, these earth forms, is manifold. To begin, they are themselves the milieu—borrowing from Teilhard, the "divine milieu"—in which we dwell as teachers and learners together. A distinction might be made here between *thinking about* and *being in* something, but a separation of these is impossible. Religious education is at best a bringing together of the two—*thinking about* that in which we *are* every moment of our lives. So, at one level, we must come to terms with the air, the earth, the fire, and the water giving us actual bodily life.

At another level, however, the very *primariness* of these earth forms, their primordial character as companions in life, enables them to stand as a litmus test of our approach to all created beings. We are related to each of these forms, and they, nonhuman as they are, are related to us. In this role, the earth forms stand for and are images of all other nonhuman reality; they are *basic* symbols, basic sacraments.

Thus, how we address, handle, or touch earth and flame and water gives clues to us about the ways in which we address, handle, or touch manufactured, artificial, yet similar things: books, pencils, chalk, oil, tea, ointment, floors, clocks, bells. The sacramental character of the basic earth forms exists as a reminder that all teaching is done through the mediation of a third being, along with the teacher and the learner—a third that is often of the earth.

Further, these forms are reminders of the primary places where religious education takes place: in communities of people, especially in families; in work and sport and artistic environments; in as many nonconsciously as consciously planned situations. At its best, schooling is only one of many possible forms in which religious learning takes place, and sometimes it is only a boundary form.[4] For, although earth forms are not always the stuff of every classroom, they are beyond argument the stuff of every life.

Finally, these earth forms continually recur in the spirituality of religious people sand are central elements in all religious ritual. One may speak of the Hindu sense of *pranha,* the goodness in the air that one breathes in and out like the scent of roses; of spittle mixed with earth, whose touch gives sight to the blind as in the miracles of Jesus; of the Spirit of God breathing over the waters and birthing Creation; of the Spirit of God arriving in Pentecostal tongues of fire; or of the candles whose flames we light in preparation for Shabbat and for Eucharist. These religious images convey a *sacramental* consciousness, a sacramental *imagination,* one that sees the holiness in things, the sacred in things, the educating capacity in things.

Dorothee Soelle tells of a pious old man in his last years who, though sound in mind, was feeble in speech. All the old man could say, and he said it repeatedly, was "Everything, everything, everything." He died with these words on his lips.

This word "everything" is a formula, a symbol for the confirmation of the totality. This kind of piety is deep in our Catholic roots, a piety that affirms everything, forgets and omits nothing.[5] The old man's word is also a formula for the wisdom that knows that nothing in existence is without the capacity to educate. And it is a symbol in our tradition for the piety and the spirituality that is demanded of religious educators in their role of handing on a sacramental way of being *in,* of being *with,* and of being *for* a Creation revered as "good."

Notes

1. Carlos Castaneda, *A Separate Reality: Further Conversations with Don Juan* (New York: Simon and Schuster, 1971), p. 4.
2. In *A.D.* 5 (May 1980): 30–31. How different this spirituality is from one that proposes "contempt for the world."
3. Ibid.
4. Gabriel Moran, *Religious Education Development* (Minneapolis: Winston Press, 1983), pp. 162–173.
5. Dorothee Soelle, *Death by Bread Alone* (Philadelphia: Fortress Press, 1978).

Additional Resources

Browning, Robert L., and Roy Al Reed. *The Sacraments in Religious Education and Liturgy*. Birmingham, AL: Religious Education Press, 1985.

Clark, Linda, Marian Roman, and Eleanor Walker. *Image-Breaking, Image-Building*. New York: The Pilgrim Press, 1981.

Donze, Mary Terese. *In My Heart Room*. Liguori, MO: Liguori Pub., 1982.

Fox, Matthew. *Breakthrough: Meister Eckhart's Creation Spirituality in the New Testament*. New York: Doubleday and Co., 1980.

_____. *Original Blessing*. Santa Fe, NM: Bear and Co., 1983.

Highwater, Jamake. *The Primal Mind*. New York: Harper and Row Pub., 1981.

Luke, Helen. *Dark Wood to White Rose*. Pecos, NM: Dove Pub., 1975.

Tooker, Elisabeth, ed. *Native North American Spirituality of the Eastern Woodlands: Sacred Myths, Dreams, Vision Speeches, Healing Formulas, Rituals and Ceremonials*. Classics of Western Spirituality Series. Ramsey, NJ: Paulist Press, 1979.

Thich Nhat Hanh. *The Miracle of Mindfulness*. Boston: Beacon Press, 1976.

Woods, Richard. *Mysterion: An Approach to Mystical Spirituality*. Chicago: Thomas More Press, 1981.

At the time of this writing, Maria Harris was the Howard Professor of Religious Education at Andover Newton Theological School in Newton, Massachusetts. Her latest work was the videotape series Teaching and the Religious Imagination *(Argus Communications)*.

War Toys

Joanne Sheehan

As we prepare to celebrate the birth of Christ, toy manufacturers are gearing up to convince children that true Christmas joy lies in getting the right toy. For little girls that means many things in pastels—ponies with hair to comb, dolls with tiny waists and big pocketbooks, and lots of furniture and clothes. For little boys that means dinosaurs that carry deadly weapons, toy grenades, and guns that shoot red pellets that "prove" you've hit the other guy. On Christmas morning children chase each other around the stable of the Prince of Peace with submachine guns and spend the evening with the latest video games doing battle with the family.

War toys are a leading category of toys sold today. These toys include action figures such as G.I. Joe, robots equipped with weapons such as transformers, laser tag games, interactive toys with weapons, and an alarming increase in realistic toy guns including battery-powered sub-machine guns and hand grenades that really explode. Promoting these toys are a large number of violent cartoons seen daily by children before and after school, and on weekends. These promotional cartoons have an average of fifty acts of violence per hour, one with as many as 114 such acts.

Characters like G.I. Joe are being sold as "Great American Heroes" and role models for children. Promoted with descriptions such as "the ultimate warrior," these toys and their cartoons make war and killing exciting to children. While there is a high level of violence in these shows, according to the National Coalition on Television Violence, rarely do people die, giving children the impression that violence is not harmful. The characters often portray racial and sexual stereotypes, promoting hatred in our society. A G.I. Joe cartoon has an "enemy" with a foreign accent who is seeking sanctuary. Women, when they are depicted, are portrayed as younger, more dependent and less active than males. The "good guys" are always physically strong, capable of beating any "enemy"—the perfect man. Many of the "evil" characters are portrayed as having disabilities. Rambo has an enemy called "Gripper," a terrorist who has a mechanical hand and an eye patch.

This article appeared in PACE 19 (1988–1989).

Dr. Arnold Goldstein, Director of the Center for Research on Aggression at the University of Syracuse states,

The playing with war toys legitimizes and makes violent behavior acceptable. It desensitizes children to the dangers of harm of violent behavior and increases the chance that they will resort to violent behavior. Probably only a small number will commit heavy-duty violence, but a large number will pick up some harmful behaviors. The degree that youngsters are learning to take pleasure from aggression decreases their ability to learn empathy, negotiation, and cooperation. Cooperative games do exist and can be fun. I would recommend that parents not allow violent toys in their homes, but purchase nonviolent toys and games.[1]

Parents and educators know firsthand the problems that arise from children playing with war toys. They become more aggressive in their behavior—with increased incidents of pushing, hitting, kicking. Children often mimic the play they see on television, therefore eliminating the creativity and cooperation needed in children's play.

Violence in our society is at an all-time high, according to FBI statistics. Increasingly teenagers are killing, being killed and committing suicide. Police deal daily with the question of whether a gun is real or not, sometimes with tragic outcomes. It is important for our society to work against this violence. Eliminating war toys and violent cartoons is a good place to start. Allowing children to have war toys and to watch these cartoons implicitly supports violence and war as solutions to problems.

One reason for the increase in violent entertainment for children is a by-product of the Reagan administration. Previous to 1980, the Federal Communications Commission did not allow cartoons promoting children's toys on the air. However, Reagan's FCC allowed such shows. In the spring of 1986, ten "action figures" were being promoted by violent cartoon shows which air seven days a week. By the fall of 1986 there were twenty-nine such cartoons, and in the fall of 1987 the toy companies added another twelve cartoons to help sell war toys. By the end of 1987 there were indications that these cartoons were not selling toys as well as they once did, and the shows began to slowly leave the air. One pressure on the industry was a bill in Congress to return children's television to pre-1982 rules. The Reagan administration vetoed that bill on November 10, 1988. Children are watching more television than ever before, with elementary school age children averaging four to five hours a day. Studies show they are being influenced by what they watch. While fewer in number, many war toy cartoon shows are still being shown, mostly on independent TV stations.

A second cause of the decline of the war toy TV shows is the rise of video games. This industry, dominated by Nintendo, has become the largest selling item in the toys category for boys, with over one billion a year in sales. Its prime market is boys at the upper age limits of the war toy market who are no longer buying G.I. Joes. Instead, they are buying video games, eighty-five percent of which have violent themes, and fifty-eight percent of which have war themes.

Another serious problem regarding children's exposure to violence is the number of violent adult shows children are watching, including violent movies on home videos. When my daughter was in the second grade her teacher asked the class how many of them had seen the Rambo movie. Six boys and one girl had already seen it. A year later I spoke in a junior high where fourteen out of sixteen seventh graders had seen "Rambo." Of the two who had not, one didn't have a VCR; the other's dad was a Vietnam veteran who knew how violent that war had been and did not want his children watching such a violent and unrealistic movie.

Dr. Benjamin Spock, noted pediatrician and peace activist, put it this way:

We are living in the most violent country in the world in terms of murders, murders within the family, rape, wife abuse and child abuse. We have one of the two largest stocks of nuclear weapons and are developing others that will be more fiendish still—and more difficult to control. Our government has been intruding ruthlessness and illegally in the affairs of other nations sometimes trying to overthrow their governments and murder their officials because it dislikes their politics. Are we doing everything to reverse these alarming trends? Quite the contrary. We are allowing our children to watch endless violence on television which we now know as a scientific fact has a progressively brutalizing effect.

We are buying for our children even more elaborate war toys—machine guns, death ray guns, tanks, war-making robots, and spaceships. We can see from the way they play that these stimulate hostile, brutal feelings even in very young children, which will gradually erode their capacities for tenderness and sympathy.

It's time we realize that we are storing up terrible trouble for ourselves, our children, and grandchildren in the future. But we can save our families, our country, and our world if we will face our problems and reverse our downward spiral. [2]

The Stop War Toys Campaign

In the summer of 1985, members of the War Resisters League/New England became alarmed by the 350 percent increase in the sale of war toys between 1982 and 1985. A Stop War Toys Campaign was created to alert others to the situation and to provide organizing ideas and resources to enable people around the country to do something about it. Coleco

215

Industries announced plans to bring out an action figure based on the violent Rambo movies soon after the Campaign was begun, giving us our first focus.

The objectives of the campaign are to alert the public to the dangers of war toys and violent cartoons and to stimulate parents, educators, therapists, organizations and the media. Our goal is to decrease the sales of war toys and violent cartoons on television. Because the popularity of war toys is a symptom of a greater acceptance of violence and militarism in our society, we hope that our campaign will sensitize people to this, enabling them to find ways to actively work to reduce the violence and militarism which permeates society.

The campaign has been successful in many ways. In four years it has grown from a small handful of concerned people to a movement that includes people in fifty states, with contacts in several other countries. Although no one group can take credit for this growth, the War Resisters League has acted as the clearinghouse—providing an organizing packet, a newsletter, coordination of International Days of Protest Against War Toys (the Friday and Saturday after Thanksgiving), and generally acts as a resource for those working on the issue.

Our first major success was the discontinuation of the Nomad doll, Rambo's Arab terrorist enemy, as a direct result of letters of protest to Coleco organized by the War Resisters League and the Arab-American Anti-Discrimination Committee. Although toy analysts predicted that the Rambo series of action figures would be popular, sales were very poor and the toys can now be found only in bargain bins. Such a success within the first year of the campaign encouraged us and reminded us that we can make a difference.

According to the Toy Manufacturers of America, action figure sales have declined two straight years, 1987 and 1988, after five years of increases. However, sales of toy guns, weapons, and accessories have risen over the last two years. In 1986, nineteen million toy guns were sold, thirty-three million in 1987, and thirty million in 1988. And in the last two years the sales of video games, eighty-five percent of them with violent themes, have grown to have the largest sales of any toys. Nintendo has been on top of Toy & Hobby World's sales list since late 1988, when they added video games to their survey.

Even though there have been successes, it is obvious that there is still a serious problem that needs to be addressed. Even companies that have traditionally made basic, constructive toys—Lego, Fisher-Price—have jumped on the war toys bandwagon and continue to create new toys with weapons.

As the campaign developed, we realized that we needed to do more than just work against war toys and violent cartoons. We began to encourage people to address some of the underlying issues. An understanding of the importance of building self-esteem and the development of creative conflict resolution skills in children is essential.

The Stop War Toys Campaign Packet contains material on war toys and violent cartoons (including studies and research findings), project and organizing ideas, materials and resource lists on countering stereotyping, safety issues, interactive toys, a petition against war toys, brochures and lists of resources including organizations, books, and audio-visuals. (This packet is available for $5 plus $2 postage from the Stop War Toys Campaign, PO Box 1093, Norwich, CT 06360.)

Children do need to learn how to deal with aggression, but there are more constructive ways to do this than through war toys. Fear, anger and feelings of low self-esteem are often at the root of aggressive behavior, behavior that is encouraged by playing with war toys and watching violent TV shows. The home and school should be places where children can build their self-esteem. Their environment should encourage communication, cooperation, and the development of creative ways to solve conflicts.

No society interested in attaining peace and justice can allow such a militarization of the young to go unchallenged. Any vision of a future without war and killing is impossible if the young are raised to be passive consumers of violence and militarism in toys, cartoons, and popular culture.

Notes

1. From Press Release of The National Coalition on Television Violence, June 11, 1985.
2. From a letter by Dr. Benjamin Spock addressed to the Stop War Toys Campaign, Sept. 13, 1987.

At the time of this writing, Joanne Sheehan, mother of two, was on the staff of War Resisters League/New England. She was a co-founder of the Stop War Toys Campaign.

Some New Thoughts on Penance

Doris Donnelly

The guesswork is over. The Pastoral Research and Practices Committee of the NCCB has done us all a big favor. It undertook an in-depth study of the Sacrament of Penance in Catholic life today and published its findings.[1] As a result, we now have facts, figures, and an analysis of data that enables—or ought to enable—us to move forward with regard to the liturgical renewal of this sacrament.

The study relied on input from various groups. Those involved with the project consulted widely and invited many constituencies to reflect on reasons behind the decline of individual confession. The study is stronger because of this approach. Another plus was the cross-disciplined orientation of the document: Anthropology, psychology and the social sciences along with theology were the combined resources. The result is an uncommon breadth and scope.

In addition, the project is just plain interesting. For example, while it is true that the reception of the sacrament has slipped over the last 25 years, this document reports that "the quality of those sacramental encounters has improved." The study also challenges the common perception that Rite 3 (communal confession with communal absolution) is being used extensively throughout the United States. The data does not support that conclusion and in fact suggests that Rite 3 is being used sparingly. Further expanded use of Rite 3 is generally favored by priests and laity; bishops seem less enthusiastic about that possibility. The document also reflects a certain degree of confusion about what is genuinely sinful. *All* groups agree on this point, with some difference in emphasis.

A word about the composition of the database is important before we survey the findings and insights of the committee. All U.S. bishops were asked to respond to a questionnaire; 42 percent did so. Of a random sample of 2,500 priests, 44 percent replied. Among laity, only those active in parish life were invited to be part of the sample. Of these, 86 percent were Catholic from birth, 62 percent attended Catholic elementary schools, 22 percent attended a Catholic college, 17 percent have masters or doctoral degrees,

---

This article appeared in PACE 20 (1991).

73 percent are married, 10.5 percent are single, 8.5 percent divorced or separated, and 7.5 percent widowed. The laity had a 35 percent response.

We know they responded. What did they say?

By far, the most instructive findings were the different reasons offered for the decline in the frequency of individual confession. Bishops tended to focus on a diminished sense of sin and a lack of clarity about the true nature of sin. The assessment offered by priests turned to the excessive guilt which motivated many confessions in the past and which is no longer operative, although they, too, acknowledged that confusion about sin was prevalent. The laity, on the other hand, suggested that the decline in individual confession had a great deal to do with their finding other ways to experience reconciliation.

All groups had something to say about priests as confessors. The bishops are aware that few workshops had been offered to clergy on the subject of reconciliation since the new *Ordo Paenitentiae* was introduced in 1974—16 years ago. They also noted that homily materials need to be prepared and that a personal conviction on the part of priests themselves regarding the value of the sacrament helps the pastoral effort. Among priests, more than two-thirds said they did not feel that they had been adequately trained to serve as confessors according to the demands of the renewed rite—*Two-thirds!* From the laity, the issue of priests elicited some potentially valuable information which affects their reception of this sacrament. For example, the largest group of laypersons responded that their involvement in parish life had made them so well known to their parish priests that they were reluctant to confess to them. In other cases, laypersons reported that confessors did not take their search for spiritual development seriously enough. Still others, although the number in this case was small, did not see the need for the priest as an intermediary in the reconciliation process.

It was encouraging in this connection to read that among the priests who responded to this survey eight percent receive the sacrament weekly; 27 percent monthly, 47 percent every two or three months, and 18 percent annually. The conclusion of the document with regard to these statistics is that 82 percent of priests in the United States receive the sacrament with some degree of frequency. Among the laity, the following information regarding the frequency of their reception of the sacrament of penance emerged: Four percent receive the sacrament weekly; five percent monthly; 17 percent every two or three months; 55 percent once or twice per year; and, 19 percent, never. Apart from the sacrament of penance, laypersons identified other ways that they experienced reconciliation—through the Eucharist, prayer, by making an act of contrition, by talking with a friend, through the corporal works of mercy, and by reading Scripture. Bishops, too, recognized that reconciliation is available through a variety of means, but they tended to emphasize the privileged sacramental encounter made possible through confession.

The Sacrament of Penance stands as a counter-cultural reality, according to this study. And if we were honest about this, is there a catechist or pastoral minister who would dispute this claim? In the first place, the influence of *individualism* has encouraged people to believe that self-determination and self-identity are the keys to personal freedom when, in fact, the Gospel suggests that self-transcendence is the means to being fully human. In the process, one would legitimately expect the development of one's consciousness to connect with other persons. Eventually, that would elicit the insight that any harm done through sin is a harm that affects others. The study aptly quotes Pope John Paul II on this issue:

> *There is no sin, not even the most intimate and secret one, the most strictly individual one, that exclusively concerns the person committing it. With greater or lesser violence, with greater or lesser harm, every sin has repercussions on the entire ecclesial body and the whole human family. (Reconciliatio et Paenitentiae, 161)*

Regrettably, these insights are not widely shared. In response to the crisis spawned by individualism, this study not only lays out convincing statistics but offers sober thoughts to ponder. For example, it wonders along with Joseph Holland whether the current enthusiasm for spirituality is not merely a disguised form of "expressive individualism."

Second, the study takes note of the issue of *pluralism* which encourages doubts about the truth claims and consequent praxis of any one group. One way pluralism affects American Catholics is when the culture proposes several options for their consideration—either moral choices or as ritual practices—and claims them all of equal worth. Given this cultural relativism, it is no surprise that people adopt positions at variance with the teaching of their own church. In many such instances, it does not seem to be important to hold firm to learned principles but rather to remain nonjudgmental toward others and toward oneself. This spirit espouses an "anything goes" philosophy which at times lessens the emphasis on repentance and conversion of heart as prerequisites for sacramental confession in the Catholic economy.

The impact of the communications media is the third cultural influence considered in this study. This virtually untapped evangelization resource frequently belittles religion and proposes decadent situations as the accepted norm of behavior, thereby desensitizing our moral inclinations. Media specialists can continue their debates about the impact of violence in promoting serious crime; in the meantime, what seems absolutely incontestable is the way the media is able to relativize our own peccadilloes by comparing them to the evils shown in the movies, on TV, and those chronicled in the newspapers. It is difficult for many people to believe their lives are in need of conversion when those guilty of far more serious crimes are pictured as blissfully happy and free from the sting of guilt.

If this is the mess we are in with regard to the sacrament of penance, what can we do about it? The NCCB Committee offers some suggestions as well as hints for creative thinking. Four insights seem particularly rich.

1. *Retrieve the tradition.*

The Roman Catholic Church holds a valuable resource in its tradition of understanding penance as "medicine for sin." Burdened down, diseased by sin, we are in need of ways to recover from our spiritual illnesses. The recovery process is aided by an enlightenment concerning our dark or "under"-side and our honest admission of what it is that stands in the way of the light of Christ penetrating our inmost beings. Identifying that "illness" or sin is difficult and risky business because it places us on the road to a realignment of our loyalties and a shifting of our priorities that will impinge on our lifestyles. The tradition says the cure is worth the price. The medicine of penance by which we cooperate with the grace of the conversion allows us to redirect our energies and get in shape, spiritually, for the new being about to be born. For those who regard penance as a medieval practice whose demise has come, the medicinal aspect of this sacrament has a message for contemporary men and women who are aware that health and wholeness is not only physical but that it involves the heart, emotions, and psyche as well.

2. *Identify places where parishes and dioceses are doing the work of reconciliation.*

Reconciliation takes place not only in reconciliation rooms in parish churches. It happens when the creative pool of imagination in a parish concerns itself with race relations in the community and acts as an agent which brings people together when other forces are pulling them apart. Engaged Encounter and Marriage Encounter, ministries to the bereaved, the separated and divorced, the alienated, and the un-churched are all forms of Christ's spirit of reconciliation in our midst.

The document from the NCCB encourages communities and dioceses to recall some of the many specific occasions when such reconciliations have occurred and to make those stories known. When the church community sponsors listening sessions for teenagers estranged from their parents, healing happens. When dioceses reach out and welcome back Catholics who have distanced themselves from the church, healing happens. When Catholics cooperate with other Christian (and non-Christian) churches in peace and justice efforts, profound symbols of healing are seen by all.

221

Reconciliation as a word needs to be taken out of the dictionary, dusted off, and renewed. It needs to stand for those many occasions when what was apart is brought together again, when what was lost is found, when what was broken is healed. What the sacrament celebrates is precisely this: That God's prodigal undeserved love *heals* relationships between brothers and sisters, in-laws, neighbors, and even those divided against ourselves.

3. *Spiritual Direction and Sacramental Confession.*

The NCCB document does us a great service by tackling the issue raised by some who have entered into relationships with "spiritual guides" to whom they disclose their ongoing relationships with God. Certainly, the experience of spiritual direction is valuable if one's growth is toward freedom, but it is not built along the same rhythm as that of the Sacrament of Penance.

Penance calls for taking ownership of our false-selves; it calls for accountability; it asks that we disengage from un-freeing behaviors; it asks for serious reckoning with sin. This kind of discovery may, of course, take place within a relationship of spiritual guidance. However, when one excuses oneself from the obligation of repentance because one has outgrown the need, then spiritual guidance may become one of the many camouflages or deflections we have learned to put in the way of repentance. In those circumstances, it needs to be named as such.

The truth of the tradition holds firm, and the document under study frames that truth well: "The more one has grown in the spiritual life, the more important recourse to the Sacrament of Penance becomes"—and not the other way around, however tempting the thought might be.

4. *Practical concerns: Training of confessors, time and place for the Sacrament of Penance.*

The study by the Pastoral Research and Practices Committee acknowledged the need—among all groups surveyed—for better training of priests to function as confessors within the Sacrament of Penance. Several recommendations are offered at the conclusion of the document to reinforce this need and to improve the preparation of seminarians and ordained priests for this ministry. Of all the suggestions, here is my favorite sentence: "All this fund of human gifts, Christian virtues, and pastoral capabilities has to be worked for and is only acquired with effort."

When all is said and done, what we learn about confessors is that, like Christians, they are made, not born. There are probably no short-circuits to becoming an effective listener, a gentle guide, and a bracing reminder of the war that wages in our hearts between good and evil. So study, up-dating, reflection, prayer, and one's own experiences as penitent all converge for the priest who celebrates this sacrament with us individually and as community. It would seem to me that a certain amount of patience from the community is called for as well, as embryonic gifts come into their fullness. And it would not seem inappropriate to ask that the community pray that their priests become effective mediators of the message of the Gospel.

A final recommendation from the Committee is a deceptively simple one: It asks that we as a community re-examine the time and place of celebrating the Sacrament of Penance. The post-Vatican II liturgical renewal called for confessions to be heard outside of the Eucharistic celebration, and surely one cannot argue with the logic of the theologians in the regard. Yet many of the parishioners surveyed indicated their preference for reinstatement of those times. This writer believes some listening and dialogue is in order on this point. Even when the laity support Advent and Lent communal celebrations, we need to be attentive to schedules and calendars of busy people. We also need to care about "opportune moments" when people desire sacramental reconciliation and it is not provided. This small issue may provide an occasion for shaping the liturgy to respond to real needs.

It has often been said that theologians ply their trade in ivory towers away from the real life of the Christian community. The document I have examined in these pages suggests that at least once in a while the community is consulted and that the results of such surveys are enlightening. A stage beyond consultation is called for now—implementing some of the proposals, putting leadership behind some suggestions, and giving penance a second chance to respond to the need in every human heart to be whole again.

Notes

1. See *Origins,* February 22, 1990.

At the time of this writing, Doris Donnelly was a professor of theology at John Carroll University in Cleveland, Ohio, and had written many articles on the Sacrament of Penance for professional and popular journals.

Should the "Original Sequence" Be Restored for Confirmation?

Joseph Martos

Having studied and written about the history of the sacraments at some length, I have been following with interest the recent debate concerning the proper time for Confirmation for persons who have been baptized in infancy. Judging by the books and articles on the subject in the past 10 years or so, it seems that the liturgically minded (if I might call them that) have been mounting an increasingly impressive argument in favor of "restoring the original sequence" of the sacraments of initiation. Yet from the perspective of history, that argument has some inherent weaknesses which, taken together, make it extremely suspect, if not fallacious.

The argument is made that the original sequence of the sacraments of initiation was Baptism-Confirmation-Eucharist, and that therefore (for various reasons, appealing to history and selected texts from Vatican II) this sequence ought to be restored, with Confirmation taking place after Baptism and before First Eucharist. The major difficulty with this argument, however, is that the words "Baptism, Confirmation, and Eucharist" do not refer to the same realities today that they referred to during the patristic period. If this is the case, then to argue that the "original sequence" ought to be "restored" is superficially plausible but ultimately specious.

What actually was the original process of Christian initiation? If we examine the New Testament record, it appears to have been adult conversion followed by immediate Baptism and then participation in the life of the community, which naturally included participation in the Breaking of Bread, or the Lord's Supper. The laying on of hands for the reception of the Holy Spirit seems to have been a charismatic practice which may have preceded or followed Baptism in water, and which may or may not have occurred in early communities, depending on whether or not they were given to charismatic prayer experiences such as speaking in tongues. (See Acts 8:14–17; 9:17–19;

This article appeared in PACE 21 (1992). It first appeared under a different title in the spring 1991 issue of GIFTS, the newsletter of the NCCB Secretariat for Laity and Family Life.

10:44–48; 19:1–7.) In other words, Confirmation, as we now have it, was not part of the "original sequence."

The proponents of the original-sequence argument actually go back only to practices that evolved by the third and fourth centuries, when many local churches did incorporate a laying on of hands and/or an anointing either before or after the immersion in water and profession of the Creed, to signify that through the initiation process the candidate was receiving the Holy Spirit. Not until after the conversion process of the catechumenate and the baptismal rituals of the Easter Vigil were the candidates allowed to participate in their first full Eucharist (the whole celebration, not just "First Communion") with the whole assembled community.[1]

Aidan Kavanagh, in his careful study of *The Apostolic Tradition* of Hippolytus (which contains a description of Christian initiation in Rome around the year 215), argues persuasively that the ceremonial action from which Confirmation developed in the West was actually little more than a "dismissal rite" in which the bishop prayed over the newly baptized and sent them forth to the Eucharistic celebration. In *Confirmation: Origins and Reform,*[2] Kavanagh uses this discovery to suggest that the rite and meaning of Confirmation are intrinsically bound to Baptism and should not be separated from it, but the historical data could just as reasonably be used to argue that there was no distinct rite of Confirmation until the fourth century, when bishops in the West created a separate rite of sealing or confirming Baptisms performed by presbyters in local parishes—a rite that took place *after* the neophytes' First Eucharist, and from which the medieval and modern practices of Confirmation actually evolved.

In early medieval Europe, infants were often baptized and given Eucharistic wine in the same ceremony. But reverence for the sacred species eventually led the Eucharistic dimension of initiation to be dropped, thus paving the way for First Communion as a separate ritual to be introduced in later childhood. Throughout the Middle Ages, Baptism alone was the prerequisite for attending and receiving the Eucharist, just as it had been during the patristic period, both before and after the bishop's blessing was separated from the initiation process. This is one reason why for centuries Confirmation fell into virtual disuse: There was no theological justification for it until Faustus of Riez claimed that it gave an "increase" of the Holy Spirit and his rationalization became generally accepted by the medieval scholastics.[3]

Granting that the present Rite of Christian Initiation of Adults is a close approximation to the process of adult initiation in the patristic period, let us now compare the stages of children's initiation today to that same historical process.

First of all, the patristic practice was primarily for adults who could make a mature and deliberate profession of faith as part of their initiation into the

Christian community. Secondarily, it was for the households (including slaves and children) of such mature persons who accepted these adults' decisions in all matters, including matters of religion. Only thirdly was it for children of baptized parents who decided (perhaps after adolescence, as in the case of St. Augustine) to espouse the faith of their parents. Infant Baptism became a universal practice only in about the fifth century, by which time postponed Confirmation had become a standard practice in the West. Therefore, to compare the Baptism and Confirmation of children today to the initiation of adults in the patristic period seems to be tenuous at best.

Secondly and related to this, Baptism during much of the patristic period referred not only to the ritual of immersion in water but also to the entire process of immersion into the life of the Christian community which was, at its conclusion, aptly symbolized by immersion in water and participation in the Eucharistic liturgy. Since the fifth century, when infant Baptism became a more normal practice, the more encompassing dimensions of Baptism were lost and the word then referred only to the liturgical rite. To argue from any similarity between infant Baptism today and adult Baptism in the early Church is to overlook the larger existential—both personal and social—dimensions of patristic Baptism, and to attribute all of the effectiveness of Baptism to the ritual immersion, which is, at bottom, a belief in ritual magic. The process of adult initiation was existentially different from today's practice of infant Baptism, even though many of the liturgical elements are similar.

Thirdly, Confirmation in the patristic period was virtually non-existent as a separate ritual until the rite which later evolved into a distinct sacrament was split off from the baptismal liturgy in Rome and other places in the East and placed after first participation in the Eucharist. To argue that postponed Confirmation must be temporally related to Baptism is thus based on a misreading of history. Even if, theologically, Confirmation is integrally related to Baptism, that relation is not to the liturgy of Baptism but to the process of Baptism, that is, to the process of becoming a mature, participating member of the Christian community.

Fourth, the Eucharist to which candidates were admitted after their Baptism (whether blessed by the bishop, as in the earlier centuries, or not, as in the later centuries) was the full Eucharistic liturgy and not simply First Communion. To be historically consistent, proponents of the original sequence would have to argue that children who are baptized in infancy should be restricted from what is today called the Liturgy of the Eucharist and not simply from going to Communion. The contemporary fact is that unless Catholic parishes provide (as many Protestant churches do) an alternative Sunday celebration for children (e.g., in Sunday school) while their parents attend the Eucharistic liturgy, there is no real parallel between the patristic practice and today's practice of allowing Catholic children to remain during the entire Mass.

A fifth and final difficulty with arguments to restore the original sequence is a more overarching problem. Very often one reads that the sacraments of initiation ought to be received in their proper order, or that Confirmation needs to be received in order for a person to be fully initiated into the Church. However, that way of posing the question makes it crucial to ask whether sacraments can properly be said to be "received" (with the exception of the Blessed Sacrament) in a way that makes sense in the context of contemporary sacramental theology.

We as Catholics commonly speak of "administering" and "receiving" the sacraments—a manner of speaking which first appeared in the neo-Platonic thinking of the patristic period, and which was taken into the Aristotelian thinking of the Middle Ages. As developed in the Scholastic theology of Thomas Aquinas and others, the sacrament that was received into the soul of the believer was a metaphysical entity *(sacramentum et res)* that was imparted by the proper performance *(ex opere operato)* of a church ritual *(sacramentum tantum)*. This is essentially a mythical and magical notion which was given intellectual respectability by being elevated to a metaphysical category in the Scholastic system.

Today, however, few sacramental or liturgical theologians employ the Scholastic system in their thinking about the sacraments, although many of them still uncritically use the language of "administering and receiving sacraments" derived from the patristic and medieval eras. As a result, many Catholics (including liturgists and religious educators) speak about "receiving Confirmation" as though through the Church ritual the sacrament was automatically received.

A more critical awareness of the use of language today would lead us to say that the sacrament *is* the ritual (what the medievals called the *sacramentum tantum),* and that what is received (given the proper disposition of the subject of the ritual) is the Holy Spirit. Technically, it is even incorrect to say that "the sacrament is celebrated," for the sacrament is the celebration itself, although this parlance has become increasingly more prevalent during the past 30 years. Strictly speaking, what is celebrated is not the ritual but what the ritual symbolizes and points to, just as an anniversary party celebrates not the party but the happy completion of a number of years of marriage, for example.

If the sacrament *is* the celebration or the ritual, however, and not a metaphysical entity bestowed by the ritual, then there is no intrinsic necessity for the ritual to be performed unless it actually signifies something new and different in the life of the person who is the subject of the ritual. To believe that it does (even when it does not) is essentially a magical belief.

227

This point needs to be made in order to disabuse ourselves of the notion that going through the ceremony of Confirmation actually does something even when there is no evidence that it does anything. The liturgically minded would like us to be persuaded that Confirmation fully initiates a person into the Christian community, but the existential question that is liable to experiential verification is: Does it do that, really? Unfortunately, neither they nor the catechetically minded (as I might term those who favor adolescent Confirmation) can adduce any evidence that this is always, or even frequently, the case. Orthodox Christians (who are chrismated in infancy) become non-participants in the church just as frequently as Catholics who are confirmed after making their First Communion.

The conclusion to be drawn from these reflections is that the ritual of Confirmation has no automatic effect such as fully initiating a person into the church, and it has no existential effect unless it actually signifies a real change in a person's life the way that being married or ordained does. To argue that Confirmation has a real effect on Christians when in fact it has no noticeable effect on their lives is to indulge in liturgical ideologizing that is far removed from the real world.

Notes

1. Austin Milner in *The Theology of Confirmation* (Notre Dame, Ind.: Fides, 1971) gives a good summary of the practices found in various regions during this period.
2. New York, N.Y.: Pueblo, 1988.
3. For this development, see Joseph Martos, *Doors to the Sacred,* 2nd ed. (Tarrytown N.Y.: Triumph Books, 1991), Chapter 7, Section 3.

At the time of this writing, Joseph Martos was associate professor of theology at Allentown College of St. Francis de Sales in Pennsylvania. He was the author of three books on the sacraments.

The Once and Future Dialogue: Christian-Jewish Relations at the Turning Point

Eugene Fisher and Leon Klenicki

1. Eugene Fisher: Dialogue's Detractors

A good friend and colleague, Rabbi A. James Rudin of the American Jewish Committee, is fond of startling his audiences with the statement that "Catholic-Jewish dialogue is the success story of the twentieth century." It is, in a sense, but perhaps only of the last **half** of the twentieth century, the first half being marked by the nadir of the two-thousand-year-old relationships, the Holocaust. It is, of course, the bottomless darkness of the *Shoah* that sets in such striking relief the otherwise small flickering light of what Christians and Jews have accomplished together since the Second Vatican Council.

One measure of a movement's success may be found in the strength of its detractors. Christian-Jewish dialogue has scores of them within both communities. One Jewish liberation theologian, for example, calls the dialogue "dead" because, presumably, insufficient numbers of its practitioners have been swayed to his own, personal brand of anti-Zionism. Conversely, one prominent official of a leading Zionist organization has condemned the dialogue for failing to uphold **his** political aims as its own. There is, one must acknowledge, an important place for both of these views **within** the dialogue—for both are necessary to a full understanding of the Jewish people's abiding relationship with the land and State of Israel. But neither view can properly be adopted by the dialogue, as, for example, a criterion for participation. Such a criterion would preclude the consideration of other legitimate Jewish viewpoints.

Within the organized religious Jewish community, likewise, there are those among the Orthodox who take a particularly strict interpretation of an almost three-decades-old article by Rabbi Joseph Soloveichik, which argued that while social cooperation with Christians is important for the common

---

This article appeared in PACE 22 (1993).

229

good, truly religious (or "theological") dialogue is impossible because faith is too "intimate" to share. This is not the place to debate the interpretation of Rabbi Soloveichik's pre-Vatican II reflections, save to say that we do not know what he would say today. When he wrote, there was no record of Jewish-Catholic dialogue—only the medieval disputations. So perhaps the time has come to review the matter or at least to interpret the Soloveichik dictum more widely, as it was originally understood, rather than more narrowly, as some in the Orthodox Jewish community would do today.

Among Christians, the internal debate over the nature and practice of dialogue is no less widespread. Many Christians of fundamentalist learning (whether Protestant or Catholic) tend to see dialogue with Jews as inevitably "watering down" the true faith, which should be about the business of saving Jews from the damnation they will no doubt undergo unless they accept Baptism. (For the record, Pope John Paul II has on numerous occasions pointed out that this is not a viable Catholic position.)

Conversely, other Christians of self-styled "radical" leanings can easily fall prey to the temptation to view dialogue with Jews as a pious distraction from the "real," which is to say, social, agenda. Still others see Christian-Jewish dialogue's trenchant "particularity" (e.g., its covenant issue) as a threat to achieving their vision of a truly "universal theology" of the world religions. The latter would see "the Jewish question" as, at best, a subset of interreligious relations in general.

This last Christian position of detraction against the particularity of the dialogue with God's people, Israel, may be just as dangerous as the ancient supersessionist-conversionist opinion of the fundamentalists. For, while fundamentalism put Scripture in a straitjacket of modern making (i.e., the "fundamental"), thus blocking the believer's direct access to the fullness of God's inspired word, the "super-universalists" simply bypass the proclamation of Scripture by rendering it functionally irrelevant. What does it mean to dialogue?

The detractors of dialogue have in general two things in common. The first is that, with some exceptions, their major proponents have had little actual involvement in the dialogue. The second is that they all measure the dialogue according to its potential to further their own *a priori* goals, whether political or religious. But dialogue, properly understood, cannot be a means to any end beyond itself. For, by definition, it is ordered to the deepening of the relationship of meaning, trust, and understanding between the parties in dialogue.

"Dialogue" does not mean two people or groups talking. The "dia" comes from the Greek root "to see through." That is, it is the *logos* that "speaks through" to the heart of the other. As Martin Buber said, dialogue exists in the "between."

One can use religious terms such as *repentance* and *reconciliation* to characterize a proper Christian attitude toward the dialogue. In dialogue, one attempts to present his or her faith as authentically and therefore as convincingly as possible. Dialogue will change the attitudes of each group toward the other, and therefore the attitudes of each toward itself—especially between Jews and Christians, so much of whose identity has been self-defined through the centuries over and against the other.

The point is not "conversion" of the other. Rather, dialogue increases our appreciation for the other precisely by enhancing our understanding of his or her essential otherness. In this way too we understand our own traditions nonpolemically and more profoundly.

While dialogue cannot as such seek any end other than its own (to increase mutual understanding and respect), communities which have been in dialogue can and should learn to act together decisively to achieve goals which are held independently but convergently by the two communities. These can be common social goals, but done now also for the sake of God's kingdom (in Hebrew, *malchuth shamayim)* and for the sake of perfecting the world (*tikkum olam*). Here, in such a process, the results of which are then brought back **into** the dialogue for mutual consideration, there may be discerned what our mystics term the divine "seeds" (Augustine) or "sparks" (the *Zohar),* the redemption of which is key to the redemption of the universe. That is one vision of the future of the dialogue.

But **first**, of course, we need much more dialogue on whether or not we Jews and Christians, after two millennia of mutually interdependent alienation, even mean the same thing anymore by the word *redemption.* Not only our divergent histories, but our essentially religious languages which reflect those histories need today to be reconciled through dialogue.

2. Leon Klenicki

The first and the twentieth centuries, nearly 2000 years ago and today, share something in common: Both are times marking a turning point in history and human spirituality.

The first century witnessed the unique religious phenomenon of the renewal of a tradition, Judaism, and the implementation of the God-people covenant relationship in new historical and social circumstances. It was a spiritual revolution inspired by the spirit of Jeremiah 31:31: God's promise of a renewed covenant and Israel adapting the word of God to its post-exilic national and spiritual experience. It was the beginning of Rabbinic Judaism that shaped Pharisaism, the rabbinic expounding of biblical thought and commandments into the realities of life.

The first century also witnessed the realization of a call: Jesus takes upon himself a vocation. It is his mission to bring humanity, or the humanity that lacks divine guidance, to God, to the discipline of a life oriented by divine law and word. Law, a word misunderstood by the Church Fathers, and commandments, in all their forms, became the faith commitment of both Rabbinic Judaism and early Christianity. Ironically, both faith communities went through history in a confrontation fostered by Christian rulers and religious leaders that hurt Judaism and the Jewish people up to modern times. Jews faced and still face in many respects the teaching of contempt, the denigration of Judaism that nurtured a social pagan anti-Semitism that culminated in the diabolic manifestation of the Holocaust.

But Christians and Jews are now facing a turning point in history. Together they are reaching the end of a century rich in scientific discoveries and equally rich in horror, the Holocaust, or the Gulag. Both faith communities are reckoning with the diabolic possibilities of the human being while searching for the presence of God in each other, the uniqueness of their creation in the Western world. Christians and Jews are encountering each other by facing God in new historical conditions.

This is a response to God's call beyond Christian-Jewish voluntary or forced alienation. It is a time of joint response to the evils of the world—to the scourge of racism and anti-Semitism, to our obligation to witness to God and the covenantal relationship daily in the community at large.

Dialogue in Action

To talk about a joint witnessing can easily become a comfortable expression of the tea-and-sympathy relationship, a moment in the dialogue, but not its goal and total meaning. Christian-Jewish witnessing of God's call means to minister together and continually to AIDS victims, to help people with jobs and not charity that merely solves temporary misery. It means to help to overcome the spiritual limitations of poverty in the West as well as in the developing nations.

A joint Christian-Jewish witnessing means to denounce and fight the corrupt leadership of countries that use donations to feed the people for their own purposes and political ambitions. Christians and Jews have to respond to social problems beyond a romanticism that in the long run has hurt the poor of the United States and of the world.

Christians and Jews need to help people to help themselves, as they do with their own children. Parents do not help sons and daughters in their late twenties as they did when they were adolescents. The same should apply to Christians and Jews caring for the less fortunate. Such concern entails a process of change in the hearts and social conditions of those who receive help and suffer economic limitations. It is a process that should take them from being receivers to becoming givers. Otherwise, Christians and Jews are triumphalistically continuing a sense of social infancy and fostering economic paternalism or maternalism.

The Need for Sharing Spirituality

The twentieth-century Christian-Jewish turning point entails a spiritual process of reckoning and a response.

The reckoning involves looking critically to the way both are presented in their educational systems, prayers, and preaching. Both Christians and Jews have to overcome the teaching of contempt. That teaching hurt their commitment and has painfully damaged Judaism for centuries. There is a need for a more accurate presentation by study, prayer, and silence, and the recognition of the Christian-Jewish mutuality.

Christians are obligated to explain New Testament texts that might project a sense of anti-Judaism at religious services and in preaching. This implies that implementation of ecclesiastical documents, both Catholic and Protestant, on Judaism and its presentation that still need to be part of the Christian liturgical and educational systems. The texts still need a cleansing or explanation of their anti-Jewish references.

Judaism needs to understand the meaning of Christianity beyond memories. Jews cannot remain mired in the memory of past pains. A Jewish understanding of Christianity after Auschwitz and Vatican II in a democratic society, and beyond theological disputations, is the beginning of a process of recognition, to recognize Christianity, to perceive it as a faith enacted in history, as a ray of God conveying to humanity an eternal message. It is a manifestation of God, with a mission and vocation to serve humanity. To recognize the vocation of Christianity to the world is not an invitation to conversion.

The recognition of Christianity entails the acceptance of "the other" in God, for God, and in a joint spiritual task of redemption. I make my own the words of Will Herberg in this respect,

Yes, each needs the other: Judaism needs Christianity, and Christianity needs Judaism. The vocation of both can be defined in common terms; to bear witness to the living God amidst the idolatries of the world. But, since the emergence of the Church, and through the emergence of the Church, this vocation has, as it were, been split in two parts. The Jew fulfills his vocation by "staying with God," "giving the world no rest so long as the world has not God"—to recall Jacques Maritain's unforgettable phrase. The Christian can fulfill his vocation only by "going out" to conquer the world for God. The Jew's vocation is to "stand," the Christian's to "go out"—both in the same cause of the kingdom of God. Judaism and Christianity thus represent one faith expressed in two religions—Judaism facing inward to the Jews, and Christianity facing outward to the gentiles, who, through it, are brought to God, and under the covenant, of Israel, and therefore cease to be gentiles in the proper sense of the term. This is the unity of Judaism and Christianity, and this is why a Jew is able to see and acknowledge Jesus in his uniqueness as the way to the Father.

The acceptance of "the other" as a person of God, the Christian as a partner in redemption, entails his or her acceptance as an equal in God and partner in God's design. The spirituality of mutuality is the beginning of spiritual healing, deeply needed by both ways—God and the world.

This is our turning point: Christians and Jews witnessing God in the world and sharing the uniqueness of their individual spiritualities.

At the time of this writing, Eugene J. Fisher was the Associate Director of the Secretariat for Ecumenical and Interreligious Affairs of the National Conference of Catholic Bishops, Washington, DC. Rabbi Leon Klenicki was the Director of the Department of Interfaith Affairs of the Anti-Defamation League of B'nai Brith, New York. He was also a co-liaison to the Vatican.

Gay and Lesbian People: A Forgotten Compassion and Justice

Jeannine Gramick, SSND

In a catechism class he was teaching several years ago, Michael Maher, a youth minister, handed out an article on gay bashing for later discussion. To his surprise, the Confirmation students questioned why such an article would be talked about in a morality class.

But Maher should not have been surprised. More than one-third of Catholic teenage boys believe that physical violence against gay and lesbian people is acceptable. About one-half of them do not believe that homosexual persons deserve respect, friendship, or justice.

The attitudes of Catholic teenage girls are slightly less negative. About one-half of the females, as compared to four-fifths of the males, feel that derogatory terms and jokes about homosexual people are acceptable. About 25 percent of the females and 60 percent of the males do not believe the Church should treat lesbian and gay persons with understanding.

These are the results that Michael Maher found in 1990 when he conducted a survey with 123 of those Confirmation candidates from six Kansas City-area parishes. He decided to do the survey after the unexpected reaction to the gay-bashing article. The high-schoolers were asked whether they agreed or disagreed with a number of statements paraphrased from Vatican and U.S. Catholic bishops' teachings. The statements centered around human rights for gay and lesbian people and the Church's responsibility to minister to them. The youth were not informed that the statements were drawn from Church teachings.

Among other findings were the following: Almost half of the group thought Catholic leaders should not speak out against derogatory terms, jokes, and physical violence toward gay and lesbian people. Almost 90 percent of the group did not believe that the Church should offer special programs for lesbian and gay people.

Although it would be scientifically inappropriate to generalize from regional data which do not represent a random sample, my experience in

This article appeared in PACE 23 (1993).

lesbian and gay ministry since 1971 and my contact with students from grade-school to university levels confirm the fact that most Catholic students are afraid or ignorant of gay and lesbian issues. In particular, they are unaware of the Church's principles of justice and compassion toward homosexual persons.

More to the Church's Teaching

The usual response to the question, "What does the Church say about homosexuality?" is "The Church condemns it." It is true that one reason why the Church officially teaches that homogenital activity is morally wrong is that no possibility of procreation exists in same-sex relationships. But there is far more to the Church's teaching on homosexuality than the mere prohibition against homogenital acts. Unfortunately, this one judgment has been used by many who call themselves Christian to justify brutalizing gay and lesbian people physically, spiritually, and emotionally.

In 1984 two Catholic high-school boys were involved in what Washington, DC, police described as one of the most brutal anti-homosexual attacks in the city's history. In a densely wooded park, the students robbed, repeatedly beat, and slashed another youth, and threatened to emasculate and kill him. In court proceedings, the prosecuting attorney cited "hatred for homosexuals" as a motive for the students' attack. The boys defended themselves by claiming that they were taught that homosexuality was "unnatural" and "displeasing to God." Their actions, they alleged, followed from their instruction.

It is vital that religious educators working in parishes and school settings make clear that the Church's position on homogenital acts is only one part of the whole body of teaching on homosexuality; this part of the teaching should not be abused to justify or condone prejudice or hatred. If the four other areas of the Church's teaching are presented as a whole, such justification would not be possible. The five areas are contained in rudimentary form in the U.S. bishops' 1976 pastoral letter on moral values and have been amplified in later Church documents. In addition to the position on homogenital activity, the four other areas include homosexual orientation, pastoral ministry, human and civil rights, and prejudice against gay and lesbian people.

Homosexual Orientation

Religious educators need a basic understanding that a homosexual orientation means erotic or romantic feelings of attraction or desire toward someone of one's own gender. Too often people interpret the word *homosexuality* to mean homogenital acts, instead of a personal sexual orientation. For example, when arguments are scrutinized in the current public debate about gays in the military, we see that often people are objecting to homosexual behavior. There are already military regulations to prohibit certain kinds of sexual behavior. The real question in this debate hinges on excluding people because of who they are: their homosexual identity.

Various Church leaders have judged a homosexual orientation in different ways. Some bishops, such as Cardinals James Hickey and Joseph Bernardin, in public letters on homosexuality in the mid-80s, characterized a homosexual orientation as being "not morally wrong in and of itself." Equivalently, other bishops, such as those from Massachusetts (1984), said that the orientation is "morally neutral."

Although the Vatican basically agrees with this moral evaluation of the orientation, the Congregation for the Doctrine of the Faith placed a negative judgment on the orientation in 1986 by calling it "an objective disorder." The word *disorder* is usually understood in a psychological sense on the popular level. Consequently, bishops, theologians, pastoral workers, and gay and lesbian people themselves criticized this description because it failed to take into account current scientific knowledge about homosexuality. Since the early 70s, psychiatry and psychology have viewed homosexuality as an alternative form of sexuality. The Vatican did not explain what it meant by the term *disorder.* Archbishop John Quinn of San Francisco tried to mollify the hurt and anger caused by this new judgment by explaining that the Vatican used philosophical, not moral or psychological, language.

It may be confusing to students and young people to elaborate on the disagreements in tone, language, and approach between the Vatican and the U.S. theological and episcopal communities, but the pastoral minister and teacher need to be aware of the differences. The Vatican's approach to homosexual persons has generally been more harsh than that from leaders on this side of the Atlantic. The U.S. bishops are attempting a delicate balancing act in wanting to demonstrate to lesbian and gay Catholics a sense of care and compassion, while at the same time trying to maintain loyalty to Roman expectations. The message to impart to students, which is accepted by the Vatican and the U.S. Church, is that "such orientation in itself, because not freely chosen, is not sinful" *(Human Sexuality 55).*

Pastoral Ministry

The Church states that the entire "Christian community should offer a special degree of pastoral understanding and care" *(To Live in Christ Jesus,* no. 52). Any effective pastoral ministry must be based on the principle that lesbian and gay persons are children of God and full members of the Church who gift the community by their lives. Jesus' words and actions invite us to remove hatred, an unforgiving heart, judgmentalism, and an elitist attitude which would exclude or ostracize any group of people. Societal pressures on gay and lesbian people have forced them to hide or deny their sexual identity, often resulting in low levels of self-worth or even suicidal feelings.

To be gospel-based, our pastoral counseling must enhance a lesbian or gay person's sense of dignity and self-esteem.

Pastoral ministry includes families who have a homosexual daughter or son, spouse or parent, brother or sister. Because people are often healed by relating to a group of peers, the Church advocates support groups in addition to individual ministry. Various models of ministry are described in a comprehensive pastoral plan entitled "Ministry and Homosexuality in the Archdiocese of San Francisco." The "Pastoral Guidelines for Ministry to Homosexuals in the Diocese of San Jose" is also an excellent resource.

Civil and Human Rights

Civil rights for lesbian and gay people have received much public attention since President Clinton's first week in office with his proposal to end the ban on gays in the military. In 1976 and again in 1990, the U.S. bishops stated that gay and lesbian people should be accorded basic human rights. Even the Vatican in 1986 noted that the intrinsic dignity of homosexual people "must always be respected in word, in action, and in law" *(Letter . . . Pastoral Care,* par. 10). The image of God in each and every human being is the foundation of Catholic social teaching on human dignity.

However, in 1992, the Vatican issued a memorandum claiming that there were certain situations, such as teaching, athletic coaching, adoptive parenting, and military recruitment, in which civil rights could be denied. Some U.S. bishops, such as Archbishops Rembert Weakland and Thomas Murphy, and Bishops Matthew Clark and Kendrick Williams, diplomatically attempted to soften the Vatican's statement. Archbishop John Quinn and Cardinal Joseph Bernardin both publicly stated that the policies in their archdioceses will continue to affirm and defend the human and civil rights of gay and lesbian persons.

In a signature advertisement in the *National Catholic Reporter* on November 13, 1992, Bishops Walter Sullivan, Thomas Gumbleton, and Charles Buswell disagreed with the Vatican outright and claimed that there were several misconceptions on which the Vatican statement was based. Bishop Thomas Gumbleton of Detroit said flatly, "I cannot in good conscience accept the statement as consistent with the Gospel, nor can I justify implementing it" (28 July 1992). Once again, there does not seem to be a unified Vatican and U.S. position regarding this area of Church teaching.

Prejudice and Homophobia

However, there is agreement regarding the need to eradicate homophobia and prejudice against lesbian and gay persons. Some bishops believe that prejudice against lesbian and gay persons is a greater infringement of the Christian moral norm than is homosexual activity (Washington State CC). The entire body of U.S. bishops has called on all Christians and citizens of good will to "confront their own fears about homosexuality and to curb the humor and discrimination that offend homosexual persons" *(Human sexuality 55).* The Vatican has stated that "it is deplorable that homosexual persons have been and are the object of violent malice in speech and action. Such treatment deserves condemnation . . . wherever it occurs" *(Letter . . . Pastoral Care,* par. 10).

It is this last area of Church teaching which priests, youth ministers, pastoral workers, and educators need to stress. Most of our students know that the Church has traditionally condemned homogenital behavior, but how many are aware that the Church condemns violence, hostility, and prejudice toward gay and lesbian people? It is imperative that teachers and religious educators try to convey this significant part of the Church's teaching on homosexuality: the moral evil of homosexual prejudice. If we waged a forceful campaign for eradicating homophobia, then gay bashing, such as occurred in Washington, DC, and teen suicides due to homosexual identity would be dramatically reduced.

Peer Pressure

Merely knowing the Church's teaching may not be sufficient to effect Christian behavior among young people toward those who are lesbian or gay. As much as I would hope otherwise, I am not sure that many students care what the Church teaches. Of course, this does not mean that the religious educator should not present this teaching and the Gospel imperative of respect for the individual on which the teaching is based. What the young do care about is what their peers think of them. They are more influenced by their peers than by adults or adult institutions. This fact was brought home to me many years ago when a woman religious invited me to address her sixth-grade class about homosexuality.

I began the class with some elementary education about what it means to be homosexually oriented. "Sexual feeling, not sexual behavior, are the clues we need to figure out our sexual orientation," I said. "No amount of sexual experimentation will help you figure out if you're gay or straight. It depends on the inside of you, not the outside, the feelings of love you have, not what you do with parts of your body," I continued. I saw that I had the students with me.

On the blackboard, I drew a line, representing the Kinsey scale, and marked seven points on it, from 0 to 6. I explained, "People in category 0 are sexually attracted to the opposite gender exclusively. The sexual attractions of people in category 6 are toward their own gender. People in the categories between the extremes feel various degrees of homosexual attraction, from slight to very strong. Probably most of us felt some homosexual feelings."

As it dawned on the students that sexual attractions toward friends of their own gender did not necessarily mean that they were gay or lesbian, I could hear an audible sigh of relief in the class. They needed to hear that the homosexual feelings they experienced were quite normal and natural. One of the deepest fears of the young is to be on the outside, displaced from the majority, isolated on the fringe. Their sense of security requires peer approval.

It seems that many of those sixth graders I met that day had experienced homosexual feelings. Knowing that their friends would not think them "queer" was a great comfort. Indeed, realizing that their friends were probably also feeling same-sex desires led them to see that labels such as "fag" and "queer" were meaningless. When they understood that these feelings were natural, they were no longer afraid of them and were willing to reevaluate their judgment about lesbian and gay people.

Only after conveying some information from psychology and sociology should the religious educator introduce the faith dimension and the teachings of the Church. Heterosexual and homosexual feelings are gifts of God which invite our wonder, respect, and gratitude. While most people probably experience some homosexual feelings, only a minority experience these feelings in a predominant way. The central message of the Gospel regarding how we should treat any minority with respect and dignity is the starting point of the faith conversation and the teaching of the Church. Our task is to call our youth to justice and compassion for a forgotten minority in the Church.

References and Suggested Readings

Congregation for the Doctrine of the Faith. *Letter to the Bishops of the Catholic Church on the Pastoral Care of Homosexual Persons.* Rome (1 October 1986).

National Conference of Catholic Bishops. *Human Sexuality: A Catholic Perspective for Education and Lifelong Learning.* Washington, DC: United States Catholic Conference, 1991.

_____. *To Live in Christ Jesus.* Washington, DC: United States Catholic Conference, 1976.

Nugent, R., and J. Gramick. *Building Bridges: Gay and Lesbian Reality and the Catholic Church.* Mystic, CT: Twenty-Third Publications, 1992.

Pfeifer, Bishop Michael. "Thoughts of Freedom, Conscience and Obedience," *Origins* (13 November 1986), 16 (22).

Washington State Catholic Conference. *Prejudice Against Homosexuals and the Ministry of the Church.* Seattle, WA, 1983.

At the time of this writing, Jeannine Gramick, SSND, was the co-founder of New Ways Ministry and co-author, with Robert Nugent, of *Building Bridges: Gay and Lesbian Reality and the Catholic Church* (Twenty-Third).

Marian Spirituality and the Psychology of Carol Gilligan

Barbara Cortese

For centuries we have held Mary, the girl who said yes to God, as a model. The work of Carol Gilligan, the psychologist at the Harvard School of Education who has studied the development of women, suggests how that Marian quality is thwarted in young girls and invites us to help them retain it.

Intimations of Immortality

Religion is a search for the meaning of life, and nowhere does the conviction that there is a design for our lives find better expression than in Psalm 139:13–14, 16.

> *For it was you who formed my inward parts;*
> *you knit me together in my mother's womb.*
> *I praise you for I am fearfully and wonderfully made. . . .*
> *Your eyes beheld my unformed substance.*
> *In your book were written all the days that were formed for me,*
> *when none of them as yet existed.*

The psalm expresses a belief not that we are predestined to a specific course of action but rather that we have each been uniquely designed to God's purposes. We understand this unique design as a vocation when we read in Isaiah 43:1, "I have called you by name." When the Blessed Julian of Norwich hears God say, "I make you to want what I want," and St. Ignatius asks, "What is your heart's desire?"—the implication is that God calls us to this vocation through the very nature of our individuality.

Coupled with this belief that we are uniquely designed to God's purposes is the belief that children are pleasing to God in a way that adults are not. The synoptic Gospels tell us that we must be like children, that the kingdom of God belongs to children, and that we must accept the kingdom as a child does or we cannot enter it (see Matthew 18:1–5, Mark 9:33–37, and Luke 18:15–17). What is the special quality that children have, that adults

---

This article appeared in PACE 23 (1994).

have lost and must recover? The context of the passages in Mark and Matthew indicate that it is humility, though it is often discussed in terms of the child's trust and dependency on God. I would like to suggest that the quality is children's ability to remain close to God's design for them.

This ability is associated with Catholic teaching on the Immaculate Conception, the belief that Mary was conceived free of original sin. Rosemary Radford Ruether, the feminist theologian, has provided an apt description of how the Marian doctrine is related to a belief in human nature that is consonant with Psalm 139:

> *The nominalists believed that the image of God was still intact in every human being. That image was the basis on which one could independently respond to God's grace. The doctrine of the Immaculate Conception provided this late medieval theology with a model of the original or unfallen state and of the natural goodness of humanity. This natural state is the image of God in every person and is the ground of redeeming grace. Mary, who never lost this state of created goodness, is the representative of "pure nature," the capacity within created nature for perfection (Radford Ruether 68).*

Ruether goes so far as to say that Mariology was criticized by the Protestant Reformation precisely because of this "exalted view of humanity." Think of a continuum that has, on one end, the Calvinist view of original sin as so pervasive that humanity is depraved—and, on the other end, the Jewish view that there is no original sin, we are simply born with good and evil inclinations which must be balanced. The Catholic view of human nature falls somewhere in the middle: We are born with original sin, but also made in the image of God and able to respond to God's grace.

Several branches of human learning indicate that this innate quality— the image of God within us, the unique design of Psalm 139—remains but is buried somewhere deep inside. The philosopher says, "To thine own self be true." A poet sings, "The child is father of the man," and psychologists talk of "the child within." What happens to this quality between childhood and adulthood that Jesus must tell us to become like children again?

In a Different Voice

I think that when Carol Gilligan says girls "go underground" at age eleven, she is accurately describing how girls lose the quality grown women must recapture. In her first book, *In a Different Voice,* Gilligan explains that because girls do not have to separate from their mothers to establish gender identity, they experience relationships as continuing. They value connectedness and develop a sense of justice that involves meeting the needs of all in order to maintain relationships. Boys, on the other hand, must separate to establish gender identity with their fathers, a process that requires autonomy and individuation. Consequently, they go on to develop relationships based on systems of rights and rules that balance the need for independence against the need for fairness.

According to Gilligan, girls go underground at about age eleven when they first realize that their values and mode of thinking are not appreciated by the surrounding culture, a culture that upholds the values of autonomy and of justice by rights and rules. Because their inner mode of thinking differs from societal expectations, girls become more and more unsure of themselves and experience increasing difficulty in formulating and expressing value judgments. At this point, they relegate their values to the personal sphere and abide by rights and rules in the public sphere.

Annunciation Spirituality

What has the work of Carol Gilligan to do with Mary of Nazareth? I would like to suggest that every girl on the verge of adolescence is like Mary just before the Angel Gabriel appeared to her. By analogy to Mary who was, via the Immaculate Conception, without sin, the girl who has not yet gone underground still bears the image of God on her soul, as described by the medieval theologians. For if, as Psalm 139 implies, we are each uniquely designed to God's purposes, the girl who has not yet gone underground is, like Mary, full of grace—that is, predisposed by her own personality to say yes to God. Poised on the brink of adolescence, a time of self-awareness, she is about to receive her vocation.

If the girl has gone underground, the image of God, of course, remains in her soul, but, we would describe it in biblical terms as a light hidden under a basket (Matthew 5:15). For if the girl has relegated her values to the personal, rather than public, sphere of her life, she cannot respond fully to the inner voice, cannot give a resounding yes to God. In these terms, Mary remained always like a young girl, Mary Ever Virgin in the metaphoric sense. For Mary's yes (the yes that enabled the Incarnation) was not that of a girl who had gone underground. Her yes was spoken with the authority of a girl who could still hear the inner voice. That is why Luke has Elizabeth say to Mary, "Blessed are you who believed that what was spoken to you by the Lord would be fulfilled" (Luke 1:45).

Making Connections

If young girls are indeed like Mary at the time of the Annunciation, what is our part—as parents, teachers, coaches, counselors, ministers—in enabling them to remain so? What will help our girls stay in contact with that inner voice, remain faithful to the unique design of Psalm 139?

In her second book, *Making Connections,* Gilligan deals with this question, although she formulates it another way:

243

It is not at all clear what it means to be a good mother or a good teacher to an adolescent girl coming of age in Western culture. The choices that women make in order to survive or to appear good in the eyes of others (and thus sustain their protection) are often at the expense of women's relationships with one another, and girls begin to observe and comment on these choices around the age of eleven or twelve (page 26).

This formulation looks cryptic until we understand what the book defines as the two problems girls face in adolescence.

The first problem is how to maintain relationships in the face of disagreements or differences. Gilligan explains that girls see only two solutions: either in being selfless (the good woman), denying their own needs and opinions, or in being selfish (the bad woman), denying others' needs and opinions. This problem is resolved when the concept of fairness is extended to include both self and others. The second problem arises when girls observe others denying that difficulties even exist in relationships (especially in women's relationships to men). It is this that leads girls to question their sense of reality, to doubt their senses, their own experience and knowledge. The resolution comes with learning to trust one's intuitive knowledge.

Finally, Gilligan says that when girls go underground they will only speak about what really concerns them when they feel that someone will **listen** and **not leave** in the face of disagreement. Listening is important because girls' sense of justice involves a response to the needs of everyone involved. Not leaving is important because girls value maintaining relationships more than autonomy or independence.

The most heartening part of *Making Connections* is the response of the teachers at Emma Willard School (where the girls were interviewed) and their comments on how they would change their teaching methods in response to the study. They were open to the findings of the study, reacted in terms of their own comparable experiences, and redefined their work in terms of the girls' values and learning styles: In short, they affirmed their students.

Here are some examples from the teachers' reflections in the closing chapter of the book (pages 286–313). One teacher who had revered scholars and acted as an authority for her students determined instead to explore the relationships in literature as an equal with her classes. Another, a math teacher who remembered she came to love her subject because it was something she shared with a beloved grandmother, decided to make mathematics more fun for her students. Several teachers realized they had separated their personal and intellectual lives, using the caring/response mode of thinking in one and the independence/rules mode in the other. They came to understand this as an unnecessary, unhealthy dichotomy in their lives, one they did not want to model for the girls in school.

244

Visitation Spirituality

Has the psychologist touched the lodestone? Will these teachers be Miss Temple to Jane Eyre, Marmee to Jo in *Little Women?* Will Carol Gilligan's work help us be Elizabeth to the Mary in our girls? For the Visitation is another example of Marian spirituality that can be understood in terms of women's psychology.

It is such an understatement to say that the Visitation is an example of Mary's selflessness, that she put aside her own concerns to go and help her kinswoman Elizabeth. This understanding is an example of how selflessness is equated with goodness for women. Not only does it ignore the historical probability that Mary went to Elizabeth for shelter, but, more importantly, it diminishes the most beautiful aspect of women's relationships, the mutual support they bring to each other.

Would Mary have gone to Elizabeth with the story of the angel and her inexplicable pregnancy if she had not perceived in Elizabeth a person who shared her values, a person who might believe her? The details in Luke's story tell us how Elizabeth was open to Mary's understanding of her situation. When Mary entered her door, Elizabeth was filled with the Holy Spirit, meaning she responded to Mary's presence from her own spirituality. The child in Elizabeth's womb jumped for joy! We recognize these experiences: When the expectant mother is excited, the baby kicks, and, the mentor is the person who is happy to see the young person, who enjoys her.

Then Elizabeth, drawing on her own comparable experience, her own expectations for her pregnancy with a holy child, recognizes the Holy One in Mary: "And how does it happen to me, that the mother of my Lord should come to me?" (Luke 1:43). It is from our own holiness, idealism, values that we recognize these traits, graces, in others. Finally, Elizabeth affirms Mary's spirituality when she says Mary is blessed because she believed what God had told her. Mary did not deny, trivialize, or keep to her private thoughts the words of the angel; instead she believed, accepted, and shared them with others.

Magnificat

If we believe that we must become again like children, if we have ever felt the loss of our own inner voice, if we have hope that the next generation can remain faithful to God's design within them, then we can think of our girls as Mary and be ourselves like Elizabeth, teaching and parenting from our own spirituality. It could just be that Carol Gilligan, in describing how girls go underground, has given us a very human understanding of how to help them retain the childlike quality Jesus says we must recapture. If we affirm our girls' values, they may be able to express that inner voice, the image of God within, and say like Mary, "My soul magnifies the Lord" (Luke 1:47).

References

Gilligan, Carol. *In a Different Voice*. Cambridge, MA: Harvard University Press, 1982.

_____. *Making Connections*. Cambridge, MA: Harvard University Press, 1990.

Radford Ruether, Rosemary. *Mary—The Feminine Face of the Church*. Philadelphia: Westminster Press, 1977.

At the time of this writing, Barbara M. Cortese was a senior administrative analyst at the University of California and a catechist at St. Jerome Parish in El Cerrito.

Strategies

Family Rites: Doin' What Comes Naturally

Gerard A. Pottebaum

Family rituals have always presented a struggle for us. I mean the kind of ritual that embraces some explicit religious statement. Even the popular advent wreath, with the accompanying readings at dinner time, doesn't amount to more than a new centerpiece for the table. And we never did catch onto the "cooking for Christ" dietary practices. The effort continues for us to do something more than give our family the appearances of being Christian by following certain popular religious practices. Let me share my reflections with you, with the intention of encouraging you to follow your instincts. I don't intend to give any formula for success in becoming a "Christian family." Nor do I pretend to describe a model, drawn from our family's experience. Heaven forbid! Not only would heaven forbid, so would our kids.

I do intend one main point: Do what comes naturally. Translated, this means that the same family isn't the same family for very long. We used to have four little children. Now one of those sweet little things is halfway through college, and the others can't wait to move on to bigger and better things. They like it here, and they don't. They used not to think of not liking it here. And we used to think that if they didn't like living together, something was wrong. We know now if something is wrong: That's when they like it here too much.

What does this have to do with family ritual-making? The experience of the family changing, of children moving on, is the main root which nourishes the most profound family rituals. The most obvious example that illustrates this evolution is the bedtime behavior.

When the child is very young, certain ritual patterns take shape. We consider ourselves religious if we pray with the child, and that can be a good thing to do. Equally important to the child is whether or not Winnie the Pooh, or whatever the favorite nighttime cuddly might be, is in bed where he is supposed to be. Also, one of the parents has to pull up the blanket in a certain way, touch or kiss the child in a certain way, each with the kind of

---

This article appeared in PACE 7 (1976).

sameness from night to night that says to the child, "God' in his heaven, and everything's all right."

As the child changes, the ritual pattern shifts. Soon you don't have to pull up the blanket. Translation: "I'm big enough to do that myself." Next Winnie the Pooh goes. Eventually, if you prayed with the child, you begin to feel the need for more grown-up prayers. You know because you suddenly find that you're the only one saying those childish things, and your child is really only tolerating you. So you pray only occasionally, and at other times advise the child that he's old enough to say his own prayers, alone. Meanwhile, you cling to one or the other nighttime ritual, even though by now the child won't let you in the bedroom; at least you say, "Goodnight. Sleep well." or a similar greeting. Sometimes you go beyond the bound and try a kiss or a tuck of the blanket to remind the child that he or she is still your child. The ritual now begins to work a reverse effect.

Before, as the child was growing up, the ritual served to draw you together. It provided a sense of security and peace to the child and to you. But after a certain age, the child finds the ritual an expression unworthy of who he or she is. The same ritual now generates a desire within the child to move on. "I'm grown up now," the child is saying as these rituals change. "The more you try to make me do those things, the more I want to get out."

Such rituals are a graceful way for parents to tell their children that they love them and for their children to acknowledge that love, without fear of hurting them by leaving their nest. This kind of communication happens automatically, not because someone taught us some ritual formula to follow, nor because it was imposed from an authority on high. Family rituals grow out of the sacred character of ordinary experience. As people in the family grow and change, so do the rituals. If the rituals don't change, then the meaning and the interpretation change.

Family ritual is not something families do to make their home seem like church. After almost twenty-five years of family life, we've finally seen that each family is not a little church. One of the struggles has been with the notion that the only rituals that "work" are the ones prescribed by the Church. After all these years, we know now that ritual is not something we do in order to make God do something that he otherwise wouldn't consider. Quite the contrary, we realize that in ritual we make tangible in symbol, gesture, and word what we have come to discover is God already having acted in our lives. Now we struggle to enrich our sensitivities to the sacred character of ordinary experience, so that we can articulate this awareness in ritual.

One of the experiences we have come to enjoy as being "religious" in this sense concerns attending to the plants and shrubs in the yard. Three of the evergreen trees were once used as our Christmas trees when the children were very young. Another tree comes from the seeds of a persimmon tree which grows on our children's grandparents' farm. Visiting the "parent" tree every Thanksgiving became an annual pilgrimage. The children were allowed to take the walk of about two miles across the fields and into the woods only if they walked the entire distance themselves. So the journey became a sign of growing up.

The visit to the persimmon tree included eating whatever persimmons still remained, as most were gone or eaten by birds by Thanksgiving. Every year the children would listen to the stories their father would tell about enjoying the persimmons from the same tree when he was growing up. And every year he would tell how eating a persimmon teaches a lesson about sharing and entering the life of another person. Persimmons when ripe have a very tender skin. Inside one finds soft sweet meat surrounding a carousel arrangement of seeds. If you bite into the skin too hard, the skin will pucker up your mouth so thoroughly that you won't be able to enjoy the sweet fruit. But if you open the fruit with care, you'll be richly rewarded. The same holds for people. If you move in on another's life without care, you may find yourself unable to enjoy the flavor there because you are too careless. If you do enter with care, you're in for a treat. Also, people, like persimmons, aren't really any good until almost rotten. Those who don't know would ordinarily throw them out.

A few years ago we decided to try raising a persimmon tree from the seeds of a persimmon that we ate. We now have a tree about three feet tall growing in our yard, some three hundred miles from the original. When we attend to it, we are attending as well to the pilgrimage of our lives which we share. When we check to see that the tree is doing all right, especially in the spring when new growth starts to show, we enjoy a sense that our life pilgrimage is doing all right. And we imagine the day when this tree will share its fruit with us, when our pilgrimage ends.

No one could have planned such a family symbol or ritual pilgrimage to a persimmon tree, of all things. Nor does anyone who notices the twig of a tree sticking up in our yard realize how much life that twig expresses. God expresses his presence in the strangest ways. He has many names. The people of old called him their Rock. Others spoke of the Lord as their Shepherd. Then there's a few of us who have discovered that he's also a persimmon tree.

As one begins to appreciate the ritual character of ordinary experience, one senses a tension between one's sensitivities for natural rites and one's experience of church-related rites. In our early family life, we translated the Church's symbol system for use at home. We judged the quality of our family's religious experience in terms of whether we remembered to burn the children's baptismal candles on their birthdays or whether we wore the little baptismal stoles that we made and decorated with our saints' symbols. We decorated the house with banners carrying various messages appropriate to the season. We brought unconsecrated hosts home for the child we were preparing for First Communion, so that she would not be distracted from the real presence of Christ by the strange taste and texture of the host. Such efforts to integrate this symbol system with our lives evolved into a reversed effort to bring our symbols and gestures from life into church, whenever that was possible and acceptable to the larger community.

Rather than help our children become accustomed to the experience of receiving a host, we encouraged them to recognize the significance of ordinary bread. Rather than worry about how long we could make each child's baptismal candle last, we discovered that birthday cake candles made a better statement of the life we celebrate, without the churchy overtones. We don't decorate the house with message-banners anymore. We now find them preachy and find ourselves chuckling when we uncover one of them in the closet. We can enjoy now just the texture and pattern of a fine fabric or tapestry. A set of photographs of the sea, the beach, rock formations, sunrises, sand oats, and vases of roses or dried weeks with intricate seed pods prompt moments of meditation, memories, and wonder.

Through all of these growing pains over the years, we've never had the problem many parents anguish over: How do you make your children go to church? That has never been one of our standards for "success," whatever "success" means when applied to personal growth of children. Two of our children are eighteen and older. They both continue to choose to participate in weekly services. Judging from the quality of the celebrations, one wonders whether or not we've "failed" because they seem able to participate without a great deal of criticism. Somehow, underneath it all, I'm hoping that they feel that we have the right to hear the Gospel preached. Even though the preaching we hear is often foreign to the Gospel, our attendance gives witness to what we presume to be the reason for our gathering: to hear God's Word and to celebrate his life with us. I'm hoping, too, that our children will not limit their perception of ritual and religious experience to what happens in church. I'm hoping they'll find in all of life expressions of praise in spite of the pain.

An appropriate summary to these reflections comes from Edward Schillebeeckx in his book *God: The Future of Man.* It may also help in your own wonderings about your family's life of worship:

> *Jesus did not give his life in a liturgical solemnity. On the contrary, in an obviously secular conflict, colored though it was by religion, he remained faithful to God and to men and gave his life for his own in a secular combination of circumstances. Calvary was not a church liturgy, but an hour of human life, which Jesus experienced as worship. In it, our redemption is to be found. We have not been redeemed by an act of pure worship, a liturgical service. Our redemption was accomplished by an act which was part of Jesus' human life, situated in history and in the world.*

"For the one of whom these things are spoken (i.e., our Lord) belonged to another tribe, from which no one ever served at the altar" (Heb. 7:13). It is possible to speak of a secular liturgy, since the author of the letter to the Hebrews applied to Jesus' self-sacrifice in the world the cultic categories of Jewish religion under the old law, thus endowing it with their sacred character. In this way the new concept of worship came into being—human life itself experienced as a liturgy or as worship of God.

The New Testament clearly lays stress on "secular worship" because the dawn of the eschatological life came with Christ. "And I saw no temple in the city, for its temple is the Lord God the Almighty and the Lamb" (Apoc. 21:22). The profane or secular can become the pure expression of mankind's peace with God, as was fully apparent in the human life of Jesus. That is why, for about three centuries, the first generations of Christians were proud of the fact that they had no churches or altars—one of the reasons why the pagans called them "atheists" or godless people.

Can we not take from the way Jesus related to his life in those times an example of the way we might relate to our life today? Faith in Jesus intensifies our human solidarity, as this faith calls for a belief in secular life as worth living. One does not enter a separate "Church reality" in order to be filled with the Spirit of Jesus. Rather by way of the ritual character of human experience, one penetrates the human experience, one penetrates the human spirit to enjoy therein a metamorphosis with the Spirit of God.

At the time of this writing, Gerard A. Pottebaum was a founder of The Tree House in Kettering, Ohio, an education consulting service and idea center for editorial, graphic arts, and environmental design talent.

The Sabbath, or Don't We Have Time?

Mary Margaret Funk

The first law of the Church reads: To keep holy the day of the Lord's resurrection; to worship God by participating in Mass every Sunday and holy day of obligation; to avoid those activities that would hinder renewal of soul and body on the Sabbath (e.g., needless work and business activities, unnecessary shopping, etc.). So, I proposed that the diocesan office not initiate any meetings for business purposes on Sunday. With agreements to disagree, it got through the staff and on to the policy makers. The motion was defeated unanimously. Is the attitude proposed in this decision related to the fact that Directors of Religious Education are liable to early burnout—even the ones that have a well-defined job description, an agreeable contract, and a supportive parish team with whom to collaborate?

Perhaps we have forgotten our tradition of observing the Sabbath. Sunday, the Day of the Lord, the Christian Sabbath, is an opportunity to celebrate, to be, to laugh, and to pray. It is sacred time, not a time to be productive, but to marvel at the works of our hands. Sunday is the single day reserved for us to be flexible for friends, longer meals, games, and liturgy. It is not just a moment to catch our breath or to rest, as it were, to make up for all the energy expended during the week; the Sabbath is an opportunity to bask in *menuha,* according to Abraham Heschel.[1] It is not a negative concept, but something real and intrinsically positive. It took a special act to create it, and the universe would be incomplete without it (p. 23). By not observing it, we are failing to participate in the "good life." It is a gift to us and sanctioned by thousands of years of tradition. It is an opportunity for peace, tranquility, and at-homeness with ourselves and others. Why do we in our culture reject it and continually make Sunday mundane?

Why do tradition-givers especially not accept this tradition? Barth pointed out that humans were created on the sixth day and the Sabbath was the seventh. Therefore, man and woman's very first day was the Sabbath. We, then, ought to consider the Sabbath the first day, not the reward at the end of a week of toil.

This article appeared in PACE 11 (1980).

But how can DREs not work on Sunday? With our elaborate programs and multi-dimensional sessions for various age groups, Sunday becomes parish day and is a "work" day for the professional catechist or liturgist. But the essence of the tradition still holds firm. Moslem, Jewish, and Christian traditions celebrate Friday, Saturday, or Sunday, and the same kind of time is celebrated. The DRE simply must take another full day, sunset to sunset, for the Lord. He/she must also reflect on the kind of programming offered for the parish on the Christian Sabbath and see to it that it reflects the character of celebration, leisure, study/reflection, and flexible time for others.

The Sabbath is not the same as the professional's day off. A day off is for maintenance. It is a day to catch up on errands and other kinds of work besides one's profession. The Sabbath, if one is to be true to the tradition, is a special kind of time. It is not a day to change things. "Things do not change on that day. There is only a difference in the dimension of time, in the relation of the universe to God. The Sabbath preceded creation and the Sabbath completed creation; it is all of the spirit that the world can bear" (p. 21).

Perhaps we neglect the Sabbath because we can't bear the holy for a complete day. The unreflected life is not worth living, said Socrates, but to live a reflective life requires a rigorous discipline of integrity. It means living a life of vulnerability of unfinished agenda on the inside and continuous bombardment of needy persons challenging one to openness and listening.

Surveys have indicated that the senior officers of major North American corporations spend up to eighty percent of their working time having discussions, either at meetings, in face-to-face conversations, or over the telephone. Assuming that they listen more than they talk—and good executives usually do—listening to other people accounts for about half of their business day. The minister who is in the business of caring for people would need to listen seventy-five percent of his/her day. But listening is an art to be cultivated. It seems reasonable, therefore, to suggest that if a minister took time to listen to beauty, time for others around him/her, and time to share celebration for one whole day every week, a more caring minister would result.

If DREs are to be tradition keepers as well as tradition givers, then observing the Sabbath is a must. So, I offer the following reasons, in ascending order, paralleling Kohlberg's moral development stages. Each stage would require a specific mode of observance. Some stages seem to contradict the others but—as the theory goes—growth is not logical but psychological. Most DREs don't act out all these stages sequentially but these *reasons* do provide a framework.

1. To observe Sunday is a law of the Church. Not to do so is to disobey and, in some measure, it is named a sin. Sinful behavior

255

is going to be punished. Sinful habits are to be a matter for the Sacrament of Reconciliation. To deny a need to rest on the seventh day could possibly have harmful consequences, even in this life, such as sickness, nervousness, lack of control, scattered and uneven relationships, maybe even depression. To continuously work and not to rest is against all the health "shoulds." Medication can "keep one going," but it has its own side effects to remind one of the benefits of a balanced life of work and leisure. If a DRE must work on programs on Sunday, then an additional day must be set aside to rest. Once out of this survival stage, DREs move to the second level of pre-conventional thinking.

2. To keep the Sabbath is the best way to start a week. It gets one refreshed, regrouped, and at one with oneself before taking on the world every week. It is a chance to pray for the things one needs and to get to know family and friends that bring one so much satisfaction in life. The Sabbath is for the family to do things together. It is time off from work so that one can get other more spiritual realities accomplished. It is obeying God's law, and it gives one a chance to go to church and perform the duties of being a Christian. Therefore, the DRE should at least see to it that Sunday afternoon and evening are free from Church work. The DRE might also take Monday off to get caught up.

3. The Sabbath is a law, and a lawful person must observe it. It means to pray, that is go to church and be off regular work. It should be a day when one doesn't have to compete with the economy. If everyone would take Sunday off, then no one would get ahead of the other person. If the diocesan office and/or the parish would not have meetings, the persons concerned could celebrate the day with family, community, or friends. No one should be forced to needlessly work on Sunday. At this stage the DRE requests the Board to change the programming to a weekday.

4. The Sabbath should be enjoyed by everyone at the same time because community can only happen when we can all get together. Sunday is a time to see friends and be seen by friends. A practicing Catholic ought to be involved with the Church on Sunday. It is good not to be known just as a Director of Religious Education. It is a time for father to be around home, mother to be home with dad and the children, and all to be free from obliga-

tions so they can do things together. At this stage the DRE refuses a contract with a parish that will not permit him/her to be with family or community on Sunday.

5. The Sabbath is a sacred tradition given as a gift to celebrate being and all the beauty of what is given. It is a stillpoint in a turning world to be at peace with oneself, with God, and with others. But given our cultures, the essence of the Sabbath might not be tied to a particular day or even to a particular celebration. It is one aspect of a balanced lifestyle with a rhythm of work, prayer, and leisure. It must be observed, but can be changed to fit the times. The Sabbath is within us and celebrated outwardly in liturgy and community sharing. At this stage a DRE might take Monday or Friday for a day of prayer and rest.

6. The Sabbath is holy. "It is not an interlude but the climax of living." The Sabbath is a bride, and its celebration is like a wedding. It is a day for the spirit. Six days the spirit is alone, disregarded, forsaken, forgotten. Working under strain, beset with worries, enmeshed in anxieties, man has no mind for ethereal beauty. But the spirit is waiting for man to join it (p. 66). It is the Day of the Lord. Every seventh day a miracle comes to pass, the resurrection of the soul, of the soul of man and of the soul of things. A medieval sage declares, "The world which was created in six days was a world without a soul. It was on the seventh day that the world was given a soul." This is why it is said, "and on the seventh day He rested *vayinnafash*" (Exodus 31:17); *nefesh* means a soul (p. 83).

The Sabbath is a day to let go and let God be God (attributed to the philosopher Pieper). It is a day good in itself and need not be explained, justified, or practical. The Sabbath is a taste of Eternal Time. For an integrated DRE perhaps this could be a part of his/her every day.

Charles Peguy in his *Basic Verities* has God speak to us about sleep. As a poet, he blends in all the stages of moral reasoning.

SLEEP
GOD SPEAKS:
I don't like the man who doesn't sleep, says God.
Sleep is the friend of man.
Sleep is the friend of God.
Sleep is perhaps the most beautiful thing I have created.
And I myself rested on the seventh day.
He whose heart is pure, sleeps. And he who sleeps has a pure heart.

At this stage a DRE would balance each day with work and prayer; leisure and discipline and the Sabbath would be a continuous experience of "I am my work" (Meister Eckhart).

Conclusion

We have no policy in Indianapolis about the diocesan office initiating meetings on Sunday or that the DRE must observe the Sabbath as well as a day off. I have been challenged to get in touch with the meaning of the Sabbath tradition. I cannot expect illness or a policy to teach me its meaning. I cannot be at rest just being around my convent or celebrating with a priest on Sunday. I must personally stand still and enter into the Sabbath by creating an at-homeness with myself and being with others as a regular event. This tradition transcends law and order, reason and productivity. It is a holy event—being with God.

Bibliography

Cox, Harvey. "Meditation and the Sabbath." *Harvard Magazine.* September, October, 1977, p. 40.

Heschel, Abraham J. *The Sabbath—Its Meaning for Modern Man.* New York: Noonday Printing Press, 1959.

Kelly, Rev. Francis, "A Meditation on the Sabbath." *Forum Newsletter,* vol. 7, #1, September, 1979.

Lakein, Alan. *How to Get Control of Your Time and Your Life.* New York: Peter H. Wyden, Inc., 1973.

Leonard, Jon N., Hofer, J.L., and Pritikin, N. *Live Longer Now—The First One Hundred Years of Your Life.* New York: Grosset and Dunlap, 1974.

Mounier, Emmanuel. *The Character of Man.* New York: Harper and Brothers, n.d.

Proceedings of the 1978 Federation of Diocesan Liturgical Commissions. "Son-Day Worship—A Pilgrim People Pause to Pray." Washington, D.C.: The Liturgical Conference.

"Sunday Eucharist." National Bulletin on Liturgy, vol. 12, #71, November-December, 1979.

"The Act of Listening." The Royal Bank of Canada, vol. 60, #1, January, 1979.

Weaver, Mary Jo. "Leisure and Mental Health: A Case for the Sabbath." Speech in Bloomington, Indiana, Department of Religious Studies, Indiana University, May, 1979.

Endnote

1. Heschel, Abraham. *The Sabbath—Its Meaning for Modern Man.* 19 Union Square West, New York, 10003, Noonday Printing Press, copyright 1959, 3rd printing 1977 ($2.95). All page numbers in text of article refer to this classic book.

At the time of this writing, Sister Mary Margaret Funk, OSB, was director of religious education in the Office of Catholic Education, Archdiocese of Indianapolis.

Preparing for
Christian-Jewish Dialogue

Eugene J. Fisher and Rabbi Leon Klenicki

Introduction: Why Dialogue?

Dialogue means "to speak through," to move between the barriers we erect to become, for a moment, the other—to experience the world and ourselves from the other's unique stance. Without dialogue, we can neither be understood nor understand ourselves.

The world today seems torn by interreligious strife. From Northern Ireland to the Middle East, the "religious factor" lies at the heart of social conflict. More particularly, anti-Semitism appears to be once again on the rise, violently in France but also in this country with the reemergence of the Ku Klux Klan and neo-Nazi movements. To such dangers, the best response is dialogue.

From a Christian point of view, dialogue with Jews is a religious mandate. Christianity finds its source and continuing spiritual inspiration in the living tradition of Judaism. Without dialogue with Jews, the Christian cannot fully know what it means today to be Christian.

The goal of a program of preparation for and participation in a dialogue encounter for adult and older adolescent groups or classes will be to overcome the initial hesitancies about engaging in religious discussion with committed believers of another faith and to begin a process of spiritual growth through dialogue that can continue throughout life. Caution: Dialogue is so much fun it can become addictive!

1. Historical Background: From Disputation

For centuries Christians and Jews have been together, sharing a geography and a universe. To be together has not always meant together-ness and peace, however—quite the contrary. A confrontation, theological and social, has tragically separated the two faith-communities until the twentieth century. The realities of this century—the challenge of total evil, the Holocaust, the murder of six million Jews in Europe, the renewal of hope, the establishment of the State of Israel, the American-Jewish experience, and

This article appeared in PACE 12 (1981–1982).

the spirituality of Vatican II—have created a new situation of inner-reckoning which opens new perspectives on the relationship of Jews and Christians. The challenge of confrontation is replaced now by the challenge of dialogue—a creative, new dimension of Christian-Jewish witnessing.

The first century separation between the rabbinic interpretation of Scripture (Halakhah, wrongly translated as "law") and that of early Christianity focused on the understanding of central points of Jewish religious thought. Debates at that time centered on such concepts as Israel's election, the meaning of "People of God," the Messiah and Messianism, the reasons for the destruction of the Jerusalem Temple, Law (Halakhah) and faith or love, and the mission of Israel vis-à-vis Jesus and his ministry. The discussion of these concepts, of central concern in both faith communities, is reflected in Apostolic literature and a few rabbinic texts, especially the Midrash or literary interpretation of the Bible. The discussions at that time did not affect, essentially, the social condition of the Jewish community.

That situation changed, however, after Constantine, when Christianity became an official faith of the Roman Empire and seriously affected Jewish communities in Europe. Over the centuries new legislation by secular power, at times upheld by ecclesiastical law, deprived Jews of many civil rights, confined them in special sections called "ghettos," and even forbade them from becoming farmers or artisans. The practice of usury was thus imposed on the Jewish community to serve the financial needs of Christian princes. It became a trademark which precipitated a popular animosity toward Jews that was expressed in murderous attacks on the ghettos, especially during Passion Week or at times of plagues or national calamities. The Crusades, a Christian attempt to recover Jerusalem and the land of Israel from Islam, was generally preceded by cruel assaults on and massacres of Jews.

The theological Christian-Jewish discussion of earlier days developed in the Middle Ages into a confrontation that often resulted in the expulsion or forced conversion of Jews. The king or bishop of a city would call for a disputation forcing rabbis and Jewish theologians to discuss with Catholic theologians the concept of Messiah, the typological references to Jesus in the Hebrew Bible, or the question of the Chosen People. The disputations of Tortosa, Barcelona, and Paris are examples of these discussions which ended in the banishment of Jews and the burning of entire collections of the Talmud, the rabbinic interpretation of the Bible.

Such theological confrontations resulted in an anti-Judaism which assigned to Israel a negative role both in history and in God's purpose. Although contradictory to Paul's thought (e.g., in Romans 9–11), this indirectly influenced the anti-Semitism of later secular societies. For example, the French Revolution and the Industrial Revolution of modern times transformed European society, changed the feudal system into a more flexible one, and incorporated new social forces into the life of the nation.

Peasants, the middle class, and ghetto Jews were incorporated in the national life of each state—yet Jews were never able to become full citizens. The prejudice of the past lived on. Later, this prejudice erupted murderously in the Holocaust. Although the systematic, scientific slaughter of European Jews, rooted in the pagan ideology of Nazism, was denounced by most Christians, some remained silent. The silence of many Christian leaders was confusing. The Nazis interpreted it as a sign of approval, and it deeply affected Jews. This silence remains today both a matter for discussion and a very painful memory.

2. Toward Dialogue: The American Experience

Dialogue has reached a unique dimension of hope and realization in the United States. The pluralistic nature of the country, the separation of church and state, and the acceptance of credal differences have contributed to create the conditions for an honest interreligious relationship. Jewish organizations devote part of their activities and programming to dialogue. The National Conference of Catholic Bishops (NCCB), among other Christian ecclesiastical organizations, has created a special Secretariat of Catholic-Jewish Relations dealing with Jews and Judaism. Many dioceses have issued guidelines for the Catholic-Jewish dialogue, incorporating new aspects of the relationship that were not considered in the Vatican II documents, as for example the delicate matter of intermarriage and the problems it raises for both faith communities. Some guidelines and NCCB documents refer to the State of Israel and Holy Zion as central in contemporary Jewish self-understanding and indispensable in understanding today's Jewish life-experience.

Special projects are taking place considering specific areas of concern. For example, the Department of Education of the United States Catholic Conference (USCC) and the Anti-Defamation League of B'nai B'rith (ADL) together have created a special program for the training of Catholic teachers called **Understanding the Jewish Experience**. The program offers special courses on Jews and Judaism from biblical times to the present, emphasizing the deep spirituality and the recent history of the Jewish people, the Holocaust and the State of Israel, and the American Jewish experience. As a result, the Archdiocese of Philadelphia has published a curriculum guide, **Abraham: Our Father in Faith**, which gives background information on the main areas dealt with in the training program **Understanding the Jewish Experience**.

The ADL and the NCCB-USCC have also developed a "Joint Working Study Group" to discuss problems affecting the two communities. The leadership of both organizations meets to discuss questions such as the political future of the Middle East, federal aid to nonpublic schools, and problems facing the Jewish community. The Archdiocese of Chicago has published a special liturgical text for interreligious purposes on the **Passover Celebration**, still another effort to encourage dialogue between the communities.

3. Contemporary Theological Aspects

Under the mandate of the Second Vatican Council declaration, **Nostra Aetate**, Christian thinkers are now seeking to bring to the surface the positive aspects of the Church's stance toward the Jewish people. Many of their questions were first raised by St. Paul in Romans 9–11. Here Paul's basic question regarding treatment of "the Law" (**nomos**), whether or not **gentiles** have to become Jews first in order to be incorporated in the Covenant through Christ, represents virtually the only treatment of the covenantal relationship between our two peoples in the New Testament.

In Romans 9–11, Paul asks how one can explain the continued existence of the Jewish people after the coming of Christ. He rejects the notion that the relationship can be defined negatively: "I ask them, has God rejected his people? Of course not! . . . In respect to the election, they are beloved by him because of the patriarchs. God's gifts and his call are irrevocable" (Rom. 11:1, 28–29). In the end, Paul affirms, "all Israel will be saved," though he refuses to give an opinion as to whether or not this will be through conversion to Christianity. He concludes with an appeal to God's "inscrutable" mysteries.

Obviously, all sorts of questions are raised here which neither Paul nor subsequent Christian thinkers have been able to answer satisfactorily. Should the Church attempt to convert the Jews or should it, as Paul suggests, refrain from such an effort "until the full number of Gentiles enter in" (Rom. 11:25)?

Obviously, such questions seriously challenge many older catechetical formulations. Christians cannot say that the Sinai covenant has been "abrogated" or "replaced" by a second Covenant in Christ. For there is a clear teaching that Covenant and Torah ("call" and "gifts") remain valid **for Jews**. Nor can Christianity proclaim with the simple certitude of the past that **all** biblical promises were "fulfilled" in Christ. For these promises included as an essential element the notion of a universal age of justice and peace for all humankind. Thus the 1974 Vatican Guidelines candidly admit that "we still await their **perfect** fulfillment in His glorious return at the end of time."

Much work, then, remains to be done. And since the questions are relational, that work can best be done in dialogue between Jews and Christians.

Jews and Christians need to begin working together on positive theological formulations that will enable them to affirm religiously the essential spiritual validity of each other's traditions. In the Middle Ages, Jewish religious thinkers such as Maimonides, Yehudah LaLev, and Jacob

Emden were able to admit that Christianity performed a sacred task in bringing the name of the One God to the Gentiles. Such assertions of validity on both sides need to be probed and developed. Can we, together, come to a sense of common or at least shared witness to the Kingdom of God for which we both long? This is the deeper meaning and hope of Christian-Jewish dialogue today.

Catholic young people and adults should be exposed to this ultimate hope as well as given a clear sense of the tragedies of the past which lie between the two faith traditions. Through the centuries, Jews and Christians have remained spiritually and historically linked, even as they have sought to deny the mystery of that bond. In this process they have influenced each other's liturgy and theology far more profoundly than either, perhaps, is quite ready to admit even now. Religiously, in God's overall plan, Jews and Christians may **need** each other whether they like it or not.

Course Outline

1) Historical Background

    a. The split between Rabbinic Judaism and the early Hebrew-Christians.

    b. Constantine and the Medieval Scene: the civil degradation of the Jewish community (ghettos and yellow badges); the disputations and Christian theological anti-Semitism.

    c. Moments of hope: mutual influence in liturgy and scholastic philosophy, etc.; the Golden Age of Spain.

    d. The reality of total evil (the Nazi Holocaust) and the renewal of hope (the creation of the State of Israel, the American Experience).

2) The American Experience

    a. The pluralistic nature of American democracy: Jews and freedom after centuries of European discrimination.

    b. Catholics and Jews together: a shared experience of immigration into a largely Protestant environment; nativism, anti-Catholicism and anti-Semitism.

    c. Community-based encounters: the national Christian-Jewish Workshops, "living room" dialogues, the cooperation between Jewish organizations and diocesan, ecumenical, and other offices on a wide range of common social issues.

3) Vatican II and the Renewal of Theological Dialogue

    a. Official Church documents: **Nostra Aetate**, 1974 Vatican Guidelines, 1975 statement of the American bishops.

    b. Traditional statements of openness: on the Jewish side, the concept of God's universal covenant through Noah with all humanity and of a role for Christianity in spreading the name of God (HaLevi, Meiri, Maimonides, Emden, Rosenzweig, Buber); on the Christian side, the papal tradition of protection of the Jews (e.g., the condemnation of the blood libel charges).

c. Recovery of Christian origins in Judaism; the continuity of biblical and modern Judaism; the permanent validity of the Jewish covenant.

d. Liturgical sharings: Seders, Yom Hashoah; the rootedness of Catholic liturgy in the synagogue service.

4) *Actual Experience in Dialogue*

a. Visit to a synagogue, guest Jewish speaker, sharing a day with a class of Jewish students, etc.

Resource Bibliography

1) *Historical Background*

Berger, D. *The Jewish-Christian Debate in the High Middle Ages.* Philadelphia: Jewish Publication Society, 1979.

Bernards, S.S., ed. *Who Is a Jew?* New York: ADL, 1967.

Flannery, E. *The Anguish of the Jews.* New York: Macmillan, 1965.

Jacob, W. *Christianity Through Jewish Eyes.* New York: Hebrew Union College, 1974.

Parkes, J. *The Conflict of the Church and the Synagogue.* Philadelphia: Jewish Publication Society, 1961.

Talmage, F., ed. *Disputation and Dialogue.* New York: KTAV/ADL, 1975.

Filmstrip: "Christians and Jews: A Troubled Brotherhood." Niles, IL: Argus Communications.

2) *The American Experience*

Anti-Defamation League of B'nai B'rith (ADL). *Catalogue of Publications* and *Face to Face: An Interreligious Bulletin* (Quarterly), 823 United Nations Plaza, New York, NY 10017.

Belth, N. *A Promise to Keep: The American Encounter with Anti-Semitism.* New York: Times Books, 1979.

Fisher, E. and Polish, D., eds. *Formation of Social Policy in the Catholic and Jewish Traditions.* Notre Dame, IN: University of Notre Dame, 1980.

Lichten, J. "Concerning Interreligious Dialogue." *The Dialogist,* Spring 1969.

Neusner, J., ed. *Understanding American Judaism.* 2 vols. New York: KTAV/ADL, 1975.

3) Vatican II and the Renewal of Theological Dialogue

Croner, H., ed. *Stepping Stones for Further Jewish-Christian Relations: An Unabridged Collection of Christian Documents.* London: Stimulus/ New York: ADL, 1977.

Croner, H. and Klenicki, L., ed. *Issues in Jewish-Christian Dialogue: Jewish Perspectives on Covenant, Mission and Witness.* New York: Paulist/London: Stimulus, 1979.

Fisher, E. *Faith Without Prejudice.* New York: Paulist, 1977.

McGarry, M.B. *Christology, After Auschwitz.* New York: Paulist, 1977.

Oesterreicher, J. "Declaration on the Relationship of the Church to Non-Christian Religions," (no. 4). In *Commentary on the Documents of Vatican II,* edited by H. Vorgrimmler. 3 vols. Herder and Herder, 1968, pp. 1–136.

Pawlikowski, J. *The Challenge of the Holocaust for Christian Theology.* New York: ADL, 1978.

_____. *Sinai and Calvary.* Benziger Sisters, 1976.

_____. *What Are They Saying About Christian-Jewish Relations?* New York: Paulist, 1980.

Thoma, C. *A Christian Theology of Judaism.* New York: Paulist/London: Stimulus, 1980.

4) Actual Experience in Dialogue

Gilbert, A. and Olson, B. *Preparing for Jewish-Christian Dialogue,* two pamphlets: "Homework for Jews" and "Homework for Christians." National Conference of Christians and Jews, 43 W. 57th St., New York, NY 10019.

At the time of this writing, Dr. Eugene Fisher was executive secretary for Catholic-Jewish Relations of the National Conference of Catholic Bishops. Rabbi Leon Klenicki was director of Jewish-Catholic Relations for the Anti-Defamation League of B'nai B'rith.

Four-Letter Words in the Classroom

Mary Reed Newland

Not long ago, one of the diocesan agencies where children come for daycare decided to initiate a series of discussions for their staff on the problem raised by these children with their sexual language and precocity. All of them come from difficult, even violent, home situations; most of them have been the victims of or witnesses to sexual acts of all kinds. These experiences are manifested in language, actions, and suggestions which often leave some of the staff breathless.

As one of the people asked to talk with the staff, it occurred to me that a similar problem, although not so extreme, exists where even unabused children and adults meet—in the classroom, the religious education program, daycare centers, and even in the family. Four-letter words are heard everywhere, and the most innocent children pick them up, using them sometimes unknowingly but often quite deliberately, if only to shock their teachers and their parents. It has been a long time since washing someone's mouth out with soap was an effective penalty for bad language, and it is common wisdom these days that to ignore a child's use of such language will most often take the pleasure out of using it. But what of the words themselves? Is there something to be said about their meaning and origin that could be helpful for teachers and parents? When one has come to terms with and understands such words, it is less difficult to work out an approach to discussing them when this is necessary.

Origin

English vocabularies began to be written down in compendiums and dictionaries in about 1540; at that time the famous obscenities which pose a problem today were dignified and acceptable words. Many of the terms for copulation which we find objectionable—words derived from Old English, French, Latin, Greek, Old German—were in common use. The word *ficken*, from Old German (meaning "to penetrate," was probably the antecedent for what is the most famous of the vulgarisms for sexual intercourse. By the

---

This article appeared in PACE 12 (1981–1982).

early 1600s, such words had slid over into slang usage and had begun to acquire a distasteful connotation among "proper" people—although Shakespeare delighted in using the current slang in his plays, to the great appreciation of his audiences. Eventually it became illegal to print such words, and, if an author was determined to use one, it had to be presented with the first and last letters only, the others being represented by asterisks. James Joyce and D.H. Lawrence tried in their novels to return the words to their original acceptability but succeeded only in getting their books condemned as obscene and banned from bookstores. Today, although dictionaries of slang print the words and provide historical background, the Oxford English Dictionary still does not list them. During World War II, the common popularity of such words pushed them beyond the category of obscenity into ordinary slang; now they have become synonyms for such expressions as "Get lost!" "messed up," and so forth. The World War II acronym for "Situation normal, all _____ up," has entered our vocabulary as the word *snafu*.

Thus four-letter words, so-called, are used in distinctly different ways. Children used to hearing such language from the adults in their lives and everywhere in their culture will pick it up without any sense of its being worse than words like "darn," "creeps," or "baloney." But when they are intended as obscenities, these words pose a different problem.

Unacceptable—But Why?

Although the rule that such language is unacceptable in the classroom ought not to need defending, "Because I said so!" does not make it clear that there are good reasons for a rule. And for the teacher who is a bit timid, fearful that there might even be bad language as well as discipline problems, it may be helpful to consider the reasons. One is not always able to think of them on the spot.

Such language is unacceptable because it is disrespectful—although that may sound quaint at a time when slangy obscenities sprinkle the conversation of all kinds of people all the time. But one of the ends of education is learning to speak—well, clearly, precisely—and, especially in religion class where the goal is to explore the love of God and his call to us to love and respect one another, vulgar language violates the reverence God would have us show one another. The journey towards maturity includes learning to discipline impulsive outbursts and to master reasonable behavior, and in a classroom one is expected to help maintain a climate where this is possible for everyone. Even when such language has become a child's customary speech (and it is the folk language of many children), it is unsuitable in a class where friendship with God and one another is meant to lead to prayer and praise.

The words themselves, oddly enough, are vulgarisms for things which are noble and good and a part of God's design. Bodily elimination, genital acts, the genitalia—these are not "dirty," even though people seem to have a proclivity for talking about them as though they were, and it is possible to shift students' focus on such language by having a class on sex education included in the religious education curriculum. (This is quite safe; we have at least three documents from the American Bishops approving it.)

Several years ago, the parents at one school in our diocese became so alarmed at the street language their children were bringing home that they themselves suggested a session on sex education for each class from grades three through eight. I was the lady chosen for the talks, and the usual giggles and snickers greeted my first mention of the word "sex." But in each case, the children's' interest in, and surprise to find, sex as a discussible topic without undertones of dirtiness, helped them to become comfortable. Going to the bathroom, which provides a score of slangy obscenities, took on another dimension when it was pointed out how splendidly the body is designed to care for itself and to eliminate harmful residues of food and drink in order to keep in good health. The idea that one best uses the specific words for both the eliminative system and our genitalia in order to talk seriously about their functions led to discussion and to questions and answers which would almost have been impossible had we depended upon the neighborhood jargon. Part of the children's change in attitude was due to the experience of having a "teacher" who could speak of the seemingly unspeakable in a manner which helped them to be at ease with a subject otherwise in the category of dirty jokes and "swearing." Following such a comfortable and informative discussion, it is much easier for a teacher to check the use of vulgar language, at least in the classroom, with a discreet reminder that such language is not only vulgar, but immature.

When Jesus was criticized for not washing his hands the required number of times before eating, he answered that it was not what went into a person that made him unclean, but what came out of the heart. Experiences in religion class, it is hoped, will help both teacher and students to open their hearts to God's love, to become more generous, loving, serving, and eager to help heal the world. The very first requirement, then, is to speak in a way that is simple, respectful, and true.

Deliberate Obscenity

A young man working in the childcare agency told of hearing a ten-year-old girl say to a five-year-old girl, "If I was a boy, I'd _____ you." "I was so startled," he said, "that I didn't know what to say so I acted as though I hadn't heard it and walked past. What would you have done?"

I think I would have gone back to talk to the older girl. I would have tried to find out first if she had meant the remark as an insult or a threat or if she was parroting something she had heard someone else say. In any case, I would have said something like, "I hope you wouldn't do that, dear, because it would be unkind and wrong. That is a vulgar word for something which, when two people like a loving mother and father do it, is good, and is called 'making love.' But it is not love when it is done without caring for what is good and right for the other person. If you meant to show love, there are lots of better ways: doing kind things, being generous, helping. To use that kind of language just to be mean is wrong because each one of us is very special and dear to God and we have to try to treat each other with respect. It isn't easy, especially when we are angry or in a bad mood, but we have to try."

Someone may say that such talk is useless to children whose ambiance is obscenity and violence, but it could be the only time they hear anyone speak of sex with respect, or of love as something besides sexual activity. When said by someone a child likes and trusts, it could introduce an attitude towards sexuality which might grow into thoughtfulness one day, even though at the moment, to save face, the response must be disdain. One can hardly say all this in the middle of class, but to speak to such a child privately is worth a try. Every teacher has had the experience of discovering that something which seemed to be totally ignored turned out, later, to have been carefully pondered. The heart longs to believe in good—that is the premise of religion class—and adults can lose by default if they will not risk what needs saying to the young.

There is little to be gained by berating children for obscene remarks (they have probably already been berated), and endless preaching is not good, but to ignore a remark that seems to call for attention is unfortunate. One need not be a professional psychologist to lovingly, respectfully, firmly correct children. The late Dr. Haim Ginott often said about parent-to-child communication that the combination of strength and humanity is powerful. The possibilities are endless: "It is disappointing to hear you say that . . .," "It would be better to say that you are angry than . . . ," "I know it is easy to slip into that kind of language but . . . ." A teacher who had once taught in the inner city said to a class which seemed to be trying to provoke her, "You know, after teaching in the inner city I probably know more of those words than you do; I don't shock, but I do find it immature and I do resent this waste of time." And there is always plain-speaking: "We have a rule in this classroom: **No objectionable language**." Interestingly enough, boys will often refrain from using vulgar language in front of women teachers; a chauvinistic attitude, perhaps, but an advantage not to be despised.

There is one more problem with respect to the kind of ribald speech the young use so matter-of-factly when it is the language of their culture: It can be very funny, and not the least of the difficulties is to keep a straight face. I remember telling a Japanese fairy tale at a story hour in the inner city, about a man who fell into the sea, was pursued by a shark, and at the last minute was awakened from his dream by a benevolent guru and sent on his way with an appropriate moral. One young person who had sat tensely on the edge of his seat waiting for the climax heard the end of the tale and, with a look of utter disbelief, commented "_____!" Who could blame him? With expectations primed by "Jaws" and "Jaws II," this denouement was a total flop.

A hundred considerations have to be given to the use of vulgar language by children if one is to decide about its indifference or deliberateness. They hear it from their families, their peers, on television, in the movies, wherever they go in their culture, so we cannot be surprised that they pick it up. For some it can be meaningless, for others an experiment in rebellion, and for still others it can be a form of violence. Its real meaning is measured by its intention. For the religion teacher the issue is precisely that—to help children form in their hearts the loving intention towards others and their world which is the presence of the Lord Jesus. Reverence, respect, peace, gentleness, and simplicity of speech are among its many fruits, slow growing, but so worth nurturing.

At the time of this writing, Mary Reed Newland was chairperson of the Committee on Adult and Home Education for the Diocese of Albany, New York. She had received three honorary degrees and the Elizabeth Seton Award, written eleven books, made numerous tapes, and lectured widely all over the country.

271

Looking for a "Peace Liturgy"? Try the Mass!

Robert W. Hovda

It is strange that we can do something every Sunday of our lives, be profoundly formed and influenced by it, and remain unconscious of its meaning—of the reasons why it has been called traditionally "the sacrament of peace," "the sacrament of love," "the sacrament of unity," and of the fact that it is the major sacrament of reconciliation, with penance being only the auxiliary.

Ritual acts are by definition habitual acts. Good liturgical celebration must have a solid foundation in traditional structures and rhythms that are programmed, repeated, expected. The profound formative effects of regular Sunday Eucharistic celebration are neither fully indicated nor fully appreciated by the mind alone. Nor can they be easily articulated in speech or in a series of statements. Their effects are broader and deeper than those which can be apprehended by reason.

Because liturgy is symbolic action, which we do together as assembly, and because its power is in proportion to its God-centeredness, its Other-centeredness, no objective or subjective examination is adequate to explore the changes in us over a long period during which these actions have been a regular part of our lives.

But we live in a culture that wants everything (including people) to be superficially and pragmatically effective, to *produce* results that are certifiable, measurable, namable. If we cannot measure a product as the end result of an activity, we tend to dismiss the activity as meaningless. That's why we have so little patience with and appreciation for works of art, human environments, play, imagination, and fantasy. All these things, like liturgy, get much too deep for our measuring devices.

Liturgies that have their roots in the Bible, the liturgies of Judaism and Christianity, are liturgies that celebrate the reign of God, the sole ultimate dominion of the God who is moving the world toward its fulfillment in a holy

---

This article appeared in PACE 15 (1984–1985).

city of justice and peace, liberation and solidarity for all. Every basic liturgical structure in that biblical tradition is, therefore, a liturgy of peace and reconciliation, among other things.

One of my regular column pieces in *Worship* magazine last year was a comment about the peculiar experience of hearing newly converted social actionists (who have been in the Church for years) asking for "peace liturgies," as if celebrations with that theme had been nonexistent up to now. These people have been regular participants in the Sunday Eucharist without ever having raised to the level of rational articulation the fact that the Mass *is* a peace liturgy, a liturgy of reconciliation, from beginning to end, top to bottom, inside and outside, *A* to *Z*—beginning with the physical fact of assembling a heterogeneous crowd and continuing through all its symbol-language of word and sacrament.

The editor of *PACE* asked me to comment further on that theme, since one hears frequently these days that our public worship is somehow remiss in not catching up with our social thought. Liturgical celebrations are indeed weak in many parishes, but that is not the reason. It seems to me the opposite is true. Our social thought and sense of social mission and responsibility have been remiss and are only now beginning to catch up to where our liturgy has been all the time. For a person familiar with the Mass and nurtured by regular participation in it suddenly to perceive a need for a "peace liturgy" is a bit like a baker standing in the midst of the morning's output (loaves of almost every size and kind) and lamenting the lack of bread.

What does it mean for a group of people to assemble once a week on Sunday, not because they are a blood family or homogeneous in some other natural way, but solely to affirm and celebrate the dominion of the one true God over all of us of different types, colors, sexes, classes, lifestyles, backgrounds, and so on? Common conversion, faith, and Baptism are all the motley crowd shares, but those three bonds are basic and decisive, uniting us on a level deeper than any of our differences and making us *ecclesia,* church. So the local Church that assembles for Mass on Sunday is already, in the very act of coming together, a peacemaking and reconciling community. Before God, all our differences fade into insignificance. Just the fact of assembling to celebrate together our common apprehension of the meaning of human existence is already an exercise and a victory in making peace.

Nor is that all. Once assembled, we celebrate the liturgy as one unit. No one of us baptized is the whole Christ, but together with our Head, *we* are Christ. As local Church we are therefore able to offer a worship to God more perfect than the worship any one of us could offer individually. "Where two or three are gathered in my name, there am I." Our communication in this Godward common prayer or liturgy or public worship is the symbol-language of word and sacrament. Symbols (the stories and parables of the Bible, the

273

common eating and drinking of the Lord's Supper) are a communication that unites, reconciles, makes peace among people who are divided by idioms, culture, and customs of many kinds.

So the first thing we do in the Eucharist is sing a common song of praise, be greeted with scriptural words by the priest or bishop who presides in our (Christ's) name, and offer our silent prayer before and our "Amen" after the common prayer of our solidarity and peace in faith that the presider utters. In other words, the first thing we do is get our eyes on our common Source, on the Almighty who has gathered us and whose grace has united all of our separate and contingent beings into one Body. All of biblical tradition—including the covenant, the law, and the prophets—is the approbation of our corporate oneness, summed up in the messianic mission:

> *Now in Christ Jesus you who once were far off have been brought near*
> *through the blood of Christ. It is he who is our peace, and who has made*
> *the two of us one by breaking down the barrier of hostility that kept us*
> *apart . . . reconciling both of us to God in one body through his cross,*
> *which put that enmity to death" (Eph. 2:13–14,16).*

After our gathering through common song and common prayer, our first major act in the Mass is the proclamation of scriptural readings with our listening and our common faith response. And then we consider a homily, which attempts to interpret the scriptural readings in terms of our current life situation and problems. The initiative is that of God's Word, a classic, symbolic word of liberation and unification, of peace, coming to us with an authority that commands obedience.

Here we are, gathered. Faith has brought us, but we are all in and of our particular worlds and cultures and ways. And in all of our worlds there is still much oppression and much division. Some of us are oppressors, some of us oppressed. Barriers and walls, prejudices and hostilities are part of the human environment we know. But, because of God's initiative and the priority of the biblical word, we can hear together the message of God's will to free us and to bring us into one. Our response is sluggish, but that is not because the message is unclear. It is because we rather like to be held hostage by the economic, political, military, and social systems under which we live (and which we have created and support). Against this constant cultural tide, the word of God is proclaimed and we give our ears, our hearts, and our assent.

In cultures riddled by oppressions of many kinds, by all sorts of pretenders to dominion and allegiance, by suspicions and prejudices and hostilities from which none of us is totally free, this little straggling community of faith on Sunday regularly bows to the word of the biblical readings, with their constant, many-faceted but univocal call to realize our freedom and our oneness in God by building the new Jerusalem, the city of peace.

And then we give thanks, again in union with our Head and in common, for the loving kindness of God which enables this faith community to be a reconciler, a peacemaker, in our world and for it. We give thanks for the very tension faith creates, its counter-cultural implications and thrust, its alternative to the status quo. We give thanks with gifts of money ("for the poor and the church"). We give thanks with gifts of bread and wine, standing for us and our corporate life as church and, by Jesus' institution, standing for the Messiah's perfect obedience to God's will and perfect acceptance of God's dominion, his body given for us and his blood shed for us, and for the forgiveness of our sins (all that oppresses and all that divides). In that eucharistic prayer, our hearts are lifted to the new possibilities of God's reign as *present,* not merely future, reality.

So, with the Lord's Prayer we ask for that forgiveness by pledging our forgiveness, our love, to all who have oppressed or excluded or harmed us. And we exchange a physical sign of peace, recognizing each other with the fresh vision of faith, as daughters and sons of one God, sisters and brothers, to whom reverence is due for God's sake (not because we have earned it). This is the foundation of all peace and of all peacemaking.

The climax comes in the sharing of the holy bread and the holy cup—communion. Nowhere else in our world, in any of our particular "worlds," is there so sacred and awesome and totally involving a symbolic action—one that lays low all walls of sex, color, class, separation, privilege, and status and invites everyone in the faith community to share and share alike. Even the sign of peace just mentioned fades before this breaking and sharing of the one Bread of Christ, this pouring and drinking from the one Cup of Christ. Their symbolism extends far beyond even Judaism and Christianity, for cultures the world over have regarded (and reflected in their languages) eating and drinking together as an act, a pledge, a sign of peace and friendship. The English word *companion* (one with whom one shares bread) is one indication of a human feeling and meaning of that deep symbolic level, more basic than our varieties of culture, language, and mores.

All this means peace, not through making us all alike, but through the reverent eyes which faith gives us. So that we see each other, including the enemy, in Christ and in God. It doesn't solve our battles. But it creates a new arena for all our common human life, our cooperation, and our struggles. It rejects the arena of violence, force, might-makes-right, and the vicious circle that arena has maintained through the history of our world thus far—one oppressor made to yield to another, a mere change of personnel, with the structures of oppression and division unchallenged.

The peace of the Mass challenges the structures and proposes the reign of God, the holy city, the new Jerusalem, the environment of a love willing to suffer even to death, so that new life can emerge, a life fit for the daughters and the sons of God. Perhaps we are only beginning to see the implications of all this for Christian mission: The fact that giving water to the thirsty now means creating systems of water supply, treatment, and distribution that serve all people equitably, not merely the rich and the powerful. Faith gives us the vision. We have to work out the practical ways to form new economic and political institutions with the rest of the human family. But the vision is important, and the vision of the Mass is peace. No fabricated "peace liturgy" could possibly match its power or its depth or its potential for the lives of those whose eyes have been touched by Christ.

At the time of this writing, Rev. Robert W. Hovda was a pastoral associate at St. Joseph's Church in Greenwich Village, New York City. A writer and lecturer on liturgical renewal, he received the Michael Mathis Award from the Notre Dame Center for Pastoral Liturgy and the Berakah Award of the North American Academy of Liturgy.

Coming into Community:
Some Ways and Means

Parker J. Palmer

Having shared my understanding of the spiritual dynamics of Christian community, I want now to suggest some practical ways and means of coming into community with one another. Please note that I do not speak of "building community" or "creating community." Community is not something we create or build. Rather, it is a gift of God, a gift pure and simple—not a goal to be achieved but a gift to be received. Even so, we can learn to receive the gift better than we usually do. We can learn to be openhanded and openhearted with each other so that the gift, when it comes, will not be rejected. The ways and means I want to share in this essay will not make community happen, but they will help open us to the God-given community that is already and always among us.

The methods I shall share here come from my ten years of living in the Quaker community called Pendle Hill, so I know them to be time-tested and true. Some of them rest on Quaker spiritual assumptions—which I shall try to make clear as I go along. But since half the members of our community of seventy are not Quakers but Protestants, Catholics, Jews, and assorted others, I know that these methods do not rely on Quaker formation for their success. The methods have the virtue of being straightforward and simple (in good Quaker style), and I shall try to describe them as such. However, precisely because of their simplicity, it is easy to overlook their profound possibilities, so I urge you to read "between the lines" as you consider each of them, imagining what they might open up in your congregation.

The first method involves sharing our life stories. It is very rare in our society—and in our churches—for people to feel that their own life stories are known. We present ourselves to each other partially and marginally, but authentic community requires that whole persons be present. Knowing each other's stories helps avoid some of the needless conflict that tears communities apart; I have found that it is impossible to hate another person when I know his or her life story well.

At Pendle Hill we use a deceptively simple device for sharing our life stories. A group of twelve or fourteen people are seated in a circle. A person

This article appeared in PACE 15 (1984–1985).

acting as moderator introduces a question to the group—a question that often seems shallow or even banal on the face of it: "What was your first pet?" "What was the first job you ever held?" "What can you remember of the time when you were about ten or twelve years old?" People are invited to answer this question as they wish (that is, we do *not* go systematically around the circle), and it is made clear that no one is required to answer. And a firm ground rule is laid down: No one may poke at or analyze or otherwise respond to anything anyone says.

The results of this simple procedure are quite amazing. No one feels pressured to speak (as one often does in a "group sharing" session); the privacy of the individual is protected. No one is threatened by the questions; they are the kinds of questions one can answer on any level of depth or self-revelation one chooses—though it is remarkable how often such a question will evoke a keenly felt answer. And no one is subjected to the often insensitive probes that people sometimes make in similar settings; no one is victimized by amateur psychoanalysis. To put it positively, people have the refreshing experience of being able to tell their story, or part of it, and to listen to the stories of others, with simple attentiveness and appreciation. And when a group convenes to do this, not once but several times over a period of weeks (or does it at the beginning of each business session), the cumulative effect is a deepening awareness of the community that is already among us.

A second simple device is doing manual work together. In my community, each of us has a daily job related to some aspect of meal preparation or housekeeping; and once a week we spend half a day together doing the larger chores of the place: raking lawns, painting a house, repairing broken windows. Though we do many other things of a communal nature, this manual work is high on the list of things that help us to discover the community that is among us.

Studies of church growth and development have revealed much the same phenomenon. The strongest sense of community in a church usually occurs during its early years. There are several reasons for this, but one is the fact that in those early, formative years there is a considerable amount of manual work to be done, and people are doing it together. There are pews to be built, a basement to be finished, a kitchen to be installed—and people show up on weeknights and Saturdays to do this work cooperatively. As years go by, the church's need for such work declines—and so does the sense of community. Someone once said that a community is a group of people who take care of their own garbage. You can interpret that on a psychological level, but it has a literal meaning as well. As soon as a community hires a janitor to take care of its garbage, it has taken a big step away from being a community and a big step toward being just another institution.

There are several reasons why doing manual work together helps us discover the community already among us. One of the biggest is that manual work serves to reveal and utilize and celebrate a range of personal gifts that many group activities ignore. Most groups are organized around activities—worship services, classes, business meetings—that require some degree of verbal skill and self-confidence in order for one to participate. Yet many people do not have verbal strengths, and as a result they feel left out of this sort of "community." Manual work gives people a chance to exercise skills other than the verbal, and it gives the verbally adept folk a chance to recall how dependent they are on these other kinds of gifts. We thus learn about both our variety and our interdependence—and, in the process, we come deeper into community with each other.

A third device we use is sharing our dilemmas and decisions with each other, seeking communal support and guidance. One of the realities that undermines community is the tendency to come to the realization that when I have a real problem—a family difficulty, a vocational crisis, or whatever—I am most alone, both because I am reluctant to share my problem with the community and because the community consequently has no mechanism for dealing with the problem I have. In other words, when everything is okay in my life, I can be in "community" with ease. But once I have a serious problem, I retreat into lonely isolation—and my morale for community suffers as a result.

At Pendle Hill we try to change that tendency by practicing something called a "clearness committee." When I have a problem, I ask five or six people I trust to serve on such a committee for me. The first step is for me to write up an account of my problem—its background, its present shape, my future prospects, hopes, and fears. After members of my committee have studied that document, they convene for up to three hours, with one member serving as recording clerk (so I may retrieve information later) and another serving as facilitator. The facilitator's main job is to enforce the single, simple rule by which a clearness committee operates: No member may say anything to me except to *ask a question.*

Please note that this rule serves to outlaw the thing that normally happens when we bring a problem to other people. Normally, we get five minutes of listening and questioning followed by an hour of advice! But, as everyone knows, advice is the last thing we need when we have a serious problem, for our task is to find our way toward our own truth. Yet our inclination to give each other advice is often indulged as a way of getting the other "off our backs." If I give you advice and you take it, I no longer need bother with you because your problem is (or should be) solved; if you don't take my advice I no longer need bother with you because you are obviously spineless, uncomprehending, or just a fool. So advice-giving works against true community, while the discipline of "hanging in there," listening and questioning with patience, brings us deeper into community with each other.

The clearness committee rests on a Quaker spiritual assumption that each of us has our own truth, our own source of guidance, deep within our souls. This is the inner light, the inward Christ, that of God in every person. We *know* what to do in any situation, but that knowledge is often layered over by parental biases or social expectations or cultural confusions. So the purpose of the clearness committee and its continual questioning is to peel back those layers, one at a time, until the person's own inner answer can be reached. We do not call on the community to solve our problems but to help us discover the solutions that lie within us.

A fourth way of coming into community with each other is to make community decisions by consensus. It is common knowledge that communities often fall apart over critical decisions—but the problem usually lies not so much in the decisions that get made as in the *way* they are made. Our way of decision-making reflects our conception of power, and our conception of power often exposes the weaknesses in our rhetoric of "community."

Many churches make decisions the same way they are made in the larger society—by majority rule. Here is a point on which Quakers differ not only from society but also from most churches: Quakers reject majority rule because they see it as a subtle but damaging form of violence. Whenever 51 percent (or 72 percent or 95 percent) of the people have their way, there is a smaller group who feel out maneuvered, tromped on, and alienated—feelings that do not help to bring us into community with each other. Furthermore, there is always the chance, however slim, that the minority "had the truth" all along. Despite its relative virtues, majority rule is neither a good way to determine truth nor a constructive means of evoking community.

So Quakers practice decision-making by consensus. Consensus does not mean that everyone in the group must go along wholeheartedly with a proposal before it becomes a decision; such a state of affairs is rare indeed. But consensus does mean that the group cannot make a decision if any one in the group feels obliged to oppose it on the grounds of values, faith, conscience, or truth. Making decisions by consensus assures that the community will move as a community, not as a broken collection of power blocs. Making decisions by consensus assures that truth, not power, is the issue, and that the minority—even the lone individual—always has a chance to speak its truth to the group.

At this point, many people who have not experienced consensual decision-making begin thinking of people they know who are difficult to deal with because of their extreme cantankerousness. If you do not let the majority rule, what is to prevent such people from continually frustrating the movement of the group? It may be that cantankerous people are born, but I doubt it; instead I think they are *made*. And one way they are made is by the politics of majority rule where the premium is put on competitiveness, not cooperation.

In a situation where majority rule is operating, I am not encouraged to listen for the strengths and appeals of the viewpoint of the "opposition." Instead, I am compelled to look for its weaknesses and supposed idiocies so that I can point them out to others and gather enough votes to defeat that opposition. When the majority rules, I am encouraged to be cantankerous. But when we are proceeding by consensus a different mood prevails. Knowing that nothing can happen if any one in the room has deep objections, I am encouraged to listen very openly and carefully for that which I can affirm and build on in another's proposal. When consensus is working at its best, the result is not a mild compromise, not the lowest common denominator, but a new synthesis, a deeper truth, which no one had foreseen. Consensual decision-making does not prompt us to be cantankerous but rather evokes the community that is already and always between us.

Again, none of these methods can "create" community. Community is a gift, and these methods can only help us receive the gift more openly and fully than we usually do. The nature of that gift is best expressed in Jesus' words, "Whenever two or three are gathered, I will be among them." With that faith, these methods become not merely gimmicks for human relations but pathways to Christian community. With that faith, we can come together without anxiety or fear to receive the gift of community that God is continually offering us.

At the time of this writing, Parker J. Palmer was teacher and writer-in-residence at Pendle Hill, a Quaker spiritual community and adult study center near Philadelphia. His writings included The Company of Strangers *and* To Know as We Are Known: A Spirituality of Education.

281

Developing a Solid Religion Curriculum for Adolescents (Part One)

Thomas Zanzig

During the past few years I have spent considerable time reflecting on the kinds of principles that might guide us as we attempt to develop religion curriculums for adolescents, both in Catholic high schools and in parish programs, that reflect the following characteristics:

- theological integrity,
- sensitivity to the developmental patterns of adolescents, and
- recognition of both the opportunities and the limitations experienced in the parish and the school settings.

Yet, my discussion is not an attempt to simply share the results of my own thinking about the development of religion curriculums. Rather, I want to stimulate *your* reflection and/or discussion with fellow DREs, volunteer teachers, representatives of parish boards, parents, and others interested in this important dimension of the educational ministry of the Church. This article presents a series of six questions for reflection and discussion, each suggesting a principle of design intended to help us focus on the religion curriculums we are currently offering our adolescents.

It should be noted that the questions for reflection are also applicable to the Catholic high school setting, and I will occasionally illustrate a point with an example relevant to a Catholic school. Given the readership of *PACE,* however, my primary focus here will be on religious education as it is encountered in the parish setting.

Questions for Reflection and Discussion

1) Does our religion curriculum for adolescents provide a clear, sequential, and integrated presentation of the essential content of the Christian story and vision?

This article appeared in PACE 16 (1985).

This question is clearly loaded and deserves some elaboration. Implicit in the question are a number of my own personal convictions about curriculum development. In and of themselves, these convictions warrant some discussion, if not debate:

a) There is a body of information about our Catholic Christian faith that is not arbitrary, and this information should be included in any curriculum that strives for theological integrity.

b) The curriculum content should unfold in a logical way, that is, with concepts in one course or at one level of the program building in a sequential way upon concepts previously introduced to the students.

c) The entire curriculum should have some unifying principle, a clearly identified and recognizable "integrating thread" that weaves and connects the curriculum's courses or levels into a reasonable whole.

As suggested, all of these convictions are open to some debate. What they refer to and critique is an unfortunately common situation: A religion curriculum in a parish—and far too often in Catholic schools as well—has been allowed to simply evolve in a haphazard and, at times, even contradictory way over the years. The resulting "curriculum" is a series of courses with no apparent relationship to one another.

Such a result will come about, for example, if units of material in a parish program or religion courses in a school are randomly incorporated into the curriculum purely on the basis of the experience or biases of individual teachers. When asked why a particular topic is part of the curriculum, the director of such a program will respond that "at one time we had a teacher who was 'into' that topic."

But the integrity of the curriculum can also be violated through omission rather than commission. That is, at times a central dimension of the Christian message might be avoided or eliminated because "we have no teacher willing to teach it." Neither including nor omitting courses purely on the basis of the experience or interests of the teachers is acceptable if one of the characteristics we seek in our religion curriculums is theological integrity.

A related point should be raised here. There is no one, universal "integrating thread" that should always be present in every religion curriculum. If such unanimity across parish programs or schools were possible or even desirable, there would be only one acceptable design for a curriculum. Such is clearly not the case.

By way of example: For quite some time, the integrating principle in many Catholic high school religion curriculums was the theme of *salvation history*. Commitment to this approach led many schools to offer a course on the Hebrew Scriptures to freshmen; the rationale for this was that all of salvation history could be understood only in light of the religious history of the Jews. (Many publishers of religion texts offer "parish versions" of their texts by simply shortening the texts to make them more usable in parish settings. Many parishes therefore adopted the salvation history approach—and the use of textbooks, for that matter—despite the fact that the unique situation of the parish setting demands different content and methodologies from those used in the high school setting. More on that in a moment.)

A more recent example of an integrating principle for designing religion curriculums has been our growing understanding of the *religious and faith development of adolescents.* Advocates of this approach base their curriculum designs on the evolving capacity of young people to understand and to personally appropriate the content and meaning of Christian faith. Both of the above approaches, as well as others, can be supported. The point here is that the leaders of a program should be able to identify what it is that integrates its courses or units of material into a reasonable curriculum.

Implicit in the discussion of this point is the question of a wide-open elective system in a religion curriculum. This is reflected in those cases, particularly in the parish setting, in which the young people themselves are allowed to unilaterally determine the topics for discussion to be included in the curriculum.

It is curious that we would rarely—perhaps never—even consider such a possibility in the teaching of any other subject or in the pursuit of any other discipline. When it comes to discussions of faith and religion, however, we assume that young people are so in touch with the questions at hand—in fact so familiar with the "answers" that faith and religion can provide for those questions—that they are capable of designing their own programs.

I am not denying at all the desirability of involving the young people *to a reasonable extent* in determining the content of a program; the next question for reflection will speak to that issue. Nor am I saying that the provision for *some* elective courses in a curriculum is not at all worthwhile; offering some electives can be very reasonable, particularly for older students. But I am suggesting that there is a body of information about our faith that we are obliged to offer in attractive ways to our young people, information that they would, on their own, claim no interest in—simply because they have had no exposure to it. (Note also that this question of a wide-open elective system comes into play in the discussion of question 3 below.)

2) Does our religion curriculum consider and reflect what we know of adolescent religious and faith development?

I will readily admit that this question demonstrates my own bias toward sensitivity to student needs and abilities as a major integrating principle for developing a curriculum. My understanding of learning theory leads me to the strong conviction that failure to take into account the developmental characteristics of the potential learners virtually guarantees failure in the attempt to teach anything, religion included. This is not to suggest, in the context of our comments above, that material such as the Hebrew Scriptures cannot be taught to freshmen (though I do have my reservations on that point).

The thrust of this principle is, however, that whatever we choose to teach at whatever grade level, the needs and abilities of the students should dictate at least *how* we teach the material. Again using our example above: If a teacher is seeking a text for teaching the Hebrew Scriptures, he or she should not simply look for a text that covers the material adequately. The text must also be attuned to the starting point of the students with whom it will be used.

Perhaps more to the point in terms of parish programming is the question of the value of using a text as a primary tool or educational method. Remember, our concern here is to be sensitive to the developmental characteristics and needs of the young people. Is it reasonable to expect young people to get excited about another textbook in their evening parish program, after having spent the entire day dealing with (or trying to avoid dealing with!) textbooks in school? Parish programs also usually lack any means of accountability, like a grading system, with which to motivate young people to read their texts outside of the program time. (An exception to the typical practice of no grading or accountability might be those programs that use acceptance or rejection for Confirmation as a means of accountability, a tactic that I would propose lacks the support of good sacramental theology!)

The typical schedule of a parish program also works against the effective use of textbooks: With students meeting no more than weekly, retention of material becomes a significant problem. The alternative suggested by some educators—actually spending valuable class time reading out of textbooks—would seem to be not only boring for the students, but also a wasted opportunity for nurturing the vitally important relationship between the young people and their adult leaders.

What is the alternative to the use of textbooks for parish programs? I think the answer is to provide creative materials *for the volunteer teachers,* thorough designs of learning experiences that guide the teachers in the use of dynamic teaching methods, which they in turn can share with their students. Group discussion activities, simulations, role-plays, films, and much more—all are enjoyable means of approaching material in ways that can capture and hold the interest of both students and teachers.
To rephrase the question at hand: Does your religion curriculum incorporate both content and learning processes that reflect a real sensitivity to the starting point of your young people?

3) In our curriculum, does understanding concepts take precedence over learning facts?

It is unfortunate that religion, like history, can be taught by having students simply memorize information, with little concern for whether or not they truly recognize and understand the significance and meaning of the concepts often hidden behind the information. This fact-oriented approach is far less likely to happen in the teaching of mathematics or the sciences; in those cases, the student's failure to understand one concept quickly shows up in the failure to understand a subsequent and dependent concept.

In the teaching of religion, though, we have to guard against the ease with which students can move from one course or unit of material to another with little comprehension of the material presented. Methods for both the presentation of material and the testing of student understanding should be sensitive to this reality.

For example, a lecture method of presentation followed by testing to determine if students simply listened well—that is, whether they can give back the information as it was presented—tends to provide facts to the students while promoting little real comprehension. Though this approach is commonly associated with the school setting, many parishes have resorted to it in their programs, particularly in the context of Confirmation preparation, when the threat of refusal of the sacrament can be used to "motivate" students. As already suggested, group processes, personal reflection, open discussion, and approaches to testing that require more reflection than memorization (e.g., essay questions or the keeping of a journal) will lead to more effective learning of the theological content.

Important to note here as well is something that was alluded to in our earlier discussion of the problems with a wide open elective system in designing a religion curriculum. It appears, from a conceptual or a theological perspective, that the integrity of a program demands that some concepts must either precede or build upon others if true understanding is to be made possible. For example, how can one discuss Christian sexual morality if one has not yet been introduced to the moral teachings of Jesus? Or how can one understand the sacraments if one has no grasp of the meaning of the Church?

When students are allowed to choose for discussion only those topics that appeal to them at the moment, they will often be forced to deal with a given topic within a conceptual vacuum, making real learning extremely unlikely. It also seems likely that many students in parish programs that are based solely on electives will, once they have completed the "attractive" courses, simply stop coming to the program. Consequently, they will never be exposed to concepts that might well have interested them if they had just been given the chance to encounter them. The key to an effective curriculum, it seems, is to design an integrated curriculum based on our mature understanding of the faith, but to offer that material with such sensitivity, creativity, and enthusiasm that young people will find it responsive to their developmental needs.

4) Are our students allowed, and even occasionally encouraged, to question, doubt, argue against, and perhaps even temporarily reject what is being taught, without fear of reprisal?

This question clearly deserves more discussion than I can give it here, so much so that I was tempted to avoid including it in this article. But I believe the question is simply too important to neglect. We have come to realize that the struggle to achieve maturity of faith nearly always demands that individuals experience what John Westerhoff calls "searching faith." The essential task of that search is for individuals to reevaluate their inherited religious beliefs, traditions, and practices in light of their increasing maturity. At some point, then, they freely choose whether or not to personally appropriate those culturally imposed religious realities into their own identities. At times this process can be very difficult, leading some individuals to a "crisis of faith;" for others the process can be relatively pain-free. In either case, the process appears to be essential to our growth as Christians. Does your religion curriculum help or hinder students in their journeys through "searching faith"?

5) Does our curriculum unfold in such a way that the students are prepared to assume personal responsibility for their continuing faith development beyond high school?

This question raises a number of related issues, among them the ultimate goals that we seek with our religion curriculum, our methodologies, and the skills we attempt to provide our young people. Further questions may help us to more clearly focus on our ultimate goals: What kind of world will our students confront as they leave high school, and does their experience in our programs provide them with the tools they will need to deal with that world as maturing Christians? These are tough questions, to be sure, but ones that get right to the heart of our efforts as religious educators of adolescents.

Consider some others: Does our curriculum develop within the students a clear sense of their Catholic identity—one that is rooted firmly in an understanding of the Gospel of Jesus as it has come to be known and proclaimed within our Catholic tradition? Are our students learning how to pray? Can they find their way around the Scriptures, and can they interpret those Scriptures (to a reasonable extent), using acceptable approaches to biblical interpretation? Can our students make moral decisions that are grounded not in legalism but in a sound understanding of the values of Jesus?

If we can answer such questions in the affirmative, we are on the right track. If not, perhaps we must reevaluate our entire religion curriculum, as well as the total ministry of our parish to and with our young people—which brings us to our last question.

6) Is our religion curriculum understood within the context of the total life of the parish community, so that it both speaks to and is enhanced by the other dimensions of parish life?

Again, the limitations of space here preclude a lengthy discussion of this very important factor in our examination of religious education in the parish or the Catholic high school. Suffice it to say that the attainment of the results implicit in question 5 above would seem to demand a commitment to a philosophy of total youth ministry in the parish—or, in the Catholic high school setting, the counterpart of youth ministry, which is campus ministry. Skills cannot simply be taught in classes; we learn what it means to live as Christians by doing it, not simply talking about it. Opportunities to engage in prayer, liturgical celebrations, retreats, service on behalf of peace and justice, peer ministry, and so on, are all vital to the adolescents' growth as Christians.

On its own, then, a religion curriculum cannot lead students to Christian maturity, regardless of how well planned and implemented it is. Its primary task is to shed intellectual light on the realities of our faith. But these realities must be experienced in other areas of our lives—in relationships with family and peers, within our own personal experiences of the presence of God in our lives, within the context of communal worship, and more.

These, then, are some of the challenging questions I would pose as we reflect on the task of developing effective religious education curriculums for our young people.

Thomas Zanzig is a consultant and an author working for Saint Mary's Press.

Ministry and Singleness

Susan Muto

For a growing number of single persons, women and men, ministry to church and society, as an expression of inclusive love, replaces marriage, as an expression of exclusive love. This is not to say that married persons are not as active in a variety of ministerial roles. It is only to stress that work—what one does for a living—absorbs a great deal of time and energy in a single person's day. An unmarried medical doctor I know makes himself available for off-duty hours, not because of sheer altruistic ideals but because, in his words, "I love to do what I do, and I don't mind giving the married guys a break." He often describes his work, as I do mine, as a form of ministry.

Ministry and Mystery

In trying to understand this word from a transcendent and not merely from a functional perspective, I have come to link in my mind "ministry" with the gifted capacity that belongs to me as a single person in the world to be more available for "service to the Mystery." Just as singleness has everything to do with who I am, so ministry has everything to do with what I do. Being single and doing for others seem to go hand in hand. I, like many others, view single persons as a tremendous force for good in the world. Would that both church and society strove to tap into this reservoir of energy rather than identifying being single only as a negative—as a state of NOT being married—or as a form of crippling loneliness or irresponsible narcissism.

The truth is that single people populate the marketplace. Many define their singleness as a state of being in transition to a committed marital relationship; others find themselves single by circumstance due to separation, divorce, or widowhood. More and more women, for example, manage single-parent families, struggling to make ends meet when child support becomes at best irregular, at worst non-existent. More so in our time than previously, women and men feel free to ask if they are perhaps called by God to live their single life as a vocation.

This article appeared in PACE 21 (1992).

Theirs is a free choice, not a coerced decision. For Christians, this call often leads to a deepening of the spiritual life. One feels a person-to-person bond with Jesus Christ, who was and remained a single person in the world devoted to following the Father's will.

To understand that one is single not because of childhood wounds or unresolved fears but because one has been called to this state of life by God is a beautiful experience, profoundly freeing and evocative of a new depth of understanding and appreciation for the spiritual meaning of ministry.

Disciplines Linking Service and Singleness

Helping one to find the link between service and singleness are some basic disciplines of the spiritual life. I call these four sure steps for a fuller Christian life, a life of likeness to Christ as suffering servant, as one who calls us friends and washes his disciples' feet.

Silence. First I encourage single persons to accept the spaces of silence in their lives as a blessing. In silence and solitude, we are able to take time to ask God the life questions that really count: "Who am I?" "What divinely-inspired direction might my life take if I have the courage to surrender to God's way with and for me?" In inner calm and stillness, we temper our tendency to be overly self-directive and become more receptive to the guidance of the Holy Spirit. In due course, as silence creates in us a space to listen, we will find that ministry becomes less a problem to be mastered and more a mystery to be lived, in and through the power of God's grace.

Reading. Second, rather than filling those silent spaces with useless bouts of worry and the birth of anxious concerns, I recommend that singles seek the word of God through spiritual reading, especially of the Scriptures and the writings of classical masters. It is wise in this regard to read books on, by, and about people who have lived their single life as a mode of service to the Most High. One text that readily comes to mind is Dat Hammarskjold's diary, *Markings*. In prose and poetry, he traces his personal negotiations with God as he strove to live as a dedicated servant, seeking peace on our troubled planet. Saints' lives can be equally inspiring. Who would not be uplifted by the single-hearted dedication of a Francis of Assisi or a Therese of Lisieux, a Dietrich Bonhoeffer or a Flannery O'Connor?

Meditation. The third step to living ministry as a mirror of the mystery is to become a reflective person who takes time to meditate, thus bringing the powers of one's intellect, memory, and will to bear on the duties and responsibilities of daily life. At times, our lives feel fragmented. It is as if we are ministering to others in several different directions all at once. Lest the confusion we feel within proliferate to the outer world, we need to stop short of exhaustion or burnout and try to see in an insightful way to what the bits and pieces of our creativity may be pointing. Once we come to understand what is causing the inner split between who we are and what we do, we can

290

begin to make some decisions to change what can be altered while trying to make the best of what is and has to be.

Prayer. At this juncture of apprehension and affirmation, one has no choice but to pray more and more faithfully for the divine guidance one needs. One strives not only to say prayers but to practice the prayer of presence. We want to be present prayerfully to God throughout our day so that we may behold and trust the Spirit's mysterious ways with us.

Prayer energizes us for ministry as no amount of mere intellectual stimulation or manual labor can. It enables us to approach our work as a form of ministry. What we do cannot be reduced to empty routine, the aim of which is only remuneration. Rather, through prayer, work becomes an ennobling opportunity to give of ourselves to others and to promote the common good of humanity.

Prayer is the bridge singles must cross if we want our work to become a mode of care and not merely a means of making money. This service orientation ought not to be an excuse to take advantage of a person just because he or she is single, nor ought it be a license to treat single persons unjustly. It is only to suggest, based on my own and others' experience, that single life can become an excuse for selfishness unless with God's help we cultivate this orientation to the otherness of the other. Without prayer and a serious commitment to deepen our spiritual life, single life runs the risk of succumbing to the narcissistic pursuit of self-gratification that kills generosity.

These four disciplines taken together—silence, spiritual reading, meditation, and prayer—protect singles from the ever present danger of losing their ministerial sensitivity to the entrapment of egocentrism. The best and only way of tempering this tendency is to bind one's life in the world to the Divine Other and to the otherness that is at the base of our capacity to be of service.

Styles and Principles of Responsible Ministry

Without going into many practical details, since these are dependent on each one's work situation, I would like to suggest some styles and principles of responsible ministry on the part of single women and men. It is essential, first of all, to respect the uniqueness or ultimate singleness of others. The best kind of ministry begins with our being responsive to the basic need in others to feel worthwhile, confirmed, and loved in their own right. It is sometimes the hardest thing in the world to resist imposing upon others our narrow image of who and what they should be. Teachers are especially influential in this regard. They can help those entrusted to their care to find the unique image of God in which they are made or they can resort to tactics of manipulation and seduction that destroy any possibility for real ministry.

Secondly, singles in the working world can create around themselves what I am fond of calling "welcoming space," where others really feel comfortable being themselves. A goal in this regard is to bless others on their journey of faith and formation, to give them a word by which they might find their way to happiness in this life. This word or gesture must arise from a heart accustomed to loving others inclusively, without a guarantee of reciprocal love in return. When we bless another, we express gratitude to God for bringing him or her forth in this world to accomplish a singular mission. Such heartfelt benediction can become a major goal of one's ministry. Any number of people may cross our path. Being single, we might be able to spend a few extra moments with them—to listen to a tale of woe or wonder, to offer a word of advice and encouragement, to show less by what we say and more by who we are that we really care about their well-being and want to give them plenty of space to grow.

For a single person, compassion is probably the best protection one has against the corrosive obstacles of narcissism, solipsism, withdrawal, and self-sufficiency carried to the extreme. This third principle of loving and responsible ministry beholds in mercy and forgiveness the vulnerable nature of the human condition. Single persons in ministry can only be compassionate to others if they have learned to feel some compassion for themselves. If there is one fault single persons must overcome, it is their tendency to beat themselves to death by overworking, by feeling guilty if they go on vacation, by falling into the trap of omni-availability. Once we accept our own less-than-perfect being, we can open our hearts to the limited yet lovable persons placed on our path.

Seeing others with compassionate eyes enables single persons to forestall some of the dehumanizing trends in contemporary society. People are children of God, not statistics. God loves us first and calls us by name. God thinks the world of us, and, I am convinced, God chooses single persons in a special way to bring this message home in a world that depersonalizes the homeless, labels the marginalized, and devalues the elderly.

Singles in Ministry

Everywhere in the world, single persons will be found standing with the poor, tending to their physical and spiritual needs, and helping others to see the ultimate oneness we all share as creatures of the same God and Father. Especially, single people who are not parents themselves evolve through experience a keen sense of the meaning of spiritual parenting, wherein they become fathers and mothers to many by laying aside self-centered desires and becoming desirous mainly of loving and serving others in Christ's name.

Obstacles to the Ministry of Singles

Undoubtedly the obstacles of rampant individualism, isolationism, and narcissism stand in the way of one's becoming a single minister who respects uniqueness, welcomes others into his or her space, and expresses compassion.

Further despoiling the service singles can offer church and society are the obstacles of rigidity, low-grade depression, and the workaholic tendency. Living alone can make a person so set in his or her ways that adaptation to or compatibility with others becomes difficult. Lacking the accountability typical of steady companionship and the need to address reciprocal lifestyles as in marriage, a single person can come to believe that there is only one means to execute a task. Stubbornness and a need to control can override the ministerial dispositions of flexibility and openness to dialogue.

While being alone occasionally is a fact of life no one can avoid, for single persons the pain of loneliness can become more prevalent than the joy of solitude. Being too much alone—fearing, for example, to go to a fine restaurant for dinner, whether or not one has a partner with whom to dine—can place singles at risk where the matter of low-grade depression is concerned. While one may not be clinically depressed or in need of medical attention or psychotherapy, one can feel as if the joy has been sucked out of life like juice from an orange. One may awaken and wonder, "What is the use? Why should I get out of bed this morning? Who cares if I am alive or dead?" One can develop a pervasively depreciative stance towards one's looks, one's gifts, seeing only lacks and the traits of a loser.

It is imperative that singles try to nip such negatives in the bud before they come into full bloom. Behind the overt symptom of ministry burnout, especially among people in the helping or service professions, resides the slow-acting poison of negative thoughts that produce poor self-images and feelings of despondency. One can become a chronic complainer and be almost without friends. Little wonder resentment takes the place of respect, envy of emulation, and competition of cooperation.

In a way, the opposite extreme of the person suffering from low-grade depression is the get-up-and-go workaholic, the person who takes pride in sleeping only a few hours a night, who feels guilty about taking time off to relax, who drives himself or herself to the point of exhaustion and dubs this "virtue that knows no bounds."

Activism pushes out creative action rooted in contemplation. The truth is that the single person who takes responsibility for a demanding ministry also needs time to enjoy stillness, to read, to reflect and pray, to study and write, to seek further education, and to grow in professional excellence.

What I am suggesting here is that single persons—in order, as it were, to justify their existence—may begin unwittingly to work themselves to death. We may allow others to take advantage of our goodwill unless we have pledged ourselves to make as a top priority the maintenance of a balance between work and worship, participation and recollection, labor and leisure.

The problem of being a single workaholic, who never says "no" for the sake of a greater "yes," is compounded because we live in a society that measures worth by means of functional accomplishment. We are what we achieve in such a climate. We are complimented when we cease to call ourselves "human beings" and instead accept the label of "human doings."

Finding the Balance

I once knew a doctor who preached to his patients the need for eight hours' rest, eight hours' work, eight hours' leisure a day—a truly balanced program that he himself, a single man, never lived. Instead, he worked 18 hours or more a day, dying in his late 40s. The same happened to a well-meaning prelate. He preached elegant sermons about how God worked for six days and rested on the seventh, but he made sure even his Sabbaths were filled with useful things to do. Burnout came for him also in his mid-40s, and he almost left the ministry.

Being in competition with oneself on the level of productivity is not only exhausting personally; it also makes it difficult to be present to others in an inspired, compassionate way. The great art is to exert oneself willingly above and beyond the call of duty—for a good cause or in the exercise of one's talents—while never neglecting the equally important values of proper rest and recreation. We need to replenish our inner resources lest we make the mistake, so prevalent in the single life, of running on empty.

There are times when we must listen to the still, small voice within, beckoning us to go away for a while, to step aside from burdensome tasks so that we can start over again with renewed energy, to heed the call to cease doing something useful and to simply be. These modes of being are not merely states in which nothing is going on. When we take distance from what we are doing to gain perspective, it is amazing how much inner, preconscious activity takes place. Now begins the work of creative reflection, of serious assessment of the here-and-now situation. Disparate thoughts may coalesce into new constellations of meaning. We can reach wise conclusions and make important decisions. These are the moments when time is pierced by the Eternal, when we create space for grace. Thus renewed, refreshed, and restored inwardly, we can give fully of ourselves to others. We can in our ministry as singles truly be messengers of the mystery.

For Further Reading

Fleming, David A. (ed.), *Fire and Cloud: An Anthology of Catholic Spirituality* (New York: Paulist Press, 1978).

Merton, Thomas, *Contemplation in a World of Action* (Garden City, NY: Image Books, 1973).

Mulholland, Robert M., *Shaped by the Word: The Power of Scripture in Spiritual Formation* (Nashville, Tenn.: The Upper Room, 1985).

Muto, Susan, *Pathways of Spiritual Living* (Petersham, Mass.: St. Bede's, 1991).

_____, *A Practical Guide to Spiritual Reading* (Denville, N.J.: Dimension Books, 1990).

_____, and Adrian van Kaam, *Practicing the Prayer of Presence* (Denville, N.J.: Dimension Books, 1980).

Underhill, Evelyn, *Practical Mysticism* (New York: E.P. Dutton, 1915).

van Kaam, Adrian, *Music of Eternity: Everyday Sounds of Fidelity* (Notre Dame, IN: Ave Maria Press, 1990).

Wells, Ronald V., *Spiritual Disciplines for Everyday Living* (Schenectady, NY: Character Research Press, 1982).

At the time of this writing, author and teacher Susan Muto was also executive director and co-founder of the Epiphany Association, 1145 Beechwood Blvd., Pittsburgh, PA 15206–4517.

"Tell Me What Your God Look Like, Celie": It Matters What Stories We Tell

Midge Miles

The symbolizing power of sacred stories has everything to do with our images and beliefs about who the Divine is, who we are before and with that Divine Other, and what our place is on this planet we call Earth. Thus, the choices we make in our use of stories are critical ones. Some sacred stories have been silenced or ignored and thus need to be told; others must be re-formed and told in new ways; still others must be created wholly new. Because of the formative power of both stories and storytellers, this article will discuss both the priestly dimension of storytelling and its prophetic dimension. I believe that every religious educator who is working for a more just and compassionate world must be aware of the seriousness of the stories we hear and the stories we tell.

The Formative Power of Storytelling

Our identities are formed by the stories we tell ourselves and one another about who we are, by the stories we embrace as our own (McFague 119–144). Before any of us told stories, we listened to stories, so that in a sense each of us becomes the story we are told to be. Or as Sallie TeSelle [McFague] writes, "The story of my life is structured by the larger stories (social, political, mythic) in which I understand my personal story to take place" (McFague 140). The familial and cultural stories we grew up with shaped our responses to such questions as: Where do I come from, who are my people, who and what is to be trusted/to be feared, who am I in relationship to all those others, what can I expect from life, and what is my role as a woman, as a man? (Christ 1–12). We are a "storied" and "storying" people. Ultimately, as John Dominic Crossan points out in *The Dark Interval: Towards a Theology of Story,* humans can no more live outside story than fish can live outside water.

The link between story and religion is a formidable one. Since ancient times, we human beings have attempted to express our deepest experiences

---

This article appeared in <u>PACE</u> 22 (1993).

of the sacred. Through story, drama, and dance, we have tried to convey what rational explanations can never do. And every attempt is incomplete, imperfect, at best a glimpse into the One we know as Mystery. Each of our sacred stories, the dramas of Moses and Miriam, of Rachel and Jacob, the parables and healing stories of Jesus, reveals yet another face of the Creator/Creating God who breathes life and love into us every day. As religious persons and communities, we tell, listen, and live into these tales as we deepen our meeting with the Holy One within ourselves.

The sacred stories of our tradition provide a cosmology that orients us personally and communally to the Divine. They provide, too, the symbols and metaphors for our image of the Divine and consequently for ourselves.

Priestly Storytelling

Religious educators are often engaged in what I call priestly storytelling, an aspect of priestly ministry that involves honoring the traditions of the religious community by bringing the past into the present through preserving its stories, acting in ritually remembered ways, and gathering in community.[1] If, for example, we rehearse a group of high school students for their contemporary presentation on the parables, prepare a fourth-grade class for its part in the Christmas Eve nativity drama, or conduct an adult Bible study, we are, in effect, saying, "Here, these, too, are the stories of your people, stories that have rinsed through the lives of countless members of this tradition for nearly two thousand years." "Stories, then, re-member us to the communities of people who belong to those stories" (see Williams 19). The power of story is what compels those of us who follow an itinerant storyteller named Jesus to continue to tell and ritually re-member ourselves to his Story.

When Priestly Storytelling Isn't Enough

Unfortunately, the primary stories of religion are not shaped by everyone's experience. The *anawim*, who include women and men of color, the aging and the differently abled, the poor and marginalized, nearly all women, those who are of other than North American immigrant or European ancestry, and the Earth herself, rarely hear their voices echoed in the stories of religion and culture. If the dialectic between story and experience is real, then we must ask "Whose experience is shaping whose story?"

From my experience conducting workshops in storytelling and spirituality as well as teaching theology in high school, I have become convinced that our religious stories are, for the most part, written, shaped, and told by storytellers who are white, male, clergy, or theologians. My point is not to dissuade religious educators from drawing on the resources of these narrative theologians and storytellers, but to suggest that their stories are simply not true enough for many of those they presume to be speaking for.

In *Diving Deep and Surfacing,* Carol Christ describes the effect of patriarchal stories on women's experience. "Women have been neither the tellers nor the shapers of their own stories . . . . Without stories she cannot understand herself, is alienated from those deeper experiences of self and world that have been called religious or spiritual . . . she is closed in silence" (Christ 1). Her words describe the "culture of silence" that is the reality not only of women but all the *anawim,* all those who are unable to tell their own tale, who inherit someone else's story and are constrained to live out inauthentic lives. This poem written by an anonymous Navaho child is a poignant example of one whose story has been silenced by the sanctioned storytellers of patriarchy:

Have you ever hurt about baskets?

I have, seeing my grandmother weaving for a long time.

Have you ever hurt about work?

I have, because my father works too hard and he tells me how hard he works.

Have you ever hurt about cattle?

I have, because my grandfather has been working on the cattle for a long time.

Have you ever hurt about school?

I have, because I learned a lot of words from school, and they are not my words.

Because my own passion has been the religious education of women, I mourn the ways textbooks on the Hebrew Scriptures devote so much attention to the history of the patriarchs but silence the stories of the women who were their raped or exploited lovers, daughters, and wives. I mourn, too, the absence of female images from children's religious stories that include tales about animals and things with characters such as, "Joshua, The Littlest Shepherd" or "Freddy, the Raindrop." If you still question the impact of imagery in shaping our spiritualities, remember this conversation from *The Color Purple:*

Then she say, "Tell me what your God look like, Celie."

"OK," I say. "He big and old and tall and gray bearded and white. He wear white robes and go barefooted."

298

"Blue eyes?" she ast.

"Sort of bluish—gray. Cool. Big though. White lashes," I say. (Walker 175).

Sacred stories, whether from the canon of biblical literature or the wider religious tradition, should provide images which both affirm our experience as we know it and stretch us toward a vision of wholeness and justice. This is what Jesus did through his use of parables, challenging his listeners to envision a different future, provoking them into hope, into seeing a better way of living and acting (Bausch).

Prophetic Storytelling

Speak up for the people who cannot speak for themselves. Protect the rights of all who are helpless, the rights of the poor and needy (Proverbs 31:8–9).

In discussing the role of the prophet, Bernice Marie-Daly writes, "The prophet calls for systemic change, a change possible only with the re-evaluation of our assumptions and categories that perpetuate injustice—not simply a reshuffling of old pieces but a real inversion of power" (Rae 100). Prophetic storytelling requires nothing less than a reevaluation of our assumptions about stories and their storytellers! We need to bring a "hermeneutics of suspicion" to our selection and telling of sacred stories, a critical perspective, in order for the whole religious community to hear the whole religious community imaged through their telling. To transform stories is nothing less than to transform our imaginations, which in turn, will transform the culture. In this manner, we can "keep alive the ministry of imagination, keep conjuring and proposing alternative futures"(Brueggemann 45).

Our Tasks as Prophetic Storytellers

(1) As an educator you are a teller of stories, a maker of form. The primary story you communicate is the one that you are. In all the ways you share stories with your listeners in ministry and in the daily narratives of conversation, claim your right and responsibility as a prophetic storyteller. Pay attention to the stories and storytellers you draw on who shape the telling of your own tale and those of the tradition, as well.

(2) Where necessary re-form and then re-tell stories, always crediting the original author, explaining that yours is an adaptation of her/his work. Create new images and metaphors which redeem the story of its sexism, racism, ageism, etc. The most frequent retelling I do is correcting the

stereotypic roles given male and female characters—still the norm in most stories, whether they're about flowers, people, or bunny rabbits.

(3) Work with diocesan staff and teachers to recognize limited or distorted symbols and imagery in your curriculum and resource materials. Contact publishers to express dismay with their narrow perception of what constitutes experience that could genuinely be described as religious.

Working with Scripture Stories

(1) Raise up and tell the biblical stories of those *anawim*, most of whom are women, whose tales are rarely the stuff of homilies or religious education curriculum.

(2) We must enter imaginatively and expand the stories of those who have been allowed to slip in sideways, at best, amid patriarchs and apostles.

(3) We must sometimes create parables, midrashim, and metaphors from our own experience "which make available the power of the tradition in new ways" (Fisher 123).

Where priestly storytelling is concerned with rooting us in the traditions and beliefs of a people, prophetic storytelling challenges the tradition to assure that the stories it tells about who we are and who our God is are genuinely religious, that they shape and are shaped by the experience of the whole community. Always an attempt to express our encounter with Divine Mystery, our sacred stories must be as richly diverse and ever-changing as Mystery itself. It is, after all, our experiences of being held and embraced by the Divine, which have impelled us throughout history to tell, dance, and sing its Story.

Questions to Consider When Choosing Stories
- Whose experience shaped this story; whose voice tells the tale?
- Whose story is silenced or distorted by the telling?
- For whom does it assume to be speaking?
- To what extent does it "speak up for those who cannot speak for themselves"?
- How shall we remember this story so that it compels us toward justice and wholeness? In what ways might/should it be re-imagined differently?[2]

Suggestions for Further Reading

Bausch, William. *Storytelling, Imagination, and Faith.* Mystic, CT: Twenty-Third Publications, 1984.

Brody, Ed, Rona Levinthall, and Jay Goldspinner, eds. *Spinning Tales, Weaving Hope: Stories of Peace, Justice, and Environment.* Philadelphia: New Society Publishers, 1991.

Kirk, Martha Ann. *Celebrations of Biblical Women's Stories: Tears, Milk, and Honey.* Kansas City, MO: Sheed and Ward, 1987.

Endnotes

1. I am indebted to Maria Harris for her descriptions of prophetic and priestly ministry.
2. My final two questions are adapted from Katherine Zappone's *The Hope for Wholeness* (Mystic, CT: Twenty-Third, 1990).

References

Bausch, William. *Storytelling, Imagination, and Faith.* Mystic, CT: Twenty-Third Publications, 1984.

Brueggemann, Walter. *The Prophetic Imagination.* Minneapolis: Augsburg/Fortress, 1978.

Christ, Carol. *Diving Deep and Surfacing: Women Writers on Spiritual Quest.* Boston: Beacon Press, 1980.

Crossan, John Dominic. *The Dark Interval: Toward a Theology of Story.* Allen, TX: Tabor (Argus), 1975.

Fisher, Kathleen. *The Inner Rainbow: The Imagination in Christian Life.* Mahwah, NJ: Paulist Press, 1983.

McFague, Sallie. *Speaking in Parables: A Study in Metaphor and Theology.* Minneapolis: Augsburg/Fortress, 1975.

Rae, Eleanor, and Bernice Marie-Daly. *Created in Her Image; Models of the Feminine Divine.* New York: Crossroad, 1990.

Walker, Alice. *The Color Purple.* New York: Washington Square Press, 1982.

Williams, Michael. "Voices from Unseen Rooms: Storytelling and Community" in *Weavings* (July/August 1990).

At the time of this writing, Midge Miles was a storyteller and adult educator, founder, and director of STORYSHOPPES and its certified training program, MINISTRY IN STORY.

Helping Children Achieve Self-Worth Through Tae Kwon Do

Roscann Klosterman, CSJ

Sacred Heart School is a small K–6 school in upstate New York. The children are from a variety of economic backgrounds, with probably half from middle to low income families. The rest range from very poor to comfortable. I have been principal here for five years, noticing after the first two years that many of the children appeared hyperactive, overly anxious, and self-defeating. They had no confidence in their own ability and no inner belief in their self-worth. They showed no sense of responsibility for their actions (their mother always forgot). At the same time that I was concerned about the lack of purpose and self-control demonstrated by our students, a young single mother came to my office to register her child for kindergarten. This mother of two was telling me about her five-year-old daughter, comparing her to her eight-year-old son. As I listened, I was quite happy the eight-year-old was not coming to Sacred Heart. This was also disturbing to me because we certainly had many children who, like her son, showed no signs of self-discipline or self-caring. As I was wondering out loud about how to reach these children, a substitute teacher came into the office. She was my first introduction to the Korean martial art of Tae Kwon Do.

Tae Kwon Do is a form of self-defense. The Western attitude toward self-defense is strictly physical. But in the East, Tae Kwon Do is a state of mind. Control of one's mind, self-restraint, kindness, and humility must accompany physical grace (Chun 8). Being proficient in technique as an end in itself is not enough for a master from the East; the art must be integrated as a "way of being-in-the-world" (Chun 8). I found this information very intriguing—especially this "way of being-in-the-world"—people trying to get in touch with their inner selves knowing their own temperament and choosing "the way" accordingly. They then would be in harmony with the universe, choosing what is creative rather than destructive.

As I spoke with the substitute teacher, she told me she had two sons who were taking lessons in Tae Kwon Do, and she herself was a red belt. Her

This article appeared in PACE 22 (1993).

sons were young at the time—in elementary school, and she hoped her sons, besides learning the physical skills, would also learn some important life skills, such as being perceptive enough to avoid persons and situations which would inhibit their growth and development. To be able to know themselves and what strengths and weaknesses they possess so that they can live life to the fullest. This is, of course, our goal as Catholic Christians—to live our lives to the full and to use our God-given potential for our good and for the good of others. "The essence of Tae Kwon Do is to make the individual aware of personal strengths and of how to apply them to the greatest advantage. In this way the individual overcomes the only real weakness: lack of faith in oneself" (Chun 19). It struck me, then, hearing those words, "our only real weakness is a lack of faith in ourselves," that this was what the children in our school were missing: belief in themselves, self-images that fortify a sense of accomplishment and their ability to make a difference in their world. Many of our children lack a sense of being somebody!

Maybe there was something to this art of Tae Kwon Do—a way of unifying body, mind, and spirit—a way to overcome self-doubt and fear, a way to be in touch with one's center and ultimately with one's God.

I visited the Tae Kwon Do school and spoke to the owner. (He teaches the traditional Korean Tae Kwon Do.) Mr. Y.J. George gave me more information: "The beginning of wisdom is for one to know what is already contained within oneself and therefore have no desire to forcefully seize it from another. Thought is made clear, action efficient, and human life, which consists in the integration of these two things, is enhanced" (Chun 9). Since it was the end of June, I decided to take lessons myself so that I could give some kind of judgment on the program. It is hard work; a person has to listen and can't allow the mind to wander. By the end of the summer, I felt this program would help the children build self-esteem, confidence, and discipline by getting in touch with themselves.

We made arrangements for Mr. George to teach the children one day a week beginning in September. I made Tae Kwon Do mandatory for all students in grades one through six. I felt the students could not handle having a choice, because they tend to quit anything that may require some work.

Class begins with stretches and jumping jacks and progresses to various self-defense techniques. Mr. George says a good work-out has nothing to do with breaking boards or what the children may see in Saturday morning cartoons or afternoon Kung Fu movies. The children do practice different kicks and punches and how to block them, but there is no sparring. According to Mr. George, traditional martial arts teaches nonviolence, and fighting is never encouraged. Mr. George stresses the spiritual and moral aspects of Tae Kwon Do. The children are required to learn the five basic tenets of Tae

Kwon Do: courtesy, integrity, self-control, perseverance, and indomitable spirit. They also learn what each tenet means and how to practice the tenets: courtesy in the lunchroom; self-control during music and art class; integrity when taking a test; to persevere when they join a team, such as basketball and not quit because they're mad at the coach, want more playing time, or don't want to practice; indomitable spirit when they are trying to learn a difficult skill—whether physical or mental.

Each workout is fifty minutes long and in silence. The children enter the gym, remove their shoes and socks, put their socks in their shoes, line them against the wall, toes toward the wall. They then line up at attention in the gym, six across and six to ten deep, without saying a word. The only ones who speak during class are Mr. George and his two or three assistants.

After the workout, which lasts about forty minutes, the children line up again (still silent) and sit on the floor with their legs crossed, hands on their knees. The children are then quizzed on the tenets and the Tae Kwon Do oath: (1) I will observe the tenets of Tae Kwon Do. (2) I will respect all instructors and all seniors. (3) I will never misuse Tae Kwon Do. (4) I will be a champion of peace and justice. (5) I will build a more peaceful world. At this time, the children may also share with the instructors how they have practiced the tenets or helped to bring peace to others either at home or in school. After the sharing, the children are quiet again for a few minutes of silence to think about themselves and what gifts and talents make them proud to be who they are. Class concludes with the Prayer of St. Francis, asking God to make them "instruments of your peace." For fifty minutes a week, the children are silent, disciplined, and peaceful.

This attitude of the children is thrilling to me. They are encouraged to do their best kicks and punches, and their inner power grows, as does their confidence. In class they must also learn patterns of punches, kicks, blocks, and stances. These patterns could be compared to dance routines and are very difficult to learn. Each pattern is named for a quality or force in nature, and the pattern is done with this element in mind. The first pattern the children learn is one of basic moves to give them an idea of what is expected. The second is called "Keon," meaning heaven and light, so, when doing this pattern, the students focus on their inner strength as good (heaven) and all encompassing (light). The third pattern is "Tae," joyfulness. This pattern elicits joy in the person as the pattern is being performed.

The children must concentrate on their moves and keep their mind centered. These patterns could be a form of meditation—keeping in mind God's creation. This centering is a beginning for the children, a way for them to learn prayer techniques for meditation and contemplation. Once they've learned to be mentally still, they can go a step further.

In their classrooms, the teacher can take ten to fifteen minutes during the day—ask the children to sit where they are most comfortable, remove their shoes if they wish, close their eyes, and just relax. A breathing exercise could then be used to help them into prayer. William O'Malley, in his article on praying, has an excellent exercise. He says to tell the children to

Take a deep breath—a really deep breath: hold it for five counts, out for five counts, in . . . out . . . think of all the air in this room; we use it then pass it on, never knowing whom it has kept alive before us; we share that life-giving force. In. Out. Now go beyond this room to the envelope of air that surrounds the whole earth; you're a part of that—leaving us, crossing the Atlantic and Asia and the Pacific and back to us. In. Out. Now as you breathe in that air say inside the innermost room of yourself: "God, my good friend. . ." and as you breathe out,. . . "somehow You are alive in me." Say it again, several times to yourself (See O'Malley 509–5113).

After allowing a few minutes for the children to pray within themselves, gently call them back—have them move quietly to their places. I believe this prayer exercise or one similar can be used with any age group, adapting it to fit the children's level. O'Malley also addresses what I have touched on earlier. "Most of the limitations on our freedom are self-imposed: enslavement to others' judgments [peer pressure]," gigantification of our shortcomings [low self-esteem], and at the root: fear. If we could just lay hold of our inner selves, we might find "the serenity to accept the things that can't be changed, the courage to change the things that can be changed, and the wisdom to know the difference."

Using Tae Kwon Do as a springboard to help build confidence, discipline, and courage, we can lead our children into centering prayer so they will have the "wisdom" to "make" a difference.

Questions for Reflection

1. We cannot give what we do not have. Therefore, how do I try to integrate or balance the physical, mental, and emotional in my own life? Am I physically active, and do I take fifteen to thirty minutes a day to be with my God in prayer?

2. Am I sensitive to the pain and insecurity our society has thrust upon our children? What am I doing to give them a sense of self-worth and an awareness of God-within?

References

Chun, Richard. *Tae Kwon Do: The Korean Martial Art*. New York: Harper & Row, 1976.

O'Malley, William J. "Praying," *America* (June 6–13, 1992).

Suggested Readings

Chun, Richard. *Advancing in Tae Kwon Do*. New York: Harper & Row Publishers, 1982.

Rhee, Jhoon, Father of U.S. Tae Kwon Do. *Chon-Ji of Tae Kwon Do Hyung*. O'Hara Publications, Inc., 1984.

At the time of this writing, Roseann Klosterman, CSJ, was principal of Sacred Heart School in Utica, NY. She was working toward her blue belt ranking in Tae Kwon Do.

DREs and the Public Schools: A Call to Action

Thomas P. Walters

Currently there are approximately three-and-a-half million Catholic children and young adults attending parish religious education programs throughout the United States. These children also attend the nation's public schools. And minimally, there are at least a million more Catholic youngsters in the public schools who don't participate in any formal religious education program. By the time both of these groups of youngsters graduate at age eighteen (if they graduate), they will have spent 11,000 hours of their lives in a public school.

The public-school system is forming and educating close to 80 percent of the children of Catholic parents in the United Sates. What is happening today in our nation's public schools will have a dramatic impact on the Catholic Church of the twenty-first century. For DREs to leave the public-school context unattended is to pass up one of the most influential factors in our young people's religious formation.

However, there is an almost instinctive negative reaction whenever religious education is mentioned in the same breath as public schooling. This is because of the long-standing concern about the separation of Church and State. But there are many ways in which DREs can involve themselves in supporting and promoting the public schools and still avoid the many educational, political, and legal potholes that surround the issue of religion and public schooling. In this article, I will highlight a number of them.

My suggestions are stepping stones into the public schools. They are not controversial, and they are do-able—right now. They are activities that call on DREs and parishioners to step outside the confines of the parish center and into the public forum. They are activities that affirm and support the many members of the Catholic community—children and adults alike— who presently find their vocational call in the nation's public schools. They are activities that can accomplish what current K–12 programs are incapable of achieving. They can make religion and religious education a visible part of everyday life.

This article appeared in PACE 22 (1993).

I have divided my suggested activities into three categories—teachers and administrators, learners, and school environment. These are followed by a short bibliography.

Teachers and Administrators

- In the fall, have a back-to-school liturgy for all of the public-school children and teachers in your parish. Model it on Catechetical Sunday, but direct it to public-school teaching and the mission of the public schools.
- Once a year, sponsor a parish dinner to honor all of the parishioners who are employed in the public schools—teachers, administrators, secretaries, custodians, nurses, counselors, coaches. Don't forget those who teach on the college and university levels.
- Request that your diocesan paper do a weekly, monthly, or yearly article on an outstanding Catholic teacher(s) in the public schools. For example, Mr. Larry Hurt, an art teacher at Ben Davis High School in Indianapolis, Indiana, is one of the 1992–93 Disney Teachers of the Year.
- Invite the principal(s) from the school(s) within your parish boundaries to address parents on how they approach the teaching of values.
- Ask some of the public-school teachers in your parish to share some "teaching tips" with those catechists who are working in classroom settings in your religious-education program.
- Invite the local public-school teachers to share periodically with the catechists on the same grade level the activities and topic of study that they are or will soon be focusing on in school.
- Have all the youngsters in the parish religious-education program or a particular grade level plan a special celebration, dinner, awards banquet, or whatever for their public school teachers.

Learners

- Put together a free tutoring program for children in the parish who may be having difficulty with math, reading, or other school subjects. These tutors could be adults or high-school youngsters who have the skill and patience to do the job well.
- Sponsor a "Getting a Summer Job" fair for the young people in the parish. Work with the school counselors in designing it.
- Have grade-level liturgies for the youngsters at the beginning of the school year. In the intercessory prayer, include the names of the various schools represented.
- If the schools have a "Student of the Month," and one of the children in the parish receives the award, make note of it in the parish bulletin and/or post his or her picture in the church vestibule. Someone from the education committee could contact the school each month to find out who the chosen students are.

- The same things as above could be done for athletes, drama club, Mcdonald's or Wendy's employees of the month, and other activities in which parish youth are involved. This type of activity is limited only by one's imagination. Remember, it's the thought that counts, and a thoughtful parish community will have an impact on its youth.
- On the other side of the coin, if youngsters do something special in the parish—raise money for a needy family, participate in a walk-a-thon, or whatever—have a representative from the parish let the public school know.
- If the school if looking for volunteers for a particular project, volunteer as members of the parish community. Own activities as parish members and not just as parents who have children in the school.
- If some children need transportation to and from school, set up a carpool. It doesn't have to be your own children; they don't even have to be children from the parish. In fact, it may be that your child doesn't need a ride. The carpool is a service offered to the community by the parish.
- Sponsor social-justice activities that the youngsters in the parish can get involved in. Check with teachers in the schools who are designing such projects and find out how the parish can help. Let the teachers and administrators know that the parish is ready and willing to help in any way possible. This witness will not be lost on the children.
- Sponsor an English as a Second Language (ESL) program, if it is needed for youngsters in the parish or in the local area. If the school is looking for volunteers to assist in such a program, take the lead and help put together a team of volunteers.
- If you have a special project that you want done in the parish, see if there is a way in which you could involve the public school. For example, if you need some art work, check with the art teacher to see if there are some students who have the talent and the interest to take on the task.

School Environment
- In your position as DRE, schedule an appointment each year with the principals of the various schools which the children and young adults in your parish attend. Explain to them your parish's programs and your willingness to help the school in any way you can.
- If possible, gather the other DREs in your school district (Catholic, Protestant, Jewish, Muslim) and try to schedule a meeting with the principals to talk about topics of interest. It is best for the religious educators to meet first and decide on the topics for discussion. It is important that these meetings be viewed not as confrontational, but as an opportunity for sharing and finding ways to be helpful to each other.
- Raise money to improve the library's holdings on world religions. Ask people in the parish to donate funds to help the schools in your district to

improve areas of the library that are in need of special attention—the religion section might be a good place to start. Each year the parish could buy copies of the Newberry winners and donate them to the library.

- Encourage the parish to start a fund for children in the public schools who are in need of clothing and food. The principals of the schools involved could identify (not by name) the needy families or student and distribute the monies or gift certificates in the name of the parish.
- When there is a controversial issue that arises in the schools, sponsor a debate. This will help the parish realize that issues that affect the community are religious-education concerns.
- Help the senior citizens in the parish organize some type of program to provide assistance to the public schools in the parish. The number of ideas they will come up with is probably surpassed only by their combined ages.
- Include some reference to the public schools each week in the general intercessions.
- Check with the schools to see if there is a special project that could be undertaken (cleaning up some outside walls, landscaping, painting a corridor) for which parishioners could volunteer their services. The presence of the parish community in the school building and in the lives of the children serves as a living reminder that the Church has a real role to play in their lives.
- Find out from school officials what your parish can do to enhance public schooling in the community.
- Put together a listing of parishioners who have special talents or are leaders in the community and who are available to speak to students or teachers in the schools. This can be a very helpful listing that exists in the community. It is also a compliment to parishioners when they are asked to volunteer their services in the name of the parish community.
- Set aside a day at the end of each school year to say "Thank you" to all in the parish who volunteered their services to the public schools.

Conclusion

For too long, public schools have received at best benign neglect from the Catholic community. It is time for this to change. It is time for religious educators, DREs in particular, to take the lead in encouraging the Catholic community to embrace the public schools. This is a call to action—a call to recognize, support, and promote the role of the public schools in the ongoing religious formation of Catholic youth.

Suggested Readings

I have found the following books both affirming of the public schools and insightful. They are well-written and are available at most bookstores.

Bloom, Jill. *Parenting Our Schools: A Hands-On Guide to Education Reform.* Boston: Little, Brown and Company, 1992. Provides the information needed to understand and take the lead in reforming our public education system.

Fiske, Edward B. *Smart Schools, Smart Kids.* New York: Simon & Schuster, 1991. Fiske, the former education editor for *The New York Times,* takes you inside some of the effective "new" schools of the 1990s. This book focuses on what is right in public schooling.

Grant, Gerald. *The World We Created at Hamilton High.* Cambridge: Harvard University Press, 1988. This book is, in the words of Art Seidenbaum of the *Los Angeles Times,* "[A] graceful, human, engaging narrative of what happened to an American high school during successive decades of optimism, integration, student upstarting, and declining results. . . . A superb case history of what is probably the noblest American dream—education for everybody." I agree.

Kidder, Tracy. *Among Schoolchildren.* Boston: Houghton Mifflin Company, 1989. Kidder takes you inside Mrs. Zajac's classroom at Kelly School in Holyoke, Massachusetts. It is a gripping and realistic account of what it is to be a teacher in today's public schools. It is a book not only about teaching, but about life.

Matthews, Jay. *Escalante: The Best Teacher in America.* New York: Henry Holt and Company, 1988. Matthews, Los Angeles bureau chief of *The Washington Post,* wrote this inspiring book about the efforts of Jaime Escalante, a math teacher at Garfield High School in East Los Angeles. It is the story of a fascinating and courageous teacher.

Schlechty, Phillip C. *Schools for the 21st Century.* San Francisco: Jossey-Bass Publishers, 1991. The author challenges us to reexamine both the structure and fundamental purpose of our nation's schools. He stresses the need for long-term commitment to the restructuring that needs to take place in the public schools. This book offers an intriguing perspective on the nature and purpose of public schooling on the verge of the twenty-first century.

Sizer, Theodore. *Horace's Compromise: The Dilemma of the American High School.* Boston: Houghton Mifflin Company, 1984. This is the oldest of the books I am recommending, but it offers five rather compelling imperatives for better schools. According to James Herndon, author of *The Way It Spozed to Be,* "Sizer reminds us that the essentials of the school are teachers, students and subjects and asks us to begin thinking about schools in which these components may flourish."

At the time of this writing, Thomas P. Walters was dean of St. Meinrad School of Theology, Indiana.

Confirmation Service: A Prerequisite or a Response?

Susan Murphy

One of the most tedious features in any adolescent Confirmation preparation program is the bookkeeping of the dreaded "service project hours." You know the routine. You line up a group of reluctant teenagers preparing for Confirmation and assign them jobs, such as cleaning the kitchen in the church hall or raking the yards of some elderly parishioners. And, for the next six months, you try to keep track of who has completed which hours, while one of the candidates tries to convince you that he shoveled someone's walk once, a year or so ago, and doesn't that count? Debit and credit. Balance the ledger.

And while your frustration has you gnawing on your desktop, you try to recall what was so spiritual about this concept anyway. The interminable parade of disinclined teenagers, resistant parishioners who believe teenagers aren't much help anyway, and parents who are convinced that their children are overburdened, is a specter to haunt even the most confident DRE. The notion of Confirmation directly following Baptism, light years before this child is your responsibility, is suddenly looking very appealing. Relative merits of infant Confirmation notwithstanding, if your parish is committed to adolescent Confirmation, then you are probably struggling with the issue of "service hours."

The Value of Service

Service could be defined as the utilization of one's energy and talent to meet a need outside of one's self. All of our lives we are either serving others or being served. The caliber of our existence is frequently defined by our willingness and ability to serve others.

Jesus responds to his apostles, who are arguing about which of them was the most important apostle, "Anyone among you who aspires to greatness must serve the rest; whoever wants to rank first among you must serve the needs of all." (Mark 10:43–44). Jesus reminds us that in order to

---

This article appeared in PACE 23 (1994).

serve him, to serve God, we must serve each other as he has served us. To have value, to reinforce one's self-esteem, a service must be more than a chore. It must be a total responsibility.

How many times has someone approached you with some gruesome chore that no one wants to do and said, "Don't you have some Confirmation kids that owe you some service hours?" Debit and credit. Balance the ledger. How could a job which no adult wants possibly impart any sense of worth to a young person? What exactly are we trying to teach our young people? That they are only worthy of the most menial errand? Do we then expect them to infer from this servile assignment that they are revered and honored members of our faith community? And we wonder why young people leave our flock in droves after they are confirmed!

The Nature of Service

Very young children are totally served by their parents and family, because they cannot care for themselves. All the needs of an infant or young children must be met by someone else. As children mature, a shift in their relationship to their world occurs. They develop the ability to perform simple tasks. This development allows children to interact bilaterally with the adult community. Children must still rely on older people to provide their most basic needs, but may concurrently contribute to their family community by performing simple chores. However, adults still define the tasks and outline the parameters of each task. This system of learning is appropriate skills for each chore. "When I was a child I used to talk like a child, think like a child, reason like a child. When I became a man I put childish ways aside" (1 Corinthians 13:11).

If we want our teenagers to think and act like adults, we need to expand how we think about the areas of their responsibilities—beyond the "chore list." If adolescent Confirmation is envisioned as a "rite of passage" into adult faith, then the parish needs to acknowledge its obligation to fully receive these young people into the adult community.

Service as a Prerequisite

One notion of adolescent Confirmation is that the privilege to be confirmed is somehow **earned**—like a place on the honor roll or a varsity letter. If one attends a number of years of religious education, writes an insightful letter to the bishop, and completes the prescribed number of service hours, the sacrament is **conferred** like a Bachelor of Arts degree. In that context, Confirmation is the finale, and the performance of service is a means to this end—a procedure with no inherent value. And too often, in this framework, the newly confirmed see their obligation to this community as fulfilled and their relationship with their parish as being concluded. Debits and credits. Balance the ledger.

If we follow the model of the Rite of Christian Initiation of Adults, we understand that Confirmation is a process of learning and faith development, as well as an initiation into the community of believers. In that realization, service is not a stepping stone to a goal, but an expression of faith—a witness to Christian life, that occurs as a **result** of the renewal of baptismal vows. The commitment, therefore, should be service to the parish **after** the sacrament, not before! And if adolescent Confirmation is, in part, an initiation into the adult faith community, then the service should be in the form of adult roles in the parish and not to those menial tasks that no one else wants.

Service as a Response

Instead of talking about service, perhaps we should be discussing "ministry." Most discussions of youth ministry involve the ways in which older parishioners minister to young parishioners. Seldom do we see our young people as ministers themselves, taking on responsibilities usually reserved for adults. And yet, if we are to communicate to our teenagers that one facet of the Sacrament of Confirmation is to make an adult commitment to their faith, then the faith community has a reciprocal obligation to fully receive these newly confirmed adults into parish life.

What kinds of ministry can adolescents do well?

1. Religious education. What teenagers lack in experience and knowledge, they make up for in enthusiasm and true affection for the younger children. More importantly, the teenager's very presence in this catechetical role is a powerful witness to the students. Most of our teenagers who choose a catechetical role for their service commitment themselves had a teenage religion teacher when they were younger.

2. Retreat team. High-school seniors are the most affective small-group facilitators at a retreat for younger adolescents. The senior retreat team meets once a month, throughout the years, developing their leadership skills and bonding with each other as a team. On the retreat weekend, retreatants, who may be just freshmen or sophomores, will discuss issues with peer-group leaders that they would never raise with adults.

3. Liturgy. Teenagers function well as lectors, Eucharistic ministers, and ushers. This is a very visible ministry that serves to persuade the assembly that the youth of the parish are spiritual, respectful, mature young people of whom the congregation may be very proud.

4. Music. Do you have a Mass in your parish schedule that needs some musical support? Very often parish budgets do not allow for a full music program at every Mass. More and more teenagers today are accomplished musicians, more than willing to learn contemporary sacred music. A group of young musicians, under the guidance of the music director, could provide the music for one of the Sunday liturgies, as long as the parish is willing to concede to electric guitars and keyboards. An accompanying benefit of this ministry could be a sudden influx of young people at this Mass.

5. Christian outreach. As part of our parish's ministry to the elderly and homebound, teenagers who chose this service are matched with a person who is confined to home because of physical limitations. The first time a teenager visits that person, he or she is accompanied by an experienced adult member of the team. After the initial visit, the teenager telephones regularly to talk with this person, visits once a week, does personal errands, and sends greeting cards. Often a very warm and lasting friendship develops that benefits the members of both generations.

6. Soup kitchen. Is your parish committed to preparing and serving a monthly or weekly meal at a nearby soup kitchen? Having a team of high-school seniors who can be counted on to be present each month relieves the amount of recruiting the parish team needs to do every month. These teenagers are strong, energetic, and bring an enthusiasm to their participation that lightens everyone's burden.

If we want to communicate to our youth that love is certainly an action, we need to provide them with the opportunities to express their spirituality in a meaningful way. In your parish there are probably many more areas where your young people could be setting their lamp on a stand, "where it gives light to all in the house. In the same way, your light must shine before [all] so that they may see goodness in your acts and give praise to your heavenly Father" (Matthew 5:15–16).

You may ask, "If teenagers have already been confirmed, how do you get them to carry out the service commitment?" The key is in the presentation. The privilege to serve the parish is reserved only to those mature enough to be initiated fully into the faith community—those who have celebrated their acceptance of God's grace and the fulfillment of their baptismal promises in the Sacrament of Confirmation. Younger adolescents are very aware of the high school seniors who are functioning in very visible adult roles in their church. Unquestionably, these teenagers perceive the taking on of important roles in the parish as a milestone in their highway to adulthood. In this setting, the service component of the Confirmation process becomes a motivator for the young people, instead of a hurdle. As Sister Kieran Sawyer said, "Confirmation is the celebration of one's willingness to be for others as Jesus was, to use one's gifts for the sake of the community, to further the growth of justice and love in the world, to give one's life in the service of others" *(Confirming the Faith,* Notre Dame, IN: Ave Maria Press, 1982, 10).

If we wish to give our young people a sense of the nobility of service to others, we must allow them to move gracefully into our spiritual life and express fully, with the characteristic passion, their singular response to the realization of God's love in their lives.

At the time of this writing, Susan Murphy directed the religious education program at Our Lady of Fatima, Sudbury, MA.

Right and Wrong: Contemporary Catholic Perspectives

Timothy E. O'Connell

When religious educators are asked to teach morality or to discuss their teaching, one often discerns a look of barely repressed terror. In many cases, it seems that the teachers are not altogether clear about their own views, theoretical or practical. Beyond that, they often experience issues of morality as charged with political energy; it is so easy to be misunderstood, to offend, to "slip." And so their first urge is to request transfer to another section, to retreat into the background, or to dumbly parrot the cagey formulations of the text.

But it need not be so. Even with all the discussions of our age, the controversies and questions, there are dependable perspectives that can undergird the teacher's efforts. This article addresses these perspectives. And with regard to a central question, the character of "right" and "wrong," it offers suggestions for the educational ministry we all cherish.

Right and Wrong

The questions we are pursuing are quite simple: What is right? And what is wrong? And why? In recent years Catholic moral theologians have spilt acres of ink on these questions. They have generated a frightening quantity of heat and, thank God, a good bit of light. Let me set the situation for you.

The sort of Catholic moral theology proposed in recent centuries, that was taught in seminaries and preached from pulpits, has been, it is fair to say, very legalistic. The moral life was understood in terms of rules, and the central dynamic of Christian living was understood as obedience, as the generous acceptance of and faithful adherence to the rules of "legitimate authority."

For some purposes, that authority was understood as the Church, or even the State. Thus, for example, many Catholics thought (think?) that there is a "rule against divorce," that it is "forbidden" to them. And for years there

This article appeared in PACE 22 (1992).

was the quite common presumption that obedience, even unquestioning acquiescence, to civil laws was an immediate and necessary consequence of Catholic religious commitment.

In other contexts, this traditional Catholic perspective understood "legitimate authority" as referring to God's own self. Thus, one would hear blithe references to the "moral law," "ethical prohibitions," the "will of God," as if moral oughts were nothing more than arbitrary divine edicts, exercises of dominative authority over human persons. In all these cases, however, what was central was that the shape and character of the appropriate Christian ethical response was the same: obedience.

There are many specific historical reasons why this view held sway. We cannot detail them here. Suffice it to say that this approach to morality was rooted in overarching perspectives on life, perspectives which justified legalism and, indeed, in some ways required it. In any case, recent decades have seen a shift. Building on quiet scholarly developments in the last century, the mid-1900s witnessed a concerted effort to break out of this legalistic mentality. If behaviors really are morally wrong, said this new approach, the reason for that wrongness cannot be simply that they are prohibited. For that would make of the Christian life an activity that is arbitrary and, ultimately, trivial and insignificant. If a behavior is morally wrong, it has to be wrong on the grounds that it is really and objectively destructive.

Conflict and Change

This "revisionist" approach was, in its core assertions, nothing else than the ancient Catholic natural law tradition stripped of its legalistic accretions and restored to its initial beauty. But, for all that, the approach did represent something new. For, in the twentieth century, we are exquisitely aware of two truths about human life. And focused attention to these truths led to nuancing of this traditional vision.

The first truth is that human persons are finite. We are not God; we are merely human. Because we are finite, all of our human choices involve the resolution of conflict. For we, quite simply, cannot do everything. To do one thing is to leave another thing undone. To serve one need is to leave another need unmet. Consequently, what makes a particular behavior morally right is the fact that it is as helpful as possible, given the alternatives. And what makes an action immoral is the fact that it is unnecessarily destructive.

Actually, even this sensitivity to conflict is not altogether new. Medieval Catholic theology emphasized the central role of prudence in the living of the Christian life. For only a prudent person can make difficult moral judgments and choices. And moral textbooks often spoke of the need for a "proportionate reason" for the toleration of evil. But what is new is the escalation of this insight into an element of general moral theory: Moral judgments always involve the resolution of conflict, and attention to proportions is unavoidably necessary. Indeed, because of this sensitivity, this revisionist perspective is sometimes called *Proportionalism.*

The second truth to which the revisionists were sensitive was that of temporality, the reality of time, of change, and of change's product: history. We live within the envelope of time. The past is not the future; what has been does not determine what will be. And consequently, although past experience teaches us much about ourselves and about what our future will be, it does not teach us everything. The possibility of something truly, powerfully new remains one of the challenges we face.

Out of that awareness, then, the revisionists asked a telling question: Given that what makes something wrong is that it is truly, objectively destructive, are there any specific behaviors that are **always** unduly destructive and, beyond that, **probably** always unduly destructive? For, if it is true that history presents us with a future that is truly, essentially new, can we ever be certain that judgments of the past will remain valid in the future, that what was destructive will remain so in times to come? Or to put this another way, granted that our morality is an **objective** morality, is it also true that it is an **unchanging** morality? Indeed, can one have an unchanging morality in a changing world?

In answer to this question, the revisionists/Proportionalists said that the best one can do is to be faithful to the complex and changing circumstances of our lives, doing as much good as possible and as little harm as necessary, tentatively trusting the past while being open to the possible newness of the future.

Response

In the 70s and 80s there was a reaction against the Proportionalists by a group of Catholic theologians and philosophers. Their position was that morality is not just a matter of balancing things. Morality is a matter of being faithful to what it means to be human. But this fidelity means that here are certain things human beings should never do. There are certain "basic goods" which should always be observed and respected. Granted that one cannot do every good thing for everybody (a point made by the Proportionalists), one should at least not do bad things to people. At least, one should leave them alone!

Now, the details of the debate between Proportionalists and the proponents of a Basic Goods approach could occupy us for hours. For our purposes, though, the key point to make is simply this: For the better part of the last ten years, these two groups have been shooting at each other, at best engaging in honest theological debate about passionately held views, at worst indulging in a shameful exercise in intellectual polemics.

319

Recently, however, a ray of hope can be seen, a tendency to move beyond the polarized camps into a synthesis of the wisdom contained in each. It is that synthesis which is really useful to those of us in religious education. I will attempt to summarize that synthesis here.

New Synthesis

The kernel of wisdom that the Basic Goods People (if I may use that term) offer and that is being espoused more and more widely is that the rock-bottom premise for Christian morality, the reason we pursue morality at all is because human persons have worth. That worth does not come from their productivity or talent or beauty or utility. It comes from the fact that they are human. Hence, the bottom-line foundation for objective morality is the non-negotiable dignity of the human person. All the proportionality in the world cannot justify trading away the intrinsic dignity of the human person. For, if one trades away that dignity, one is trading away the very reason for the moral enterprise itself.

On the other hand, the gift that the Proportionalists bring becomes clear when we begin to activate ourselves to positively care for persons, when we decide to respond to the intrinsic dignity of person by acts of caring love. The way we actually do that is by trying to do as much good as possible and as little harm as necessary, by responding to the complex and interdependent realities of the situation with creativity and compassion, by assessing the available alternatives with an awareness of the dimensions of conflict and change.

So the Basic Goods People define the terrain and then the Proportionalists offer the strategy. Let me rephrase this in a way that will be helpful to religious educators. The insight of the Basic Goods People, that the bottom line of morality is a positive respect for human dignity, expresses itself in the "consistent ethic of life." In our complicated and conflictual world, we may not be able to do all good things for all people (indeed, we surely cannot). And we may even need to defend ourselves against those who would attack us. But at least, as an absolute minimum, we can "leave people alone!"

But if this is true, then this consistent ethic of life can, in turn, be expressed through an absolute prohibition. Granted that there may be many behavioral alternatives, many possible solutions to the ethical conundrums that face us, one solution is always the wrong solution: the direct killing of the innocent. The reason why it is wrong is that the very premise for morality is concern for persons. And the one intervention that can never express concern for the person is elimination of the person. In this act (and only in this act) is the internal contradiction: "I love you so much, I'm going to kill you!" That simply will not do if we claim to be articulating a Christian understanding or morality.

So this is the starting place for our Christian morality. Expressed positively, it is the consistent ethic of life, respect for human life. Expressed negatively, it is the prohibition of the direct killing of the innocent. Then, when we go beyond this starting point and try to figure out how to be good caretakers of ourselves and of one another in a complex world, we do that with proportion. Or, as our Catholic tradition puts it, we exercise the virtue of prudence.

Religious Education

So in this area of "right and wrong," we have moved out of a recent legalistic tradition into a heated battle between two alternative paths of development and then out of that battle into the possibility of a new synthesis, an understanding that can shape our work in religious education. Let me give two examples.

First, this understanding of right and wrong suggests that we ought to focus much more on values than we do on norms. In talking about objective morality, there are two languages one can use: those of values and those of norms. To use the language of norms is not necessarily to fall into the legalism discussed earlier. For example, I can tell you: "Don't break the speed limit," and be expressing the wisdom I have accumulated about the objective destructiveness of speeding. And sometimes the use of strong normative language can help to communicate to one's listeners the depth of one's convictions about the destructiveness of particular behaviors.

But even if it is legitimate, the use of norms is dangerous, for it dares the listener to imagine an exception, to propose a conflictual situation in which the norm would not express the morally correct thing to do. So, for example, someone might respond: "But, if I'm driving a friend to the hospital in the middle of the night, I ought to break the speed limit." If I succumb to the temptation to debate that exception, I will be distracted from the really important point I was trying to make: that speeding is a dangerous thing.

Therefore, it is usually more productive to use the language of values. When we articulate the things we cherish, we invite participation from our listeners. We direct their attention to important matters which they might otherwise overlook. And, in the long run, we thereby more effectively serve our deeper aim: to call believers to a more complete life of effective interpersonal service.

Second, we should put more energy into the development of activities which help our students develop the skills of moral judgment. I have mentioned how the virtue of prudence is central to the living of the moral life. Note that prudence is a **virtue.** In Catholic theology, virtues are moral **habits.** And habits, properly understood, are human skills of living. So part of our business as religious educators is facilitating the development of these skills in our students.

321

Doing this, though, may involve many things. It may mean the more extensive use of cases. It may mean encouraging students to retrieve and mine their past experiences, to appropriate more fully the values that have informed their lives and to become increasingly intentional about ways of acting. It may mean orchestrating supplementary experiences, situations in which students can "try on" new ways of behaving. The common practice of involving students in social service projects is not just a pleasant frill in a program of religious education. Rather, it is an astute strategy for the development of Christian virtues, for the increasingly clear understanding of Christian values. And facilitating the growth of these moral "skills" will surely mean the introduction to the students of models of moral living, women and men who incarnate the commitments and approaches that we wish to commend.

Conclusion

In all this, then, the religious educator will express a rich understanding of his or her role. Giving answers is only part of our job (though a worthy part, if we honestly have answers). More importantly, we facilitate moral growth. We nurture the Christian life which belongs to our students, for which they are ultimately responsible, and about which we share abiding, faith-filled concern.

To say this, coincidentally, may be another way of presenting the central truth of objective morality which we saw earlier: the unequivocal dignity of all human persons. That truth represents the key to right and wrong. It is also, it seems, the key to the ministry of religious education.

At the time of this writing, Timothy E. O'Connell was Professor of Moral Theology and Director of the Institute of Pastoral Studies, Loyola University, Chicago.

Faithfulness and Film: Movies and Childhood

Joseph Cunneen

For educators and pastoral ministers, the most significant function of movies is not how they may be used in programs for children, but how much they have to teach us about those mysterious beings whom we wish to serve. Of course, children are an obvious subject of films—Lumiere's brief sequence, "Baby Having a Snack," was shown at the *Salon Indien* in Paris in 1895, at the very beginning of cinema—but there is a great danger of smiling complacently and not really looking at what they show. Instead, we should use the best of these filmed images of childhood to gain a deeper understanding of our young charges.

Even those too young to have lived through the period when Shirley Temple was the biggest international star know how captivating children can be. My family wouldn't have missed one of her pictures when I was growing up—Shirley was almost unbelievably talented and provided innocent pleasure for millions—but Ingmar Bergman is not thinking of them when he says, "To make films is to descend, by way of its deepest roots, into the world of childhood." Although Shirley became rich and famous and audiences were entertained, on a more serious level, both were exploited. Shirley surrendered her childhood when she became conscious of what she had to do to "win us over," and we were too easily reassured that dimples and an ability to tap-dance could overcome all problems. In the process, the spontaneity of a child's glance got lost.

The lesson for us is that Hollywood didn't really value the child; it wanted to create a star. There was no sinister intent, and I do not have a formula for using children in movies. It is a strange business to explain to a six-year-old, for example, that in this scene the child has been abandoned by his father. My instinct would be to preserve the immediacy of "the first time" and always use unknowns, but it is certainly understandable that producers would want to draw on demonstrated talent and to capitalize on bonds established with audiences on the basis of an earlier role. In any case,

This article appeared in PACE 24 (1994).

323

directors who work with children have an immense responsibility; the best of them unconsciously draw on evangelical language in stressing the need to become like children if one is to communicate successfully with young performers.

It is hardly surprising that the most powerful film images of children will be captured by directors who remain in contact with their own childhood. And, as with Dickens, their children, while immensely appealing, are never simply "cute." The autobiographical element has been fictionalized, but Chaplin's rapport with Jackie Coogan in *The Kid* is hardly fortuitous. The desperate poverty of the London slum in which he grew up and his abandonment by his father when still an infant help prepare the hobo for that instinctive fraternity with the boy he finds on the sidewalk. Laughter and tears are shrewdly combined, and a dream sequence supports the idea that cinema itself reflects a dream of reconciliation between humanity and the world of childhood. In his dream Charlie is transported into a paradise where conflicts and resentments between children, adults, and policemen have all disappeared. Probably the point most worth noticing in *The Kid* is that it is not just a matter of Charlie taking care of the little boy, but of the boy taking care of Charlie—they heal each other's wounds. As Henri Agel said, "If Charlot gives the kid what is best in him and rescues him from the hell that was waiting for him, the kid permits Charlot to reach the deepest part of himself."

One does not have to embrace a naive opposition between nature and civilization to be struck by the fact that film images of education and adult authority show that they are experienced by the child as a kind of repression. As a longtime teacher full of good intentions, I find sobering the video of Jean Vigo's French classic of schoolboy life, *Zero for Conduct* (1931), in which, from the very first shots, the point of view is that of the children. Even allowing for obvious differences from an earlier situation which accepted physical punishment, those who have not completely forgotten their own classroom days will recognize something painfully familiar in the boys' faces as they register blind submission to law.

Again, the director, orphaned at twelve, when his anarchist father died in prison under mysterious circumstances, is drawing on an especially painful childhood. But even those of us with far happier memories will surely recall painful encounters in which the child in us was squelched by the necessities of conformity. The explosion that greets the release from school at the end of the day, even in middle-class neighborhoods served by progressive teachers, suggest that Vigo's sequence of a study period that ends in total anarchy is illuminating rather than perverse. Few of us, I suspect, beat our students, but if we are not to impose on them—and imposition is all the sadder if the subject is religion—we need to make deeper contact with their point of view. All through *Zero for Conduct* the adult world and the world of childhood cross, but they never come together. The attack on officials during a school celebration is not random violence but a critique of pomp and elaborate etiquette, the pretentious side of authority that childhood cannot accept. In the near-surrealistic atmosphere suggested by Vigo, at the end the boys escape from the roof, a dream-like deliverance from a world weighed down by an insupportable burden—the absence of childhood.

"Film," Jacques Vallet says, "creates a universe with specific laws, in which the child emerges from its chrysalis on a screen of light. . . . In a society built according to the aspirations and demands of the adult, movies assure children of the fundamental power of representation, raised to the level of art." No one has taken this effort to capture childhood on film more seriously than Francois Truffaut. Predictably, he warns against using children as artificial decorations. "Since children automatically bring poetry with them, I believe one should avoid introducing poetic elements in a film about childhood, so that the poetry is born of itself as a kind of excess. . . . I find more poetry in a sequence showing a child doing the dishes then in one that dresses the child in velvet and shows him gathering flowers in a garden to the accompaniment of Mozart."

In Truffaut's *400 Blows,* the camera dogs the steps of Antoine, a solitary child without support from a family structure; we look through his eyes at the devastation and drabness around him. Antoine is a juvenile delinquent who would test anyone's patience, but most of all he is a rascal in need of tenderness. Although Truffaut denies that the movie is simply autobiographical, he is remembering his childhood, and like a child, he is looking at the world as if for the first time. Antoine is like so many kids no one takes an interest in—which is why Truffaut was interested. One has to watch closely: Antoine's revolt is shown in the smallest movements, in apparently insignificant bits of mischief. Because childhood speaks so authentically, we are awakened to its liberty, and we, too, see things as if for the first time. Truffaut makes us accomplices as Antoine passes along the forbidden pin-up photo underneath the desk of his classmate, sulks in silence at home, indulges in horseplay at the neighborhood movie theater, and finally escapes from the juvenile correction center. Then there is the desperate race to the sea, a sudden awakening of joy, as the camera observes the unstudied movements of Antoine (Jean-Pierre Leaud), bathed in sunlight, frolicking on the sand, far from the artificial light of a movie studio.

Jean Collet points to the original way in which Truffaut handles the scene with the psychologist at the correction center.

*Notice that we do not see the psychologist in the dialogue with Antoine; we hear the voice-off. But Antoine looks at **us**, he looks straight into the lens as if he were answering our questions. . . .Such a presentation radically modifies our relation to what is shown—and hence, our function as spectators. Antoine's fixed glance at the lens makes us uneasy witnesses of a confession, challenging us and calling for a response. We feel responsible. We are unable to forget, in that instant, that the camera exists. In contrast, the young actor is in the process of forgetting it—his innocence is unbearable. We have to do something. **The links woven between spectator and actor are more serious than before. The spectator will become the consciousness of the actor.***

Many other movies of childhood can be useful reminders that the reconciliation of the child—including the child in ourselves—and the adult is central to our hopes for the world and the coming of the kingdom. Truffaut's own *Wild Child* (the story of a painful initiation into civilization of a child who had grown up in the forest), Charles Laughton's *The Night of the Hunter,* and John Ford's *How Green Was My Valley* quickly come to mind. Vittorio de Sica's *Bicycle Thief* is particularly revealing regarding the role of the child in film, even though the story is essentially about Ricci, whose bicycle has been stolen and who needs one for his job. As Andre Bazin says, "It is the child who gives the adventure of the worker its ethical dimension. . . . Leave him out and you would summarize it in the same way. Bruno's role is simply to trot along beside his father. But he is the intimate witness, the particular chorus attached to the tragedy." When Ricci is humiliated after trying to grab a bicycle (to replace the one taken from him), Bruno puts his hand in his father's. At a moment like this, in which such an instinctive gesture evokes our childhood sense of solidarity, we are no longer looking at a film; it is the film that is looking at us.

The most powerful films about childhood are usually inappropriate for young children because they deal with that painful process which leads to its conclusion. Of course, our Christian ideal is not that of Peter Pan: Children need to enter the adult world. But we need movies with their special capacity to remind us of the vulnerability of children—and of the child that remains in us. Let me offer an idea for a movie sequence which sums up much of what I am saying.

The situation is one in which we have failed a child, overreacting to his unruliness or her stubbornness, perhaps because we were tired or simply found it difficult to provide an explanation for the question one of them asked us. The camera captures the disbelief in the child's eyes, the loss of some degree of illusion in our wisdom or goodness, a head turning away in pain and humiliation. The camera shifts to record our awkward attempt to regain control, to assume a mask of dignity, gathering our belongings as we prepare to leave the room. The camera returns to the child, still in pain, but looking back at us, perhaps with some unconscious sense that we, too, regret what has happened. The sequence is meant to suggest that, in spite of our adult pretensions, there is a hand ready to be placed in ours, that our very salvation is linked to that of the child. Can we bear to watch it?

At the time of this writing, Joseph Cunneen was editor of Cross Currents and a professor at Mercy College, Dobbs Ferry, NY.

African Folktales and Catechetical Instruction

Cyprian Davis, OSB

Folktales are a major characteristic of African cultures. Like the many African proverbs, the folktales embody popular wisdom and often present a lesson in ethics. As part of the popular culture, they represent a certain worldview and reveal certain cultural values. The African continent is immense and the ethnic groups are numerous, but many folktales are strikingly similar, existing in similar versions in diverse parts of Africa. The recounting of the tale is an honored task, and the audience is not a passive on-looker.

Folktales as a text can have different levels of meaning. For the religious education teacher in the United States, this can provide an opportunity to reach African-American students and to enrich the background of all the students. They can supply an "Afrocentric" background to the Catholic school classroom. In fact, many of these folktales actually crossed the Atlantic in the days of slavery and were reconstituted in the southern United States. This is the origin of the famous "Uncle Remus" stories which Joel Chandler Harris heard in the slave quarters, copied down, and published in the last century.

Some African-American teachers have begun to recount these African folktales to audiences of children with the same verve and vitality that the African storyteller uses. Roger Abrahams, in the introduction to his collection of African folktales, states: "Storytelling—as pure narration—seldom arises by itself in this part of the world. Stories involve a singing, a dancing, and acting-out of themselves" (Abrahams 8–9).

The storyteller is part of the dynamic of the folktale. The storyteller makes the tale come alive and invites the audience to participate. As a result the tales can have a pedagogical import, that is, a rule of conduct is demonstrated and a lesson for life is acknowledged. This makes the African folktale an excellent tool for the religion teacher teaching Christian values and ethics to children in an African-American setting.

This article appeared in PACE 24 (1995).

The Power of the Tongue

A famous tale is the account of the hunter who goes out into the forest and finds an old dried up human skull. The hunter asks the skull, "What brought you here?" The skull answers, "Talking brought me here." The hunter runs back to the king to tell him that there was a talking skull in the bush. Guards are sent back with the hunter to see if he was telling the truth. They are charged to kill the hunter if he has lied. The hunter returns to the skull and tries to get the skull to speak again. His effort is fruitless. The skull will not speak. At the end of the day the hunter is put to death. As soon as the guards leave, the skull asks the dead hunter's head, What brought you here?" The dead hunter's head answers, "Talking brought me here."

This version is that of the Nupe people in Nigeria. According to Abrahams, a version of this story is to be found among many African peoples (1–2). It also crossed the ocean and came to the United States. Zora Neale Hurston, who did pioneering work in the area of African-American folklore, gives another version of this folktale of the talking skull in her book, *Mules and Men* (184–185). The hunter has been transformed into a Black man named High Walker who goes into a cemetery, holds converse with the bones, and discovers the skull who admits that his own mouth had brought him to the cemetery and that Walker's mouth would do the same for him unless he took care. With this, High Walker goes back and tells some of the white men about a talking skull. They do not believe him, and High Walker rashly says that they can cut off his head if it is not true. A white man accompanies High Walker back to the skull. The skull will not speak, High Walker loses his head, and in the aftermath the skull says to the head of High Walker that he had warned him that his mouth would bring him there.

The point of the African tale and the African-American version is that too much talking can get one into trouble. The present writer has often used it to explain how the historian must work. The researcher must know how to search for evidence everywhere. With perseverance, one can scour the territory and, with the right questions, allow old bones and skulls to speak.

Morality Tales

Many tales that end with a moral twist ask the audience for a decision. An example is a tale from the Mende people in West Africa. Two strangers are welcomed into a village for a night's lodging. They are warned, however, that no one in the village is allowed to snore during sleep. Those who snore will be put to death. That night one of the strangers begins to snore. His companion awakes, hears him, and also hears the villagers sharpening their knives. To drown out his friend's snoring, the second companion begins to sing. He sings so loudly and so well that the villagers drop their knives, take up their drums, and begin to dance. The next day the chief of the village gratefully presses a full purse into their hands for the night's celebration. On their way from the village, the strangers begin to argue about who should get the larger portion. The snorer claims it because, as he sees it, his companion would not have sung had he not snored. The other counters that without his song the snorer would have been killed. The resolution is left up to the audience. This story might illustrate how each person has his or her gifts. And the benefits of these gifts should be equally divided. In the human family, we all need each other and each other's contributions in order to live and in order to profit from our gifts (Feldmann, "The Two Strangers," 200–201).

The same lesson is taught negatively in the story of a tug of war between the elephant and the hippopotamus, cleverly arranged by the tortoise. Tortoise, like the hare, the rabbit, and the spider, is one of the tricksters. Found in all folklore, the trickster is a rogue or a scamp who gets the better of others by his cleverness, but at the same time often teaches a lesson. Both the hippopotamus and the elephant had minimized the importance of the tortoise by calling attention to his small size and lack of strength. Therefore, the latter challenges each of the giant animals to a tug of war, arranging the matter so that, unknowingly, they would be pulling against each other. At the height of the contest, tortoise cuts the vine, causing each animal to fall back. convinced that tortoise was pulling at the other end of the vine, both elephant and hippopotamus agree that size has nothing to do with strength. Tortoise used this subterfuge to entitle himself to be called their friend and equal. The question to the audience is whether they were truly equal.

The moral of this tale, of course, is that a clever, intelligent mind is more powerful than brute strength. In the religion class, it might lead to a discussion about honesty and deception, with further thought on how people willingly deceive themselves. Perhaps the most important lesson in a religion class might be the fact that none of us is strong unless we pull together and not pull apart (Abrahams, "A Tug-of-War," 208–211). It might also lead to a discussion on how winning does not always mean that someone else must lose.

A lesson about prejudice is exemplified by two folktales. An Ethiopian tale recounts what happens when the lion, the leopard, the hyena, and the donkey agree that conditions have become very bad because one of them had sinned. So they decide on a public confession. The lion confessed that he had caught a young bull and eaten him; the leopard confessed that he had eaten a goat, and the hyena had entered a village and stolen a chicken, which he ate. After each confession, the animals, having a healthy respect for the strength of each one, discounted the confession, agreeing in each case that it was no sin. Finally, the donkey made his confession. He acknowledged that he had nibbled the grass beside the road when his owner had stopped to chat with a friend. None of the animals respected the donkey and so they quickly agreed that this was indeed a sin and that he was the cause of all of their troubles. They attacked the donkey and ate him (Courlander, "The Donkey Who Sinned," 542). The lesson in the causes of prejudice is obvious. Unpopular peoples and groups are readily blamed and persecuted for situations for which they are neither responsible nor the cause.

The meaning of the brotherhood and sisterhood of all peoples is taught by the animals in a Bakongo folktale. A crocodile makes several fruitless attempts to eat a plump hen whom he spies on the river bank. Every time he gets ready to open his jaws and snatch up the tasty morsel, the hen cries out, "Oh, brother, don't." This unnerves the crocodile so badly that he loses the opportunity for a meal. He does not understand how he could possible be a brother to the hen. He is so upset that he sets out to ask God the meaning of this. On the way, he runs into the great lizard and tells him what is happening. The lizard warns the crocodile that he risks embarrassing himself if he asks how he could possibly be the hen's brother. The lizard goes on to point out that just as the hen lays eggs, so both the duck and the turtle live in water and lay eggs, and lizards do the same. And this is also the case with the crocodile. All are brothers and sisters in a sense (Feldmann, "Why the Crocodile Does Not Eat the Hen," 179–180).

Universal Truths

The folktales include more than a single moral conclusion. Some lead to broad conclusions about virtue and right conduct. Four African folktales draw a conclusion that is a profound human truth. The first one, from the Bura people in West Africa, has a theme common to many folktales all over the world. A father advertises the hand of his daughter in marriage to the suitor who successfully accomplishes a difficult task. In this instance, a father promises his daughter to the hunter who can bring him a live deer. Two friends arrive together to vie for the prize. One of them is a renowned and skilled hunter who has a tremendous desire to win the hand of the maiden. His companion is not so ardent nor so determined. Both enter the forest together, but the less determined finally gives up the chase and sits down to sleep. He thinks that chasing after a live deer to marry a maiden is silly. His companion, however, because of skill and determination finally catches a live deer. Carrying the deer around his neck, the great hunter and his companion return to the village.

The father of the bride-to-be welcomes them back. Puzzled as to why the second youth did not catch a wild deer, the father turns the question of his daughter's hand in marriage over to the decision of the village council. The council deliberates and decides to give the daughter in marriage to the young man who was not as determined and who sat down and fell asleep.

331

The council admits that the hunter who bagged the deer was truly a brave man "with a great heart." They note, however, that with such determination he would stop at nothing to achieve his end. He would not listen to others who might give him advice. If his wife did wrong and he began to beat his wife, he would not listen to a member of the community who might plead on her behalf. So they rejected him. The companion is seen as one who would be willing to listen and thereby modify his actions. If they were to plead for the wife, he would heed their request. They saw him as one who is good and gentle (Feldmann, "The Son-in-law," 202–205).

The writer has used this folktale in retreat conferences. Oftentimes the reaction has been one of anger and some resentment. The father is judged to have treated the hunter unfairly because he had caught the deer. The folktale reveals, on the other hand, a cultural value that is typically African. Community values, village consensus, and human qualities are more important than the outcome of a contest. Ultimately, the community makes the decision regarding the marriage of a daughter. Happiness is more important than the rules of the game because, again, winning is not everything. Perhaps most typical is the insight into personality. Strong-willed and determined people are too often not easy to deal with. Flexibility can be a greater asset than iron determination.

If flexibility is part of wisdom, so is prudence, that is, the ability to discern the right and carry it out. In another Ethiopian tale, the wife goes to a shaman or witch doctor to ask him for a potion so that she might regain the affections of her husband. The shaman tells her that he will need three hairs from the mane of a living lion. The wife, after much thought, figures out how she can get three hairs from the mane of a lion that often came by her village. She brings him a lamb for his meal each day and practically tames him. It reaches the point where the lion is willing to lay his head on her lap. when this trust is complete, she carefully plucks out three hairs from his mane and takes them to the surprised shaman. When he hears how she had been able to accomplish this feat, he says to her that, in the same way that she tamed the lion, so should she tame her husband (Rutherford 69–70). Prudence and patience enable one to choose the best methods to accomplish an end. Patience also provides the willingness to work it through. Nothing is accomplished overnight. Life itself is something that one must learn to tame if one is patient enough to change it little by little.

Wisdom also means not making the same mistake twice. In another folktale, the white man (symbol of colonialism) has come upon a snake trapped beneath a large rock. At the pleading of the snake, the man lifts up the rock to let it go free. The snake then prepares to bite the man, who remonstrates with him, pointing out that he had freed it. They agree to go to someone who is wise for a second opinion. Thus they ask a hyena. The hyena, who also wants to eat the man, sides with the snake. The snake prepares to bite him again. Still, the white man seeks a third opinion and asks the jackal. When the jackal says that he does not understand how the rock could have possibly pinned down the snake, he persuades the snake to lie down again and let the white man cover him up. Once the snake is pinned down again, the jackal forces the man to leave him there despite the snake's pleadings (Abrahams 138–139). The teacher might point out a corollary in the Gospel of Matthew: "Be wise as serpents and innocent as doves." (Matthew 10:16).

Finally, there is the Hausa folktale from northern Nigeria in which a wealthy Moslem leader discovers a boy who had been struck down by his father and left half dead. The father was a wretchedly poor man making his living by digging for rodents. The wealthy Moslem chief takes the boy to his home, cleans him up, feeds him, gives him fine clothes, and treats him as a son. The boy is instructed by his foster father in the ways of wealth and prodigality that is part of the lifestyle of the sons of the other wealthy Moslem princes. Eventually the boy's real father discovers his son dressed in fine clothes. He demands that he return. The climax is reached when the wealthy Moslem prince takes the boy and the father into the jungle, produces a sword, and then tells the boy that he must take the sword and kill one of them. The story is to be completed by members of the audience. Which man should he kill—his real father who treated him so badly or the wealthy benefactor who gave him wealth and position and treated him like his son (Abrahams, "Who Should He Kill?" 117–118).

The story does present a moral dilemma, but it has another lesson beyond the question of what makes fatherhood. This lesson is the necessity of making decisions and that decisions have permanent consequences. This story might have a special meaning in a class of older teenagers where the question of fatherhood and its implication is something very realistic. Many of the young men might already be fathers. Both young men and young women may have an experience of the "absent father" who has affected their lives. This folktale, moreover, has implications regarding God as Father as presented both in the Old and New Testaments. God has sought us out and made us his sons and daughters. He has given us inestimable gifts. In the Old Testament the choice is between God and the false gods of the nations. In the New Testament it is between God and the world with its allurements.

A Spiritual Application

Humor and comedy is not lacking, as in the story of the Ashanti people that is extremely amusing. It's about a farmer who one day went to his fields to dig up some yams. One of the yams proceeded to chide him because he had never bothered to weed there before. The yam ends by telling the farmer to go away and leave it alone. The farmer thought the cow was talking to him, but the dog spoke up to say that it was not the cow who spoke but the

333

yam. Thus begins an extraordinary tale of inanimate objects and one dog speaking to humans and thereby frightening them out of their wits. The story ends with the frightened men telling their story to the chief, who is not at all impressed by their tale, until he in turn is accosted by a piece of talking furniture. The charm of the story is in the humor. But is there a deeper meaning? Perhaps it says something about the African concept of being and how all things share in being in varying degrees. To my ears, however, the story has always said something about prayer and listening to God. All things speak to us of God, and the habit of prayer must finally lead to the habit of listening.

There are several collections of African folktales available today. Two of the best are *A Treasury of African Folklore*, edited by Harold Courlander, and *African Folktales*, edited by Roger Abrahams. The collection made by Courlander is valuable because it also includes other African oral literature, such as myths, historical legends, epics, and proverbs. Abrahams has a wide selection of myths and tales with an excellent introduction and bibliography. Finally, there is a paperback edition by Paul Radin of a work originally published in 1952, *African Folktales and Sculpture*, New York: Bollingen Foundation, Inc. The paperback edition is entitled *African Folktales*, New York: Schocken Books, 1983.

References

Abrahams, Roger, editor. *African Folktales, Traditional Stories of the Black World.* New York; Pantheon Books, 1983.

Courlander, Harold, editor. *A Treasury of African Folklore.* New York: Crown Publishers Inc., 1975.

Feldmann, Susan, editor. *African Myths and Tales.* New York: Dell Publishing Co. Inc., 1963.

Hurston, Zora Neale. *Mules and Men.* Philadelphia: J.B. Lippincott Co., 1963.

Rutherford, Peggy. *African Voices,* New York: Vanguard Press, 1960.

At the time of this writing, Cyprian Davis OSB was professor of history at Saint Meinrad School of Theology.

Subscription Offer

PACE (Professional Approaches for Christian Educators) is a professional periodical filled with insightful articles written by:

- Thomas Groome
- Maria Harris
- Neil Parent
- Bishop Kenneth Untener
- Berard Marthaler
- and many more renowned authors

Topics range from AIDS education, liturgical programs, religious education, youth retreats, and other insightful topics.

Published eight times a year (September through April), **PACE** is a periodical you won't want to miss!

☐ YES! Please sign me up for my one year subscription to PACE at the rate of $75.00—$20.00 off the regular price of $95.00.

Name _____

Parish/School/Library _____

Address _____

City/State/Zip _____

Phone (   ) _____

BROWN-ROA

A Division of Harcourt Brace & Company
P.O. Box 1028
Dubuque IA 52004-1028
Phone 800/922-7696